Autocracy and Redistribution
The Politics of Land Reform

When and why do countries redistribute land to the landless? What political purposes does land reform serve, and what place does it have in today's world? A long-standing literature that dates back to Aristotle and is echoed in important recent works holds that redistribution should be both more prevalent and more targeted at the poor under democracy. Yet comprehensive historical data to test this claim has been lacking. This book shows that land redistribution – the most consequential form of redistribution in the developing world – occurs more often under dictatorship than democracy. It offers a novel theory of land reform and develops a typology of land reform policies. Michael Albertus leverages original data from around the world dating back to 1900 to extensively test this theory using statistical analysis and case studies of key countries, such as Egypt, Peru, Venezuela, and Zimbabwe. These findings call for rethinking much of the common wisdom about redistribution and political regimes.

Michael Albertus is Assistant Professor of Political Science at the University of Chicago. His research interests include redistribution, political regime transitions and regime stability, politics under dictatorship, clientelism, and conflict. Albertus's most recent work has been published in journals such as the *British Journal of Political Science*, *Journal of Conflict Resolution*, *Comparative Political Studies*, *Economics & Politics*, and *Comparative Politics*. He has also conducted extensive field research throughout Latin America.

D1224183

Cambridge Studies in Comparative Politics

General Editors
Kathleen Thelen *Massachusetts Institute of Technology*
Erik Wibbels *Duke University*

Associate Editors
Robert H. Bates *Harvard University*
Gary Cox *Stanford University*
Thad Dunning *University of California, Berkeley*
Anna Grzymala-Busse *University of Michigan, Ann Arbor*
Stephen Hanson *The College of William and Mary*
Torben Iversen *Harvard University*
Stathis Kalyvas *Yale University*
Margaret Levi *Stanford University*
Peter Lange *Duke University*
Helen Milner *Princeton University*
Frances Rosenbluth *Yale University*
Susan Stokes *Yale University*

(Continued after the Index)

Autocracy and Redistribution

The Politics of Land Reform

MICHAEL ALBERTUS
University of Chicago

CAMBRIDGE
UNIVERSITY PRESS

CAMBRIDGE
UNIVERSITY PRESS

32 Avenue of the Americas, New York NY 10013-2473, USA

Cambridge University Press is part of the University of Cambridge.

It furthers the University's mission by disseminating knowledge in the pursuit of education, learning and research at the highest international levels of excellence.

www.cambridge.org
Information on this title: www.cambridge.org/9781107514300

First published 2015

A catalogue record for this publication is available from the British Library

Library of Congress Cataloguing in Publication data
Albertus,Michael, 1983–
Autocracy and redistribution : the politics of land reform / Michael Albertus.
   pages cm. – (Cambridge studies in comparative politics)
Includes bibliographical references and index.
ISBN 978-1-107-10655-0 (hardback) – ISBN 978-1-107-51430-0 (paperback)
1. Land reform – Political aspects.   2. Land reform – Developing countries – History.
3. Developing countries – Politics and government.   I. Title.
HD1332.A43   2015
333.3´1091724–dc23   2015012675

ISBN 978-1-107-51430-0 Paperback

Contents

List of Tables

List of Figures

Acknowledgments

This book has its deepest roots in my early graduate work at Stanford University, although it only truly sprouted wings after numerous trips to the field and seemingly endless input and support from colleagues and mentors. I have consequently accumulated enormous intellectual and personal debts in its production.

Perhaps my greatest debt is to David Laitin. His ability to nurture the seed of a good intuition is unsurpassable. When I first found that autocratic regimes redistribute more land than democratic ones, he immediately grasped on to the finding and urged me to develop it. Over the next five years, he taught me how to plumb the depths of a topic while keeping it broadly relevant and testing its generalizability – essential skills for any scholar of comparative politics. His mastery of the intellectual topography of the discipline constantly prodded me to engage with the big questions while paying plenty of attention to nitty-gritty details.

The rest of my dissertation committee – Jim Fearon, Steve Haber, and Jonathan Rodden – was equally indispensable. Jim, as always, cut straight to the heart of any inconsistency or shortcoming in my logic. Steve helped critically shape my understanding of the politics of authoritarian regimes as well as the limits of what we currently know. And Jonathan was an endless font of suggestions about framing the project and how to make the most out of the data that I had to test the theory. This committee supported not only my work on what would ultimately become this book but also the related bits and pieces that have trickled out in other venues.

My other colleagues and peers at Stanford gave me invaluable feedback along the way. Beatriz Magaloni and Alberto Diaz-Cayeros helped shape my understanding of Mexico's land reform and pushed me to consider the coercive and clientelistic aspects of land redistribution as experienced by beneficiaries. Barry Weingast encouraged my thinking on institutional constraints to rule under both democracy and autocracy. Lisa Blaydes and Karen Jusko provided helpful early suggestions about turning the project into a book. My fellow graduate students and close friends Thomas Brambor and Victor Menaldo sounded out numerous iterations of my early ideas and generously provided comments without fail.

My colleagues at the University of Chicago energetically and enthusiastically brought me into the fold after graduate school. I have benefited enormously from the insights of Gary Herrigel, Ben Lessing, Stan Markus, John McCormick, Monika Nalepa, Tianna Paschel, Alberto Simpser, Betsy Sinclair, Dan Slater, Paul Staniland, Lisa Wedeen, and Dali Yang. The indefatigable Dan Slater read several versions of various parts of the manuscript and provided incredibly detailed and thoughtful comments and critiques that are inextricably woven throughout the text. He has been a champion of the project and the rest of my work since I first came to Chicago; for this, I am eternally grateful. John has, on many occasions, left me pondering big questions about the nature of democracy, how it might work versus how it often does, and how the masses can possibly tame elites when the deck is stacked so heavily against them. Lisa provided me with comparative perspective on several Middle Eastern land reforms and encouraged me to think carefully through the role of foreign powers in shaping and even imposing land reform agendas. Paul gave me cogent and crucial advice on reorganizing parts of the manuscript in the wake of my book workshop. Monika provided detailed and extremely helpful suggestions about how to revise the manuscript in response to reviews.

My department at Chicago, and Cathy Cohen in particular as chair, also supported an exceptionally fruitful workshop for the book manuscript. As key participants of that workshop, David Brown, Kevin Morrison, Guillermo Trejo, and Daniel Ziblatt read the manuscript in incredible detail and gave me invaluable advice and suggestions that helped improve it dramatically. Their devotion to ideas and scholarship, as well as their public-spiritedness, represent the best of our profession. I owe all of them a deep debt of gratitude. I am also appreciative of the participation and feedback of my colleagues and the graduate students at the workshop.

Beyond the outsized influence of these individuals on the final manuscript, countless others also shaped my thinking along the way. Of particular note are Ben Ansell, Reo Matsuzaki, Jim Robinson, and Milan Svolik, all of whom provided insightful comments on the project. Reo read the first few iterations of the early chapters of the book while we were both postdoctoral Fellows at Stanford's Center on Democracy, Development, and the Rule of Law. Various parts of the project similarly benefited from the comments of Pablo Beramendi, Rikhil Bhavnani, Cathy Boone, José Cheibub, Michael Coppedge, Scott Gehlbach, Hein Goemans, Gretchen Helmke, Wendy Hunter, Ollie Kaplan, Ethan Kapstein, Terry Karl, Herb Klein, Bethany Lacina, Scott Mainwaring, Aila Matanock, Enrique Mayer, Cynthia McClintock, Vicky Murillo, Ana de la O, Daniel Ortega, Maggie Peters, Guillermo Rosas, Jake Shapiro, Ali

Valenzuela, Nikki Velasco, Jeremy Wallace, Jeremy Weinstein, and Kurt Weyland. I also thank the many workshop and seminar participants at the Juan
March Institute, Stanford University, University of California-Berkeley, University of Chicago, University of Illinois, University of Notre Dame, University
of Rochester, University of Texas-Austin, University of Wisconsin-Madison,
and Washington University–St. Louis for their critical and constructive
comments.

Equally important to the final product were anonymous manuscript review-
ers for Cambridge University Press and Oxford University Press who provided
excellent and thoughtful reviews. The manuscript is undoubtedly better as a
result, hopefully to a degree equal to their expectations. I thank Lew Bateman at
Cambridge and David McBride at Oxford for soliciting such brilliant reviews,
and for doing so in such short order. Lew has been a fantastic editor – responsive, deft, and quick – at every stage of the process. Erik Wibbels and Kathleen
Thelen enthusiastically brought me into the Cambridge Studies in Comparative
Politics series, for which I am honored and thankful.

This manuscript could never have been written without the vast quantities
of data that I have collected on land reform. Such an undertaking is daunting
in retrospect. I never would have conceived it even possible without the enthu-
siastic and emphatic call of an early mentor, J. David Singer of the University of
Michigan, to systematically collect data in an effort to form a better empirical –
and consequently theoretical – understanding of the world around us. His dedication to political science as science served as a siren's call as I was completing
degrees in electrical engineering and mathematics. Jim Morrow and Paul Huth
further encouraged my initial foray into political science, generously sharing
their time with me and providing feedback on my thesis of a quality far beyond
my undergraduate expectations.

A special thanks goes to those who facilitated data collection at a host of land
reform agencies, including the Instituto Nacional de Reforma Agraria (INRA)
in Bolivia, the Instituto Nacional de Colonização e Reforma Agrária (INCRA)
in Brazil, the Servicio Agrícola y Ganadero (SAG) in Chile, the Instituto Colom-
biano de Desarrollo Rural (INCODER) in Colombia, the Instituto Nacional de
Desarrollo Agrario (INDA) in Ecuador, the Registro Agrario Nacional (RAN)
in Mexico, the Comisión de Formalización de la Propiedad Informal (COFO-
PRI) in Peru, the Instituto Nacional de Colonización (INC) in Uruguay, and the
Instituto Nacional de Tierras (INTi) in Venezuela. These were the lifeblood of
my data collection, along with archival work. The dedicated people working at
these agencies taught me volumes during my field research about the varieties of
land reform, the process of land reform, and the inner workings of how reform
programs are implemented and how they are hijacked or hobbled. Without the
insights of many bureaucrats with their sleeves rolled up, such as Edgar Pajares
(COFOPRI), Juan Alvarez (SAG), Napoleón Jaramillo (INDA), Noel Miranda
(INTi), and Juan de Dios Fernández (INRA), the accounts of land reform in
this book would be conceptually much thinner.

Similarly vital were the experts I interviewed and engaged with during my field research throughout Latin America, among whom I would especially like to thank Carlos Balderrama, Olivier Delahaye, Román Duque, Absalón Machado, Carlos Machado, Genaro Méndez, and Esteban Sanjinés. Discussions with countless land reform beneficiaries, whose voices are often surprisingly absent from the assessments of these programs, critically helped shape my understanding and views on the long-term impacts of land reform as redistribution. I would like to thank all of those whose lives have been profoundly marked by land reform who shared their precious time and experiences with me on long bus rides, in their homes or fields, in the waiting rooms at land reform agencies, at corner stores, or in public squares. Beyond these important individuals, national statistics agencies, archives, and libraries too numerous to list augmented my data collection in Bolivia, Chile, Colombia, Ecuador, Mexico, Peru, Uruguay, Venezuela, and, of course, the United States.

Generous funding and institutional support backed the research that is foundational to this book. My fieldwork and data coding were funded by two Stanford University Graduate Research Opportunity grants, a Diversity Dissertation Research Opportunity grant from Stanford's Office of the Vice Provost for Graduate Education, an Ayacucho Foundation grant accompanied by generous institutional support from Venezuela's Instituto de Estudios Superiores de Administración as facilitated by Francisco Monaldi and Michael Penfold, Stanford's Center on International Conflict and Negotiation, and a grant from the University of Chicago's Social Sciences Division. An O'Bie Shultz Dissertation Completion grant and a predoctoral fellowship from the Stanford Institute of Economic Policy Research helped fund my final year of graduate school, allowing me to focus on my research. Larry Diamond and the Stanford Center on Democracy, Development, and the Rule of Law provided a home for me as a postdoctoral Fellow and the time to complete data collection and compilation and to start converting what was then a dissertation paper into a much more involved book project.

Able research assistance was provided by Frank Alarcón, Mark Deming, Victor Gay, and Bogdan Popescu. Frank was invaluable in gathering and compiling materials for the case studies in Chapter 8. Mark and Bogdan assiduously took on the task of coding coalitional splits between political and landed elites across the entire world since 1900 and aided in wrestling with the conceptual issues associated with applying this framework to substantive contexts that are very different from those in Latin America. We met countless times to discuss the cases, which also helped with the honing of the theoretical formulation behind elite splits. Victor happily agreed to review the formal model in Chapter 3 and generously aided in the graphical depiction of the model equilibria.

Selected parts of Chapter 6 previously appeared in my 2015 article "Explaining Patterns of Redistribution under Autocracy: The Case of Peru's Revolution from Above," *Latin American Research Review* 50(2): 107–134, © 2015 by the Latin American Studies Association. Related versions of some materials in Chapter 7 were published in my 2013 article "Vote Buying with Multiple Distributive Goods," *Comparative Political Studies* 46(9): 1082–1111, doi: 10.1177/0010414012463897. Elements of Chapter 3 were published in my 2012 article "If You're Against Them You're with Us: The Effect of Expropriation on Autocratic Survival," *Comparative Political Studies* 45(8): 973–1003, doi: 10.1177/0010414011428593. I thank the publishers of these journals for their permission to draw from this work.

Last, but hardly least, I thank all of my friends and family for their gracious and stalwart support. An unusually close group of friends, especially though hardly exclusively "The Club," has long supported me, laughed with me, provided counsel, adventured with me, reminded me not to take myself too seriously, and accepted many of the crazy ideas I have had or pursued. Chelo Perales has been a lively, sage, and engaging teacher of many things Latin American since I first met her at Stanford, and she is now a great and irreplaceable friend.

I have also been incredibly lucky when it comes to family, and I dedicate this book to them. My parents, Anne and Steve, inspired me from a young age to learn and to question. They also taught through example a deep dedication to social justice and service to others. It is hard to imagine my route to the present without such constant role models and unfailing champions on my behalf. My siblings, Julie, Paul, Jim, and Daniel, have been my closest and most important companions throughout the years. They have always encouraged me to reach higher, to live a reflective and engaged life, and to laugh and have fun, and they have accompanied me time and again into the natural spaces of this world to which I have grown so attached. I am humbled to walk among them. I met my wife, Ally Stewart, at the end of graduate school at Stanford, and my life has been richer every day since because of her. Her spirit of adventure, authenticity, and enthusiasm is infectious. She has been steadfastly supportive in every way I could have imagined, and in many ways I could not have imagined. The words of a profound Machado verse that Chelo taught me are even more exciting with Ally to journey with: "[C]aminante, no hay camino, se hace camino al andar."

1

Introduction

What are the political conditions under which land reform occurs? When is land reform redistributive, and what political purposes does it serve? Who are the chief beneficiaries of reform? And what place, if any, does land reform have in today's world?

Land reform dates back at least to the time of Solon and Pisistratus in sixth-century BC Greece. Distributional questions related to land use and ownership were at the heart of the French Revolution, the emancipation of the serfs in Russia, and countless long-standing social movements in the developing world. And land reform continues in the present day in countries such as Brazil, the Philippines, South Africa, and Venezuela. US President John F. Kennedy encapsulated the imperative of land reform in the Americas when he announced the 1961 Alliance for Progress, highlighting the need for countries to "improve the productivity and use of their land, wipe out disease, attack archaic tax and land tenure structures, provide educational opportunities, and offer a broad range of projects designed to make the benefits of increasing abundance available to all."

The answers that I provide to these important questions depart from much of the common wisdom about the rural sector that political scientists, economists, and sociologists hold dear. First and foremost is the observation that the most redistributive variety of land reform occurs under autocratic rule, not under democracy. Indeed, the spread of democracy has undermined land redistribution and left many disregarded rural populations cast adrift. This implies a second novel observation: in spite of the conclusions of influential scholars such as Barrington Moore and Alexander Gerschenkron, democracy has rarely been threatening to landowners. Indeed, democracy has not infrequently been a friend and savior of large landowners. Although democracy does not forestall all types of land reform, it tables land redistribution – the greatest threat to landed elites. Third, the focus on popular mobilization and the perception that mobilization drives redistribution is at least partly misplaced. Intra-elite

1

conflict and institutional constraints to rule largely determine where and when redistributive land reform occurs. Popular mobilization only rarely yields land redistribution directly; much more frequently, it directs the scope and targeting of redistribution once an opening for redistribution has been created. Finally, land reform is hardly dead. Negotiated land reform and land colonization – and to a lesser extent land redistribution – is ongoing in many developing countries, and rural populations will continue to press for reform. But if land reform is to have a chance at effectively tackling rural poverty and landlessness in the future, it needs a major overhaul.

This book is dedicated to developing and explaining these findings. My main argument, from which these conclusions stem, is that redistributive land reform occurs when there is a coalitional split between ruling political elites and landed elites alongside low institutional constraints to rule. A coalitional split provides political elites with the incentives to eliminate a powerful rival elite outgroup while simultaneously currying the favor of regime insiders. But a coalitional split is not enough; land reform is an onerous process that requires the sustained cooperation of a wide range of political actors. Redistributive land reform therefore also necessitates the concentration of power most often found under autocracy if landed elites are to be stymied from acting as a cog in the wheel of reform. Institutional constraints simply provide too many toeholds for landed elites to leverage their influence and obstruct reform. The less redistributive types of land reform – negotiated land reform, which compensates owners at market rates, and land colonization – operate under logics distinct from those of land redistribution. Foreign aid, wealth, and popular pressure from below have a greater impact on those types of land reform.

LAND, LAND REFORM, AND THE RURAL SECTOR

Land is the chief productive asset for the world's rural poor. Most of the rural poor, and some of the urban poor as well, depend on agriculture as their main source of income (Lipton 2009, 148). Land also serves as social insurance in the developing world. It provides not only employment and income but also sustenance, a place to live, insurance for infirmity and age, and security for future generations. Land reform in developing countries is therefore viewed as a type of affirmative action or as a substitute for income and employment transfers that is analogous to the Western European welfare state (e.g., Thiesenhusen 1989).

Yet throughout most of the past several hundred years and most of the history of settled agriculture during which there was surplus, the majority of rural people have been dependent on local landlords for access to land, inputs, and credit. Rural inhabitants frequently worked small plots of land at the discretion of a local landlord who required labor on the landlord's property in exchange.

Take the case of Bolivia prior to the 1952 revolution. The largest 6 percent of landowners held 92 percent of the entire country's farmland. Most highland peasants operated under the system of *colonato*, wherein workers were given a small house and a plot on a hacienda for subsistence farming in exchange for labor on the landlord's fields, often 5–6 days per week in the growing season and every day of the harvest (Thiesenhusen 1995, 54). On top of this, domestic service was required in the landlord's house. Women often served as maids and men as busboys or deliverymen. As one priest put it in 1870, "the Indian continues to be considered by us as a degenerate being born to serve, to be employed without pay in the vilest of occupations" (Condarco Morales 1965, 37). Where land was not a limiting factor, peasants were allowed to plant in unoccupied territories but were mandated to turn over a portion of their crops and livestock to the landlord. Landlords that did not reserve land for themselves to be farmed by peasants instead often imposed taxes. Physical abuse and exploitation of peasants was common. A fieldworker from the Inter-American Committee for Agricultural Development reported the following on the eve of the revolution:

So the patrón [landlord] would say to the headman (*jilacata*): "this man is working badly – give him the lash" – and calling his people together he would say – "come, now, my son, down you get. Come along, headman, three lashes for this lad, three of the best!" So the headman would give him three strokes and if they were not hard enough then the patrón himself would thrash the headman, saying: "This is the way to thrash and this is how thou'llt thrash the workers, so that they feel it as thou art feeling it now." (Pearse 1972, 269).

Colonos were kept in debt peonage and therefore lacked freedom of movement. They were sold with the land.

Landlords in Bolivia justified the status quo with arguments of racial superiority, economic necessity, and the imperative of social order. All of this was lacquered over with a touch of cynical paternalism, as the differing post–land reform accounts by a landlord and a service tenant from the same former estate indicate:

Patrón: "In my estate, we gave equal treatment to whites and to *indios*. All of the *indios* were well loved. When they needed something they would come and ask: 'Master, lend me the so-and-so' and we gave them all they asked for. More than this, my father arranged their marriages. He would grab hold of a peasant and ask him whom he wanted to marry, and no matter whether the one he chose was widowed or single, my father would immediately make them marry. It was a splendid life – and see what it has come to now!"

Peasant: "Before, we were slaves because we were stupid, we didn't understand what was going on. We didn't have anybody to defend us and we were afraid to do anything for fear that the patrón would beat us. We didn't know why we were beaten. We didn't know about our rights." (Muratorio 1966, 5).

Asymmetric and in some cases feudal relationships like those that defined the *colonato* in Bolivia clearly delineate social class. They also have important political implications, not least of which is the ability of powerful landowners to exclude rural workers from the franchise or to influence rural workers' votes (Baland and Robinson 2008; Moore 1966; Ziblatt 2009). Agrarian institutions "are one of the best outward manifestations of social class: they reflect status within society, they reflect privilege, they reflect power" (Thiesenhusen 1989, 31). Land is therefore also fertile ground for contentious politics. Unequal or weak agrarian institutions and skewed landholding patterns are linked to land conflicts in diverse contexts across the world (e.g., Albertus and Kaplan 2013; Boone 2013; Paige 1975; Russett 1964; Wood 2000).

The impact of rural relationships on society in developing states has been enormous, and it continues to be so today. In 1950, 71 percent of the world's population was rural. As of 2010, 49 percent of the world's population was rural. In most of sub-Saharan Africa today, the level of ruralization is similar to that in Western Europe around 1850 and to that in most of Latin America around 1900, and rural populations are continuing to grow (Boone 2013). Poverty is concentrated in these rural areas. Slightly more than three-quarters of the 1.2 billion people in extreme poverty (the "dollar-poor") were rural in 2002 (Lipton 2009, 148). Furthermore, the overwhelming majority of the rural population works in agriculture. Roughly 67 percent of the world's economically active population worked in agriculture in 1950, and that figure remained at 45 percent in 2000 (FAO 2000).

Land reform can fundamentally transform the material and social well-being of the poor. Although definitions of land reform vary, most share in common one often-stated end: the reduction of rural poverty by transferring the control of farmland to the land-poor. Land reform can increase the well-being of rural workers by increasing income from land for the land-poor, raising the demand for labor, and creating farm enterprise opportunities (Lipton 2009). It can simultaneously contribute to agricultural growth, given that small farms are typically more productive than large farms (e.g., Berry and Cline 1979; Deininger 2003). Furthermore, by redefining the relationship between rural inhabitants and landlords, land reform enhances social inclusion, converting the poor into more equal citizens with greater political clout. Land reform therefore represents an economically important and politically charged type of redistribution that amounts to what Huntington (1968, 299) calls a "reordering of basic social relationships." It is perhaps the most consequential form of social and economic redistribution in agrarian societies – certainly much more consequential than income redistribution.

The effects of land reform are not limited to the rural sector. Increased rural income often spills over to increases in non–farm income as input suppliers gain business and consumption increases. Land reform can even have economy-wide effects as the retarding influence of inequality wanes (Alesina and Rodrik 1994; Vollrath and Erickson 2007).

The legacy of land reform bears witness to its transformative potential. Land reform has contributed considerably to the decline in the economic and social oppression of the rural poor. It has affected at least 1.5 billion people since 1945

(Lipton 2009, 1). Land reforms under Gamal Abdel Nasser in Egypt, Mengistu Haile Mariam in Ethiopia, and Robert Mugabe in Zimbabwe attacked landed elite interests, as did the elimination of the zamindars in India and land collectivization in Tanzania. Radical land reforms implemented by the United States in Taiwan, Korea, and Japan led to the destruction of the landed classes and a fundamental social and economic reformation as large landholders were destroyed in favor of smallholders (Walinsky 1977). China, Russia, and much of Eastern Europe under communism expropriated landed elites and collectivized property only to later decollectivize in a relatively egalitarian manner (King 1973; Lipton 2009, 283).

Even Western European countries, such as France and the Netherlands, witnessed major land reforms during the nineteenth century that are seen as key milestones in their political and economic modernization (Swinnen 2002). Similarly, land reform in southern Italy following World War II targeted large estates for redistribution among peasants and transformed the semi-feudal rural social structure (King 1973).[1] Other examples abound in cases as diverse as Iran, Iraq, Nepal, Pakistan, the Philippines, and Vietnam (see, e.g., Borras 2007; El-Ghonemy 2002; Herring 1983; Tai 1974). As Lipton (2009, 7) writes, land redistribution in favor of the rural poor "has spread much further, and with more success, than is widely believed." By contrast, where land reform has been absent, the poorest half of rural workers typically control less than 10 percent of the farmland (Lipton 2009, 2).

Land reform has also played a key role in empowering indigenous and minority communities in many countries. The physical recognition of historical land claims has been a motivating force behind a host of social movements by populations that are facing discrimination and seek formal recognition, cultural autonomy, or policies of affirmative action. South Africa, for instance, instituted a market-based land reform following the end of apartheid that provides state support to restitute lands to blacks dispossessed through racially discriminatory practices such as the Native Land Act (Thwala 2006). Similar efforts to restitute land to blacks dispossessed during colonialism are also under way in Kenya and Zimbabwe. Yashar (1999, 83) details how many major land reforms in Latin America prior to the onset of neoliberalism provided space for the reemergence of indigenous leaders, the reconstitution of communities, and the institutionalization of indigenous community practices and identities at the local level. Although some of these gains were eroded following democratization and the adoption of neoliberal policies, marginalized indigenous groups and rural Afro-Latino communities that descended from runaway slaves have recently organized in many Latin American states to gain collective land rights that strengthen their identity and traditions (Hooker 2005).

---

[1] By contrast, Spain's failed attempt at land redistribution during the Second Republic led to the persistence of the agrarian aristocracy among the "Grandes de España." See, e.g., Malefakis (1970).

Of course, land reform is not always transformative. Radical attempts at reform can be watered down, gutted, or countered. Landed elites can try to subdivide their land among relatives and friends in an effort to evade landholding ceilings or to inflate their perceived family size to qualify for higher land-retaining thresholds, as some landed elites did in West Bengal (Bardhan and Mookherjee 2010). Large landowners can marshal influence with local judges, the police, and even militias to keep land reform laws from affecting them, as many did in Brazil and Colombia (Albertus, Brambor, and Ceneviva 2015; LeGrand 1986). And landed elites who cannot wiggle out of land expropriation but who have diversified assets can sometimes relocate to cities and continue to exert influence over policy in other economic sectors. Furthermore, low state capacity can hobble reform implementation. Weak state penetration into the periphery can raise the cost and decrease the efficacy of reform, as occurred under Ferdinand Marcos in the Philippines. Land reforms can also be entirely derailed. Landed interests can capture or influence legislators to reverse the terms of land reform; in some cases, land-concentrating policies are cynically advanced under the banner of "land reform." Landed elites can also directly threaten the executive by leveraging their economic power or an alliance with the military.

The primary – but not exclusive – empirical focus of this book is Latin America. The history of land reform and political development in the region makes it an ideal testing ground for theory on the conditions under which reform is implemented. Latin America inherited a legacy of lopsided and semi-feudal land ownership following Spanish and Portuguese colonization (de Janvry 1981; Thiesenhusen 1989). Following independence, land long remained a key component of net wealth for both rich and poor and a major economic foundation of political power and social prestige for ruling elites (Barraclough 1973). Although only 21 percent of the population was rural in 2010, more than 50 percent was rural before 1961. The majority of the economically active population was employed in agriculture in fourteen of nineteen countries in Latin America in 1950. The same number of countries had more than 40 percent of the economically active population employed in agriculture in 1970. Yet the vast majority of these rural laborers were poor. A mere 10 percent of the population in Latin America owned 90 percent of the land even in the 1960s (Lapp 2004, 2).

Political variation in the region against this backdrop of inequality has provided a wide range of institutional arrangements under which land reform could be pursued. Every country in Latin America has experienced both autocratic and democratic rule since the early twentieth century. Institutional variation has also been wide within these regime types. There have been long periods of single-party rule under dictatorship, as in Mexico and Paraguay, as well as many episodes of military dictatorship and unelected civilian rule. Democracy has been characterized by periods of presidentialism and parliamentarism, varying degrees of judicial independence, single legislative chambers and bicameralism, and differing levels of malapportionment. Furthermore, most countries in the region, as exemplified by Argentina, Brazil, Ecuador, Honduras, and Peru, have oscillated between democracy and various forms of dictatorship.[2]

Under what political conditions has land reform been implemented? How has it been structured, and who has benefited from it? What are the consequences of land reform in these countries? Thiesenhusen (1995) denigrates many of the cases of land reform in Latin America as little more than "broken promises" when they are measured according to their intended goals. Rather than eliminating haciendas by redistributing them to peasants, de Janvry (1981) argues that many agrarian reforms accelerated the modernization and transformation of the hacienda system. Kay (1998) echoes this thesis, contending that although a host of Latin American countries implemented substantial land redistribution, the majority of reforms ultimately favored the development of capitalist farming by the 1990s.

Yet despite the large literature on land reform, this conclusion is incomplete. There has been no scholarly work that uses a cross-national comparative framework to empirically analyze the political foundations and outcomes of these programs. Furthermore, many accounts of land reform's failures reach this conclusion by treating partial reforms as failures or by focusing exclusively on direct rich-poor transfers. But as Lipton (2009, 281) argues, "Enormous social changes, challenging *some* 'rural tyrants' and placing land and power in the hands of *some* of the rural 'masses' for the first time in centuries, should not be written down – or written off – because they fail to meet exaggerated targets or expectations." No land reform program could possibly resolve all forms of rural poverty at once and eliminate every large- and medium-sized landholder. Nor could a reform program redistribute all targeted land simultaneously. Problems of noncompliance, finite administrative funding, and limited state capacity imply that some groups will inevitably be untouched by reform efforts. Finally, even reforms that are subsequently undone or undermined merit attention, even if they do not yield long-standing or widespread changes; the unraveling of reform may occur because of factors distinct from those that led to reform in the first place.

The lack of systematic empirical evidence is one major reason why existing scholarship comes to widely varying conclusions about the causes and successes of land reform. Research to date has also often failed to conceptually distinguish between the types of reforms that have occurred, thereby conflating dissimilar policies.

CLASSIFYING AND MEASURING LAND REFORM

This book makes sense of some of the disparate findings in the land reform literature by developing a typology of land reform – focusing on the source of

---

[2] The findings in following chapters are not simply driven by the relative lack of stability in some Latin American democracies or other potentially unique regional features. A global analysis of land reform in Chapter 8 yields findings that closely parallel those for Latin America.

land and how it is acquired or incorporated by the state for the purposes of reform – and then systematically collecting data across this typology for all of Latin America since 1930. The book also provides a framework for understanding the different conditions under which governments are likely to implement one type of land reform instead of another. It consequently fills a major gap in the study of comparative politics. Land reform has been dramatically understudied despite the fact that land is at the center of rural life and rural politics.

Land reform encompasses a variety of policies: land expropriation and redistribution, negotiated transfers from the private market, colonization programs, land titling, tenure reforms, and the generation of private land markets.[3] I focus on three analytically distinct policies of reform that are oriented at physically transferring the ownership of land: redistribution, negotiation, and colonization.[4] I define land redistribution as the undercompensated or uncompensated expropriation of land from the private sector and the redistribution of that land to the land-poor. Land negotiation is the acquisition of land from the private sector with market-value or above-market-value compensation and its subsequent transfer to the land-poor. Land colonization is the state-directed transfer of state-owned land to settlers.

Coding the physical area of land transferred through these policies provides the clearest picture to date of the extensive scope and character of land reform in Latin America. A total of 128 million hectares, or 1.28 million km^2, of land was expropriated and redistributed in Latin America from 1930 to 2008. There were 37 million hectares transferred through compensated land negotiations and another 106 million hectares transferred through land colonization. A total of 14 percent of all of the land in Latin America – 271 million hectares – transferred hands between 1930 and 2008 as a result of these three types of land

---

[3] The term "land reform" is used by some scholars to refer to a subset of the broader policies that constitute agrarian reform. These broader policies may include, but are not limited to, the provision of credits, inputs, infrastructure (e.g., irrigation), marketing assistance, and services directed at the rural sector (see, e.g., Deininger 2003; Thiesenhusen 1989; Tuma 1965). Although I discuss many of these consequential policies, a systematic analysis of them is beyond the scope of this book.

[4] This is not to say that other land reform policies are unimportant or that they are not redistributive. Land tenure reforms, such as the modification of leasing laws or revisions of the terms for distributing surplus production from sharecropping, for instance, can certainly influence rural welfare (see, e.g., Swinnen 2002), as can securing land tenure via titling or other mechanisms (see, e.g., De Soto 2003; Deininger 2003; Galiani and Schargrodsky 2010). Similarly, progressive taxes on agricultural land, while presently and historically very low (Binswanger-Mkhize, Bourguignon, and van den Brink 2009; Bird and Slack 2004), may prompt "voluntary" land reform by encouraging more efficient land use and spurring changes to land tenure (see, e.g., Binswanger-Mkhize et al. 2009). Nonetheless, the physical transfer of land ownership is at the core of land reform and holds the potential to be the most redistributive reform method, both because of its economic importance as the transfer of assets (plus future income) and because of its implications for rural social relationships. The land reform literature has therefore long focused primarily on land transfer programs as the most consequential reform policy and as an indicator of total land reform effort (see, e.g., Tai 1974, 11–13).

reform. This represents an area nearly the size of all of Western and Northern Europe or the equivalent of roughly 1.5 times the land area of Mexico. Given that most land reform focused on arable or cultivable regions, *more than half of all the cultivable land in Latin America* transferred hands through land reform.

Bolivia, Chile, Cuba, the Dominican Republic, El Salvador, Guatemala, Honduras, Mexico, Nicaragua, Panama, and Peru all implemented considerable land redistribution programs. These programs had a significant impact on landed elites and the welfare of rural inhabitants. Brazil, Colombia, Costa Rica, Paraguay, and Venezuela did less redistributive reforms, focusing more on negotiated land transfers with full compensation to landowners than on expropriation and redistribution. Bolivia, Brazil, Colombia, Ecuador, Honduras, and Venezuela all had large land colonization programs to grant state-owned land to rural colonizers, some of which complemented other land reform policies and others of which served as substitutes to alleviate demographic pressure on privately held land. Furthermore, land tenure reforms abolishing feudalistic tenure arrangements, such as *pongeaje* (Bolivia), *huasipungaje* (Ecuador), *inquilinaje* (Chile), *peonaje acasillado* (Mexico), and *yanaconaje* (Peru), destroyed some of the most exploitative labor conditions and enabled peasants to increase their political and social independence vis-à-vis landlords. As Mayer (2009, 3) writes of General Velasco's land reform in late 1960s Peru: "[I]t was the first government ever to execute significant income distribution in a society of great inequalities. It completed the abolition of all forms of servitude in rural estates, a momentous shift in the history of the Andes, akin to the abolition of slavery in the Americas."

Land reform was also blocked or reduced in scope by landed interests in a number of cases. Landed elites watered down reform in countries such as Colombia and Costa Rica, and they almost entirely blocked it in Argentina and Uruguay.

There is significant variation in the timing and pace of land reform in the region. Early land redistribution began in Mexico following its 1917 constitution. Land negotiation began in Uruguay in the 1920s and continued in the 1930s, when Colombia began purchasing private land for redistribution in conflictive areas, Chile expanded land colonization, and the Dominican Republic began land redistribution. Land redistribution, negotiation, and colonization continued at comparatively low levels until the late 1950s with Cuba's large-scale expropriation. Land reform efforts increased in many countries in the 1960s. Rafael Trujillo's extensive holdings in the Dominican Republic were expropriated in 1961 following his assassination. Land reform laws were passed in the early 1960s in Colombia, Costa Rica, Honduras, Guatemala, and Venezuela, but all of these countries relied on land negotiation and colonization instead of expropriation with the exception of Honduras, which was under military rule in the 1970s. The late 1960s witnessed increasing reformism in Chile and Mexico as well as under military generals in Bolivia, Brazil, Ecuador, Panama, Paraguay, and Peru. Land reform remained very active in the 1970s.

Land redistribution declined in a host of countries during the 1980s. Yet land reform persisted in the 1990s and 2000s, primarily but not exclusively in the form of land negotiation and colonization. Land reform during this most recent period has been dominated by Bolivia, Brazil, Colombia, and Venezuela. There was also substantial trailing reform (the *rezago agrario*) in Mexico after the officially declared end of reform in 1992, most prominently in response to the Zapatista Uprising. Land reform then reentered the political debate in the mid- to late 2000s in several countries.

Land reform is, of course, hardly limited to Latin America. To test the gen- eralizability of my main theoretical argument explaining land redistribution, I also present data on every episode of land redistribution across the world since 1900. I code more than fifty episodes of land redistribution beyond Latin Amer- ica across roughly a third of all countries, spanning every region of the world. Many more countries than this have undertaken large-scale programs of land colonization and land negotiation, and still others experienced reform prior to the last century.

THE POLITICS OF REDISTRIBUTION

Land reform is only one potential redistributive policy that governments might pursue to benefit the poor. There is a large literature on redistribution that pro- vides a series of important insights into the political underpinnings of socially redistributive policy. What does this literature tell us about when governments implement equality-enhancing reforms?

One particularly influential argument comes from social conflict theory. Social conflict theory anticipates that democracies should be more likely than autocracies to adopt policies that will benefit the majority of citizens (e.g., Acemoglu and Robinson 2006; Boix 2003). Rooted in Meltzer and Richard's (1981) median voter model of tax rates, social conflict theory argues that majority rule allows poorer citizens to exert greater influence over the polit- ical economy than the oligarchy, therefore narrowing the income gap between the rich and poor through progressive social policies. As Acemoglu and Robin- son (2006, 104) write, "[T]he median voter, who becomes poorer relative to the mean [with franchise extension], prefers greater tax rates and more redis- tribution."

This thesis echoes the classic arguments of Aristotle, Alexis de Tocqueville, and *The Federalist* Papers. Aristotle (1992, 192), for instance, stated, "Where men rule because of the possession of wealth, whether their number be large or small, that is oligarchy, and when the poor rule, that is democracy." For Aristotle, this had important implications for public policy, particularly because the rich in a society were few in number compared to the poor. Democracy was therefore tantamount to redistribution: "In democracies all share in all things, in oligarchies the opposing practice prevails" (Aristotle 1992, 415).

Acemoglu and Robinson (2006) and Boix (2003), the most prominent recent contributions to social conflict theory, generate predictions about overall levels of redistribution but do not directly test them. These authors instead focus on explaining transitions to democracy and the duration of democratic rule as a function of the level of inequality in a society, where inequality captures the implicit demand for redistribution from the masses. For Boix (2003), higher inequality threatens greater redistribution under democracy and therefore generates greater elite resistance to democratic rule. This undermines both democratization and democratic consolidation: "When a society is acutely unequal, no constitutional rule can sustain democracy" (Boix 2003, 15). Acemoglu and Robinson (2006), by contrast, argue that democratization occurs at medium levels of inequality when there is a credible and transitory threat of revolt by the masses. At low levels of inequality, there is no demand for democracy, and at high levels, the ruling elites have too much to lose and will always choose to repress. Acemoglu and Robinson's prediction for democratic consolidation is nonetheless similar to that of Boix: the redistributive threat linked to higher rates of inequality undermines democracy by providing incentives for elite-led coups.

Yet inequality and democracy are much more compatible empirically than is predicted by social conflict theory, casting doubt on the assumptions these authors make about the redistributive implications of political regimes. Although the distribution of income is right-skewed throughout the world, redistribution from the rich to the poor does not appear to be any higher in democracies than it is in autocracies (Ross 2006; Scheve and Stasavage 2011; Slater, Smith, and Nair 2014).[5] Economic elites have disproportionate influence over economic policy in many of the world's poorest democracies (Keefer 2004; Rajan 2009). Furthermore, many democratic transitions occur despite high inequality (Haggard and Kaufman 2012). And democracy is not associated with redistribution even at the highest levels of inequality (Iversen and Soskice 2009; Morrison 2009; Mulligan, Gil, and Sala-i-Martin 2004; Perotti 1996; Rodríguez 2004).

Many Latin American states bring into high relief the weak empirical support for theoretical predictions about the importance of relative equality – or even medium levels of inequality – in democratic transition and consolidation. Most countries in Latin America transitioned to democracy despite exceedingly high rates of income inequality, and now many of these states are deepening their democratic institutions amid persistent inequality (Schmitter 2010).

Democracy in Latin America, set against a backdrop of inequality, is even more puzzling under current theory given that land was long a principal economic foundation for the political and social power of ruling elites

---

[5] This point is also consistent with Ansell and Samuels (2010), Freeman and Quinn (2012), and Haggard and Kaufman (2012).

(Barraclough 1973). As a fixed, illiquid asset that cannot be moved abroad to avoid the reach of the state, *landholding heightens the redistributive fears of the elite in an unequal society* in which land rather than capital constitutes an important part of elite wealth (Boix 2003). When elites hold high-specificity assets such as land, democratization should be far less likely given lower costs of repression relative to the expected tax burden for elites (Acemoglu and Robinson 2006; Ansell and Samuels 2010; Boix 2003). Landholding should also undercut democratic consolidation by lowering the costs for landed elites of mounting a coup (Acemoglu and Robinson 2006; Boix 2003). Finally, because the concentration of wealth in a society is typically much greater than the concentration of income (Piketty 2014), the potential redistribution of assets such as land is much more politically consequential than income redistribution, a fact that few empirical tests of theories of redistribution consider.

Several well-documented empirical observations provide evidence that the elite actors critical to democratic transition do not always fear its hypothesized redistributive consequences. Despite the fact that there is often pressure from below for political reform (Przeworski 2009; Wood 2000), concrete steps toward democracy, such as scheduling elections and relinquishing control over the security apparatus, are often initiated by elites themselves (Collier 1999; Karl 1990; Lizzeri and Persico 2004; O'Donnell and Schmitter 1986). Moreover, a democratic transition is more likely if elites manage to negotiate a constitutional framework that continues to protect their interests after they exit (Albertus and Menaldo 2014; Inman and Rubenfeld 2005; Negretto 2006). Institutional features such as checks and balances (Henisz 2000; Tsebelis 2002), malapportionment (Horiuchi 2004; Snyder and Samuels 2004), and the proscription of leftist parties (Mainwaring 1999) can be built into constitutions in order to protect property rights and reduce policy volatility. In Western Europe during the nineteenth and early twentieth centuries, democratization proceeded in gradual, calculated steps intended to appease economic elites' fear of radical political change (see, e.g., Boix 2010; Dahl 1971; Ziblatt 2006). Similarly, the economically powerful accepted democracy in Latin America when their interests were protected by conservative parties (Rueschemeyer, Stephens, and Stephens 1992) or favored through counter-majoritarian rules (e.g., Snyder and Samuels 2004). Schmitter (2010, 20) argues that democratization in many Latin American states came once elites "began to realize that their interests would be better protected under democracy than they had been under authoritarianism."

There are three literatures that help explain the lack of a general relationship between democracy and redistribution. The first is a new generation of social conflict theory that argues that even after a transition, elites may circumvent democratic institutions to capture policymaking and block redistribution (Acemoglu and Robinson 2008). If elites' de facto power persists after democratization, they can engage in vote buying or clientelism that fractionalizes the political power of the poor (Keefer 2007; Ziblatt 2009). The ability of elites to maintain excessive influence over policymaking under democracy echoes long-standing concerns about oligarchs undermining plebiscitary democracy that date at least to Niccolò Machiavelli's analysis of ancient Rome (McCormick 2011).

The second literature is power resources theory, one of the dominant explanations for the variation in the size and scope of the welfare state in OECD countries. Korpi (1983), Stephens (1979), and others argue that strong unions are needed to compress wage and salary distributions and to lower market inequality, and that social democratic parties will deliver redistributive social policy.[6] Yet in marked contrast to the OECD (Iversen and Soskice 2006), strong unions and effective social democratic parties are lacking in much of the developing world. The weaker bargaining position of workers in the developing world, along with globalization, may limit the effect of democracy on certain redistributive policies (Avelino, Brown, and Hunter 2005; Rudra 2002). And partisanship has little explanatory power over redistribution in many developing countries (see, e.g., Huber, Mustillo, and Stephens 2008).

The third literature, which is not explicitly focused on redistribution, stems from North's (1990) watershed neoclassical theory of the state. Authors in this tradition emphasize that in autocracies, a lack of formal institutions and commitment mechanisms – factors critical to making property rights protection credible – facilitates expropriation in these regimes (e.g., North and Weingast 1989; Olson 1993). Democratic institutions, by contrast, create checks and balances that tie the hands of leaders who may otherwise violate property rights through major policy changes. This literature therefore shifts the focus toward horizontal constraints and away from political incentives. It consequently struggles to explain why some unconstrained rulers but not others violate elite property rights, and why these violations sometimes take the form of redistribution as opposed to predation, which merely lines the pockets of rulers or facilitates their parochial interests (e.g., warfighting).

The contributions from these three literatures all underscore the recognition that the explanation of redistribution through social conflict theory is incomplete, but they leave us with no robust alternative framework for understanding when and where redistribution should occur, especially in developing countries. This book offers a step in the direction of building a new foundation for explaining the politics of redistribution.

THE LAND REFORM PUZZLE

The literature on land reform supports the notion that elites can capture or disproportionately influence the policymaking process under democracy to undercut redistribution (e.g., Huntington 1968). But the balance of findings in this

---

[6] Iversen and Soskice (2009) argue that these factors have deeper roots in economic coordination (especially in guilds and rural cooperatives) and the limited proportional representation systems of the nineteenth and early twentieth centuries.

literature also highlights a fundamental disjuncture between general theory on redistribution and actual outcomes. Neither social conflict theory nor its recent correctives provide a framework to make sense of the empirical fact that land redistribution has been *substantially greater under autocracy than under democracy*. This finding sits more at ease with the literature on property rights protection – which many political economists seem to forget when bringing the median voter model to bear on questions of redistribution – although it would be quite a stretch to say that the property rights literature provides a satisfying explanation for patterns of land redistribution (or for other types of redistribution).

Land reform under democracy should, however, be an easy case for social conflict theory. As discussed earlier in this chapter, when land inequality and asset specificity are extremely high – *as is the case in nearly all of the rural sector in Latin America* – democratic transition, when it comes, should yield major land reform. This prediction is only strengthened by the fact that land reform can make an important contribution to economic growth by creating greater equality of holdings (Alesina and Rodrik 1994; Lipton 2009), as it did in Japan, South Korea, and Taiwan. In fact, Bardhan and Mookherjee (2010) suggest in their careful study of West Bengal that land reform is one of the few developmental policies in which the trade-off between equity and growth can be avoided. Land reform should therefore be politically attractive for demo-cratic politicians seeking votes (Lapp 2004). Yet land reform under democracy in Latin America is massively and systematically lower than what theories of redistribution would lead us to expect.

Extant theory also fails to shed light on why some autocracies distribute land while others do not. These patterns are particularly puzzling under existing theories of redistribution given that "[a]grarian reforms have generally been the outcome of political changes from above" (Kay 1998, 15). Although the process of reform is often influenced by social pressures from below, the lack of strong peasant unions and the rural dispersion of peasants has meant that "few agrarian reforms in Latin America were the direct result of peasant uprisings" (Kay 1998, 15).

The literature on land reform brings us closer to understanding the patterns of reform that are perplexing under more general theories of redistribution. For instance, Huntington (1968, 388) famously argues that "pluralistic politics and parliamentary rule are often incompatible with effective land reforms." And in a sweeping volume that analyzes the history of land reform in eight countries, Tai (1974, 473) similarly concludes that successful reform is more likely where "political power is concentrated in one political party or a small group of leaders."

Yet these seminal contributions – in a manner that parallels the property rights protection literature's predictions regarding rights violations – speak more to the broad patterns of land reform than to the causal mechanisms that trigger reform in some instances and not others. They also fail to distinguish between different types of land reform. Take Huntington's (1968) argument about pluralistic politics and legislatures acting as the "graveyards" of land reform. Although I find evidence consistent with this claim, its obverse – that the absence of pluralistic politics yields land reform – is not true. There are many cases of narrow autocratic regimes that do not implement land reform. I develop a theory for why some of these regimes pursue land reform while others do not. Huntington's focus on the role of legislatures in blocking land reform is also too narrow; reform may be effectively forestalled by an executive, the bureaucracy, or the judiciary as well. Finally, Huntington fails to differentiate theoretically between different types of land reform, instead basing his conclusions primarily (but not exclusively) on land redistribution. Yet land negotiation and colonization operate under distinct logics. Both of these types of reform frequently occur despite pluralistic politics and robust legislatures, conditions that Huntington would consider inimical to land reform. The shortcomings of Tai's work parallel those of Huntington.

Furthermore, the land reform literature is not unified on the patterns of reform. El-Ghonemy (2002), for instance, argues that an authoritarian approach to land reform has yielded the most consequential results, similar to Huntington's and Tai's arguments. Yet Lapp (2004) maintains that land reform is instead most likely when there is a democratic opening that expands the franchise and institutionalized political parties are competing for new rural voters. Thiesenhusen (1995) contends that major reforms occur only in the wake of revolution when newly enfranchised peasants demand reform and overwhelm a landlord class already weakened by war and economic decline, and minor reforms occur when governments seek foreign funding or want to undercut opposition from below. Hirschman (1963) argues that "divide and reform" tactics can yield reform when politicians confront a fractionalized array of landowners and other elites, opening the possibility of a "revolution by stealth." Powelson and Stock (1990) hold that, with the exception of nineteenth-century reforms in Europe and Japan, land reform occurs without peasant pressure when a government either has already conquered the landed aristocracy or is an elected minority with a compassion for the peasantry. Although Paige (1975) focuses primarily on explaining forms of peasant collective action, he envisions three paths to land reform: revolutionary nationalist movements in agrarian economies with settler (typically former colonial) estates, socialist movements that yield revolution in reaction to sharecropping systems, and the initiatives of reformist political parties that spark agrarian movements in commercial hacienda systems. The socialist movement path echoes Tuma's (1965) and Skocpol's (1979) emphasis on the revolutionary road to reform. Yet it contrasts with de Janvry's (1981) conclusion that many 1960s land reforms were implemented from above to undercut peasant revolts and stabilize capitalist relations.

Nearly all of these diverse explanations for land reform contrast with existing general theories of redistribution. They also underscore the need for further basic research on two questions. First, what are the political conditions under which various types of land reform occur? And second, how might these findings contribute to the refinement of existing theory?

In answering these questions, this book casts doubt on the fundamental assumption that drives social conflict theory: that redistribution should be both higher and more targeted at the poor under democracy. Instead, by endogenizing the heterogeneous preferences of elites, it builds a theory of land redistribution that can explain the political conditions most conducive to reform. Given the relative lack of powerful class-based social democratic parties in Latin America and the relatively few established peasant unions that mimic the dense networks of labor unions that push for redistributive social policy in the OECD, this book also sheds light on the scope conditions of power resources theory. Although the patterns of land redistribution are influenced by pressure from below, it is intra-elite competition that largely determines when, where, and how land reform occurs.

SUMMARY OF THE ARGUMENT

The main argument of this book is that for land redistribution to occur, it requires those in government to have both the incentive and the capacity to implement redistribution. There must first be a *coalitional split* between landed elites and ruling political elites that gives political elites an incentive to cut landed elites out of power. The concentration of power under autocracy makes land redistribution more likely but does not guarantee it. Once there is a coalitional split that provides ruling political elites with the incentive to pursue land redistribution, there must also be *low institutional constraints* in order for land redistribution to be carried out. The implementation of land redistribution requires the sustained cooperation of a wide range of political actors and sufficient administrative capacity.[7] The opposition of a small number of actors can jeopardize reform: if the executive opposes reform, the legislature cuts off funding, the judiciary raises legal barriers, or the bureaucracy is corrupt or unorganized, redistributive land reform efforts will fail. Landed elites, of course, can affect the likelihood of a failed reform by influencing *any* of these actors to obstruct reform. Land redistribution therefore operates as a type of veto gauntlet: the support of a wide range of actors is required for action. The creation of new institutions and agencies cannot circumvent an otherwise onerous process. There is no back door to land redistribution. The institutional constraints to policymaking under democracy make redistributive land reform by a democratic regime unlikely.

I find strong empirical evidence in support of this theory in later chapters. The findings hold both in the descriptive statistics and in a host of regression

---

[7] I therefore depart from political economy literature that conflates low institutional constraints with low institutional capacity and high constraints with high capacity.

models regardless of the estimation strategy. The results are also robust to accounting for a series of alternative explanations of land redistribution that are offered in the literature: left-wing ideology, development trends and contagion spillovers, foreign aid and other forms of foreign influence, the long-term legacies of geographical endowments, economic openness, fluctuations in land value, the outsized influence of revolutionary regimes, autocratic regime types, and the level of economic inequality. Although these alternative explanations may help account for isolated instances of redistribution, their broader explanatory power is uniformly poor and always plays second fiddle to elite splits and institutional constraints. Finally, the results hold when including country fixed effects to address unobserved country specific time-invariant heterogeneity and when using instrumental variables estimation to account for potential endogeneity in elite splits and institutional constraints.

Successful land redistribution serves two powerful, complementary functions from the perspective of ruling political elites. First and foremost, it weakens or even destroys landed elites and the potential threat they pose to political elites and their support group over the longer term. Second, it generates resources to undercut the threat of instability from below by providing land for redistribution to the rural poor. As Huntington (1968, 292) memorably quipped, "He who controls the countryside controls the country." Once the supply side is satisfied and there is a political opening for land redistribution, pressure from below can influence the scope and spatial patterns of reform. This is because resistance and protest by the masses can raise the costs of ruling (Scott 1985). It can also threaten political stability and even spark revolution (Acemoglu and Robinson 2006; Boix 2003). Providing selective incentives to the masses or pursuing populist policies such as distributing land can reduce resistance and yield valuable support for the regime (Levine 1998). Land redistribution is therefore rarely initiated to put the genie of revolution back in the bottle, but it does provide an opportunity to build peasant dependencies and ease the pacification of the countryside.

The land reform typology that I develop aids in the testing of my argument. In contrast to land redistribution, which presents a clear threat to landed elites, land negotiation poses at most a mild threat, and land colonization poses no threat at all. I therefore anticipate that a coalitional split between landed and political elites alongside low institutional constraints should be less important for land negotiation and irrelevant for land colonization. Instead, other factors, such as foreign aid, wealth, and popular pressure from below, should have a greater impact on these types of land reform. I elaborate on the logic of land negotiation and land colonization in Chapters 4, 5, and 7.

Incentives for Redistribution

Political elites often have strong incentives to redistribute under democracy. As the franchise is extended and the relatively poor masses are empowered, both social conflict theory and power resources theory suggest that these new voters will be able to translate their preferences into policy. In agrarian societies where landed elites disproportionately control access to land, politicians will seek office by courting rural voters with the promise of land reform (Lapp 2004; Swinnen 2002). Because rural voters greatly outnumber landed elites, stable political coalitions can be built without relying on the support of landed elites. Of course, factors such as cross-cutting cleavages and clientelism can be used instrumentally by landed elites to insert themselves into political coalitions alongside rural voters, which undercuts the incentives for land redistribution.

Political elites under autocracy can also have strong incentives to redistribute. Whereas landed elites may have considerable influence that can be translated into political power in autocratic regimes, as suggested by social conflict theory, they cannot always ensure that their interests will be upheld. Why do some dictators and their autocratic coalitions faithfully uphold the interests of powerful landed elites and not others? The key determinant of whether autocratic political elites will turn on landed elites is the level of *coalitional overlap* between (i) ruling political elites and the allies that comprise their initial support coalition and (ii) landed elites.[8] The members of the initial support coalition can be landed or other economic elites; they can also be cliques of military officers or larger social groups, such as labor unions or peasant organizations. These coalitional dynamics are the political origins of redistribution.

When the ruling political elite's initial support coalition is composed of members of the landed elite or depends on landed elites for key financial, logistical, or repressive support, political elites are unlikely to expropriate these individuals for fear of undercutting their only supporters and therefore all but guaranteeing their overthrow. By contrast, when the initial support coalition is not composed of landed elites and is not dependent on or allied with them, the expropriation of landed elites is one powerful policy that ruling political elites can employ to reduce their political insecurity and remain in office longer, because it eliminates rivals with long-standing power. And given the initial support coalition's tenuous position at the outset of a new regime (Bueno de Mesquita et al. 2003), the political elite's demonstration that they will not rely on other economic elites, such as landed elites, for their chief political support signals to this key coalition a credible commitment to future rents from political power. The initial support coalition can therefore benefit from expropriation by gaining credible access to future power and rents – and should strongly advocate for it – even if its members are not the recipients of the expropriated assets.

---

[8] Haber (2006) refers to the initial support coalition as a "launching organization." I distinguish this term from the governing coalition on which the political elites rely once their rule stabilizes, because the groups composing the governing coalition may differ from those in the initial coalition.

Capacity for Redistribution

Existing theories of redistribution focus primarily on government incentives to pursue redistribution. There is less attention paid to the capacity for policy implementation. Yet the ability to execute policy plays a key role in redistributive outcomes. Furthermore, this ability is correlated with regime type.

Although both democracies and autocracies can have political *incentives* to pursue redistribution, democratic leaders often face prohibitively restrictive *institutional constraints* to redistribution. Democratic institutions frequently build heterogeneous interests and powers into government, creating checks and balances that require large coalitions to support major policy changes such as redistributive reforms. Indeed, this type of horizontal accountability is at the heart of James Madison's vision of democratic constraints in *The Federalist* Papers (Madison, Hamilton, and Jay [1788] 1998). It also underpins Adam Smith's conclusion that "[c]ivil Government, so far as it is instituted for the security of property, is in reality instituted for the defence of the rich against the poor" (Smith [1776] 1863, 321).

Social conflict theory and power resources theory face a conceptual problem in focusing on what Dahl (1971) calls the participation or inclusiveness dimension of democracy while downplaying horizontal constraints. This leads to majoritarian predictions of policy outcomes. Although Dahl himself largely sidelines constraints, he nonetheless recognizes that adding a contestation dimension to participation "increases the number of individuals, groups, and interests whose preferences have to be considered in policymaking" (Dahl 1971, 14). Slater (2013) takes this one step further, noting wide variation in horizontal constraints among democracies and highlighting the capacity of horizontal constraints to restrain policymakers. These constraints are always at risk of clashing with the participatory demands of the relatively excluded.

The key role of horizontal constraints in the credible protection of property rights is at the heart of North's (1990) influential neoclassical theory of the state and Olson's (1993) view of the state as a "stationary bandit." Because the absence of formal institutions and commitment mechanisms in autocracies makes it easier for a regime to violate or redefine property rights, players with a stake in the game will act to alter the structure of decision making to construct third-party enforcement of contracts and to eliminate the unfettered ability of the sovereign to confiscate assets (see also North and Weingast 1989).

The literature on economic policy reform is no stranger to these conclusions. Most of this literature holds that when institutional constraints to policymaking are higher, it is less likely that significant policy changes will be enacted (e.g., Henisz 2000; Tsebelis 2002). Haggard and Kaufman (1995), for instance, demonstrate that fragmented political systems decrease the likelihood of major economic reform. Franzese (2002) similarly demonstrates how greater numbers of veto players slow fiscal adjustments to negative economic shocks. Applied to land redistribution, this literature implies that a larger number of veto players will set the stage for more heterogeneous interests within any legislature, administration, and bureaucracy, all of whose support is necessary for the implementation of a serious reform but which are also susceptible to obstruction by landed interests (Tai 1974; Thiesenhusen 1989). Even if a reform program is successfully initiated by one democratic administration, political changes in a subsequent administration may block its implementation (Herring 1983).

Of course, the strong horizontal checks and balances envisioned by the Federalists pose normative and practical difficulties for political accountability and citizen inclusivity. With the rare exception of more radical forms of popular, majoritarian, or plebiscitary democracy, elites can often block redistribution under democracy through direct representation in the legislature, placement in the judiciary, elite capture of elected officials, judges, or bureaucrats, and clientelism.[9]

This discussion about horizontal constraints in democracy implies that democracies are less likely to implement redistributive reform programs than autocracies, provided that a dictator is more empowered by autocracy than the landless are empowered by democracy. Yet the policy reform literature is less clear on when low constraints will actually lead to reform; it offers factors that range from partisan advantage to ideology to the simple desire by incumbents to line their own pockets. I argue that when leaders face *fewer institutional constraints* and need only small coalitions to support reform, changes such as large-scale redistribution can be implemented more rapidly and with less resistance from other government branches or agencies *if a leader has the coalitional incentives to pursue such changes.* A ruling political elite that is restrained by few institutional veto points and is motivated to displace traditional landed elites is better able to coherently leverage state resources to effect redistribution than one who necessitates compromise and coordination with potentially opposing political actors. Redistributive reform is therefore more likely to happen under a strong, determined autocratic political elite than under democracy.

ROAD MAP OF THE BOOK

The layout of the book is as follows. Chapter 2 defines the main political actors that bargain over land reform: landed elites, ruling political elites, and the rural poor. Economic, social, and political factors combine to constitute these actors. This chapter then takes an important further step toward understanding the deeper political roots of redistribution by theorizing the origins of coalitional splits between ruling political elites and landed elites. Drives for state autonomy (especially by the military and by secularizing political elites), a developing and

---

[9] One of the most prominent examples of the tension between the demand for popular sovereignty through majoritarian democracy and the constraints of Madisonian democracy is Carl Schmitt's (1923) argument for the failings of parliamentary democracy in interwar Europe and the notion that emergency conditions justified the imposition of dictatorial rule in Weimar Germany.

diversifying economy, ethnic differences, and foreign occupation can all generate elite splits.

Chapter 3 develops a theory to explain the conditions under which land reform occurs. This chapter first details the political process of land reform, outlining the steps required to create and implement an effective land reform and the players and institutions involved in this process. It then examines how the various political actors interact within this process to either push for or block land reform. Chapter 3 also builds a formal model of the theoretical argument and analytically examines how several key parameters – such as the coalitional overlap between political and landed elites and the capacity of landed elites to capture democratic policymaking – affect the likelihood of land redistribution. It does so while also introducing several additional components that capture the broader political environment in which land reform decisions are made: dynamic decision making, simultaneous policies of redistribution captured through taxes and transfers, coup threats by the landed elite, the threat of revolt by the rural poor, and the costs associated with political conflict. The model demonstrates that land redistribution is more likely to occur under autocratic rule. Whereas a popular democracy instituted by the masses may implement land redistribution, democratic transitions are more typically captured by elites who construct safeguards against redistribution under democracy. The model also shows that the likelihood of land redistribution increases as the coalitional split between the landed elite and the political elite widens and that land redistribution is more likely when the rural poor form a more credible threat of revolt.

Chapter 4 provides a framework for differentiating and measuring analytically distinct land reform policies. There is a large case study literature on land reform and a number of insightful compilations of reform analyses (e.g., Barraclough 1973; Binswanger-Mkhize, Bourguignon, and van den Brink 2009; Dorner 1992; Rosset, Patel, and Courville 2006; Thiesenhusen 1989). Yet although these works provide key insights into land reform policies, it is hard to draw broader inferences from them in the absence of a systematic coding of land policies and land transfers in a manner that is cross-country comparable and spans a sufficient time period. What precisely constitutes land reform? Have land reform policies changed over time and, if so, how? Where and when has land reform been implemented most intensely, and what consequences has it had? Chapter 4 addresses these questions. This chapter codes country-year level data on land transfers for all of Latin America between 1930 and 2008. I focus on three main policies of reform: redistribution, negotiation, and colonization. These policies are defined and detailed in turn, and I discuss the redistributive nature of each of them.

Chapter 5 presents a series of empirical analyses of land reform to test the theoretical predictions presented in Chapter 3. Chapter 5 therefore contributes to an explanation of why land reform occurred in some countries and not others, why it took the form that it did, and why it occurred at certain points in time. I find that land redistribution is most likely to occur when there are both coalitional splits between political and landed elites as well as low institutional constraints to rule. Pressure from below and revolution are also robustly linked to land redistribution, but they have less impact on the magnitude of redistribution and rarely yield substantial redistribution absent elite splits and low institutional constraints. These factors instead tend to impact the scope and targeting of redistribution once a political opening has been created. The findings are robust to accounting for a host of alternative explanations, including ideology, development trends and spillover effects, foreign influence, geographical endowments, globalization in the form of economic openness, declining land value, the disproportionate impact of revolutionary regimes, autocratic regime types, and economic inequality. They are also robust to using instrumental variables estimation to account for potential endogeneity in elite splits and institutional constraints. Consistent with the theory, I also find that less redistributive land reforms, such as land negotiation and land colonization, are less strongly associated with elite splits and lower institutional constraints. The Chapter 5 findings indicate that those elites that are assumed under existing theory to be most opposed to redistribution and therefore to democracy – landowners – often fare worse under autocracy than they do under democracy.

Chapters 6 and 7 turn to within-country variation in land reform in order to examine the theory's causal mechanisms and to test the observable implications of the theory. In doing so, these chapters ultimately help demonstrate the theory's internal validity. They also show the usefulness of the theory in generating an understanding of the spatial and temporal variation in land reform *within* as well as *across* countries.

Chapter 6 examines in depth an episode of redistributive land reform under military rule in Peru. This chapter first details, in line with the theory, the economic and political conditions that led to land reform at a particular moment. It then unpacks the coalitional politics that generated a split between landed elites and ruling political elites, which in turn made large-scale land redistribution politically attractive for the military. Finally, Chapter 6 sheds light on how land reform was used to target landed elites as well as on which groups of peasants received land and why. Prior to 1968, the Peruvian military had long been manipulated by powerful landed elites who had regulated its budget and training curriculum, called on it to overthrow threatening democratic regimes, and then used their ownership of the press and lucrative export sector to coordinate opposition and pressure military rulers who deviated from their desired policies. The military dictators Juan Velasco Alvarado and Francisco Morales Bermúdez and their political allies consequently sought to "break the back of the oligarchy" with a wide-ranging land reform program aimed at diminishing elite influence over the military's institutions, budget, and actions. A subnational analysis of the roughly 15,000 properties that were expropriated and redistributed from 1968 to 1980 – constituting 45 percent of all agricultural land in the country – demonstrates that the military targeted its land reform program to destroy the largest, most influential landowners. Land was redistributed to "middle-class" peasants that had worked on expropriated estates and had the greatest potential to organize against the regime had the reform excluded them or been broadened.

Chapter 7 examines how institutional constraints blocked land redistribution in favor of land negotiation and colonization in Venezuela from 1958 until the 1990s. It also explains how Hugo Chávez brought land redistribution back to the table. This chapter first provides a broad overview, within the framework of the theory, of why land reform occurred in Venezuela when it did as well as why it was structured in certain ways. It then moves a step further to conduct subnational analyses on all land transfers under the Punto Fijo era of democracy from 1958 until the 1990s and on all land beneficiaries under Hugo Chávez's new land reform program. Venezuela's first major agrarian reform law was passed in 1960, and from 1960 to 1991, roughly 8.2 million hectares of property passed through the hands of the government – more than half of the cultivable land in the country. Yet landed elites who helped craft the reform law used their influence within democratic institutions to block land redistribution in favor of excessively compensated land negotiation and land colonization. The two principal political parties then used land that had been acquired through the reform as a distributive tool to build party support among newly enfranchised rural voters in a clientelistic fashion. Land reform fizzled in the 1990s. Then Hugo Chávez brought land reform back to the agenda in the 2000s, transforming the Punto Fijo era style of reform into land redistribution as part of his "Bolivarian Revolution." As institutional constraints weakened under Chávez and Nicolás Maduro, land reform grew teeth. Venezuela's land reform now represents the largest land redistribution program in the Western Hemisphere.

Chapter 8 places land reform in Latin America in comparative perspective. The chief aim of the chapter is to explore whether the dynamics that have driven policies and patterns of land redistribution in Latin America also operate in other contexts. To that end, it introduces a complete account of all cases of redistributive land reform that have occurred outside of Latin America since 1900 as well as the conditions under which these reforms have occurred. I document fifty-four episodes of land redistribution across forty-five countries outside of Latin America since 1900, spanning every region of the world. Together with Latin America, more than one-third of all the countries in the world experienced redistributive land reform in the past century. More than 80 percent of redistributive land reforms beyond Latin America occurred when there was a coalitional split between political and landed elites alongside low institutional constraints to rule. This relationship remains robust in a series of regressions. The chapter then conducts a structured comparison of elite splits, institutional constraints, and land reform across four specific cases in four different regions: Egypt, Hungary, Taiwan, and Zimbabwe. A process-tracing exercise in each of these cases demonstrates further support for the causal mechanisms that link low institutional constraints and elite splits to redistributive land reform.

Chapter 9 concludes the book. This chapter briefly recounts my basic theoretical argument and findings and subsequently explains how and why they challenge some of the commonly held wisdoms about the rural sector. It then discusses whether land redistribution is entirely unique from other types of redistribution or whether the theoretical argument has purchase in explaining other major types of redistribution. Although there has been surprisingly little broadly comparative empirical research on many types of redistribution, suggestive evidence indicates that the expropriation and distribution of the assets of natural resource and financial firms, legal changes that extended certain human rights (e.g., the abolition of forced servitude), the centralization and expansion of access to primary education, and even early welfare state initiatives that established social insurance, minimum wages, maximum hours, and corporate profit sharing in much of Europe often occurred when institutional constraints were low and leaders were split from major economic interests. If indeed this is generalizable, these findings would represent the most comprehensive challenge to existing theory on redistribution to date and should cause a dramatic rethinking of the scope of both social conflict theory and power resources theory.

Chapter 9 subsequently examines some of the problematic normative implications of the main finding: that land redistribution occurs most often under dictatorship. If the rural poor are destined for the greatest material gain under repressive regimes, should we simply hold our noses and prescribe dictatorship for early stages of development? What is to be done for those countries that have become democratic yet never cowed landed elites? Fortunately, the rural sector need not be left in the lurch as the world becomes more democratic. The experiences of Brazil, Colombia, the Philippines, South Africa, and Venezuela demonstrate that land negotiation and land colonization can effectively get land to the tiller. But if the world is serious about tackling rural poverty, landlessness, and rural unrest, these programs need a major shot in the arm. The current attempts to address these issues are the equivalent of using a bucket of water to douse a burning house. The most practical and effective solutions for fixing these programs include providing vastly more funding from the top down, opening a parallel reform track that operates from the bottom up by harnessing existing technology and forms of service provision, and creating new standards or having international agencies such as the World Bank provide a blessing over "land redistribution light," which would facilitate quicker reform without engendering capital flight by enabling "fair" rather than market-value compensation to expropriated landowners.

Finally, Chapter 9 explores some of the long-term consequences of land reform for economic growth, rural stability, the growth of human capital, and the foundations of political regimes. Now that this book offers the first comparable dataset on land reform, spanning a long period of time and a host of countries, these relationships can be empirically tested in a more direct manner than ever before. Furthermore, some of these literatures would do well to incorporate insights from the theory presented in this book. Class-based models of democracy, for instance, should incorporate intra-elite splits that enable political elites who directly hold power to act separately from landed or other economic elites outside of government. An elite that is wary of potentially volatile autocratic rule may be more likely to push for democracy from a position of strength, thereby undercutting the hypothesized link between democracy and equality.

2

Actors, Interests, and the Origins of Elite Splits

This chapter begins laying the foundation for a theory of land reform. I first define the main political actors that impact reform outcomes: landed elites, ruling political elites, and the rural poor. I detail how these actors are constituted and what their preferences are. Although I focus on these actors in the Latin American context, their relevance is far from limited to this region. I consequently provide extensions regarding how to conceive of them in other contexts.

This chapter also examines in depth the origins of splits between landed and ruling political elites. While much of the current general theory on redistribution collapses elites into one monolithic actor, I argue that splits among elites are crucial for providing the incentives for land redistribution. Furthermore, elite splits are far from uncommon. I demonstrate that a range of circumstances can give rise to splits between landed elites and ruling political elites: drives for state autonomy (especially by the military or by secularizing and developmentally oriented political elites), a diversifying economy, ethnic difference, and foreign occupation. Recognizing these splits brings us closer to explaining observed patterns of redistribution. And theorizing where elite splits originate is a major step toward understanding the deeper political origins of redistribution.

LANDED ELITES, RULING POLITICAL ELITES, AND THE RURAL POOR IN LATIN AMERICA

From the time of colonization until the early twentieth century, most Latin American countries were characterized by extreme social and economic inequality rooted in the skewed distribution and use of land. More than half of the population in Latin America was rural until 1960. Yet the vast majority of rural laborers were poor. The poorest half of rural workers in most countries throughout the region typically held less than 5 percent of the land. Landed elites, by contrast, were very powerful. The richest 2–3 percent of large landowners typically commanded ownership of most of a country's land. Landed elites also used their authority to influence the behavior and even the movement of the rural workers who lived on their estates (Baland and Robinson 2008; Barraclough 1973). Against this backdrop, there was also a turbulent political environment. Frequent political transitions in many countries brought to power political elites with widely divergent coalitions and agendas. Ruling political elites were at times allied with landed elites and at other times directly in conflict with them.

Landed elites, ruling political elites, and the rural poor are hardly the only social groups that matter for land reform outcomes. Political parties, urban workers, bureaucrats, and foreign actors can also influence land reform, either directly or through alliances with or against these other groups. Yet we can go a long way toward understanding what drives the dynamics of land reform with a simplified and stylized focus on the principal players that impact reform. Interactions between landed elites, ruling political elites, and the rural poor have led to most of the major social changes related to land in the region. To be sure, the state, the bureaucracy, and political institutions play a key role in influencing how and whether redistribution actually occurs as a consequence of these interactions. I turn to this point in detail later in this chapter and in Chapter 3. Chapters 5 and 8 return to the role of foreign actors. But first I describe the main actors and their preferences.

Landed Elites

The first critical actor in my stylized model is the landed elite. These individuals enjoy selective property rights that grant them special privileges and, often, flows of rents. Landed elites own land as a "livelihood,...as financial security (e.g. as a hedge against inflation), as a transfer of wealth across the generations, and as a resource for consumption purposes (e.g. country estates held by urban elites for leisure purposes)" (Ellis 1992, 196). Because of the versatility of land, many economic elites in Latin America have historically held some landed interest as a component of their net assets.[1] Landed elites seek first and foremost to protect their property rights and maintain their land. Cohesion within this group is underpinned by a shared interest in preventing land redistribution.

Landed elites in most Latin American countries have been small in number but command substantial economic power through extensive landholdings and the control of labor. This further contributes to their social cohesiveness and ability to act collectively. The outsized power of landed elites can in many cases be traced back to colonial times, when the Spanish and Portuguese crowns granted extensive tracts of land to colonizers and the church as well as the right to use indigenous populations as resident laborers (Barraclough 1973). This arrangement led to the widespread *latifundio-minifundio* system, in which

---

[1] See, e.g., Gilbert (1977, 344) for a discussion of the Peruvian case.

indigenous peasants worked for landlords and could subsistence farm on their own small plots when they were not otherwise occupied (Thiesenhusen 1995, 70). Subsequent developments, such as the granting of large landholdings to key military figures in the independence movements and disentailment laws that enabled already powerful elites to usurp remaining indigenous lands, often reinforced unequal landholding patterns. To be sure, there are distinctions between large landowners, such as those who are engaged in labor-intensive agriculture versus those who are not (e.g., Moore 1966; Rueschemeyer, Stephens, and Stephens 1992). Nonetheless, landowners tend to circle the wagons as a group in the face of threats to their properties.

Chile is one illustrative example of the power and perpetuation of landed elites. Large estates predominated in Chile at the end of the nineteenth century and into the early twentieth century as a result of the enormous land grants (*mercedes*) and trusts (*encomiendas*) that had been given to conquistadors and other Spanish families by the crown centuries earlier. *Encomienda* owners were allowed to use the labor of the population in their jurisdiction. By the early 1800s, most of these consolidated estates were used for cattle ranching for domestic consumption, but the opening of new export markets in the mid- to late 1800s brought a shift to wheat farming, which required more labor.[2] Landowners established large resident workforces on their property, spurring *inquilinaje*, a "quasi-feudal patron-client institution that was a central feature of Chile's agrarian structure for nearly a century" (Thome 1989, 218). These *inquilinos* formed a growing rural middle class, and although they began as renters, displacing day laborers (peons and slaves) who became temporary and migrant workers, the *inquilinos* gradually lost their relative independence and became dependent laborers (Thome 1989, 219–220). By 1928, a mere 2.5 percent of landowners held 78 percent of the arable land (Thiesenhusen 1995, 89–90). And with the exception of mine owners, large landowners had the highest per capita income of any social group in Chile in the late nineteenth century (Rodríguez Weber 2009).

McBride (1936) provides a stark picture of Chile in the early twentieth century as "a twentieth-century people still preserving a feudal society; a republic based on the equality of man, yet with a blue-blood aristocracy and a servile class as distinctly separated as in any of the monarchies of the Old World." Large landowners coordinated to defend their power and landholdings through organizations such as the powerful Sociedad Nacional de Agricultura, which yielded several presidents and persisted in a similar fashion until the 1960s with the stated intent of "defending the interests of agriculture against public powers and popular opinion."

---

[2] One of these new markets was San Francisco, because the Gold Rush brought a major population center to the western United States – which was much more easily reachable from the port of Valparaíso – for the first time.

The Chilean case is typical of the dominance of large landowners during this period. According to Bolivia's 1950 census, 92 percent of the farmland was owned by 6 percent of owners, whereas the smallest 80 percent of farms controlled only 1 percent of the land. Agriculture took place mainly on large haciendas, and landlords often kept peasants in debt peonage and sold them with their land. The concentration of land in sparsely populated Paraguay at the outset of the twentieth century was even more extreme. The state had sold off nearly 90 percent of all national land in the wake of the War of the Triple Alliance (1865–1870) in order to raise revenue. The land was obtained by a small number of corporations (many of which were foreign-owned) and Paraguayan elite (Carter and Galeano 1995, 51–53). In eastern Paraguay, eleven landowners held 5.5 million hectares, and sixty individuals and enterprises had obtained nearly the entire Paraguayan Chaco, which is more than 20 million hectares (Kleinpenning 1984, 165).

Table 2.1 provides statistics on the landholdings of the largest and smallest landholders for most countries in Latin America during the 1950–1970 period. The table indicates a clear pattern: landowners in most countries in Latin America were relatively few in number and very wealthy. The largest 2–5 percent of landowners in most of these countries held more than half – and in some cases closer to 80 percent – of the total land around 1950. The smallest 50 percent of landholders were often relegated to less than 5 percent of the land and in some cases as little as 1 percent. Large landowners also frequently controlled, or at least influenced, the mobility of a substantial portion of agricultural labor through various forms of debt peonage, anti-vagrancy laws, control over access to information, paternalistic tenancy arrangements, and influence over the police and judiciary. The most oppressive among them leaned on coercion and repression to ensure a supply of non-wage or servile labor (see, e.g., Rueschemeyer, Stephens, and Stephens 1992). But attempts to manipulate and control workers were hardly limited to this set of landowners.

That landed elites were small in number and very wealthy contributed to their social coherence as a group. Landed elite families often intermarried and were in frequent contact at exclusive country clubs and private events. In the case of El Salvador, Almeida (2008, 37) writes that "[b]etween 1913 and 1927, interlocking family clans with large landholdings dominated the Salvadorean polity." In Argentina, large landowner participation in elite social clubs such as the Sociedad Rural Argentina, the Jockey Club, the Club del Progreso, the Club Social, and the Círculo de Armas yielded tight social and familial bonds that often paid off politically (Figueroa and Leiras 2014). In Peru, the core of the oligarchy until the 1960s was the well-known "forty families": a group of traditional landed elites that dominated the major primary export sectors. Gilbert (1977) traces the lineages of several of these prominent families, demonstrating close-knit social ties, business collaborations, and marriages between families that were organized cognatically and functioned as corporate groups.

TABLE 2.1. *Land Distribution in Latin America, 1950–1970*

Country	Year	Less than 5 Hectares				More than 200 Hectares			
		Number of Holdings	% of Holdings	Area of Holdings (Ha.)	% Area of Holdings	Number of Holdings	% of Holdings	Area of Holdings (Ha.)	% Area of Holdings
Bolivia	1950	51,000	60.0	74,000	0.2	9,400	11.1	31,910,000	97.4
Brazil	1950	458,000	22.2	1,170,000	0.5	170,000	8.2	175,286,000	75.5
	1960	1,033,000	30.9	2,537,000	1.0	190,000	5.7	174,579,000	69.9
	1970	1,801,000	36.7	3,897,000	1.3	236,000	4.8	195,292,000	66.4
Colombia	1954	505,000	55.0	927,000	3.3	23,000	2.5	15,848,000	57.1
	1960	757,000	62.6	1,239,000	4.5	21,000	1.7	15,047,000	55.0
	1971	701,000	59.6	1,147,000	3.7	24,000	2.0	17,355,000	56.0
Costa Rica	1950	17,000	39.5	37,000	2.0	1,100	2.6	972,000	53.6
	1963	25,000	38.5	53,000	2.0	1,600	2.5	1,355,000	50.8
	1973	40,000	48.8	59,000	1.9	2,800	3.4	1,701,000	54.5
Cuba	1946	32,000	20.0	85,700	0.9	20,700	12.9	6,448,000	71.0
Dominican Rep.	1950	210,000	76.4	318,000	13.7	1,000	0.4	851,000	36.6
	1960	385,000	86.1	472,000	20.9	800	0.2	778,000	34.5
	1971	235,000	77.0	352,000	12.9	1,400	0.5	1,048,000	38.3
Ecuador	1954	251,000	73.0	432,000	7.2	3,200	0.9	3,400,000	56.7
	1974	336,000	64.7	539,000	6.8	6,000	1.2	3,127,000	39.3

Country	Year							
El Salvador	1950	140,000	80.5	190,000	12.4	1,000	0.6	618,000	40.4
	1961	190,000	84.8	232,000	14.9	1,000	0.4	589,000	37.8
	1971	282,000	88.7	283,000	19.5	700	0.2	410,000	28.2
Honduras	1952	88,000	56.4	202,000	8.1	1,300	0.8	953,000	38.0
	1974	125,000	64.1	240,000	9.1	1,500	0.8	892,000	33.9
Mexico	1950	1,004,000	72.6	1,363,000	0.9	55,000	4.0	131,995,000	90.7
	1960	900,000	65.9	1,328,000	0.8	68,000	5.0	152,467,000	90.2
	1970	609,000	59.7	881,000	0.6	64,000	6.3	125,598,000	89.8
Panama	1950	45,000	52.9	96,000	8.3	400	0.5	308,000	26.6
	1960	44,000	46.3	95,000	5.3	900	0.9	560,000	31.0
	1971	64,000	55.7	77,000	3.7	1,300	1.1	718,000	34.2
Peru	1961	728,000	83.7	1,036,000	5.8	6,000	0.7	14,302,000	80.7
	1972	1,105,000	79.4	1,560,000	6.6	8,000	0.6	16,858,000	71.6
Uruguay	1951	11,000	12.9	29,000	0.2	14,000	16.5		
	1961	12,000	13.8	34,000	0.2	15,000	17.2	14,457,000	85.1
	1970	11,000	14.3	30,000	0.2	14,000	18.2	14,338,000	86.8
Venezuela	1961	160,000	50.0	278,000	1.1	13,000	4.1	22,265,000	85.6
	1971	126,000	43.8	342,000	1.3	17,000	5.9	22,492,000	85.0

Sources: Author's calculations based on FAO 1981; Ministerio de Asuntos Campesinos y Agropecuarios 1951 (Bolivia); Hendrix 1996 (Cuba).

31

A similar situation operated in many other countries, such as Bolivia and Paraguay, as well.

The coherence of landed elites has declined in some ways with development as younger generations migrate to cities and landowners leverage their economic clout to enter the industrial sector. Yet those who have remained in possession of large tracts of land continue to be united at the very least by the desire to defend their landholdings, and they often have dense social and business networks that mimic earlier forms of organization. Albertus, Brambor, and Ceneviva (2015), for instance, document the web of personal, business, and political connections that underpin large landowner and agribusiness organization in contemporary Brazil.

While landed elites seek to protect their property rights and land ownership, I do not impose any assumptions about their preferences toward the types of political arrangements that yield this end. Much of the literature concludes that landlords are systematically antidemocratic because they fear that the majority would vote to expropriate them, and therefore landed elites support dictatorship over democracy (Acemoglu and Robinson 2006; Ansell and Samuels 2010; Boix 2003; Gerschenkron 1946; Ziblatt 2008). A narrower variant of this hypothesis suggests that landed elites who are devoted to labor-intensive or labor-repressive agriculture are an obstacle to democracy (Mahoney 2003; Moore 1966; Rueschemeyer et al. 1992; Wood 2000). Yet a host of examples demonstrate that these conclusions – especially the broader former one – are at best only partially correct.[3] Although landed elites may oppose a majoritarian democracy with few checks and balances, they have incentives to support a Madisonian-style democracy that protects minority property rights, particularly when the threat of expropriation under autocracy is high.[4]

Many democratic transitions in Latin America had the support of landed elites who helped craft democratic institutions. Examples include Colombia's democratization under the National Front in 1958 (Albertus and Kaplan 2013), Venezuela's transition under the 1958 Punto Fijo agreement (Albertus 2013), Peru's 1956 transition (Gilbert 1977), Brazil's 1985 transition (Weyland 1996), and a host of other transitions in Argentina, Ecuador, and Honduras. As Payne (1992, 19) writes in the case of Brazil's transition from military rule: "[L]andholders are unlikely to deliberately undermine the democratic transition since they have retained both influence and protection throughout that political process." Furthermore, it would be a stretch to argue that in none of these cases were landed elites labor-dependent. The recent deterioration of democracy in several countries in the region yields newer evidence that is

---

[3] For a summary of critiques and revisions to Moore's (1966) narrower conclusion about the antidemocratic nature of labor-repressive landowners, see Mahoney (2003).

[4] One illustrative example is the Philippines, where large landowners were more supportive of institutionally constrained democratic regimes in the 1960s and 1990s than they were of Ferdinand Marcos's less predictable autocratic rule during the New Society (Slater 2010).

consistent with the overarching point: large landowners and agribusiness in Venezuela, Bolivia, and Ecuador are among the most vocal proponents of more independent judiciaries and stronger constraints to executive rule in these countries.

Ruling Political Elites

The ruling political elite is the second major actor. The ruling political elite is composed of key military players and civilian politicians as well as important political appointees, and it is normally headed by an elected executive under democracy and a dictator or junta under autocracy. Although there may be conflicts and machinations even within the political elite, what they share is the power and organizational capacity to run the government. Ruling political elites control the state apparatus and therefore wield a credible threat of violence. This control enables them to grant, withdraw, and modify property rights. They also have broad policymaking influence, which affects citizens' welfare and economic choices. Political elites primarily seek to remain in office or to obtain greater power and autonomy for the institutions they represent (see, e.g., Geddes 2003).

In contrast to landed elites, ruling political elites are much more likely to have diverse social origins. This is true under both democracy and dictatorship. Although there may be overlap between landed elites and ruling political elites, such overlap is rarely complete. How the divergence between landed and political elites is manifested in land reform policies, however, depends on the structure of institutions – a point taken up in Chapter 3.

Under democracy, ruling political elites are comprised of elected politicians and appointees to key government and agency positions.[5] Among elected politicians, I restrict the focus to the executive branch.[6] The executive branch is the main catalyst of land reform initiatives. Legislators may be powerful political players but are typically second movers when it comes to land reform. Whereas reform will certainly fail if the executive opposes it, legislative opposition sometimes but not always spells the death of land reform. Key political appointees include those who occupy cabinet positions and the appointed leadership of the main agencies, if indeed these individuals are appointed.[7] These are all critical

---

[5] For an in-depth discussion of the concept of political elites, see, e.g., Parry (2005).

[6] These are nationally elected officials, although subnationally elected officials (e.g., governors) may also theoretically play an important role in decentralized or federal political systems to the extent that they have the authority to initiate and implement major policies, such as land reform. India is perhaps the best example. Subnationally elected leaders did not play a considerable role in land reform initiation in Latin America during the period covered by this study.

[7] There is variation among democracies in terms of whether (and how many) top officials and bureaucrats in key agencies are appointed versus internally promoted. These figures nonetheless play an important political role in the implementation of policy (see, e.g., Aberbach, Putnam, and Rockman 1981).

players surrounding the executive that influence the decisions of whether and how to formulate a land reform program.

As I discuss in detail in Chapter 3, elected politicians outside of the executive as well as judges and bureaucrats that rise to key posts via internal promotion can attempt to promote or forestall land reform. Their ability to do so, however, depends on the distribution of power among political institutions. I therefore treat this as a distinct variable in the theoretical argument elaborated in Chapter 3.

Democratic political elites are typically quite socially diverse. This is the result of relatively broad and open selection mechanisms and the nature of elections. By definition, the ability to contest elections under democracy is more open than it is under dictatorship. Politicians can and do arise not only from elite families but also from middle- and lower-class backgrounds. Furthermore, politicians are often elected from or affiliated with geographically distinct districts that vary in how urban they are, their level of development, their racial and ethnic composition, and many other dimensions. Representatives of diverse interests are likely to reflect many of those differences in office.

Under dictatorship, the ruling political elite is composed of key military players and civilian politicians along with appointees to powerful government and agency positions and is headed by a dictator or junta. The precise makeup of the ruling political elite depends in part on the type of dictatorship (see, e.g., Geddes 2003). Political elites in single-party dictatorships are those who staff the party's central committee and politburo along with those delegated to control powerful ministries. Political elites in military and personalist dictatorships are members of a relatively small circle of top military officers, civilians, and close advisors or administrators.

Recent research suggests that under dictatorship, pseudo-democratic institutions such as legislatures and opposition parties may contain key actors that serve to check an autocrat's rule (e.g., Gandhi 2008). This depends on their function. Whereas in some cases these institutions are used to simply co-opt restive groups within the population, in other cases autocratic rulers are forced to create such institutions to provide an avenue for powerful individuals to credibly check their power (Magaloni 2008). As with the case of democratic political elites outside of the executive discussed earlier in this section, I do not treat these powerful individuals in the same way as top autocratic political elites for the purposes of the theory. I instead consider their ability to check executive decisions through formal channels as a separate variable.

There is substantial variation in the social origins and diversity of ruling political elites under dictatorship. Some groups of autocratic political elites are relatively homogenous and integrated to a particular class or social interest, whereas others are very heterogeneous.

Consider the example of the political elite that ruled Venezuela from 1945 until early 1948. In 1945, a coalition of disaffected military officers and civilians united to overthrow the dictator Isaías Medina Angarita. The successful conspirators subsequently formed a seven-member ruling junta (Junta Revolucionaria de Gobierno) staffed by four civilians from the formerly repressed political party Acción Democrática (AD), an independent civilian, and two military officers from the self-fashioned Unión Patriótica Militar (UPM). AD leader Rómulo Betancourt presided over the junta. Many of the civilians were former student leaders from the Generation of '28, and they included a doctor, a political organizer, a teacher's union leader, a formerly exiled politician, and a lawyer. None was from an oligarchic family. The two military officers – one of whom would later overturn a subsequent election in a coup – were a French-educated engineer and a captain who had attended the Escuela Militar de Venezuela. The two military officers were part of the larger UPM (led by thirteen members), which opposed Medina's rule and wanted increased pay, better equipment, and more predictable promotions. The junta appointed a series of military and civilian cabinet officials who were equally socially varied. These individuals represented the two chief groups that comprised the initial support coalition of the regime: the UPM and Betancourt's ascendant political party, Acción Democrática. Table 2.2 provides an overview of the key ruling political elites of the regime.

Venezuela is far from being unique in having a diverse group of political elites ruling under nondemocracy. When Castelo Branco ousted João Goulart from power in Brazil in a 1964 military coup, post-coup policymaking was dominated by military officers and civilian technicians associated with the Higher War School (ESG) (Ames 1976, 264). The ESG had heavy joint military-civilian participation and wide recruitment from the middle class. Civilians were drawn from education, industry, communications, and banking. Mexico's post-revolutionary regime was built from key leaders of the three main factions that had jockeyed for power during the Mexican Revolution: small farmers from central Mexico, represented by Emiliano Zapata; the fledgling labor movement, represented politically by Pancho Villa; and a contingent of merchants, mine owners, and ranchers from Mexico's northern states, represented by Alvaro Obregón (Albertus and Menaldo 2012a). Paraguay's Revolutionary Febrerista Party, which seized power under Colonel Rafael Franco in 1936, was composed of soldiers, veterans, peasants, and students (Lewis 2006). Similarly heterogeneous coalitions were built in autocratic regimes in El Salvador, Bolivia, Ecuador, and elsewhere.

Heterogeneity among ruling political elites under dictatorship is in part a function of military recruitment, given that the military plays a key role in nondemocratic regimes. Military officers are often socially varied because they are recruited from a range of class backgrounds (Janowitz 1977). Just as Western militaries that were built on feudal aristocratic and upper-class personnel shifted toward middle-class recruitment during the nineteenth century, so too have the majority of Latin American military officers been of middle-class origin since the end of the nineteenth century (Nun 1976). Among the generals, brigadiers, and admirals in mid-twentieth-century Argentina, for example,

TABLE 2.2. *Key Ruling Political Elites in Venezuela, 1945–1948*

Members and Backgrounds of Junta Revolucionaria de Gobierno	Key Ruling Political Elites	Initial Support Coalition
1. Rómulo Betancourt (AD): former student leader; exiled several times; founded AD in 1941	1. Junta members	1. Acción Democrática (AD): popular political party founded by Betancourt and populated with middle-class activists
2. Carlos Delgado Chalbaud (UPM): raised in exile in France; engineer and military officer	2. Cabinet members a. Carlos Morales b. Carlos D'Ascoli c. Juan Pablo Pérez Alfonso d. Luis Lander e. Eduardo Mendoza Goiticoa f. Valmore Rodríguez g. Humberto García Arocha	2. Unión Patriótica Militar (UPM): group of disaffected military officers who opposed Medina's rule and wanted increased pay, better equipment, and more predictable promotions; founded by Captain Mario Vargas and led by Marcos Pérez Jiménez
3. Mario Vargas (UPM): career military officer; attended the Escuela Militar de Venezuela		
4. Gonzalo Barrios (AD): raised in Barquisimeto; doctorate from UCV; elected Senator in Portuguesa prior to exile; helped form AD		
5. Luis Beltrán Prieto (AD): raised in Nueva Esparta; doctorate from UCV; founded first national teachers union		
6. Raúl Leoni (AD): raised in Bolívar; former student leader; lawyer		
7. Edmundo Fernández (Independent): born in Caracas; jailed as student leader; doctor		

Note: AD indicates membership in Acción Democrática. UPM indicates membership in the Unión Patriótica Militar. These political elites handed over power to Rómulo Gallegos, who was inaugurated in 1948.

23 percent were from traditional families, nearly half were from middle- and upper-middle-class families, and 25 percent were from the lower middle class (Nun 1976, 53). Brazil exhibited a similar pattern during that period. The trend toward recruitment of the military from the middle and lower middle classes has continued over time throughout the region because interstate rivalry and

intrastate rivals have played large roles in military expansion and state building more generally (Thies 2005).

This shift toward middle-class officers is not unique to the West or to Latin America. It was mirrored in militaries in the Middle East in the mid-twentieth century (Bill 1969) and in Asia and sub-Saharan Africa (Janowitz 1977), although the social bases of recruitment in the latter were more variegated. Janowitz (1977, 125–126) attributes broad social recruitment in these regions to the lack of a tradition of feudalism and land inheritance that long grafted aristocratic families to the upper echelons of the military in Western Europe.

Varied patterns of social recruitment help explain why "the military have only exceptionally shown a tendency to act as the representatives of the oligarchy" (Nun 1976, 71). Militaries much more frequently pursue their own corporate interests (Albertus 2015a; Nordlinger 1977; Slater, Smith, and Nair 2014), which may only occasionally align with those of landed or other economic elites. This empirical fact is of course a significant departure from recent literature such as Acemoglu and Robinson (2001, 2006) and Boix (2003), who assume that those who hold power under dictatorship are the rich. Yet it is key for understanding the conditions under which large-scale land reform occurs.

While ruling political elites have their own incentives separate from those of the landed elite or the rural poor, their incentives can nonetheless be aligned to protect the rights and interests of the landed elite when political elites are directly drawn from the landed elite or when the support coalitions of political elites incorporate landed elites or allies of landed elites. Prominent examples include the Pinochet regime in Chile and parties under the National Front in Colombia. In Colombia, both the Liberals and Conservatives long had strong landowner membership (Zamosc 1986). Landowners from both parties were empowered in government under the National Front pact when democracy was reestablished in 1958. Indeed, members of the Federation of Colombian Cattle Ranchers and other powerful agricultural interests were given positions on the Agrarian Reform Committee board, which made high-level policy decisions on land reform (Albertus and Kaplan 2013). Although Lleras Restrepo (president, 1966–1970) attempted to broaden his popular base of support at the expense of large landowners (Zamosc 1986, 47–51), his efforts at reform were thwarted by the resistance of large landowners from both parties (Dugas 2000, 91). Large landowners and politicians then struck a formal agreement (the Chicoral Pact) to table significant land reform after the dissolution of the National Front.

Landed elites can also at times act as the puppet masters of ruling political elites. For instance, the Aspillaga family in Peru, a powerful north coast planter family that owned Cayalti, one of Peru's largest sugar plantations, made a massive contribution to Luis Miguel Sánchez Cerro's campaign for the presidency in 1931. Sánchez Cerro toppled the long-time military dictator Augusto Leguía in 1930 in a coup. Leguía had persecuted the Aspillagas for years. Heavily backing Sánchez Cerro in the election he arranged was an opportunity to turn the page. It also kept the family largely out of open and direct political involve-ment, consistent with Ramón Aspillaga's written counsel to his brothers to be "involved in everything, but visible nowhere" (Gilbert 1977, 96). The Aspilla-gas then organized a fundraising drive among a committee of fellow oligarchs to subdue rebellions and uprisings that threatened Sánchez Cerro's rule, hosted honorary events at Cayalti for the military, and even gave Sánchez Cerro the use of their private railroad to move troops to the country's interior (Gilbert 1977, 182). In exchange, Sánchez Cerro repressed political activity and labor organizing that threatened Cayalti and other major plantations and turned a blind eye as the Aspillagas bribed local officials to imprison and deport labor agitators (Gilbert 1977, 181). Other oligarchic families that had major landed interests and had backed Sánchez Cerro such as the Prados also benefited under his rule.

The policy preferences of ruling political elites and landed elites, however, are not always shared. Ruling political elites have an incentive to undermine the power of landed elites when their preferences diverge. And even if political elites have incentives to protect the property rights of landed elites, resulting in an overlap in policy preferences, this does not mean that these property rights cannot be rapidly withdrawn later.

Rural Poor

The third actor is the mass of the rural poor. The rural poor are far greater in number than either landed elites or ruling political elites. Although only 21 percent of the region's population was rural in 2010, more than 50 percent was rural before 1961. Figure 2.1 shows that the majority of the economically active population was employed in agriculture in fourteen of nineteen countries in Latin America in 1950. The same number of countries had more than 40 per-cent of the economically active population employed in agriculture in 1970 and a host of individuals that lived in small towns and supplemented their primary income via agricultural labor. Yet the vast majority of rural laborers were poor. As Table 2.1 indicates, it was not uncommon around 1950 for 60–70 percent of the smallest landowners in a country to hold less than one-tenth of the land.

The rural poor are a more diverse group than landed elites and are often differentiated by the form of their tenancy or labor (see, e.g., Paige 1975). Smallholders, renters, squatters, sharecroppers, day laborers, indigenous com-munities, and peons can simultaneously coexist in a single national agrarian economy. Peru is one illuminating example. Of the 16 million hectares of land in holdings larger than 5 hectares surveyed during the 1961 census, approx-imately 11 million hectares were privately owned and occupied, largely by landed elites (see Table 2.1). There were 2 million hectares in rental arrange-ments (typically resident laborers on larger properties), 70,000 hectares under sharecropping, 70,000 hectares in feudal (*yanaconaje*) arrangements, 2 million hectares in indigenous communities, and the rest in forms of mixed tenancy.

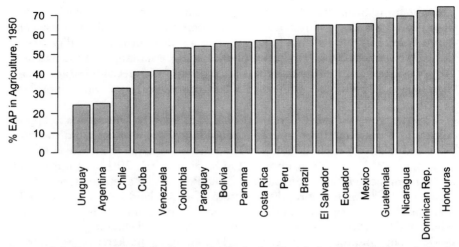

FIGURE 2.1. Percentage of the Economically Active Population in Agriculture in Latin America, 1950. *Note:* Data on the economically active population in agriculture are taken from the Oxford Latin American Economic History Database.

Similarly wide-ranging forms of tenancy could be found throughout the region prior to major land reforms.

Although the rural poor are fairly diverse, they are united by a common and powerful goal: to improve their well-being via increased access to land. The most secure form of land access is ownership. The rural poor therefore support land reform in substantial majorities, even if their electorally expressed preferences may at times be somewhat different because of factors such as clientelism.[8] The actual implementation of land reform in many contexts provides prima facie evidence for why diverse groups of peasants may rationally unite in support of reform: major land reforms typically benefit several distinct social groups of peasants simultaneously. Cuba's 1959 Agrarian Reform Law, for instance, gave preference over land redistribution to tenants, sharecroppers, and squatters simultaneously (Thomas 1971).

What if some subset of rural dwellers opposes – or at least does not actively support – land reform? Huntington (1968), for instance, writes that peasants may either be revolutionary or a conservative force that supports the status quo. Ansell and Samuels (2010) similarly argue that smallholders will support democratic constraints on government to protect their property rights. These authors envision that landholders with secure tenure will oppose changes

---

[8] This is even true when ongoing land reforms have problems or shortcomings that disadvantage peasants over the longer term. For instance, Mexico's 1988 national agrarian survey (*Encuesta nacional agropecuaria ejidal*) demonstrates overwhelming support for continued land redistribution despite manifest problems with the Partido Revolucionario Institucional's (PRI) manipulation of peasant voters. See also, e.g., Albertus et al. (2014).

brought by reform. For Huntington, such landholders are primarily indigenous groups with long-standing and secure communal landholdings. Ansell and
Samuels refer to middle-class landowners in a society of land equality. Yet by
the early twentieth century in Latin America, indigenous landholdings had been
largely usurped and land equality was nonexistent.[9] Neither of these arguments
therefore undermines the claim that the bulk of the rural poor will support land
reform.

The one group outside of landed elites that at times had incentives to oppose
reform in Latin America – middle landholders – was distinct from the rural
poor and relatively small in number. The ratio of peasants to middle landowners around 1950 varied from about 3:1 in Brazil to nearly 20:1 in countries such
as the Dominican Republic, El Salvador, and Peru, and it averaged around 10:1
(FAO 1981).[10] Furthermore, the structure of many land reforms – especially
high landholding ceilings – undermined opposition from middle landowners,
who stood to benefit from the destruction of large landed elites (e.g., via reduced
land pressure and the opening of formerly dominated markets) as well as from
the ancillary programs associated with land reform, such as subsidized inputs,
marketing, and the development of infrastructure. Middle landowners often
supported smaller land reform programs and the early stages of major reforms,
before which landholding ceilings were sometimes subsequently lowered to
affect middle landowners (e.g., in Peru and Cuba). Article 6 of Cuba's 1959
reform, for instance, authorized expropriation of medium-sized holdings but
was not initially enforced because of its political repercussions: "[A]n alliance
between the large and middle landlords would have almost certainly been
forged," which would have threatened the reform (O'Connor 1968, 171). Middle landowners nonetheless often ultimately get swept aside with landed elites
in major land reforms. Cuba's 1959 Agrarian Reform Law was followed in
1963 by the Second Agrarian Reform that expropriated medium-sized landholdings. The interests of middle landowners therefore align at times with the
rural poor and at other times with landed elites, but they are rarely so consequential as to catalyze or entirely forestall land reform. They are consequently
not treated as a separate actor.

Although the rural poor will typically support land redistribution in large
numbers, as discussed earlier in this section, this does not of course imply that
they will be able to act effectively or that reform will necessarily occur. Marx

---

[9] Even in Costa Rica and Uruguay, countries with relatively higher equality of landholdings, land
inequality remained. Both countries ultimately faced rural conflicts that pressed for land reform.

[10] Peasants here are counted as landholders with fewer than 20 hectares of land, and middle
landowners are those who hold between 20 and 200 hectares. These ratios are substantially
higher when accounting for landless agricultural wage laborers or for the fact that 20 hectares is
relatively small for some crops that require extensive planting areas. Middle landowners should
therefore not be confused with the median landholder, which typically held fewer than 5 hectares
of land (see Table 2.1). As is discussed in Chapter 3, land reform programs rarely track the preferences of the median landholder.

([1852] 1963, 123–124) famously denigrated the lack of solidarity among the French peasantry in the 1840s as follows:

The small-holding peasants form an enormous mass whose members live in similar conditions but without entering into manifold relations with each other. Their mode of production isolates them from one another instead of bringing them into mutual intercourse. The isolation is furthered by France's poor means of communication and the poverty of the peasants...Thus the great mass of the French nation is formed by the simple addition of homologous magnitudes, much as potatoes in a sack form a sack of potatoes...Insofar as there is merely a local interconnection among these small-holding peasants...and the identity of their interests forms no community, no national bond, and no political organization among them, they do not constitute a class. They are therefore incapable of asserting their class interest in their own name.

Although peasants are clearly not always as innocuous as sacks of potatoes, there are a host of barriers to rural collective action. Chief among these are paternalistic and repressive forms of land tenure, geographic dispersion, clientelism, and mechanisms of control over information, basic needs, and even freedom of movement.

The Bolivian *colonato* described in Chapter 1 was one of the more extreme, inhumane tenure systems. Yet repressive land tenure systems are unfortunately far from rare. Haciendas dominated much of the rural sector in Mexico in the nineteenth and early twentieth centuries. These landholdings evolved from Spanish land grants to notables (*mercedes*) as well as grants of jurisdictions to individuals (*encomiendas* and *repartimientos*) that included both villages and peasants. Grantees were allowed to levy taxes and demand labor from the villagers who lived within their land grant. Haciendas varied in size and were generally smaller in areas of the south, where rainfall is greater and land is more fertile, and much larger in the more arid regions of the north. Peasant residents on haciendas (*peones*) typically were each given an individual plot in exchange for labor on the hacienda – often six days a week – and a predefined share of the harvest (Thiesenhusen 1995, 31). The wives and daughters of male *peones* performed household tasks for the landowner. Landowners typically monopolized the provision of basic goods and services (e.g., food, medicine, and church services) and were able to charge extortionate prices by restricting peasants from finding alternative sources outside the hacienda. This resulted in constantly ballooning debt for *peones*, which shackled them in a paternalistic relationship with the *patrón* that they could not easily escape (Thiesenhusen 1995, 31–32). The children of *peones* then inherited this crippling debt. The historian Frank Tannenbaum (1962, 80) provides a succinct and damning summary of this system: "The hacienda is a society under private auspices. It is an entire social system and it governs the life of those attached to it from cradle to grave."

Clientelism and control over information can also impede rural collective action. Prior to the Peruvian military's seizure of power in 1968 and subsequent land reform program, for instance, the state did not fund schools in highland *latifundios*. Peasant education depended on a landlord building schools and encouraging education. Yet few landlords did so because literacy requirements prevented illiterates from voting (Handelman 1975, 41–42). Of those peasants that could vote, landlords influenced their votes not only through fear and intimidation but also by forbidding outsiders from entering their hacienda and manipulating and restricting information so peasants were either unaware of parties not favored by the landlord or were mistaken about candidates' political affiliations (McClintock 1983, 130–131). Landowners used peasant unions instrumentally, firing or bribing incipient union leaders and influencing leadership selection, which yielded malleable leaders who could demobilize peasants or influence their votes (McClintock 1983, 131). In these ways, landlords attempted to deliver electoral support for preferred anti–land reform candidates who were their allies or even relatives (Handelman 1975, 45).

Guatemala's early history demonstrates several additional mechanisms of control over rural laborers that undermined collective action. During the colonial era in Guatemala, as in many Latin American countries, indigenous communities were resettled in centralized *encomiendas* to increase extraction and facilitate control over the population. Liberal generals in the late 1800s expropriated the remaining communal indigenous lands in the lowlands and sold off state land to domestic and foreign ventures to encourage an agro-export economy based on coffee (Wittman and Saldivar-Tanaka 2006). Indigenous communities forced to marginal lands in remote areas of the western highlands were largely cut off from the lowland areas they had previously used to seasonally grow corn and consequently became increasingly dependent on seasonal wage earnings. The demand for seasonal labor simultaneously increased as coffee estates and the production of tropical lowland crops expanded. The *colonato* system was therefore adopted on many coffee estates along with the continued use of debt peonage. When the latter was abolished in 1934, it was replaced in short order by an anti-vagrancy law that required individuals with fewer than 2.8 hectares of titled land to work 100–150 days per year as wage laborers or face punishment (Wittman and Saldivar-Tanaka 2006, 27). These severe restrictions on movement applied to most of the indigenous population.

Although the collective action problem facing the rural poor can often only be overcome by mobilization from above, coordination points, exogenous shocks, and organizational innovations can at times enable the poor to act collectively. Table 2.3 lists all major cases of large-scale rural protest and organization from 1910 to 2008. Numerous smaller peasant organizations, unions, and limited or unorganized movements are not listed in Table 2.3.

Every country in Latin America has experienced at least one episode of major rural protest or peasant organization. The large-scale and sometimes violent displacement of indigenous groups via land enclosures were countered by land invasions and rural unrest in Mexico toward the end of the Porfiriato (Sanderson 1984) and in frontier regions in Colombia in the 1920s–1930s

TABLE 2.3. *Cases of Large-Scale Rural Protest and Organization in Latin America, 1910–2008*

Country	Event	Years	Regions Affected	Outcome
Argentina	Grito de Alcorta strike	1912	Southern Santa Fe	Agrarian Federation of Argentina formed
Bolivia	Land invasions, strikes	1940s–mid 1950s	Various	1952 revolution, MNR seizes power
	Protests, demonstrations	Early 1980s	Various	Agricultural credits and CNRA representation
	Marches, protests, blockades	1990–present	Nationwide	Indigenous lands recognition, political reform
Brazil	Peasant Leagues movement	Late 1950s–early 1960s	Spread from Pernambuco	Won right to unionize, then repressed
	Movement of Landless Farmers	Late 1950s–early 1960s	Rio Grande do Sul	Won right to unionize, then repressed
	Movement of Landless Rural Workers	1980s–present	Nationwide	Intermittent repression and land grants
Chile	Protests, land invasions, unionization	1970–1973	Nationwide	Expropriation criteria relaxed, then repression
	Mapuche protests, strikes, land invasions	Early 1990s–present	South	Limited land grants, expanded rights, repression
Colombia	Land invasions, strikes	Late 1920s–early 1930s	Northern departments	Local repression
	La Violencia	1947–1960	Nationwide	Civil war with over 200,000 killed
	ANUC land invasions	Early 1970s	Various	Repression and land titling
Costa Rica	Land invasions	Late 1950s–early 1960s	Various	1961 Law of Land and Colonization

(*continued*)

TABLE 2.3 (*continued*)

Country	Event	Years	Regions Affected	Outcome
Cuba	Rural insurgency	1953–1959	Spread from Oriente	Cuban revolution and land reform
Dominican Republic	Land invasions, rural organizing	Mid 1960s–mid 1970s	Nationwide	Little action followed by 1972 agrarian laws
Ecuador	CONAIE uprisings, blockades	1986–present	Nationwide	Indigenous lands recognition, political reform
El Salvador	Land invasions; mass revolt	1930–1932	Spread from west	Violent repression, especially after 1932 coup
	Mass rallies and counter-protests	1976–1977	Nationwide	Repression, UCS fails under FARO pressure
Guatemala	Rural insurgency	Early 1960s–1980s	Various	Repression
	Marches, sit-ins, land occupations	1986–1989	Nationwide	Limited land transfers, land commission
	Land invasions	Mid-1990s	Various	Land trust fund via civil war peace accords
	Land invasions, protests	Early 2000s	Various	Repression, limited land transfers
Honduras	Banana strike	1954	Various	Wage increase, rural trade union legalization
	Union protests; land invasions	Early 1970s	Various	López Arellano coup and reform
	FUNACAMH protests	1979–1980	Various	Reform slowed, INA director replaced

44

Country	Movement/Event	Years	Location	Outcome
Mexico	Land invasions, rural insurgency	1911-1920	Various; less in north	Mexican revolution and 1917 land reform
	Land invasions, demonstrations	1960s-early 1970s	Primarily in north	Land transfers, local repression
	Zapatista uprising	1994-2000s	Chiapas	Limited land transfers, repression
Nicaragua	Sandino guerrilla campaign	Late 1920s-early 1930s	Various	Negotiated settlement, amnesty and land grant
	Land invasions; FSLN uprising	1960s-early 1980s	Various	Civil war, overthrow of Somozas, land reform
Panama	Panama Boston Coconut Co. protests	1957	Veraguas	Repression and fractionalization
Paraguay	Protests, Christian Agrarian Leagues	1960-1976	Spread from south	Repression
Peru	Farmers' union movement	1958-1963	La Convención, Lares	Repression, limited land grants
	Peasant strikes, land invasions	1963-64	Southern Andes	Repression
	Rural insurgency	1965	Andes	Repression
	Shining Path insurgency	1980-1992	Various	Repression
Uruguay	Tupamaros rural insurgency	Late 1960s-early 1970s	Various	Repression, disbanding of peasant unions
Venezuela	Land invasions, protests, unionization	1958-late 1980s	Nationwide	Land transfers and political incorporation

Sources: Argentina: Guido Pastorino (1971); Bolivia: Muñoz and Lavadenz (1997), Yashar (2005); Brazil: Ondetti (2008); Chile: Aylwin (2005); Thome (1989); Colombia: LeGrand (1986), Zamosc (1986); Costa Rica: Seligson (1980); Cuba: Valdés Paz (1997); Dominican Republic: Stanfield (1989); Ecuador: Yashar (2005); El Salvador: Almeida (2008); Guatemala: Granovsky-Larsen (2010), Sandoval (1992); Honduras: Stringer (1989), Thorpe (1991); Mexico: Eisenstadt (2011), Walsh Sanderson (1984); Nicaragua: Thiesenhusen (1995); Panama: Gandásegui (1985); Paraguay: González Casanova (1985); Peru: Albertus (2015), Hunefeldt (1997); Uruguay: González Casanova (1985); Venezuela: Lapp (2004).

(LeGrand 1986). These culminated in revolution in the case of Mexico. An economic shock galvanized the rural poor in El Salvador in the early 1930s. Landlessness increased and wages decreased as a result of the global depression, sparking rural mobilization and sporadic land invasions (Almeida 2008, 41–43). The government reacted by banning public gatherings and "communist" meetings and associations. A military coup followed, along with a mass peasant and worker uprising in 1932 that was violently repressed. Similar economic pressures led to the poor tenant farmers' Peasant Leagues movement in the Brazilian sugarcane region of Pernambuco as well as pressure for land reform in other Brazilian states such as Rio Grande do Sul (Ondetti 2008, 11).

Sporadic protests and uprisings were replaced by more coherent, if not always successful, rural movements in many Latin American countries as peasants became more politically active and systematically organized. Exploitation by the United Fruit Company and other large agribusinesses contributed to rural strikes and protests in Honduras and Guatemala in the 1940s–1950s that eventually resulted in the legalization of rural unions and land reforms. A similar pattern occurred in Panama in the 1950s and 1960s. Peasant unions formed as part of Venezuela's land reform beginning in the 1960s. Land invasions shook the southern Peruvian Andes from 1963 to 1964, and they later spread in Brazil, where they were led by the Movimento dos Trabalhadores Rurais Sem Terra (MST). They were also part and parcel of Bolivia's defining 1952 revolution. In some cases – Colombia, Cuba, Mexico, Nicaragua, Peru, and Uruguay – land grievances spurred rural-based insurgencies. Table 2.3 indicates that peasant pressure for land reform is ongoing in many countries.

Elites that are confronted with rural pressure for land reform can respond in several ways. Landed elites and political elites can join together to repress rural movements with the help of the military or police (e.g., Peru and Panama in the early 1960s, El Salvador in the 1970s). Faced with this threat, the rural poor can attempt to overthrow both political and landed elites and directly seize power to expropriate landed elites. Successful popular revolutions of this type are rare.[11] In other cases – those that give rise to most major land reforms – ruling political elites can take up the cause of the rural poor and expropriate landed elites in favor of the rural poor.

When rural movements do not represent a threat to systemic stability but are widespread, elites may be willing or forced to tolerate them. These movements can become long-standing rural tools of pressure and mobilization. As Table 2.3 indicates, Bolivia, Brazil, Chile, and Ecuador have large and sophisticated peasant organizations that continue to pressure for land reform. Beyond these cases, Colombia, Guatemala, Honduras, Mexico, Nicaragua, Paraguay,

---

[11] Furthermore, revolution itself does not necessarily yield large-scale land redistribution. In Bolivia, for instance, the Communists were originally opposed to land reform. Redistribution came instead when political elites pushed top Movimiento Nacionalista Revolucionario (MNR) leaders to destroy landed elites. They also faced an implicit threat of further protests by peasants if they failed to do so.

Peru, and Venezuela all have rural groups that are currently pushing for reform through demonstrations and land occupations.

This suggests a "middle route" of peasant pressure between the extremes of "sacks of potatoes" and revolution. This middle route consists of street protests, marches, blockades, targeted land invasions, political organization, and other everyday forms of resistance that make completely ignoring rural demands costly. Take for instance the large-scale protests, strikes, and street blockades that swept across Colombia in mid-2013 beginning in the rural sector. Tens of thousands of peasant farmers across a host of production sectors took to the streets and blockaded food supplies to demand more support for small-scale agriculture in the form of subsidies and rural infrastructure. After weeks of ignoring the protests and claiming they had been infiltrated by the Fuerzas Armadas Revolucionarias de Colombia (FARC), the government sat down with peasants to negotiate a pact for rural development.

LANDED ELITES, RULING POLITICAL ELITES, AND THE RURAL POOR BEYOND LATIN AMERICA

To what extent does the description of landed elites, ruling political elites, and the rural poor in the previous section apply to regions beyond Latin America? The variation in the composition of the ruling political elite outside of Latin America, although significant, is mostly in the substance of *who* holds power rather than *how* power is held; the definition of ruling political elites is sufficiently capacious to accommodate the key political actors under democracy and dictatorship in their range of forms across the world. Perhaps the best way to answer this question is therefore through the lens of land tenure arrangements that define the relationship between landed elites and the rural poor.

Although the incidence of different types of land tenure varies substantially around the world, there is a remarkably widespread distinction between landed elites and the rural poor as social groups. This is because of the high rates of land inequality. Latin America as a region has the most unequal distribution of land, but other developing regions – and particularly countries that have not implemented large-scale land redistribution – also have high levels of land inequality, often as a legacy of extractive colonial institutions. South and Southeast Asia, North Africa, the Middle East, and southern and eastern regions of sub-Saharan Africa are all notable for historically high land inequality (Frankema 2010). Europe and East Asia also had high rates of land inequality prior to redistributive land reforms. Skewed landholding distributions contribute to well-defined groups of landed elites and rural poor and also to a wider gulf between them. Griffin, Khan, and Ickowitz (2002, 288) explain:

The economic effect of concentrated land ownership in a context of small, fragmented, local labour markets is to give large landowners a high degree of monopsony power in the labour markets in which they operate. That is, most rural people either work for the local landowner or they work for no one. This monopsony power, in turn, lies at the root of "surplus labour," production inefficiency and rural poverty.

This problem was reflected in the widespread feudal and semi-feudal agrarian institutions in Europe and Russia prior to industrialization (Brenner 1976; Tuma 1965) and subsequently in the high rates of land leasing by farmers relative to ownership (Swinnen 2002). The landed elite had a strong upper hand on the rural poor even where traditional feudalism was weak or nonexistent. In East Asian countries such as Japan, Taiwan, Korea, China, and Vietnam prior to World War II, very high rates of tenancy at exorbitant rental rates supported a small landlord class (Griffin, Khan, and Ickowitz 2002). The World Bank (1975) labeled these "feudalistic landlord-tenant systems" in practice, similar to those in Latin America. Griffin et al. (2002, 305) write that in South Korea, "49 percent of farmers were pure tenants and 35 percent were part tenants. Rents were 50–60 percent of the crop, leases were oral and insecure and evictions were common. Tenants were responsible for all costs of cultivation ... Purchases of land by tenants were virtually impossible." The picture was largely similar – and endured substantially longer – in Southeast Asia in countries such as the Philippines, Malaysia, Thailand, and Vietnam (Fredericks and Wells 1978). High rates of tenancy with high rental prices alongside absentee landlordism and sharecropping also prevailed in much of the Middle East and North Africa at least until the mid-twentieth century (El-Ghonemy 2002). The political and economic advantages that concentrated land ownership granted to large landowners contributed to their coherence as an elite group and social class. The rural poor, for their part, were comprised of renters, squatters, sharecroppers, wage laborers, indigenous communities, and smallholders.

The region in which the character and composition of landed elites and the rural poor diverge most from Latin America and the regions discussed earlier in this section is sub-Saharan Africa. There, customary and communal ownership systems are widespread (Boone 2013; Griffin et al. 2002).[12] Although there are a number of countries in the region where market-based private ownership is substantial (e.g., South Africa, Zimbabwe, Namibia, and Lesotho), authority-based systems are the norm. This situation is reinforced by the lack of national land registries and cadastres. It also has implications for conceiving of landed elites as a coherent social actor given that rural land access is often formally controlled by the state. Even if the state respects some sort of "customary practice" at the local level, such arrangements are often ad hoc, subject to contestation, and locally geographically fixed (Boone 2009). Yet the absence of a landholding aristocracy or a clearly defined landed elite does not mean that rural life in much of the region is egalitarian; it is not. Chiefs, elders, and lineage heads were empowered under colonial administrations with the broad authority to

---

[12] These ownership systems are also widespread in several countries outside of Africa, such as Papua New Guinea and the Solomon Islands.

allocate and reallocate land within their domain. Although many postcolonial governments eliminated some of the most influential local rulers and bolstered secular local government, they usually preserved chiefly and "neotraditional" authority (Boone 2013, 47). Rural dwellers, for their part, are mostly small-holders given the historically high land-person ratio, although landless wage labor is increasing (Griffin et al. 2002).

THE ORIGINS OF ELITE SPLITS

When do elite splits occur such that landed elites and ruling political elites can be considered separate actors with independent interests? Why can landed elites not simply buy off ruling political elites and make them predictably execute landed elite preferences? After all, several recent influential contributions to the literature on democratization and redistribution assume that dictators act as faithful agents of a unified economic elite (Acemoglu and Robinson 2001, 2006; Boix 2003).[13] In the context of agrarian economies, these theories imply that ruling political elites will act as perfect agents of landed elites, either because they *are* landed elites or because landed elites directly appoint or otherwise provide the material foundation for their rule.

Unless all ruling political elites are landed elites – an exceedingly rare scenario not borne out in any of the cases under study – then landed elites will at best face a principal-agent problem. The fact that ruling political elites control the state apparatus and have informational advantages means that even if landed elites install a particular set of political elites in power, landed elites will nonetheless face difficulties in controlling the behavior of political elites and their rotation in office.

Still more threatening is the possibility that the interests of ruling political elites fundamentally differ from those of landed elites. Divergent interests between these two sets of elites are most likely to occur under four circumstances. The first is the drive for greater state autonomy, typically initiated either by the military as its recruitment becomes wider and more diverse or by secularizing and developmentally oriented political elites. The second circumstance is a diversifying economy in which the agricultural sector plays a diminishing role. The third is an ethnically fractionalized country where large landowners are an ethnic minority. The final is foreign occupation.[14]

---

[13] Although Acemoglu and Robinson (2006) explore deviations from this assumption in several extensions of their model of democratization, it nonetheless drives their baseline model and conclusions.

[14] While these factors contribute to diminishing the overlap between political and landed elites, they are not necessarily deterministic in causing a particular set of ruling political elites to attempt to undermine landed elites via land reform. A sufficiently well-organized and powerful group of landed elites could always attempt to launch into power a sympathetic set of political elites. Nonetheless, the likelihood of doing so decreases substantially under these circumstances.

Drives for State Autonomy

The first circumstance that is ripe for a bifurcation of interests between ruling political elites and landed elites is the drive for greater state autonomy. The classic Marxist view of the state is that it operates as an instrument of coercion on behalf of the dominant economic class. The interests of the state and those of elites are inextricably fused; there is no agency slack. Marx ([1848] 1998, 51) did not mince words when he famously wrote that "the executive of the modern state is but a committee for managing the common affairs of the whole bourgeoisie." The strong version of the theory of the "structural dependence of the state on capital" argues that this claim holds regardless of who the state managers are and whom they represent, how the state is organized, and even whether or not elites act collectively (Przeworski and Wallerstein 1988, 12). Furthermore, structural dependence binds all groups in society.

The counterpoint to the Marxist conception of the state holds that the state is much more than simply an arena in which elites express demands. The influential German scholar Max Weber, for instance, argued that states have administrative, legal, extractive, and coercive functions that are autonomous of the interests of social groups. Skocpol's seminal work on "bringing the state back in" echoes Weber. Marxist theorists, Skocpol (1985, 25) contends, miss the fact that "the structures and activities of states profoundly condition" the political expression of class interests by influencing "the capacities classes have for achieving consciousness, organization, and representation."

Evidence for a structural dependence of the state on elite interests is mixed. On the one hand, a host of well-known scholars dating back to Vilfredo Pareto, Robert Michels, and Gaetano Mosca have argued that oligarchs have historically dominated political life by overwhelming other groups in society. Prominent current models of democratization argue that this relationship prevails frequently enough to be used as a starting point for theory (e.g., Acemoglu and Robinson 2001; Boix 2003). The literature on state capture bolsters this point by demonstrating that economic elites often "capture the state" to shape the fundamental rules of the economic game to their advantage through policymaking, laws, and favorable regulations (e.g., Hellman, Jones, and Kaufmann 2003; Winters 2011). This was an abiding concern in the transition to capitalism for Eastern Europe and for states of the former Soviet Union after the fall of communism.

On the other hand, a host of empirical contributions provide strong evidence of variation in elite interests that implies competition for control over policymaking (e.g., Ansell and Samuels 2014), and of the capacity of the state to divorce itself from elite interests entirely (e.g., Albertus and Menaldo 2012a; Stepan 1978; Trimberger 1978). Furthermore, Skocpol's (1979) analysis of major revolutionary transformations demonstrates how the structures and activities of monarchical bureaucratic states actually shaped the political capacities of landed upper classes rather than simply being an outgrowth of landed interests.

This discussion suggests that the overlap in interests between the state and elites can vary substantially. Furthermore, a scenario in which state and elite interests are fused provides strong incentives for potentially powerful actors separate from the bourgeoisie and proletariat to push for a more autonomous state apparatus that can serve an architectural role in the polity (Stepan 1978).

One group that commonly spearheads the drive for state autonomy is the military given its key role in establishing and sustaining political regimes. Yet how does the military divorce itself from elites and develop its own interests?

A typical path is diversity in military recruitment, which erodes the overlap in affinities between military officers and economic elites. The increasing demands of modern warfare on militaries necessitated broader recruitment from beyond the families of elites (Janowitz 1977). A large literature suggests that the social origins of military officers are critical in transforming the military's goals and identity. Germani and Silvert (1961, 80) note that "military politics inevitably and invariably involve identification with wider social interests and ideologies. The patterning of these identifications depends in important measure on the social origins of the officer corps and the social mobility functions which the military institution may serve." Nordlinger (1970, 1142) reiterates this point in his analysis of the effects of the increasingly middle-class orientations of "officer-politicians": "Pre-adult socialization experiences, family connections by birth or marriage, social contracts, status aspirations, property ownership, business connections, political relationships – these factors bind the officers to the middle class' interests and lead them to identify with its values and members." The social origins of the military are also key to Trimberger's analysis of the autonomy of the state apparatus. Relative autonomy is achieved when those who hold high civil or military posts are not recruited from the dominant classes and do not form close personal or economic ties with dominant classes after assuming office (Trimberger 1978, 4).

A second path to a more independent military, distinct in some but not all ways from recruitment, is socialization. Stepan (1978), for instance, points to the nationalist socialization of "new military professionals" as a key factor in the distancing of the military from elite interests. This dovetails with the assessments by Nordlinger (1977) and Geddes (2003) of the military as a corporate body with its own concerns.

The social differentiation of the officer corps and its transformation into a more autonomous institution is at the heart of Trimberger's (1978) analysis of "revolutions from above" and Huntington's classic treatment of praetorianism. Huntington (1968, 203) argues that militaries are frequently key forces for progressive change in the demise of oligarchy or traditional monarchy: "In these early stages of political modernization, the military officers play a highly modernizing and progressive role. They challenge the oligarchy, and they promote social and economic reform."

The phenomenon of politically autonomous militaries with the willingness to introduce large-scale changes that attack preexisting economic elites is not uncommon.[15] Middle-class military groups pushed ruling generals and juntas whom they had empowered to implement radical programs of social reform at the expense of the oligarchy in Chile and Brazil in the 1920s and in Bolivia, Venezuela, El Salvador, Panama, the Dominican Republic, and Ecuador during and after World War II. Modernizing, redistributive military takeovers occurred in Turkey in the 1920s, Thailand in 1932, Syria in 1949, Egypt in 1952, and Iraq, Pakistan, and Burma in 1958 (Huntington 1968, 203–221). A similar pattern occurred under a host of populist dictators in West Africa following independence (Bienen 1985). Politically autonomous militaries were a prominent feature rather than an anomaly of the political landscape in these and many other cases. And in several cases of revolution such as those in the USSR, China, Cuba, and Mexico, politically autonomous militaries that had been formed out of rebellions rather than state-directed recruitment seized the state and created political parties that attacked elite interests.[16]

Landed elites are well aware of the potential threat posed by a more autonomous military. Take the case of Peru. As the military expanded recruitment to the middle and lower middle classes in the 1940s and 1950s, elites continually attempted to modify the military's changing progressive curriculum and regulate its budget in an effort to diminish its capacity to act independently of elite interests (McClintock 1981, 49; Gilbert 1977).

Another group that often pushes for greater state autonomy is a secularizing and developmentally oriented political elite. These elites have incentives to press for state autonomy when churches and religious figures are economically powerful and influential in the state apparatus.

Churches in the nineteenth and early twentieth centuries were powerful actors in Europe (Lipset and Rokkan 1967; Ziblatt 2013), Latin America (Gill 1998), and beyond (Ansell and Lindvall 2013). In some places such as Iran, the outsized influence of religion on the state remains preeminent (Gill and Keshavarzian 1999). Churches were involved in welfare provision and local schooling (Ansell and Lindvall 2013; Gill and Keshavarzian 1999) and have

---

[15] That military drives for state autonomy can generate elite splits does not imply that most regimes that evidence elite splits are military dictatorships. On the one hand, the military can form the backbone of a diverse array of autocratic regimes that split from elite interests; and on the other hand, military drives for state autonomy are not the only path to elite splits. See Chapter 5 for a further empirical discussion of elite splits and military regimes in Latin America.

[16] To the extent that a dominant political party develops in response to the introduction of mass electoral politics rather than being forged by a politically autonomous military (e.g., the United Malays National Organisation (UMNO) in Malaysia) and such a party leverages popular support to embark on a drive for state autonomy, this could provide another mechanism through which political elites and landed elites diverge. Yet given that land reform is initiated in most cases at the outset of a new regime characterized by an elite split, and is therefore either prior to or coterminous with the creation of a dominant party, the military often plays a crucial early role even if a dominant party later becomes important.

been large landowners – allying with or even comprising the landed elite (e.g., Gill 1998; Ziblatt 2013).

Several examples illustrate the role of the church as a large landholder. The Catholic Church was the largest landowner and largest single asset holder in Mexico until the mid-1800s (Gill and Keshavarzian 1999; Otero 1989). In Ecuador in the nineteenth and early twentieth centuries, the Catholic Church was a major landholder with an enormous array of haciendas (Haney and Haney 1987). In both of these cases there was early conflict between the church and peasant communities over the control of land. In the Philippines prior to the Spanish-American War, the large haciendas (primarily sugar plantations in the Negros region) were predominantly owned by the Spanish Catholic orders (Matsuzaki 2011). Prior to the mid-nineteenth-century Carlist Wars in Spain, the church was one of the largest landowners along with the nobles and communes, holding some 12 million acres of land (Brenan 1990, 108). This phenomenon is not limited to the Catholic Church. The Buddhist Church and clergy, for instance, were one of the largest owners of land and herds in Mongolia alongside the nobility through the 1920s (Bawden 1968). And Islamic educational institutions were major landowners in postcolonial Indonesia.

Ascendant liberal and secularizing political elites in many countries sought to undercut the rival power of the church by nationalizing or redistributing church property. Gill (1998, 65) writes that "[i]n Latin America, the primary asset under contention between church and state was land." In Mexico, the Liberal reforms of 1857 (especially the Ley Lerdo) provided the legal instruments to expropriate church land; expropriation was then carried out on a massive scale over the ensuing decades (Otero 1989).[17] Ecclesiastical properties not specifically used for religious purposes and held by community interests – both diocesan landholdings and land held by religious orders – were made illegal (Gill and Keshavarzian 1999). In Ecuador, Eloy Alfaro's "Liberal Revolution" seized a large portion of the church's vast landholdings in the Sierra through the 1907 Ley de Manos Muertos, which confiscated clerical property and rented it to wealthy farmers (Haney and Haney 1987, 2). The state consequently came to control nearly 20 percent of the Sierra in haciendas that comprised the Asistencia Social. Liberal reforms in Spain in the 1830s sold off church land wholesale (Brenan 1990). In Mongolia, the People's Revolutionary Party led a drive for secularization to marginalize Buddhist clergy by seizing their land and herds in an effort at "the total elimination of the economic power of the Church" (Bawden 1968, 323).

The conflict between secularizing political elites and landed elites has parallels in other types of reform. Liberals and Social Democrats in the nineteenth century, for instance, sought to nationalize and secularize primary education as a way to reduce the influence of the church (Ansell and Lindvall 2013).

---

[17] The Ley Lerdo also led to the large-scale appropriation of peasant lands by private actors (e.g., Thiesenhusen 1995).

Bismarck stoked state-church conflict in Germany when he introduced welfare reform (Esping-Andersen 1990). In Turkey, Ataturk leaned on Western-
oriented bureaucratic and intellectual elites as he abolished the caliphate, closed
religious schools, shut down Islamic courts, and switched the alphabet from
Arabic to Roman to complicate the ability of future generations to access traditional religious texts (Huntington 1968). With the support of liberal reformers in Iran, Reza Shah attacked the political power of the clergy in the late
1920s and 1930s by creating national education, property registration, and
judicial systems, thereby wresting these functions from the Shi'ite hierarchy
(Gill and Keshavarzian 1999). And similarly in Chile, conflict between liberal
state reformers and the Catholic Church in the mid-1800s resulted in secular
public education, greater religious freedoms, and finally the end of the church's
monopoly over marriages, birth and death records, and cemeteries with the
leyes laicos of the 1880s.

The Catholic Church was stripped of the vast bulk of its landholdings in
Latin America by the early twentieth century (Gill 1998).[18] For this reason, I
do not consider the Catholic Church as either a separate actor or as a major
player among the landed elite in the period of analysis here. State-church conflict after the early twentieth century occurred along a number of dimensions,
but property was not chief among them.

Diversifying Economy

The second condition that contributes to a divergence between ruling political
elites and landed elites is a developing economy in which other sectors compete
with or displace the primacy of agriculture. A diverse economy increases the
likelihood that ruling political elites will be drawn from outside of the landed
elite. Take for example an urbanizing country in which a burgeoning industrial
sector develops in cities. The resultant rising middle class and set of industrial
elites will have interests that are distinct from those of landed elites (Ansell
and Samuels 2010; Llavador and Oxoby 2005). They will also have greater
de facto political power that comes with marshaling more economic resources.
This increases the likelihood that modernization will stir demands for political
representation via democratization (Ansell and Samuels 2010; Moore 1966).
Political elites under democracy will then represent the interests of urban constituents as the strength of rural powerbrokers wanes. Even if democratization
is delayed, the likelihood of overlapping interests between ruling political elites
and landed elites still declines as the economy diversifies away from agriculture (Llavador and Oxoby 2005). Rising actors in these circumstances, such as

---

[18] Consistent with the theory developed in Chapter 3, expropriation of church land typically
occurred where there was a coalitional split between ruling political elites and the church alongside low institutional constraints. The church was destroyed as a landowner under dictators and
periods of oligarchic rule.

industrial elites, will gain the capacity to construct successful coup coalitions and autocratic regimes that exclude landed elites from power.

It is important to emphasize that ruling political elites and landed elites can diverge even in largely agrarian economies where military recruitment and promotion is biased toward elites. As long as ruling political elites are not all landed elites, they have incentives to reduce the ability of landed elites to influence them. Guatemala under Jorge Ubico is a case in point. Ubico was born into an elite family and received his military commission largely through political ties. Although Ubico cultivated Guatemala's relationship with the United Fruit Company after rising to power in a sham election in 1931, he took several steps to lessen his dependence on the strength of traditional landed elites. Ubico rotated appointed governors and abolished debt peonage, cancelling peasant debts to landlords (Berger 1992, 26–30). Ubico nonetheless did little to diversify Guatemala's heavily agricultural economy.

Ethnic Difference

A divergence between ruling political elites and landed elites is also more likely when there is ethnic fractionalization in a country and large landowners are an ethnic minority. Shared identity and interests between landed elites and ruling political elites are reduced when a set of political elites from a different ethnic group than that of landed elites obtains office. It also raises political elites' out-group apprehension. A host of literature demonstrates that interethnic and out-group interactions are less cooperative than within-group interactions (e.g., Albertus, Fenner, and Slater 2015; Chen and Li 2009; Habyarimana et al. 2007). Ruling political elites that hail from groups other than an ethnic minority comprised of wealthy landowners may harbor indignities if they are considered of lower rank in a rigid social ordering (Horowitz 1985), have ambitions to enhance their power or status by mobilizing their ethnic group (Gagnon 1995), or hold anger and frustration because their group members have witnessed curtailed economic development and career opportunities as a result of their ethnicity (Gellner 1983).

Take for example a country in which ethnic minority landowners live in the most agriculturally productive geographic region, while other groups are distributed among nascent cities, on large estates as workers, and in parts of the countryside where land is of marginal quality. A ruling political elite without ties to large landowners will have few incentives to consistently uphold landowner interests. This was precisely what occurred in Estonia and Latvia during World War I. The minority German-speaking nobility, which had roots in the Teutonic Order, had presided over a manorial estate system in the Baltic countryside that dominated the Estonian- and Latvian-speaking peasantry well after the abolition of serfdom in the early 1800s. These nobles had successfully inserted themselves into the Russian Empire's provincial government to forestall change. Assemblies of the nobles, known as *Landtags*, formed the cornerstone of local administration in accordance with the Code of Local Laws of the Ostsee Guberniyas and enjoyed self-rule not subject to the governor's endorsement (Andreyeva 2008). Yet the Baltic German nobility swiftly lost favor in 1916 with rising Estonian and Latvian nationalism and anti-German sentiment caused by World War I. Russia abolished all privileges for manorial lords in July 1916 without compensation.

Colonization in parts of Africa led to similar conditions of ethnic minority dominance in land ownership as European settlers seized large swaths of land from indigenous populations. Griffin et al. (2002, 292) write that "colonial penetration led to a high degree of land ownership concentration and a displacement of the African population to less fertile or more arid land and to land more distant from markets." The situation on the eve of decolonization was scandalous. Some 22,000 primarily French colonizers in Algeria held nearly half of all cultivated land and produced one-third of the grain, one-quarter of the wine, and half of the vegetables in the country; the remainder of the land was divided between roughly 630,000 Algerian families (Ashford 1969, 190). In Tunisia, 6,600 French and Italian colonizers held 18 percent of all cultivated land and accounted for 40 percent of the agricultural output (Simmons 1970, 456–457). A mere 6,000 white commercial farmers came to hold 42 percent of the agricultural land in Zimbabwe and produced 90 percent of the country's marketable food (Palmer 1990, 165). In South Africa, 60,000 white farmers held 86 percent of all farmland, with the remaining poor-quality land divvied up among 13 million blacks (Lahiff 2009, 170). Decolonization in these and other countries on the continent abruptly introduced an elite split between the wealthy European landowners that had long been influential under colonial rule and the indigenous political elites that took power for the first time since colonial occupation.

Foreign Occupation

A final circumstance that gives rise to a split between ruling political elite interests and landed elite interests is foreign occupation. Occupying armies and the negotiated extrication agreements they leave in their wake can dramatically impact the welfare of landed elites. This is particularly true when foreign forces take the place of local political elites.[19] Occupying forces then operate according to their own interests, using coercion and socialization to elicit compliance

---

[19] Foreign occupation can also give rise to an elite split if occupiers layer themselves in a sufficiently intrusive manner over existing political, bureaucratic, and military hierarchies while indigenous landed elites continue to dominate the countryside according to their own interests. Of course, many cases of indirect colonial rule yielded a tight alliance between colonial occupiers, indigenous political elites, and powerful local landowners who served as administrators or extractive intermediaries (see, e.g., Mamdani 1996). This latter arrangement is not generative of elite splits.

in implementing policies consistent with the occupier's preferences (e.g., Iken-berry and Kupchan 1990). These interests are typically distinct from those of landed elites. And they are not simply an artifact of ideology: the divergence in interests between US occupiers and Japanese landowners after World War II was as strong as that between Soviet occupiers and Hungarian landowners or that between the invading Kuomintang (KMT) in Taiwan and indigenous Tai-wanese landowners. Of course, foreign occupation also impacts the *capacity* of those making policy to operate autonomously since preceding political institu-tions are often circumvented or disbanded. The structure of institutions is a key factor in land reform outcomes that I discuss in greater detail in Chapter 3.

One illustrative case of foreign occupation is the KMT occupation of Tai-wan as it retreated from mainland China during the Chinese Civil War. When they arrived in Taiwan, "the KMT leadership included no representatives of the local landed gentry" (Tai 1974, 91). Furthermore, Roy (2003, 100) notes that "few KMT officials had large landholdings on the island" and that wealthy Taiwanese landlords "lacked the influence to forestall a land reform program favored by a Mainlander-dominated government that had little reason to pro-tect the interests of local landlords."

A host of foreign occupations have mirrored the Taiwan case in their intro-duction of a clear split between occupying authorities and local landed elites. Japan imposed its political authority over indigenous landed elites in several of its colonies (e.g., Palau) prior to World War II (Yoo and Steckel 2012). The United States did the same during its occupation of Japan, South Korea, and Germany in the wake of World War II. In Japan, the presence of the Supreme Commander for the Allied Powers eclipsed the power of domestic political elites that had long been allied with the landlord class (Kawagoe 1993). US occupiers in Germany eliminated despotic elites and fostered a new political leadership not beholden to old domestic economic interests (Montgomery 1957). Soviets did the same with the displacement of the Junker landed nobility in eastern Ger-many under the slogan "Junkerland in Bauernhand (Junker land into farmers' hands)." Similarly, at the end of the US Civil War, the North's military occupa-tion of the South excluded the white plantation elite. Land reform then followed under the banner of "forty acres and a mule" (McPherson 1964). General Sher-man's Order No. 15 put a land confiscation and distribution program in march for freed slaves that was subsequently deepened by the Freedman's Bureau Act of March 3, 1865.[20]

Foreign occupation also introduced a split from local landed elites in Afghanistan during the 1980s under the Soviets and in many Eastern European countries at the close of World War II. Take the case of Hungary. To start, many pre-war landowners were absent when the war ended (Marrese 1983). The Red

---

[20] The program was quickly reversed, however, by Andrew Johnson after Abraham Lincoln was assassinated.

Army occupation of Hungary completed the split between the provisional government and these landowners: "[T]he representatives of the aristocratic and gentry classes were excluded from parliament and the state administration" (Varga 2009, 225).

Common Regional Paths to Elite Splits

Some routes to a coalitional split between landed and ruling political elites are more likely than others in a particular region or country. How do elite splits tend to develop in different regions through these various paths? As the discussion and examples in this chapter suggest, drives for state autonomy and economic shifts away from agriculture have been at the root of many coalitional splits between landed and ruling political elites in Latin America, Western Europe, the Middle East, and South and Southeast Asia. Ethnic differences, in turn, have played a key role in elite splits in parts of Eastern Europe, North Africa, sub-Saharan Africa, and increasingly in Latin America in countries such as Bolivia and Ecuador. Lastly, foreign occupation has driven many of the consequential elite splits in East Asia and Eastern Europe. Although there are certainly country-specific deviations, these patterns reflect the most common regional routes to elite splits.

CONCLUSION

This chapter has laid the groundwork for a theory of land reform. The first important step was to define the main actors that determine land reform outcomes: the landed elite, ruling political elite, and rural poor. Splitting elite actors into two groups is key for explaining why and when land redistribution occurs. There must be a coalitional split with landed elites for ruling political elites to implement land redistribution. When landed elites form the cornerstone of the political elite's support coalition, land redistribution is politically self-defeating.

Splits between ruling political elites and landed elites are more likely when the economy shifts away from agriculture, when there is a salient ethnic difference between landed elites and the rest of society, or when there is foreign occupation. Drives for state autonomy also enhance the likelihood of a divergence in interests between landed and ruling political elites. The military frequently leads these drives as recruitment beyond the ranks of landed elites erodes the overlap in affinities between these groups. Another group that often pushes for greater state autonomy is a secularizing and developmentally oriented political elite.

A large literature supports the argument in this chapter that ruling political elites and economic elites often have disparate interests. Although this is taken for granted under popular democratic rule – a concern dating back at least to Aristotle and Alexis de Tocqueville – autocratic political elites and powerful economic elites outside of government frequently have different interests that are manifested under dictatorship as well (Bermeo 2010; Conaghan and Malloy 1994; Esping-Andersen 1990; Geddes 2003; Janowitz 1977; Neuhouser 1996; Stepan 1971, 1978, 1988). Indeed, some ruling political elites have strong incentives to destroy the potential threat that preexisting economic elites pose to their rule. Chapter 3 builds from these insights to generate a theory of land reform.

3

A Theory of Land Reform

This chapter develops a theory of land reform in several steps. First, it outlines the political process of land reform. It then details how the chief political actors interact within this process to either push for or block land reform. Finally, it formalizes the logic in a game theoretic model that captures the dynamic decision making of key actors and demonstrates how changes in key parameters impact redistributive land reform outcomes.

The discussion shows that large-scale changes in redistributive policy such as land redistribution are more difficult to achieve when there are more institutional constraints to political rule. The opposition of a small number of institutional actors can jeopardize reform: if the executive opposes reform, the legislature cuts off funding, or the bureaucracy is corrupt or unorganized, redistributive land reform efforts will fall flat. Because land redistribution requires significant political concentration and administrative capacity, it is more likely to occur under autocratic rule. Only when democracy is highly majoritarian – a rare circumstance – can democratic political elites implement land redistribution.

That the structural conditions for land redistribution are more propitious under autocracy, however, does not imply that reform is deterministic under these regimes. Landed elites may wield considerable political power. For land redistribution to be implemented on a large scale, there must therefore be a coalitional split between ruling political elites and landed elites that spurs ruling political elites to attack the foundations of landed elite power.

Destroying landed elites can reduce the potential threat they pose to ruling political elites over the longer term if their interests are not satisfied or if they fear the intentions of political elites. It also signals the ruling political elite's reliance on their support coalition – the group that brings them into power – instead of on landed elites, thereby reducing the threat of an insider coup. Granting land from former landed elites to the rural poor can then undercut the threat of instability from below by buying the support of key groups of the population that have the capacity to organize anti-regime resistance. These political origins of redistribution captured by the theory therefore provide an explanation for the targets and the beneficiaries of land redistribution. Land redistribution functions as a two-pronged strategy by ruling political elites to protract their rule under dictatorship. It aids ruling political elites first in consolidating their coalition and then in eliminating external threats.

Less redistributive types of land reform such as land negotiation and land colonization are not driven by the same political logic. Whereas land redistribution presents a clear threat to landed elites, land negotiation poses a mild threat at best and land colonization poses no threat at all. Consequently, while land redistribution should be associated with lower institutional constraints and a coalitional split between political and landed elites, this is far less true of land negotiation or land colonization.

The theory crucially relaxes one of the key assumptions of recent influential models of redistribution – that elites are a unitary actor. It instead conceives of three groups: ruling political elites, landed elites, and the rural poor. The formal model builds from the insights at the outset of this chapter to introduce and make explicit several more elements of the political economy of land reform. The model treats decision making as a dynamic process, considers other forms of redistribution beyond land redistribution, endogenizes landed elite coup threats and the likelihood of revolt by the rural poor, and introduces costs to political conflict.

The key theoretical prediction that land redistribution is more likely to occur under autocratic rule than under democracy holds in the more complex and complete set of actors' calculations in the model. The model also provides straightforward predictions about the prospects for land redistribution under democracy. Whereas a popular democracy instituted by the masses may implement land redistribution, democratic transitions are more typically captured by elites who construct safeguards against redistribution under democracy.

The model also advances several other testable predictions. The likelihood of land reform increases as the coalitional split between the landed elite and the political elite widens. Land redistribution is also more likely when the rural poor form a more credible threat of revolt. In order for ruling political elites to demonstrate their loyalty to the coalition that brought them to power when that coalition is distinct from landed elites, political elites will pursue the expropriation of landed elites. The land that is seized will then be redistributed to the rural poor to forestall the threat of a popular uprising. The model therefore makes sense of both the targets and the beneficiaries of expropriation. It also yields a clear set of observable implications that are tested empirically in Chapter 5.

THE CREATION AND IMPLEMENTATION OF LAND REFORM LAWS

How do landed elites, ruling political elites, and the rural poor interact to produce or obstruct land reform? To answer this question, it is first necessary to outline the steps and institutional participation required to create and implement an effective land reform. Although the ways in which these steps are implemented vary by case, all of the steps listed in Table 3.1 are required for successful land redistribution and land negotiation. The process is somewhat less onerous for land colonization, given that land colonization does not require acquiring land from private owners.

A land reform law must first be mooted and passed. Under democracy, this requires legislative and executive approval; under autocracy, it may be done by decree with the support of a dictator or a junta's support coalition. Second, the government must identify landowners who meet the criteria for being affected by the reform. This requires identifying owners that have holdings above a specified threshold if landholding ceilings are established. It otherwise requires identifying production output or tenure relations if compliance with the "social function" of land is the reform guideline. Third, the government must create or authorize an entity to administer the land reform. Fourth, a supporting legal framework for the adjudication of ownership and affectation claims must

TABLE 3.1. *Required Steps to Create and Implement Land Reform*

Land Reform Step	Actors Required
1) Pass a land reform law	Executive; possibly legislature
2) Identify those landowners who meet the criteria for being affected by the reform	Landed elites and potential beneficiaries where land registry is incomplete
3) Create or authorize an entity empowered to administer the reform	Executive; likely legislature
4) Create a legal framework for the adjudication of ownership and affectation claims in support of the reform	Executive; judiciary
5) Take possession of land subject to reform, either through expropriation or some purchasing mechanism (direct negotiation, auction, etc.)	Effective bureaucracy or military loyal to the executive
6) Assign land in the reform sector to eligible beneficiaries	Effective bureaucracy or military loyal to the executive; supportive beneficiaries
7) Enforce the new status quo distribution of land	Effective bureaucracy; loyal military; no political turnover that empowers landed elite
8) [Optional] Provide inputs, credits, and infrastructure to support beneficiaries	Legislature; possibly executive

be established. Fifth, the government or land beneficiaries must take possession of the land that is subject to reform. This may be done through abrupt
land seizures or expropriation or, in the case of a less redistributive reform,
through some purchasing mechanism (e.g., direct negotiation or auction). Sixth,
the government must assign land in the reform sector to eligible beneficiaries.
And finally, the new status quo distribution of land must be enforced. As an
additional step, the government may provide inputs, credits, and infrastructure to support beneficiaries so they can successfully transition to sustained
operation.

The sequence of actions required to pass and implement a land reform faces
evident and considerable political hurdles. The first step requires political will
on the part of the executive and possibly a legislature. Any efforts toward
reform will ultimately be stifled if the executive has no incentive to engage
in land reform. Legislative support is likewise indispensable if land reform is
to be a legislated law rather than an executive decree. The presence of landed
elites in government makes legislative majorities that support reform more difficult to build, particularly in a bicameral setting or where malapportionment
favors rural areas, as is typical in Latin America (Snyder and Samuels 2004).
Even landed elites that are not directly involved in government can wield considerable pressure on the legislature to block reform through lobbying or other
forms of influence (see, e.g., Acemoglu and Robinson 2008).

Effective implementation is far from assured even if a land reform law is
passed. Indeed, the intended scope of land reform often fizzles in the face of
insurmountable political obstacles in the implementation phase. A land cadastre aids in identifying landowners that meet the criteria for being affected by
reform (Kain and Baigent 1992), but to the extent that it is incomplete or inac-
curate, the identification of land subject to affectation requires either the support of landed elites to truthfully report holdings or the support of potential
beneficiaries to use local knowledge to report on excessive landholdings. Creating an entity empowered to administer a land reform necessitates an executive
who has the capacity to create a land agency or to vest land reform powers in an
existing agency. It may also require the support of a legislative body to support
this move with legislation and/or sufficient funding. Creating a legal framework
requires either the executive branch to create a system of land reform courts
or an existing judicial system that is willing to enforce land reform laws. Taking physical possession of the land subject to reform requires state power, in
the form of either an effective bureaucracy or a military loyal to the executive, and sufficient funding to conduct land seizures or purchases while preventing conflict. Assigning land to eligible beneficiaries again requires an effective bureaucracy or loyal military and a set of beneficiaries that support the
reform. Enforcement of the new status quo distribution of land similarly calls
for bureaucratic and/or military support. Finally, providing further inputs and
infrastructure to beneficiaries requires legislative action and funding to support
new land recipients.

Table 3.1 makes apparent that the institutions that are required to operate together to pass and successfully implement land reform are diverse. At a minimum, the executive, legislature, and bureaucracy must act in concert. Reform also requires the support of the judiciary and the military in some cases. In addition to these institutions, the cooperation of beneficiaries and even landed elites themselves can help hasten the reform and ensure its efficacy. The next section details how the distribution of power within the political system impacts the likelihood of land reform.

The process of land reform – and particularly land redistribution – is therefore quite protracted and involved, much more so than many other types of redistribution such as fiscal redistribution. There are at least four reasons why this is the case. First, the legal infrastructure is more onerous if individuals targeted with land expropriation can challenge their claims. This is fundamentally different from setting tax rates for which individuals do not challenge the legality of their individual tax burden. Second, because land reform targets assets over income, and the former are typically more concentrated than the latter, land reform frequently targets especially wealthy landowners. Smallholders and the landless are not reform targets even though it may be easier to extract from them. Yet targeting a coherent and powerful social class rather than a broader swath of society, as is done with income or consumption taxes, makes elite collective action more likely. Capture of the institutions that are required to act to implement reform is therefore more probable. This raises a third consideration: that military loyalty and effectiveness are more often important for land reform than fiscal redistribution. The military comes into play in enforcing land reform and aiding the bureaucracy in transferring property in spite of potential resistance, which can vary from foot-dragging to violence. This is less typically the case with fiscal redistribution. Finally, and related to this previous point, there is no way around physical asset transfers in land redistribution or negotiation. Governments can do an end run around enforcing individual compliance for taxes by relying on a smaller number of employers for withholding if there is a large formal employment sector. The same cannot be done with land. There is no way to avoid the necessity of physical acquisition. This process is more difficult and costly and requires the compliance of bureaucrats and the military.

It is important to note that the steps and actors that are required to pass and implement land reform differ if land reform focuses on the purchase of land from private owners or the granting of state-owned land to individuals rather than on forcible expropriation and redistribution. It is not necessary to identify owners if land is distributed from state holdings. A legal framework for the adjudication of ownership and affectation claims is less burdensome on the judicial system if full compensation reduces resistance or if the main source of land is state-owned property. Similarly, the physical seizure of land is obviated if land is purchased voluntarily from private owners or distributed from state holdings, although in the former case land still needs to be acquired from the private sector. Finally, assigning land to beneficiaries and enforcing the new status quo distribution of holdings is more easily accomplished by the bureaucracy without military support if land is not seized from some owners and then transferred to others.

All of these differences from land redistribution make land negotiation and land colonization easier to implement, because landed elite interests are less affected and the number and involvement of institutions that are required to enact reform is lower. The purchase of land from private owners and the granting of state-owned land to individuals also requires the active participation of fewer players outside government institutions, because compliance from landed elites and beneficiaries when targeting properties for reform becomes less critical.

Although land redistribution differs from other types of land reform and from typical fiscal redistribution in the ways just discussed, it does more closely parallel the introduction of major redistributive programs that require broad institutional agreement, target a narrow and powerful set of social actors, and are difficult to reverse. Examples of such programs include the expropriation and distribution of the assets of natural resource and financial firms, legal changes that extend human rights, such as the elimination of forced servitude, the centralization and expansion of access to education, and even early welfare state initiatives that established social insurance and introduced progressive income taxes for the first time. I discuss several of these other types of redistribution in Chapter 9 with an eye to whether such reforms are consistent with the theory I introduce later in this chapter.

A THEORY OF REDISTRIBUTIVE LAND REFORM

The previous section indicates that the support of a wide range of institutions is required to create and implement an effective redistributive land reform. Landed elites can affect the likelihood of reform by influencing any of these institutions in order to obstruct reform. This section draws on these insights to build a theory of land redistribution. Unless otherwise indicated, the discussion of land reform in the remainder of the chapter refers to the most redistributive and consequential type of reform: land redistribution.

There are two chief factors that determine whether redistributive land reform will occur. The first is the institutional concentration of political power. Political regimes exhibit wide variation in how the institutions necessary for creating and implementing an effective land reform are populated or influenced by political elites, landed elites, and the rural poor. The lower institutional constraints that characterize autocracy increase the likelihood that land reform can be successfully implemented. Among democracies, majoritarian forms of democracy with fewer veto points face fewer institutional constraints to redistribution and therefore are more likely to redistribute than democracies characterized by heavy checks and balances. The second key factor that affects land reform is the coalitional split between landed elites and ruling political elites.

Land reform is unlikely absent a significant split between these actors. But the prospects for land reform are high when the interests of these actors diverge in the presence of few institutional constraints. The remainder of this chapter develops this argument in detail.

Land Reform and the Concentration of Power

Democratic institutions are frequently occupied by heterogeneous actors and characterized by considerable inertia. Legislatures are composed of individuals elected from geographically disperse districts that span urban-rural, rich-poor, religious, ethnic, or other cleavages that are correlated with political preferences. The legislature may be filled through staggered elections or through elections that are offset from executive elections, thereby empowering legislators who represent changing political preferences or cyclical turnout patterns within society (Anzia 2011). The executive is elected through a different voting mechanism than the legislature. The same underlying preferences within society can therefore generate divergent interests between the legislature and the executive (Cox 1997). The executive and the legislature inherit a judiciary elected or appointed under previous officeholders, though they may appoint new judges. Finally, the executive may appoint top bureaucrats and civil servants but also often inherits most of them upon assuming office. In short, the likelihood that political elites or the rural poor solely command these institutions to the exclusion of landed elites is very low.

This is true even in parliamentary systems, where institutional constellations – particularly the legislature and the executive – are not based on checks and balances. Although key veto players in the executive and the legislature may be on the same side of a policy proposal, there are still several obstacles to reform. The first is gaining the support of the other key actors in the reform process: the bureaucracy, the judiciary, and even the military where necessary. These actors can forestall reform even if the executive and the legislature are in agreement. The second obstacle is the necessity of bargaining within a governing coalition. If landholders, for instance, are important governing coalition partners, then they may threaten the stability of the coalition when their own economic interests are at stake.

While the likelihood of democratic gridlock is high, it is nonetheless conceivable that democratic institutions can avoid capture by landed elite interests in exceptional circumstances. The most likely scenario is one in which the masses play a key role in overturning autocracy or unraveling constraints to majoritarianism. Popular revolutions that overturn elites or force elites into rushed transition bargains are more likely to yield pro-majority democratic constitutions that redefine the political game in favor of the poor (Albertus and Menaldo 2014). Guatemala's 1945 transition is one example. Mass protests and popular pressure ousted General Jorge Ubico from office in 1944 and set the stage for democratic elections, which were won by Juan José Arévalo. A new constitution stipulating that land must fill a social function was adopted in 1945. It allowed for the expropriation of uncultivated *latifundios* while simultaneously providing protection of productive land as well as municipal and communal land. This legal infrastructure reduced legislative and bureaucratic barriers and set the stage for a more comprehensive land reform under Arévalo's successor, Jacobo Arbenz.

Yet although democratic institutions can avoid gridlock and capture by landed elites by reducing institutional constraints as in the case of Guatemala, such an outcome is rare. Economic elites more frequently play a key role in democratic transitions and construct counter-majoritarian measures that enable institutional capture by heterogeneous actors who are capable of blocking major reforms even when electoral majorities favor reform.

Under dictatorship, by contrast, institutions are more likely to be occupied by a small set of ruling political elites that cohere around a dictator or junta (Bueno de Mesquita et al. 2003). With the exception of regularized rotation within single-party regimes (Magaloni 2006), these institutions are subject to overhaul when one group of political elites is ousted in favor of another. This yields greater variance in the policies implemented under dictatorship. It also implies that autocratic regimes, though far from unconstrained by their support coalitions (Albertus and Menaldo 2012b; Bueno de Mesquita et al. 2003; Svolik 2009), are typically less *institutionally* constrained in the policies they pursue than democracies (e.g., Olson 1993). The dictator may disband the legislature, stack it with critical regime players, or use it to co-opt opposition within society (Gandhi and Przeworski 2006).[1] The judiciary may be dismissed, undercut, or packed with supporters (Helmke and Ríos-Figueroa 2011).[2] A new autocratic regime may clear out the bureaucracy and re-staff it with supporters or create parallel civil servants in new agencies to undermine the powers of the existing bureaucracy. Finally, the military may gain a key role in implementing policy at the expense of other institutions. Many of the institutional constraints to the land reform process that operate under democracy are therefore circumvented when an incoming autocratic regime refashions institutions to bolster its own rule.

There are thus two very different implications that dictatorship has for land reform depending on the coalitional overlap between ruling political elites and landed elites. Land reform will not even be attempted where landed elites are allied with the ruling political elite and its support coalition. By contrast, where landed elites are excluded from the regime, attempts at land reform are likely to yield large-scale reforms that destroy those landed elites.

Although both democratic executives and autocratic regimes at times have political incentives to pursue land redistribution, the argument just presented

---

[1] The legislature may also develop as a check to the dictator. See, e.g., Wright (2008).
[2] When the judiciary is used to ease the task of ruling under autocracy, it may also develop powers of its own, albeit limited ones (Moustafa 2007).

suggests that democratic regimes should on average be less likely than autocratic regimes to implement redistributive land reform programs. Democratic
institutions typically build a larger number of veto points into government that
require large coalitions to support major policy changes such as redistributive reforms (Henisz 2000; Tsebelis 2002). This is true even in the rare circumstances when electoral supermajorities render partisan constraints weak. A
greater number of veto points enables the empowerment of more heterogeneous
interests among the legislature, administration, and bureaucracy, all of whose
support is necessary for the implementation of a serious reform but all of which
are also susceptible to obstruction by landed interests (Tai 1974; Thiesenhusen
1989, 1995). Even if a given democratic administration successfully adopts a
reform program, perhaps as a result of temporary electoral popularity, political
changes in a subsequent administration may block its implementation (Herring
1983). By contrast, a ruling political elite that faces few veto points and is motivated by its political coalition to displace traditional landed elites is better able
to coherently leverage state resources to implement redistribution than one that
necessitates compromise and coordination with potentially opposing political
actors.

This argument contrasts sharply with recent research that anticipates greater
redistribution under democratic rule (e.g., Acemoglu and Robinson 2006; Boix
2003). Yet is consistent with many case-based observations from accounts of
land reform. As Huntington (1968, 388) argues, "Pluralistic politics and parliamentary rule are often incompatible with effective land reforms." Successful
reform is instead more likely where "political power is concentrated in one
political party or a small group of leaders" (Tai 1974, 473).

The idea that redistribution may be harder to carry out under democracy
also finds support in the literature detailing how landed elites in rural societies protect their interests under democracy by forging elite-biased pacts during
transitions (Karl 1990; O'Donnell and Schmitter 1986) and creating favorable
democratic rules. Institutional features such as checks and balances (Henisz
2000; Tsebelis 2002), malapportionment (Horiuchi 2004; Snyder and Samuels
2004), and the proscription of leftist parties (Mainwaring 1999) can be built
into constitutions to protect property rights and reduce policy volatility. In fact,
democracy in Latin America has often only been accepted by elites after their
political interests have been guaranteed under democratic institutions.

Mechanisms of Landed Elite Obstruction

Several of the primary ways in which landed elites may block land redistribution under democracy include direct representation in the legislature, elite
capture of elected officials, judges, or bureaucrats, and the use of clientelism
to undercut reform support by the rural poor. The election of landed elites to
government makes legislative majorities that support reform difficult to build.
This is particularly true in a bicameral setting or where elite-biased malapportionment favors rural areas, as is not uncommon (Snyder and Samuels 2004).

Landed elites can directly scuttle reform through the legislature by voting against the passage of a reform law, failing to fund its implementation, or raising the legal barriers for expropriation and redistribution. Huntington (1968, 388–389) argues that because "elected parliaments are usually dominated by landowning interests" in modernizing countries, legislatures have "traditionally been the graveyards of land reform measures."[3]

Landed elite representation via a legislature is less capable of forestalling major initiatives under dictatorship. If a legislature is actually present under autocracy and it is used to co-opt opposition elites (Gandhi and Przeworski 2006), then giving these opposition figures (in this case, landed elites) rents or exemptions can reduce their resistance to the regime and undercut the ability of those elites to act collectively to oppose major policies. If, by contrast, landed elites are regime allies and are incorporated into a legislature or party to make power sharing credible (Magaloni 2008), then the fact that these elites are regime allies is what inhibits land redistribution rather than the presence of a legislature per se.

A host of examples demonstrate how the election of landed elites can result in failed land reform initiatives under democracy. Costa Rica's legislature also blocked land reform efforts in the 1950s. In 1951 in Costa Rica, José Figueres's National Liberation Party (PLN) pushed for a land reform, advocating for the social function of property. A special legislative commission was named to study state land policies, and it published four draft laws in 1952 (Rowles 1985, 160–161). Following Figueres's election in 1953, the PLN drafted a new Law of Land and Colonization, but after going through various committees it was voted down in the Legislative Assembly by Figueres's opposition and the conservative arm of the PLN. João Goulart's attempts at implementing reform were similarly stymied in Brazil in the early 1960s. Goulart's proposals were repeatedly blocked by Congress, as was his attempt to circumvent Congress. Peru's President Fernando Belaúnde successfully passed a land reform law through Congress in 1964, but landholding interests added so many loopholes and exceptions that it was ineffective in practice (Cleaves and Scurrah 1980, 41).

Even if landed elites are not directly in government under democracy, they may be able to wield considerable pressure on the legislature or bureaucracy to block reform through lobbying (e.g., Acemoglu and Robinson 2008; Rodríguez 2004) or other forms of capture and influence (e.g., Rajan and Ramcharan 2011; Ziblatt 2009). Elite groups that are narrow in scope and wield considerable resources, such as landowners, are well equipped to gain links of institutional access to the state (Weyland 1996). Landed elites often have alliances with and even relatives in the legislature, administration, and bureaucracy. By advocating on behalf of sympathetic candidates and government workers and aiding their placement in government, landowners can gain powerful

---

[3] This tension can be traced back at least to ancient Rome, when Tiberius Gracchus attempted to implement an agrarian reform despite opposition and a veto from the Senate (Tuma 1965).

linkages in order to influence policy. Elected officials or government agencies that attempt to initiate reform may then be stymied by captured legislators or bureaucrats whose support is necessary to implement reform but who may support narrow interests, guard established procedures, or resist encroachment on their jurisdiction. Although landed elites can also attempt to capture bureaucrats or politicians under autocracy, their ability to do so rests on their relationship with the regime. When the regime is antagonistic to landed elites, it can directly repress their attempts to buy influence and can also subvert or eliminate politicians and bureaucrats that are connected to landed elites and serve as a conduit for landed elite influence.

Several examples illustrate the capacity of unelected landed interests to undermine reform initiatives under democracy. The negotiations surrounding the passage of Colombia's Social Agrarian Reform Act of 1961, for instance, were strongly impacted by powerful landed elites. These elites ensured that high-level policy decisions were made by the Agrarian Reform Committee board, which drew mainly from the landed elite. The board included members of the National Ranchers Federation (FEDENAG) and other agricultural interests (Zamosc 1986). The implementation of the reform through regional project zones was therefore strongly impacted by landed elite resistance (Duff 1968). Local land reform councils mimicked the structure of the central governing board and were consequently also influenced by landed interests. Large landowners similarly played an important role in drafting the legal basis of Venezuela's Agrarian Reform Law of 1960 in cooperation with the major political parties (Powell 1964, 84). And in Brazil following the return to democracy, José Sarney's ambitious National Agrarian Reform Plan (1985–1989) was met by heavy pressure from landholders and their allies in the military and the government, which resulted in "substantive changes in agrarian reform policy (e.g., the focus on public over private land distribution and the increase in compensation to landholders)" (Payne 1992, 15).

Landed elites can also use clientelism and vote buying to undercut support for land reform among the rural poor. Traditional land tenure relations long enabled landlords to use patron-client relations to dominate electoral competition (Baland and Robinson 2008; Lapp 2004). Large landowners can pursue their interests in this way even if they are not themselves elected to government and do not directly lobby or influence officials. Landowners can achieve favorable electoral outcomes by buying votes or pressuring voters in an effort to shift the preferences of the median rural voter toward large landowner preferences. These strategies are particularly attractive under democracy, where the median voter is poorer and where elections are more important for determining policy outcomes than in autocracy. Although members of the enfranchised poor have strong incentives to vote for redistribution (Meltzer and Richard 1981), elites can more easily buy their votes at low prices given that the poor will value a fixed, one-time economic benefit more than wealthier voters due to the diminishing marginal utility of income (see, e.g., Dixit and Londregan 1996). Under autocratic regimes where the franchise is restricted or eliminated, vote buying by landed elites is similar to the forms of influence and bribery discussed earlier in this chapter. Not only is it more expensive, but its success also depends on whether landed elites are incorporated into the support coalition of the regime.

The long history of clientelism and vote buying demonstrates how landed elites can shift electoral support for land reform. For example, prior to the 1958 introduction of the secret ballot in Chile, landowners could monitor the votes of their workers and punish them if they voted for candidates not supported by their *patrón* (Baland and Robinson 2008). The situation was similar in Peru until 1968. Many landlords attempted to keep their peasant workers illiterate and therefore ineligible to vote (Handelman 1975). Others influenced the votes of their peasant workers through fear, intimidation, and campaigns of misinformation (McClintock 1983).

Land Reform and Elite Splits

Redistributive land reform requires the sustained cooperation of a wide range of political actors. Political elites under popular, majoritarian democracy can pursue land redistribution consistent with the preferences of their constituents given the inability of landed elites to obstruct reform through institutional checks. Much more frequently, however, landed elites will block land redistribution under democracy through direct representation in the legislature, elite capture of elected officials, judges, or bureaucrats, and clientelism. Redistributive reform is consequently more likely to happen under a determined autocratic political elite.

Yet if redistributive land reform is more likely to occur under autocracy, why is reform implemented in some autocratic regimes and not others? Why do autocratic political elites and their coalitions sometimes faithfully uphold the interests of powerful landed elites and at other times attempt to destroy landed elites through expropriation and redistribution?

Expropriation as a Strategic Tool to Destroy Rivals and Win Insider Support

The key determinant of whether ruling political elites will decide to break with landed elites is the degree of coalitional overlap between (i) ruling political elites and the allies that comprise their initial support coalition and (ii) landed elites. It is here that the political origins of redistribution lie. Uncertainty about leader intentions is often very high at the beginning of a new autocratic regime. This matters most for members of the ruling political elite as well as their initial support coalition, the group that brings the political elite to power. The initial support coalition can be comprised of cliques of military officers, social groups such as labor unions or peasant organizations, or even landed or other economic elites.[4] Although the initial support coalition brings the political elites

---

[4] Under democracy, a political elite's initial support coalition is typically a political party or a coalition of parties.

into power, its rights in the new regime and the tools it can use to defend those rights are undefined (Bueno de Mesquita et al. 2003). If uncertainty persists and these rights remain undefined, power may shift to a subset of political elites (e.g., the dictator and a few close allies) and enable those political elites to betray the broader initial support coalition. Ruling political elites may seize such an advantage in an effort to divorce themselves from dependence on an otherwise powerful constituency and to allow themselves to diversify their support.

An autocratic political elite will be motivated to target the landed elite with redistribution when the coalitional overlap between these groups is low. The ruling political elite's expropriation of landed elites in this case can preserve the ability of the political elite to act independently in the future by eliminating rivals with long-standing power. From the perspective of political elites, landed elites and other economic elites may not be the most reliable support base. Powerful economic elites who control the media, access to foreign exchange, food production for urban consumption, and key domestic industries can turn on political elites and attempt to oust them. This gives ruling political elites an incentive to do an end run around these economic elites and, in concert with their support coalition, to appeal to other groups in society such as the rural poor. Low coalitional overlap provides an opening to seize this opportunity to lock in a political advantage into the future by destroying or severely weakening landed elites.

The ruling political elite's initial support coalition also benefits from this policy when its members are distinct from the landed elite. Redistribution away from current landed elites reveals that ruling political elites favor the political support of the initial coalition that brought them to office over the support of landed elites: if a conflict were to arise between these groups, political elites would choose these "regime insiders" over landed elites because political elites are willing to tolerate the loss of rents and political support from landed elites. A ruling political elite that fails to redistribute in these circumstances will therefore either be ousted by its support coalition or pay steep costs to insulate itself from an internal coup. For a ruling political elite that plans to maintain landed elites intact as a hedge against its initial support coalition or to enjoy the rents those landed elites would deliver, expropriating land is too costly. Yet the failure to do so provides information about the political elite's intentions: the initial support coalition should infer that the political elite should not be trusted.

It bears emphasizing that the initial support coalition can benefit from land expropriation even if land is not redistributed directly to them – a logic that departs from the typical assumption in the literature that redistribution is done for the direct material recipients of a good.

The destruction of landed elites serves the critical functions of destroying a potentially threatening rival and credibly signaling the ruling political elite's reliance on its support coalition. The support coalition can then leverage its favored position with the regime to capture rents from industry, build the

TABLE 3.2. *Land Redistribution and Ruling Political Elite Survival*

	ISC ≠ Landed Elite	ISC = Landed Elite
Ruling political elite redistributes land	Tenure extended	Tenure reduced (probability of coup high)
Ruling political elite does not redistribute land	Tenure reduced	Tenure extended as puppets OR political elites are rotated in and out of office

Note: ISC = initial support coalition of the ruling political elite.

military, or otherwise pursue its own interests while investing less in hedging against or attempting to oust a duplicitous ruling elite.

Of course, it is far from certain that ruling political elites will successfully establish a credible commitment to their supporters. Yet the turbulent history of dictatorships suggests that their ability to do is critical to their survival in office. Resolving this uncertainty is particularly important given that the most serious threat that ruling political elites face emanates from *within*, rather than outside of, their support coalition (Geddes 2003; Haber 2006; Svolik 2009).

Table 3.2 displays the predicted outcomes of a ruling political elite's tenure in office as a result of its initial support coalition's overlap with landed elites and its decision about whether to expropriate landed elites. The range of intersection between the initial support coalition and the landed elite is listed in the columns. The initial support coalition and the landed elite can either be perfectly overlapping, which indicates that the initial support coalition *is* the landed elite, or they can be disjointed, which indicates that at least some subset of the initial support coalition is not drawn from the landed elite. The table's rows display the actions the ruling political elite can take: to expropriate landed elites and redistribute their property or to not do so.

As the upper left box of Table 3.2 indicates, the expropriation of landed elites is one effective policy that ruling political elites can employ to reduce their political insecurity and remain in office longer when the initial support coalition is not composed of landed elites. As Chapters 5–8 demonstrate, there is a long history of ruling political elites expropriating and harassing landed and other economic elites under dictatorship in Latin America and elsewhere.

A ruling political elite that fails to expropriate landed elites when the latter do not make up part of the initial support coalition, by contrast, risks alienating the members who are in the coalition. The bottom left box of Table 3.2 indicates that the consequence of this scenario is an increased likelihood that the ruling political elite will be ousted from power.

Now consider the right half of Table 3.2. When the ruling political elite's initial support coalition is composed entirely of members of the landed elite, a ruling political elite that expropriates these individuals will sweep the rug out from under its own feet. This outcome is therefore unlikely. One of two outcomes may result if the ruling political elite instead chooses not to expropriate. First, the ruling political elite may indefinitely play the role of a puppet and serve as the faithful agent of the landed elite. Second, the ruling political elite may be one of several groups of political elites who are rotated in and out of office to prevent them from consolidating power and thereby threatening the landed elite.

Redistribution and the Consolidation of Autocratic Rule

Land expropriation not only eliminates landed elite rivals of ruling political elites and demonstrates loyalty to the political elite's initial support coalition when its members are distinct from landed elites. It also serves the complementary function of providing resources to reduce pressure from below and to win the support of the rural poor while also locking them into political dependency. Because key groups of the rural poor may have the potential to organize resistance if their interests are neglected, the threat of revolution or rebellion by the masses remains a salient concern (Acemoglu and Robinson 2006; Boix 2003). Even everyday forms of resistance and protest that fall far short of a revolutionary threat can raise the costs of ruling (Scott 1985). Although the ruling political elite may attempt to divide and conquer the masses or terrorize them into submission (Acemoglu, Robinson, and Verdier 2004; Haber 2006), successful autocratic regimes often relegate coercion to a last resort. Providing selective incentives to the rural poor or pursuing populist policies can reduce resistance and yield valuable support (Levine 1998; Smith 2005). Land redistribution also has the additional benefit of fixing rural populations to specific areas and enabling the activation of a new set of often cheaper tools (e.g., credits and inputs) that can be used to develop dependency on the state – a point I return to later in this chapter.

The distribution of land in particular also helps solve what might otherwise pose a commitment problem for ruling political elites if the beneficiaries of their redistributive policies may be weakened in the future. Once the ruling political elite expropriates one group of society in favor of another, the latter may fear it will later itself become a target (Neuhouser 1996). Yet land distribution is far more difficult to reverse than the granting of government jobs, cash payments, conditional cash transfers, or benefits such as tax breaks or social spending. Once land is distributed it is difficult to take back and redistribute again (Tai 1974), which makes it a "sticky" form of redistribution. Physically removing occupants risks protests and violence. Retaking redistributed land is therefore rarely done under the same political regime. To the contrary, land redistribution typically represents a commitment on the part of the state to beneficiaries.

Converting rural laborers to smallholders through land redistribution can also turn otherwise aggrieved peasants into a stabilizing force that supports the status quo over movements that threaten property ownership (Ansell and Samuels 2010; Huntington 1968; Paige 1975). The sticky nature of land redistribution often spurs beneficiaries to expand their time horizons and to consider the intergenerational implications of their decisions about the occupation and exploitation of their land. This reduces the likelihood of active resistance and builds popular support for the regime over challengers that promise a return to the status quo ante and over populist alternatives that offer further reform at the expense of current beneficiaries.

Existing research demonstrates that autocratic political elites that face potential opposition or require cooperation from important groups in society to sustain their rule will be more likely to deliver favorable policies to these groups (e.g., Gandhi and Przeworski 2006). Smith (2005), for example, demonstrates how Suharto's incorporation of powerful social organizations into a central structure enabled the delivery of patronage to millions, funded largely from increased taxes on preexisting elites. Similarly, UMNO met the burgeoning redistributive demands of Malay popular sectors after the 1969 riots through increased spending financed by elites and the middle class (Slater 2010). Dictators can also court the lower classes at the expense of elites through pro-poor social programs, as was demonstrated by Ne Win in Burma (Huntington 1968; Nordlinger 1977) and Jerry Rawlings in Ghana (Bienen 1985). These patterns are also evident in the distribution of land in rural societies. Land reform in Peru and Mexico, for instance, granted land to peasant communities that had a greater capacity to organize resistance against the regime (i.e., to "middle-class" laborers and in locales where land pressure was higher) and then created cooperatives and collectives that could be more easily monitored and manipulated politically than a large number of diverse smallholders (Albertus 2015a; Albertus et al. 2014).

TWO ILLUSTRATIVE CASES: THE DOMINICAN REPUBLIC AND MEXICO

A host of examples demonstrate how land redistribution can serve the purposes of autocratic political elites in ways that are consistent with the theory. I briefly outline two illustrative examples: the Dominican Republic under Rafael Trujillo and Mexico under the Partido Revolucionario Institucional (PRI).

Prior to seizing power in the Dominican Republic, Trujillo was the commander of the powerful National Army. Empowered by the US occupation of the country and shunned by the middle and upper classes, which opposed the occupation, the military was relatively autonomous from landed and other economic elite influence (Turits 2003, 80–81). The chief threats to the Trujillo regime's early rule were regional landed elites and political gangs that seized weapons and resisted Trujillo's rule. Although most of these were quickly crushed, domestic and foreign commercial agriculturalists began to enclose large land areas, expelling peasants and increasing the likelihood that dispossessed laborers would return to supporting local elites and gangs, resuscitating the chief threats to Trujillo's rule.

Trujillo orchestrated several large-scale programs to distribute, legalize, and temporarily cede land to peasants (Turits 2003, 82). At the same time that Trujillo was extending a colonization program under Law 758, he also began in 1934 a long-standing land distribution campaign that sought to provide free access to idle land on the basis of contracts. Although the state gave peasants access to privately owned land via contract, in most cases the land never had to be returned (Turits 2003, 97–98). Additional land simultaneously came from *terrenos comuneros,* or communal land that had failed to secure "prescription rights," or legal ownership, to its enclosures. The main target was land held by individuals and companies that had created large enclosures and used fake titles or tried to get prescription rights but had failed. Trujillo used this and the colonization program to create a peasant base of support and "consolidate his regime by securing popular acceptance in the countryside" (Turits 2003, 81). Colonization and redistribution programs continued fairly steadily between 1935 and 1950 (Maríñez 1993, 41–43).

Post-revolutionary Mexico is another example of large-scale expropriation and redistribution away from powerful landed and other economic elites undertaken by an autocratic regime. Plutarco Calles took power shortly after the Mexican Revolution. The members of his initial support coalition emerged from the three main factions that jockeyed for power during the Mexican Revolution after Porfirio Diaz relinquished power in 1911 following thirty years of rule. The first faction consisted of small farmers from central Mexico, represented by Emiliano Zapata. These peasants had lost their land during the Porfiriato. Meanwhile, the development of mining, railroads, and manufacturing under Diaz had generated a fledgling labor movement that was severely repressed during the Porfiriato. It was represented politically by Pancho Villa. Finally, because Diaz had favored an elite group of industrialists and bankers, a contingent of merchants, mine owners, and ranchers from Mexico's northern states, represented by Alvaro Obregón, opposed the monopoly rights granted to Mexico City's new powerbrokers.

Mexico cycled through a series of leaders in the wake of the revolution that alienated one or more of these factions and consequently failed to consolidate power. But in 1924, Calles rose to power and quickly courted these constituencies. Calles and his political coalition thus began to seriously attack landed elites by redistributing some 3.2 million hectares of land during his official term from 1924 to 1928.[5] This placated the faction of his support coalition that was composed of politically influential, mobilized peasants. Calles also chose to tax the rich by adopting progressive income taxation – the first Mexican president to do so. The Tax Law of 1924 instituted a federal income tax on individual income and corporate profits. Finally, to cement political support among labor, Calles appointed the head of the most important national labor organization (CROM) as Minister of Industry, Commerce, and Labor. Increases in wages

---

[5] On regional variation in land redistribution under the PRI, see Albertus et al. (2014) and Chapter 5.

and benefits were then mandated for CROM workers, in essence expropriating capital and redistributing it to labor. This strategy paid off: Calles proceeded to handpick several puppets as successors and ruled behind the scenes for ten years. The short-term result was that Calles's rule was bolstered by mitigating uncertainty about whether he would remain loyal to his initial support coalition. In the longer term, a stable autocratic dynasty emerged as a by-product of the institutions he adopted to address a new generation of commitment problems associated with the transition to newly empowered elites.

A FORMAL MODEL OF REDISTRIBUTIVE LAND REFORM

This section develops a formal model of the theory outlined earlier in the chapter to construct a more comprehensive picture of the political environment in which land redistribution policies are contested. First, the model treats decision making as a dynamic process in which actors anticipate the reactions of other actors and behave accordingly. Second, it builds a more complete picture of the distributional consequences of regimes. Regimes can implement not only land redistribution but also fiscal redistribution via taxes and transfers, and actors form preferences over both types of redistribution. Third, the model endogenizes the likelihood that landed elites will attempt a coup against political elites when faced with land redistribution and the likelihood that the rural poor will revolt absent land redistribution. The probability that these actors will succeed in challenging political elites is modeled as a function of the current resources they command. Lastly, the model introduces costs to political conflict.

The model builds from key models of regime change by Acemoglu and Robinson (2006) and Boix (2003) that are rooted in the redistributive implications of regimes. It also builds from more recent work by Ansell and Samuels (2014) that adapts several key assumptions in the literature on redistribution and regimes to recent empirical evidence. One main departure from the Acemoglu and Robinson (2006) and Boix (2003) models is that elites are split into the two groups discussed earlier in this chapter and in Chapter 2: ruling political elites and landed elites. This is also distinct from Ansell and Samuels (2014), who focus on competition between landed elites and an ascendant urban bourgeoisie. Also in contrast to these earlier models, the model presented here places emphasis on both asset and income redistribution, thereby capturing a wider and often more consequential range of redistribution. Lastly, the model emphasizes the political origins of redistribution in addition to the economic origins at the heart of these other models of regime change. Additional departures from these models are discussed in depth later in this chapter.

The Economy and Initial Endowments

The model conceives of a country with three main groups: the ruling political elite (P), the landed elite (L), and the rural poor (R). The chief productive asset in the economy is land. The landed elite and the rural poor both earn their income from land. Ruling political elites capture rents from the control of key government agencies or state institutions such as the military. These rents are extracted from the revenue generated by land and therefore compete with the income that the landed elite and the rural poor earn. They may simply represent government consumption such as military funding or the creation and operation of state-owned enterprises in the pursuit of industrialization. Rents can also be captured via the control of permits or licensing, export controls, currency manipulation, restrictions on property rights, agricultural marketing boards, and other policies or actions that disproportionately favor either the landed elite or the rural poor (see, e.g., Bates 1981; Shleifer and Vishny 1998). Rent-seeking is present under all forms of government.

Under dictatorship, the ruling political elite directly holds power and has a share λ of the population. The total population is normalized to one. The landed elite and the rural poor constitute a combined share $1 - \lambda$ of the population. Of this, the landed elite makes up μ and the rural poor comprise $1 - \mu$. The political elite therefore has a population $\pi_P = \lambda$, the landed elite has $\pi_L = \mu(1 - \lambda)$, and the rural poor have $\pi_R = (1 - \mu)(1 - \lambda)$. The rural poor makes up the majority of the population, such that $\pi_R > 1/2$.

The total amount of production in the economy is normalized to equal one. Productive assets are divided between land and the control over institutions that yield rents. The landed elite and rural poor divide the income $1 - r$ from land, whereas the ruling political elite earns r in rent extraction. In the absence of any rent seeking ($r = 0$), the landed elite as a group would obtain β income from land, whereas the rural poor would obtain $(1 - \beta)$ in income from land. A higher value of β for a fixed population $\mu(1 - \lambda)$ of landed elite therefore indicates higher land inequality. But when rents are strictly positive in value, the income for the landed elite and the rural poor is reduced. A share α of these resources comes from the landed elite, and a share $1 - \alpha$ comes from the rural poor. The landed elite as a group thus earns $\beta - \alpha r$ in income, whereas the rural poor earn $(1 - \beta) - (1 - \alpha)r$.

The parameter α captures the coalitional split between the ruling political elite and the landed elite. When α is large, the political elite operates at the expense of the landed elite. When α is small and overlap is therefore high, the political elite's earnings primarily come at the expense of the rural poor. Initial endowments generate income with constant returns. Figure 3.1 displays each group's income within the economy described.

To calculate individual earnings, we divide group income by each group's population. Because political elites earn income only from rents, the income of individuals that comprise the ruling political elite is $y_{Pi} = \frac{r}{\pi_P} = \frac{r}{\lambda}$. Individual earnings for members of the landed elite are calculated as the group's income β less αr, divided by the total population of landed elites $\mu(1 - \lambda)$, or $y_{Li} = \frac{\beta - \alpha r}{\pi_L} = \frac{\beta - \alpha r}{\mu(1-\lambda)}$. Members of the rural poor have individual earnings $(1 - \beta)$ derived from the agricultural sector minus a share $(1 - \alpha)r$ captured by the

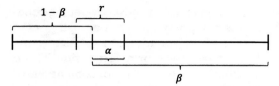

FIGURE 3.1. An Economy of the Landed Elite, Ruling Political Elite, and Rural Poor. *Note:* The landed elite as a group have income $\beta - \alpha r$, the political elite collectively have r, and the rural poor have $(1 - \beta) - (1 - \alpha)r$.

political elite, divided by the total population of rural poor $(1 - \mu)(1 - \lambda)$: $y_{Ri} = \frac{(1-\beta)-(1-\alpha)r}{\pi_R} = \frac{(1-\beta)-(1-\alpha)r}{(1-\mu)(1-\lambda)}$. Average income $\bar{y}$ is therefore equal to one.

The model assumes that members of the landed elite and ruling political elite are wealthier than members of the rural poor. Furthermore, members of the rural poor earn less than the average income $\bar{y}$ (i.e., $y_{Ri} < \bar{y}$).[6]

Political Regimes and Redistribution

This section builds from the economic structure and actors defined earlier in this chapter to examine actor preferences for the choice over land redistribution and the type of political regime. Political regimes create rules for which groups will determine policies of redistribution – including land redistribution, taxation, and spending – and how these decisions will be made. The main actors know the distributional consequences of regimes and choose strategies that will best satisfy their own interests given how other actors behave. We must therefore define the outcomes under various political regimes, especially the optimal tax rate, how tax revenues are distributed, whether or not there is land redistribution, and who the winners and losers of land redistribution are.

The model incorporates the fact that regimes can redistribute not only *income* but also *assets*. Many models of redistribution focus solely on individuals' income (e.g. Acemoglu and Robinson 2006; Ansell and Samuels 2010; Boix 2003). Yet the underlying assets that generate income are a key foundation of economic and political life. Indeed, in rural societies where land inequality is high and the ratio of assets to income is large for elites, land redistribution poses a bigger threat than taxation. It simultaneously holds greater promise for the poor than progressive government spending. The reason is simple: landholding provides a stream of income rather than a one-time payment. Individuals that earn income from land will do so as long as they own it; those who do not own land will never reap income from it. The importance of asset redistribution is compounded by the fact that the redistribution of income via taxation and

---

[6] A sufficient but not necessary condition for this to hold is the following: $\beta + (1 - \alpha)r \in [.5, 1]$ This implies that land is equally productive in generating tax revenues.

progressive spending has historically been quite low in most developing countries (e.g., Sokoloff and Zolt 2007). This is not only the result of high rates of evasion and exemptions; statutory rates themselves are also low. As a result, remaining wealth disparities provide an ample target for redistribution. This is not to say that the taxation and redistribution of income is not contentious or relevant for political dynamics. Rather, it is not the only form of redistribution over which individuals form preferences.

Redistribution under Autocracy

In an autocracy, the masses are excluded from the decision-making process and elites set policy. There are few institutional constraints to their decision making. I assume that the ruling political elite taxes the income of both the landed elite and the rural poor at a nonnegative rate of $\tau_P \in [0,1]$ and appropriate the revenue for themselves. This builds on literature that suggests predatory and extractive policies including taxation under autocracy (e.g., Ansell and Samuels 2014; Olson 1993). Without loss of generality, I assume the political elite taxes landed elites and the rural poor at the same rate and that the tax revenue generated does not vary with average land parcel size.[7] The revenue collected is redistributed as a lump sum to members of the political elite. There is a deadweight cost of taxation $C(\tau_P)$ given potential evasion and distortions in incentives to produce. I assume, for all of the regimes that follow, that there are no costs when there is no taxation, that costs increase with the tax rate (i.e., $C'(\cdot) > 0$), and that costs increase more rapidly as the tax rate increases (i.e., $C''(\cdot) > 0$).

Ruling political elites choose the tax rate that maximizes their utility when they are in power. For a given member of the political elite, this can be expressed as follows:

$$\max_{\tau_P} U_{Pi}(\tau_P) = y_{Pi} + (\tau_P - C(\tau_P)) \left(\frac{y_R + y_L}{\lambda} \right)$$

Maximizing this expression yields an optimal tax choice τ_P^* given by:

$$C'(\tau_P^*) = 1$$

The ruling political elite therefore increases the tax rate until the marginal cost equals the marginal benefit, which is one.[8]

If the landed elite launches a successful coup, it will seize power and set the tax rate. Landed elites will, similarly to political elites, levy taxes on the other two groups and keep the revenue for themselves. They choose a tax rate as follows:

$$\max_{\tau_L} U_{Li}(\tau_L) = y_{Li} + (\tau_L - C(\tau_L)) \left(\frac{y_R + y_P}{\mu(1 - \lambda)} \right)$$

---

[7] This implies that land is equally productive in generating tax revenues.
[8] There is an interior solution provided that $C'(0) < 1$.

As with the political elite, maximizing this expression yields an optimal tax choice τ_L^* given by:

$$C'(\tau_L^*) = 1$$

The landed elite therefore sets the tax rate at the point at which the marginal cost equals the marginal benefit.[9] It is possible that the landed elite, upon seizing power, may just replace the dictator and a small, key subset of political elites and then relegate the task of ruling to this more favorable political elite that will set a tax rate consistent with the landed elite's optimal rate. In either case, the bulk of political elites are not destroyed as actors – they simply no longer set redistributive policies, and their earnings may therefore be reduced via taxation.[10]

The assumption that autocratic incumbents will tax those out of power and capture the revenue for themselves is a clear departure from the influential models of democratization and redistribution put forth by Boix (2003) and Acemoglu and Robinson (2006). These authors assume that there is an isomorphism between those in power under autocracy and the rich. A host of work, however, demonstrates that autocratic regimes often tax the rich in addition to the poor (Albertus and Menaldo 2014; Levi 1989; Olson 1993; Slater 2010). As a result, recent models such as that in Ansell and Samuels (2014) incorporate the notion of a positive tax rate under autocracy. In either case, the comparative statics of the model detailed later in this chapter are similar if we assume instead that the ruling political elite and the landed elite tax only the rural poor and not other elites when they are in power, or if we assume that elites in power do not levy any taxes at all.

In addition to setting the tax rate, ruling political elites will also decide whether or not to redistribute the landed elite's property to the rural poor. Low institutional constraints facilitate the implementation of their decision. Expropriation can help the political elite preserve its ability to act independently in the future by weakening or eliminating rivals with long-standing power. Pursuing redistribution may, however, be costly: threatening the power and status of landed elites risks stoking a coup by those same landed interests. Yet the failure to redistribute also carries political risks. If the initial support coalition that brought the ruling political elite to power is distinct from the landed elite, it

---

[9] As with the political elite, there is an interior solution as long as $C'(0) < 1$.

[10] This assumption becomes apparent if we think of political elites as relatively resilient actors, for which there is considerable evidence. These actors are rarely liquidated wholesale when they are displaced from directly holding power; rather, their influence (and rents) may wane as those who seize power change policy. Take for example the Egyptian military, which had long sustained Hosni Mubarak's rule and temporarily ruled in his wake but whose power persisted amid revolution and the tumultuous transition to and from Mohamed Morsi. In a democratic context, displaced political elites are often opposition party leaders. Entirely eliminating the political elite's income when it is displaced has little consequence for the comparative statics of the model.

requires a demonstration of the political elite's willingness to adopt favorable property rights for its members. This coalition will push for land redistribution to destroy the landed elite as a potential future threat to its power. A ruling political elite that fails to redistribute in these circumstances will therefore either be ousted by its support coalition or pay steep costs to insulate itself from an internal coup. As the literature indicates, a variety of tactics could be used to insulate against the threat of overthrow, such as creating multiple layered security forces (see, e.g., Haber 2006). I introduce this into the model as a cost of coup insulation. Without loss of generality, I assume the political elite pays no coup-proofing costs against its internal support coalition (ISC) if it chooses to redistribute but pays a cost c_{Pi}^{ISC} if it fails to redistribute.

Redistribution under Popular (Majoritarian) Democracy

The political economy of popular democracy differs considerably from that of autocracy. If ruling political elites fail to redistribute land and the rural poor overthrow them in a successful revolt without the help of the landed elite, then the rural poor will establish a popular, majoritarian democracy. The median voter under popular democracy is a member of the rural poor. Because landed elites comprise a relatively small minority of the population and institutional constraints are low, the rural poor are likely to capture the veto points in government that enable them to appropriate the landed elite's property and therefore the source of their income. The rural poor's representation in government, along with the inability of landed elites to insert themselves as veto players that can block reform, leads the rural poor to fully expropriate landed elites and divide the land among themselves. Their income therefore becomes $y_{RDi} = (1 - r)/(1 - \mu)(1 - \lambda)$. Landed elites lose their income entirely.[11]

The rural poor will then determine a nonnegative tax rate $\tau_R \in [0,1]$ proportional to income following the decision to redistribute land. Given the majoritarian nature of institutions, taxation follows the Meltzer and Richard (1981) framework. All groups in society are taxed. The revenue collected is then redistributed as a lump sum to all citizens. There is a deadweight cost of taxation $C(\tau_R)$. Each citizen therefore receives a transfer $T_R = (\tau_R - C(\tau_R))\bar{y}$, where $\bar{y}$ is the average income in the society. As with dictatorship, I assume that there are no costs when there is no taxation under democracy, that costs increase with the tax rate (i.e., $C'(\cdot) > 0$), and that the costs increase more rapidly as the tax rate increases (i.e., $C''(\cdot) > 0$).

The rural poor under popular democracy will choose the tax rate that maximizes their utility as follows:

$$\max_{\tau_R} U_{Ri}(\tau_R) = (1 - \tau_R)y_{RDi} + (\tau_R - C(\tau_R))\bar{y} \tag{1}$$

---

[11] Converting landed elites into members of the rural poor rather than having them destroyed as actors following land redistribution would yield them a small transfer under democracy and make them fear popular democracy marginally less.

Maximizing this expression yields an optimal tax choice τ_R^* given by:

$$C'(\tau_R^*) = 1 - \frac{1-r}{(1-\mu)(1-\lambda)} \tag{2}$$

Equation 2 illustrates an important comparative static.[12] As r increases, indicating that the political elite captures higher rents, the right side of Equation 2 increases. For Equation 2 to hold, τ_R^* must change so that the left side increases as well. Given that $C''(\cdot) > 0$, an increase in τ_R^* yields an increase in the left side of Equation 2. The tax rate therefore goes up when political elites have higher income. As $1 - r$ increases, members of the rural poor will have gained more by appropriating a larger land sector from landed elites to themselves. A higher $1 - r$ therefore decreases the right side of Equation 2 and implies that τ_R^* must change so that the left side also decreases. Because the rural poor are now wealthier after having captured more land, they will set a lower tax rate.

Redistribution under Elite-Biased Democracy

A democracy in which the rural poor overthrow the ruling political elite and set the tax rate is not the only outcome in which the majority has a hand in ruling. Seeing the rural poor revolt, or anticipating such an outcome, the landed elite can also actively aid them in jointly overthrowing the political elite. The likelihood of achieving democracy in this case is higher than if the rural poor revolt alone because of the resources the landed elite can bring to bear to make protest successful. Yet the role landed elites play in establishing democracy also gives them influence under that regime that is disproportionate to their numbers alone. Cross-class alliances and political pacts that are forged in the process of pushing for political change are only made credible by establishing mechanisms whereby elites can replicate their strength under democracy and block large-scale policy changes that threaten them. Common mechanisms include electoral system engineering, malapportionment, the banning of left-wing parties, lobbying, and clientelism (Albertus and Menaldo 2014).

I capture the outsized influence of elites in democratic politics in two ways. First, because landed elites push for high institutional constraints and can then use formal rules and informal influence to capture key elements of the legislature, judiciary, or bureaucracy, they will be able to insert themselves as effective veto players in at least one institution necessary for the passage or implementation of a land reform that redistributes their landholdings. Since the presence of landed elites in any key veto points can forestall redistributive land reform (see Table 3.1 on the steps of land reform), land redistribution is much less likely under such a regime than it is under a popular democracy. This approach therefore acknowledges that while popular democracy may be redistributive,

---

[12] The condition for an interior solution in Equation 2 is $C'(0) < 1 - \frac{1-r}{(1-\mu)(1-\lambda)}$. Otherwise the tax rate is zero.

democracy is more frequently captured by elites who can block the policies that pose the largest threat to them.

Second, when landed elites collaborate with the rural poor to jointly establish democracy, both of these groups will be able to affect the subsequent equilibrium tax rate τ_J. Elites will not typically be able to undermine all forms of redistribution under democracy. Yet their ability to influence the extent of redistribution increases with their political influence. I capture this notion in a straightforward way by calculating the tax rate under elite-biased democracy using a weighted sum of the preferences of both the landed elite and rural poor, where the weights are determined by the relative political power of each group.[13] If the preferences of the landed elite are weighted by δ and those of the rural poor are weighted by $1 - \delta$, then the resulting tax rate is chosen as follows:

$$\max_{\tau_J}(1 - \delta)(1 - \mu)(1 - \lambda)((1 - \tau_J)y_{Ri} + (\tau_J - C(\tau_J))\bar{y})$$

$$+ \delta\mu(1 - \lambda)((1 - \tau_J)y_{Li} + (\tau_J - C(\tau_J)) \bar{y}) \tag{3}$$

Maximizing this expression yields an optimal tax choice τ_J^* given by:

$$C'(\tau_J^*) = 1 - \frac{(1 - \delta)((1 - \beta) - (1 - \alpha)r) + \delta(\beta - \alpha r)}{(1 - \delta)(1 - \mu)(1 - \lambda) + \delta\mu(1 - \lambda)} \tag{4}$$

Note that when the landed elite does not influence the tax rate ($\delta = 0$), Equation 4 simply captures the optimal tax rate in a popular democracy where the rural poor have not expropriated landed elites and divided the landed elite's land (and resultant income) among themselves. The tax rate is set by the median voter, who is a member of the rural poor.

Because landed elites had a hand in jointly establishing democracy along with the rural poor, however, they hold political power that is disproportionate to their numbers alone. Equation 4 illustrates several intuitive comparative statics that reflect this.[14] As δ increases, the right side of Equation 4 decreases. For $C'(\tau_J^*)$ to decrease as well, τ_J^* must decline, indicating that $\partial\tau_J^*(\delta)/\partial\delta < 0$.

This implies that the tax rate will decline as the relative power of landed elites increases under democracy. The effects of an increase in land inequality on the tax rate, however, depend on the strength of elites. When $\delta > 1/2$, an increase in β yields a decrease in τ_J^*. But for a fixed $\delta < 1/2$, which indicates that elites have relatively less influence than the rural poor, an increase in β results in a higher equilibrium tax rate. This dynamic is therefore similar to that which operates in a popular democracy, as detailed in the previous section. The effects of a larger split α between the political and landed elite on the tax rate are similarly conditional on the power of landed elites under democracy.

---

[13] This idea builds from an extension of Acemoglu and Robinson's (2006) basic model.

[14] There is an interior solution to Equation 4 if $C'(0) < 1 - \frac{(1-\delta)((1-\beta)-(1-\alpha)r)+\delta(\beta-\alpha r)}{(1-\delta)(1-\mu)(1-\lambda)+\delta\mu(1-\lambda)}$. Otherwise the tax rate is set at zero.

When the preferences of landed elites are disproportionately powerful under democracy such that $\delta > 1/2$, an increase in α raises τ_j^*, because a higher α increases the income of the rural poor relative to the landed elite. Yet when $\delta < 1/2$, an increase in α lowers τ_j^*. The interpretation is intuitive: a higher α translates into greater income for the rural poor, which leads them to choose a lower tax rate when they have more influence over the tax rate.

A Two-Group Model of Land Redistribution under Autocracy

Having detailed the structure of redistribution when different social groups control politics, I now examine how changes in key factors such as the coalitional overlap between ruling political elites and landed elites and the relative political power of landed elites under democracy impact the strategies chosen by each group. These strategies ultimately determine whether or not land redistribution occurs.

I begin with a two-group game between the ruling political elite and the landed elite. Figure 3.2 depicts the structure of the game. In the background stage prior to the game, a group of political elites has seized power with the assistance of an initial support coalition and has established an autocratic regime. The ruling political elite begins by choosing whether or not to redistribute the landed elite's property to the rural poor. If it chooses to redistribute land, the landed elite must then choose whether to launch a coup against the political elite and install a new autocratic regime that represents its own interests.

We can use backward induction to solve for the subgame perfect Nash equilibria of the game. A particular equilibrium is characterized by the payoff functions and the strategies for each of the players such that none of them have an incentive to deviate. In what follows, I assume that all members of each group are identical, so that the choice of one member of a group will be the same as the choice of all other members of that group given the same set of conditions. I focus the discussion only on pure strategy equilibria.

The first step in solving for the model equilibria is to determine whether or not landed elites will attempt a coup against the ruling political elite when faced with land redistribution. They will do so if their expected utility when launching a coup exceeds that of not launching a coup. This depends in part on their probability of victory. Following Ansell and Samuels (2014), I model the probability of victory as a function of the relative income of the conflictive groups. I assume that all agents are risk neutral in their preferences. In particular, I express p_L as $p_L(y_L, y_P)$, which is increasing in the income y_L of the landed elite and decreasing in the income y_P of the political elite. The intuition is straightforward: a wealthier landed elite is more likely to prevail in a coup against the political elite. Conversely, a wealthier political elite is more likely to successfully fight off a coup attempt by the landed elite.

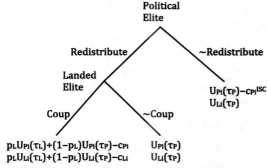

FIGURE 3.2. Intra-Elite Splits and Land Redistribution.

The costs of launching a coup also factor into the landed elite's calculation of whether to launch a coup to unseat the incumbent political elite. The cost of launching a coup to members of the landed elite is c_{Li}. The ruling political elite must also pay a cost c_{Pi} of fighting off a coup attempt. I do not restrict the coup costs to each group to be either identical or ordered in a specific way.

The landed elite will attempt a coup against the ruling political elite when faced with land redistribution when the following coup function is positive, where $U^L(\tau_L)$ is written as U_{Li}^L and $U^L(\tau_P)$ is written as $U_L i^{(P|R)}$: $C_i = p_L U_L i^L + (1 - p_L)U_L i^{(P|R)} - c_L i - U_L i^{(P|R)}$. Rearranging this equation and substituting for the utility functions yields $C_i = p_L(\frac{(\beta-\alpha r)(1-\tau_L^*+C(\tau_L^*))+(\tau_L^*-C(\tau_L^*))}{\mu(1-\lambda)}) - c_{Li}.$[15] The expression in the parentheses is positive. This indicates that if the likelihood and payoffs of a successful coup attempt are high relative to its costs, the coup constraint is met and the landed elite will launch a coup against the political elite when confronted with land redistribution. The landed elite will otherwise acquiesce.

How does C_i change with an increase in the coalitional split α between the ruling political elite and the landed elite? An increase in α decreases the likelihood that landed elites will attempt a coup when faced with expropriation of their land. It does so by making the likelihood of winning an attempted coup lower given smaller pre-coup income and by decreasing the payoffs from winning in a coup.[16] A decrease in α, by contrast, increases the likelihood of a coup by landed elites when they are faced with land expropriation. Their

---

[15] See Appendix A for the utility functions.

[16] We can see this more formally by taking the derivative of C_i with respect to α: $\frac{\partial C_i}{\partial \alpha} = \frac{\partial p_L}{\partial \alpha}(\frac{(\beta-\alpha r)(1-\tau_L^*+C(\tau_L^*))+(\tau_L^*-C(\tau_L^*))}{\mu(1-\lambda)}) - p_L \frac{r(1-\tau_L^*+C(\tau_L^*))}{\mu(1-\lambda)}$. Both terms on the right side of this equation are negative given that $\partial p_L/\partial \alpha < 0$. While $\partial C_i/\partial \alpha < 0$, an increase in the wealth of landed elites via an increase in β encourages landed elites to pursue a coup rather than to acquiesce to land redistribution (i.e., $\partial C_i/\partial \beta > 0$).

credible coup threat gives them considerable influence over the choices made by the political elite even though they do not directly hold power.

Given the strategy pursued by the landed elite, when will ruling political elites choose to redistribute land? The political elite will redistribute land if the following land redistribution function is positive: $LR_i = p_L U_{Pi}^L + (1 - p_L)U_{Pi}^{P|R} - c_{pi} - U_P^{P|\sim R}$, which can also be written as $LR_i = p_L U_{Pi}^L + (1 - p_L)U_{Pi}^{P|R} - c_{pi} - (U_{Pi}^{P|R} - c_{Pi}^{ISC})$. LR_i reflects the expected utility of choosing to redistribute land in spite of a credible coup threat from landed elites compared to the expected utility of not redistributing land.[17] Note that $U_{Pi}^{P|\sim R}$ differs from $U_{Pi}^{P|R}$ in a way that reflects the ruling political elite's need to satisfy its initial support coalition in order to forestall an internal coup threat. If the initial support coalition that brought the political elite to power is distinct from the landed elite, its members will push for land redistribution to destroy the landed elites as a long-term rival threat to their power. Undercutting the landed elite eliminates the possibility that the ruling political elite will choose to abandon its initial support coalition in the future in favor of pursuing policies that benefit landed elites. It also mitigates the likelihood that the political elite will be toppled at some point by landed elites who retain their political strength by maintaining their land. A ruling political elite that fails to redistribute in these circumstances must consequently pay a high cost to insulate itself from an internal coup. The costs the political elite pays to insulate itself from a coup by its initial support coalition are an increasing function of the coalitional split with the landed elite, so that c_{Pi}^{ISC} can be written as $c_{Pi}^{ISC}(\alpha)$.[18]

Rearranging the land redistribution equation and substituting for the utility functions yields $LR_i = p_L(\frac{-r\tau_L^* - (\tau_p^* - C(\tau_p^*))(1-r)}{\lambda}) + c_{Pi}^{ISC} - c_{pi}$. How does the likelihood of the ruling political elite choosing land redistribution change with an increase in the coalitional split α between the political and landed elite? Taking the derivative of LR_i with respect to α indicates that an increase in α leads to an increase in the likelihood that the ruling political elite will redistribute land from the landed elite. This operates through (i) a decreased likelihood that the landed elite will be able to launch a successful coup to displace the political elite when faced with expropriation ($\partial p_L / \partial \alpha < 0$), and (ii) a higher cost of having to coup proof against an internal threat from the political elite's initial support coalition. The following proposition summarizes this

---

[17] I only consider the case of a credible coup threat. If the landed elite choose not to attempt a coup when faced with land redistribution, the political elite will always redistribute land and the game ends.

[18] I assume that the political elite's costs of coup insulation against the initial support coalition are zero when the political elite's land redistribution choice is consistent with the coalition's preferences. The threat from the initial support coalition could alternatively be modeled as a probability of internal coup, in which the political elite is replaced by another political elite and the game is repeated.

result. Proofs for this and subsequent propositions are located at the end of this chapter in Appendix A.

Proposition 1. *An increase in the coalitional split α between the ruling political elite and the landed elite increases the likelihood that the political elite will implement land reform.*

A Three-Group Model of Land Redistribution

The two-group model of land redistribution demonstrates how coalitional overlap between the key supporters of the ruling political elite and the members of the landed elite influences whether the ruling political elite will pursue land redistribution under autocracy. Yet the rural poor often also play an important role land reform dynamics. Absent significant reform under dictatorship, the rural poor may push for democracy as a way to gain influence over policy formation and increase the likelihood of redistribution in their favor. This has two main consequences. On the one hand, it increases the likelihood that the political elite under dictatorship will choose to redistribute land in order to stay in power and forestall a challenge by the rural poor in the absence of reform. But if conditions are such that ruling political elites still have incentives to forego land reform (e.g., if landed elites are organized), it also introduces the possibility that a revolt by the masses will lead to the establishment of democracy in which the median voter will vote to redistribute land or at least to raise taxes on members of the outgoing political elite.

Figure 3.3 displays the structure of the three-group extensive form game and the payouts for the ruling political elite, landed elite, and rural poor. The rural

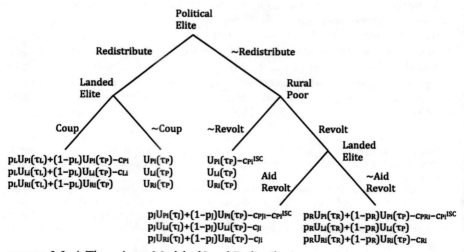

FIGURE 3.3. A Three-Actor Model of Land Redistribution.

poor can now revolt and attempt to establish a democratic regime if the ruling political elite fails to redistribute land under autocracy. Revolt may take the form of rapid revolution but can also involve a series of building strikes and popular protests or the formation of an insurgent rebellion that forces the regime's exit. When the rural poor successfully revolt without the aid or interference of the landed elite, they will set up a popular democracy with few institutional constraints in which the median voter will vote to redistribute the property of the landed elite in the rural poor's favor. Such an outcome is rare, however. The landed elite, anticipating this outcome under a popular democratic regime, can join the rural poor in pushing for democracy. This increases the likelihood of democracy, which is favorable to the rural poor, but it comes in exchange for increased influence by landed elites under democracy. When landed elites play a foundational role in democratization, they are able to construct higher institutional constraints and then capture key veto points under the ensuing regime such that they can preclude serious land reform implementation. But they cannot block all types of redistribution. The rural poor will be able to gain some influence over the tax rate. The extent to which they choose the tax rate is nonetheless limited by the outsized political influence landed elites gain in the transition process.[19]

As with the two-group model, we can solve the game depicted in Figure 3.3 using backward induction. We begin with the subgame between the landed elite and the rural poor.

The Landed Elite/Rural Poor Subgame

Democracy can possibly be achieved in the model depicted in Figure 3.3 if the rural poor choose to revolt. The landed elite can then choose whether or not to aid the rural poor in an effort to overturn the status quo. If the rural poor revolt alone, they will succeed in establishing a popular democracy with a probability of $p_R = p_R(y_R, y_P)$, which is increasing in the income y_R of the rural poor and decreasing in the income y_P of the political elite. If the landed elite aid the rural poor in joint revolt in an effort to gain political influence under democracy, they will succeed with a probability of $p_J > p_R$. Because the landed elite have considerable resources that they can bring to bear in opposing the political elite, democratization is more likely in a joint revolt than if the rural poor revolt alone. I model the likelihood of victory p_J as $p_J(y_L + y_R, y_P)$, because the rural poor and landed elites are now fighting on the same side against the political elite.

---

[19] Extending the model to enable ruling political elites to forego land redistribution and directly extend the franchise to the rural poor (which then set policy) without the latter revolting has countervailing effects. It gives landed elites more incentives to aid the rural poor in revolt so the latter do not strike a side deal with the political elite. This reduces the likelihood of land redistribution. It also broadens the circumstances under which political elites lose office, thereby giving them greater incentives to redistribute land.

The rural poor and landed elite also pay a cost if they choose to revolt. Members of the rural poor pay a cost c_{Ri} if they revolt alone. The ruling political elite must pay a cost c_{PRi} of fighting off an attempted revolt by the rural poor. If the landed elite aid the rural poor in revolt, both groups will suffer a cost $c_{Ji} <$ c_{Ri}, which is smaller than the cost paid by the rural poor if they revolt alone. The ruling political elite pay a cost c_{PJi} of fighting against a joint revolt by the rural poor and the landed elite.

The landed elite will then choose to aid the rural poor in the attempt to push for democratization if the following joint revolt function is positive, where $U^L(\tau_J)$ is written as U^J_{Li}, $U^L(\tau_p)$ is written as U^P_{Li}, and $U^L(\tau_R)$ is written as U^R_{Li} : $J_i = p_J U^J_{Li} + (p_R - p_J)U^P_{Li} - p_R U^R_{Li} - c_{Ji}$.[20] In other words, the landed elite will choose to aid the rural poor when the expected payoff of living in a jointly established democracy minus the foregone advantage that joint revolt affords to reducing the likelihood of living in a dictatorship under the political elite is greater than the expected payoff of living in a revolutionary democracy.

It is important to note that there exist some p_J, p_R, δ, and c_{Ji} such that J_i will be positive. This becomes evident if we rewrite J_i as follows: $J_i = p_J(U^J_{Li} - U^P_{Li}) + p_R U^P_{Li} - c_{Ji}$. Landed elites prefer jointly established democracy to living under the political elite because they gain more influence over the tax rate and also receive a transfer. The expression in the parentheses of this equation is therefore positive. Provided the costs of fighting a joint revolt against the political elite c_{Ji} are not too high relative to the likelihood of winning in a revolt, the landed elite will prefer to aid the rural poor in democratization rather than leave the rural poor to fight alone. As $p_J \to p_R$ from above, the landed elite simply calculate whether the benefits of influence over tax policy in democracy less the costs of revolt outweigh being expropriated in a popular democracy that is established via revolution. As $p_R \to 0$, the landed elite will aid the rural poor, provided that the expected payoffs of doing so outweigh accepting the status quo under the political elite's dictatorship.

One key parameter of interest that drives the landed elite's decision about whether to join the rural poor in pushing for democracy is the degree of political power it expects to marshal after the transition. We can formally examine how this influences the landed elite's decision by taking the derivative of J_i with respect to δ after substituting for the utility functions. Doing so confirms our intuition: $\partial J_i / \partial \delta > 0$, and therefore higher levels of political influence by the landed elite under a jointly established democracy increase the likelihood that it will join the rural poor in a self-interested revolt against the political elite. These findings yield the following lemma.

---

[20] Given that the ruling political elite choose not to redistribute land in this subgame, this subsection uses the notation U^P_{Li} to signify $U^{P|\sim R}_{Li}$ and U^P_{Ri} to signify $U^{P|\sim R}_{Ri}$.

Lemma 1. *When the landed elite enjoys a higher level of political influence δ under democracy, it will be more likely to join the rural poor in a joint revolt against the ruling political elite.*

Lemma 1 clearly contradicts Boix's dictum that "[b]ig landowners oppose democracy of necessity" because of fear of expropriation (Boix 2003, 37). Similarly, Mahoney (2003, 146) argues that labor-dependent landowners are the "most consistently anti-democratic force," a claim echoed by Gerschenkron (1946), Moore (1966), Karl (1987), Acemoglu and Robinson (2006), and Ansell and Samuels (2010). The model here, by contrast, shows that landed elites may have an incentive to aid the rural poor in pushing for a democracy that they can strongly influence when they fear that the rural poor may successfully establish a democracy on their own that functions against the interests of landed elites. Although big landowners will therefore oppose popular democracy, as anticipated by these authors, they may nonetheless embrace a democracy in which they help write the rules. Landlords are willing to go along with, and even initiate, democracy if it means capturing veto points so they can block large-scale redistribution of their property and have greater control over the tax rate.

Many democratic transitions in Latin America are emblematic of this dynamic. Colombia transitioned to democracy under the National Front pact in 1958 when the Liberals and Conservatives united to overthrow the increasingly populist and charismatic military dictator Gustavo Rojas Pinilla, who ruled over widespread conflict in the countryside. The powerful landowner presence in both parties played a key role in crafting democracy and in influencing its subsequent operation, as demonstrated by their outsized role in the design of the Social Agrarian Reform Act of 1961 (Albertus and Kaplan 2013). Venezuela's transition to democracy under the 1958 Punto Fijo Pact was guided by political leaders and powerful economic interests – including large landowners – that agreed to strong institutional constraints after a period of military rule that culminated in strikes and burgeoning land invasions (Albertus 2013). Landowners in Brazil stepped aside as military rule weakened and social movements strengthened in the early 1980s, but they retained both influence and protection throughout the 1985 democratic transition and then leveraged that influence to win favorable rules and a constitution that protected productive private property from expropriation (Payne 1992). A host of transitions to democracy in countries such as Argentina, Ecuador, Honduras, and Peru also reflect these dynamics.

Having examined the landed elite's choice of whether or not to aid the rural poor in revolt, we can now turn to how the rural poor decide whether or not to revolt. Consider the case in which the landed elite will choose to aid the rural poor in the push for democratization if the rural poor revolt. The rural poor will then choose to revolt if the revolt function R_i is positive: $R_i = p_J U_{Ri}^J + (1 - p_J)U_{Ri}^P - c_{Ji} - U_{Ri}^P$.

Higher levels of political influence for the landed elite under a jointly established democracy make revolt less attractive for the rural poor when they will be aided by the landed elite because of the lack of land redistribution and the diminished tax rate that will be set under democracy as δ increases (i.e., $\partial R_i / \partial \delta < 0$). Nonetheless, there exist some p_J, δ, and c_{Ji} such that the rural poor will rebel even when they anticipate that the landed elite will co-opt the revolt and steer the democratization process in favor of the landed elite. This is evident by rearranging R_i and writing out the utility functions: $R_i = p_J((\tau_p^* - \tau_j^*(\frac{((1-\beta)-(1-\alpha)r)}{(1-\mu)(1-\lambda)}) + (\tau_j^* - C(\tau_j^*))) - c_{Ji}$. We know that $\tau_P^* > \tau_j^*$, because otherwise the landed elite would never have an incentive to set its own tax rate. The expression in the parentheses is therefore positive.

The rural poor are not simply duped into arriving at an elite-biased democracy. To the contrary, such an arrangement may be preferable to living under repressive dictatorship, even if it does not result in land redistribution. This is because the rural poor will have some influence over the tax rate in an elite-biased democracy.

Now consider the case in which the expected utility of the landed elite is higher when it does not aid the rural poor in a revolt. The revolt function R_i for the rural poor is now redefined as follows: $R_i = p_R U_{Ri}^R + (1 - p_R) U_{Ri}^P - c_{Ri} - U_{Ri}^P$. When R_i is positive, the rural poor will revolt in an effort to establish popular democracy. Because $U_{Ri}^R > U_{Ri}^P$, there exist some p_R, τ_R^*, and c_{Ri} such that the rural poor will in fact revolt in the absence of aid from the landed elite.

Are the rural poor more likely to revolt against a ruling political elite that does not redistribute land when they are aided by the landed elite in their push for democratization or when they are left to fight alone? By definition, $p_J > p_R$ and $c_{Ri} > c_{Ji}$. Given the barriers to collective action that make popular revolution so rare, the increased likelihood of democracy when a revolt is joined by the landed elite can be preferable to a popular revolt that is much more probable to fail. At the same time, the costs of revolt are lower when the rural poor are aided by the landed elite. Only when the difference between these costs or the difference between the probabilities of revolt success are low and the payoff of a popular democracy is very high relative to a jointly established democracy would the poor prefer to revolt alone than to revolt jointly with landed elites. The rarity of these circumstances is reflected in the fact that in very few cases – in Latin America, most notably Chile in the late 1960s to early 1970s and Guatemala in the late 1940s and early 1950s – have the rural poor successfully established a redistributive democracy in which there was large-scale land redistribution.[21]

---

[21] In both of these cases, democracy was cut short in coups supported by landed elites, and the subsequent ruling political elite did not engage in large-scale land redistribution in favor of the poor. If this dynamic was incorporated into the model, it would be another contributing factor in favor of jointly established democracy rather than popular democracy.

Bringing this conclusion together with the possibility of land reform under autocracy, which is greater in the three-group model than it is in the two-group model because of the threat of a challenge from below absent reform, yields the following proposition:

Proposition 2. *Land reform is more likely under autocracy with few institutional constraints than it is under democracy, provided that the rural poor are unorganized relative to landed elites.*

If $p_J \gg p_R$ or $c_{Ri} \gg c_{Ji}$, a revolt by the rural poor to establish a majoritarian democracy in which they redistribute land to themselves is unlikely. And although a higher level of political influence δ by the landed elite under a joint democracy makes solo revolt more attractive, it also increases the likelihood that landed elites will hijack any revolt attempt in an effort to install an elite-biased democracy, which tables land redistribution. Provided that political elites have real incentives for land redistribution under autocracy – indeed, the discussion and proofs in the following sections indicate that these incentives are higher than they are in the two-group model when adding in the consequences of democratization – this implies that redistribution is more likely under autocracy than it is under democracy.

The Ruling Political Elite's Decision to Redistribute Land

I now examine how the dynamics between the rural poor and the landed elite in the absence of land redistribution affect the ruling political elite's decision of whether to redistribute land. In contrast to the game depicted in Figure 3.2, political elites in the Figure 3.3 game face the threat of possible revolt if they do not redistribute land.

When the rural poor are induced to acquiesce if faced with no land redistribution, the land redistribution function will be: $LR_i = p_L U_{Pi}^L + (1 - p_L)U_{Pi}^{P|R} - c_{Pi} - (U_{Pi}^{P|R} - c_{Pi}^{ISC})$.[22] Because the rural poor will not revolt, the game is identical to that in Figure 3.2 from the perspective of the political elite. As a result, the ruling political elite's choice to redistribute land varies with the coalitional split α between the political elite and the landed elite in the same way as in the two-player game. In particular, a larger coalitional split increases the likelihood that the political elite will pursue land redistribution ($\partial LR_i / \partial \alpha > 0$).

How does the likelihood of land redistribution change when the rural poor have incentives to revolt in the absence of redistribution? It depends on whether the landed elite will join in the revolt. When the landed elite does not aid the

---

[22] As with the two-group model, the ruling political elite's choice to forego land redistribution in this game is always weighed against the expected utility of redistributing land despite an attempted coup by the landed elite. Absent this coup threat, the political elite will always choose to redistribute land.

rural poor in a joint push for democracy, the land redistribution function is written as follows: $LR_i = p_L U_{Pi}^L + (1 - p_L)U_{Pi}^{P|R} - c_{Pi} - (p_R U_{Pi}^R + (1 - p_R)U_{Pi}^{P|R} - c_{PRi} - c_{Pi}^{ISC})$.[23] Taking the derivative of the land redistribution function with respect to α again yields $\partial LR_i/\partial \alpha > 0$. A higher split between the political elite and the landed elite increases the political elite's incentives to pursue land redistribution. There is an extra factor now pushing the political elite to redistribute: the revolutionary threat from the masses. Whereas a higher α decreases the likelihood that the poor will win in a revolt because of the reduction in their income, it nonetheless introduces the possibility that the political elite will have to pay a positive tax rate under popular democracy if a revolution is successful.

The ruling political elite's calculation of whether or not to redistribute land is again different when the rural poor will revolt in the absence of redistribution and the landed elite aid the rural poor in a joint push for democracy. In this case, the land redistribution function is: $LR_i = p_L U_{Pi}^L + (1 - p_L)U_{Pi}^{P|R} - c_{Pi} - (p_J U_{Pi}^J + (1 - p_J)U_{Pi}^{P|R} - c_{PJi} - c_{Pi}^{ISC}$. Failure to redistribute requires the political elite to incur a cost c_{PJi} when attempting to fight off a joint revolt by the landed elite and rural poor. The cost of fighting off both groups is plausibly higher than fighting the rural poor alone, and the likelihood of a successful joint revolt is higher than that of a revolt by the rural poor alone. Counterbalancing this effect to a degree, however, is the fact that the tax rate levied on the political elite if democracy is established in part by landed elites is lower than that which it would pay under a popular democracy.

The degree of the coalitional split α between the political elite and the landed elite also has potentially countervailing effects on the land redistribution function as the split varies. Intuitively, when landed elites have more political power under a jointly established democracy but earn less as α increases, they will raise the tax rate. This is bad for political elites if they are rich relative to landed elites but good if they are poor relative to landed elites. When landed elites have less political power under democracy and earn less as α increases, the rural poor will lower the tax rate because they are earning more. This is beneficial for a relatively wealthy political elite but worse for a political elite that is relatively poorer.

Regardless of how an increase in α affects the tax rate under a jointly established democracy, the net effect of a higher coalitional split on land redistribution is likely positive because of two other effects. A higher value of α decreases the likelihood of a successful coup attempt by the landed elite if the political elite redistributes, and it also raises the costs of coup proofing against a threat

---

[23] I therefore assume that the ruling political elite pay the coup insulation cost c_{Pi}^{ISC} when it fails to redistribute prior to any potential revolt by the rural poor.

from the political elite's support coalition if the political elite fails to redistribute. Both of these factors encourage the ruling political elite to redistribute land. Furthermore, they are likely to operate more strongly than the potential enticement of a relatively lower tax rate under democracy; after all, political elites pay no taxes when they hold the reins of power themselves.

The results regarding the effects of coalitional splits on land redistribution are therefore summarized as follows.

Proposition 3. *An increase in the coalitional split α between the ruling political elite and the landed elite has the following effects on the likelihood of land reform:*

(a) *When the rural poor will not revolt absent land reform, a larger coalitional split increases the likelihood that the ruling political elite will implement land reform.*

(b) *When the rural poor will revolt alone absent land reform, a larger coalitional split increases the likelihood that the ruling political elite will implement land reform.*

(c) *When the rural poor will revolt absent land reform and the landed elite will aid them in a joint push for democracy, a larger coalitional split increases the likelihood that the ruling political elite will implement land reform.*[24]

Proposition 3 for the three-group game therefore supports Proposition 1. As with the other propositions, proofs for this proposition are located at the end of this chapter in Appendix A.

Equilibria of the Model
There are five distinct equilibria of the game: stable land redistribution under dictatorship, land redistribution amid attempted coups by landed elites, status quo dictatorship absent land redistribution, popular revolt and land redistribution under democracy, and elite-biased democratization without land redistribution. Figure 3.4 plots these equilibria across the range of possible values for two model parameters that are key in shaping land redistribution outcomes: the coalitional split between ruling political elites and landed elites α and the landed elite's level of political influence under democracy δ.

The equilibria in Figure 3.4 are calculated while holding other model parameters fixed. In this example, the landed elite as a group control 52 percent of the land in the economy, although they cede part of their income to political

---

[24] As discussed previously, Proposition 3C holds under the plausible assumption that the potential enticement of a relatively lower tax rate under a jointly established democracy when not implementing land reform is small relative to the increased incentives for land reform that result from a weaker landed elite and a higher cost of coup proofing against a threat from the political elite's support coalition.

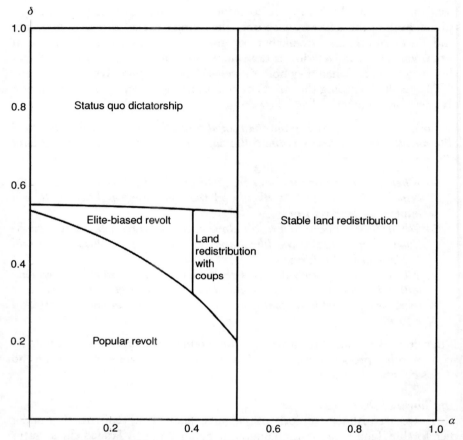

FIGURE 3.4. Model Equilibria. *Note:* Parameters of the simulation are as follows: $\beta = 0.52$; $r = 0.2$; $\pi_P = 0.02$; $\pi_L = 0.05$; $\pi_R = 0.93$; $c_L = 0.22$; $c_J = 0.05$; $c_R = 0.1$; $c_P = 0.5$; $c_{PR} = 0.1$; $c_{PJ} = 0.1$; $c_P^{ISC}(\alpha) = \alpha$; $\tau_P^* = 0$; $\tau_L^* = 0$; $\tau_R^* = 0$; $C(\tau_J) = \tau^2$. Costs of fighting are expressed as a fraction of income. τ_J^* is a function of δ. p_L, p_R, and p_J are calculated as the difference between the income of the challengers and the income of the political elite, bounded by 0 and 1.

elites (the amount of which depends on α), whose rents constitute 20 percent of the economy. The landed elite constitutes 5 percent of the population, the ruling political elite represents 2 percent of the population, and the rural poor comprises the remaining 93 percent. The coup costs for landed elites are 22 percent of their income, joint revolution costs 5 percent of their income, and solo revolt by the rural poor costs 10 percent of their income. Ruling political elites fighting off a landed elite coup suffer a 50 percent loss to their income, and they lose 10 percent of their income fighting off a popular revolution or joint revolution. The cost of internal coup proofing for the political elite when not redistributing land is $c_P^{ISC}(\alpha) = \alpha$. The probabilities for winning in a coup or revolt are calculated as the difference between the income of the challengers and the income of the political elite (bounded by 0 and 1). The tax rate is assumed to be 0 for simplicity under dictatorship and popular democracy and is a function of δ under elite-biased democracy (bounded by 0 and 1), calculated according to Equation 4 with the functional form for the costs of taxation being the tax squared.[25]

Land redistribution by the political elite under autocracy takes place when there is a large coalitional split between ruling political elites and landed elites. The insider threat to political elites is strong enough to spur land redistribution regardless of the threat of a landed elite coup. This is the rightmost region of Figure 3.4.

As the coalitional split decays, other equilibria open up depending on the level of δ. The rural poor have little to gain from a joint revolt when the landed elite would dominate political life under a jointly established democracy (i.e., when δ is high). When the insider threat to the political elite is sufficiently low and the likelihood of a successful landed elite coup is higher as a result of greater income, status quo dictatorship without land redistribution prevails. As δ declines and α is still sufficiently small, a joint revolt by the landed elite and rural poor becomes the most likely outcome. Jointly established democracy tables land redistribution for the landed elite but provides some degree of fiscal redistribution to render democracy attractive to the rural poor. A powerful off-the-path threat of a landed elite coup deters the political elite from attempting land redistribution to pacify the rural poor. As internal coup proofing becomes more costly and the likelihood of a landed elite coup victory becomes weaker when δ is still at middling levels, the ruling political elite becomes willing to redistribute land while running the risk of a coup by the landed elite. Finally, when both δ and α are very small, a popular revolt by the rural poor and subsequent land redistribution becomes possible. Low δ presents the rural poor with the possibility of establishing higher taxes and land redistribution under democracy. Landed elites cannot capture democracy. And political elites face low internal coup-proofing costs and a credible threat of a coup from landed elites if they choose to redistribute land. As discussed earlier in the chapter, this last equilibria – in which landed elites can exert strong influence over dictatorship but none at all over a new democracy – is relatively rare.

---

[25] With the other parameters as listed and $\alpha = 0.5$, the tax rate under elite-biased democracy varies from 0.34 when $\delta = 0$ to 0 when δ surpasses roughly 0.6.

STRATEGIES OF LAND REDISTRIBUTION

Although the formal model can explain *when* redistributive land reform is pursued, it is silent on *how* land reform is actually implemented. I discuss here several salient characteristics of land reform programs.

Strategies of Expropriation: Divide and Conquer

A leader's decision to expropriate landed elites can bolster the loyalty of that leader's initial support coalition and can eliminate potentially threatening landed elite rivals, but expropriation itself can be a dangerous process. Landed elites targeted with expropriation will attempt to resist or evade expropriation and may even act collectively to launch a coup. Land expropriation is therefore often done piecemeal by winnowing down landed elites so that they do not form a unified front of resistance.

The divide and conquer strategy of land expropriation that targets subgroups of landed elites to avoid triggering a reactionary coup is evident in many cases of land redistribution. In order to more effectively target landed elites while reducing their collective resistance, General Velasco's regime in Peru adopted a policy of stealth, creating landholding ceilings that became gradually stricter over time and winnowing elites by setting those under the limits against those above them, then later redefining the rules (McClintock 1983). One expropriated landowner from Trujillo, José de la Puente Haya, summarized Velasco's strategy as follows:

They used the technique of slicing up the cake in stages (*la rebanada*). When they started with the big ones, the sugar estates, people thought, "Wow." The government would then announce, "We will stop here." So smaller owners said to themselves, "I am safe, I am small, it is only against the big ones." After that they went after the medium-sized farms and the small ones still felt that they would not be touched. In this way any coordinated resistance was undermined (Mayer 2009, 95).

The first stage of the Cuban land reform similarly proceeded slowly in order to isolate those opposed to the law. The reform "gave the government a powerful instrument by which it could arbitrarily impoverish or ruin its enemies; and perhaps the reform was intended from the beginning as a first step towards further expropriation" (Thomas 1971, 1217). Indeed, the reform deepened several years after the revolution, expropriating medium-sized landholders that had previously supported the expropriation of larger landholders.

In Bolivia and Mexico, rather than expropriating many estates at once, the infrastructure of the land reform process was set up so that organized groups of peasants could request the transfer of particular properties, which complicated the ability of landowners to predict the timing and precise outcome of their fates. And in the less redistributive reform in Colombia, the savvy head of the National Agrarian Committee, Carlos Lleras Restrepo, used "divide and reform" tactics to pressure wealthy absentee landowners while engaging modernizing landowners (Hirschman 1963).

Strategies of Redistribution: Petitioning Processes and (Lack of) Land Titles

Land redistribution to rural workers can win the support of non-elite groups that have the potential to organize resistance to the regime if their interests are neglected. Many land reforms, however – such as those in Bolivia, Guatemala, Mexico, and Venezuela – are structured with seemingly peculiar features such as demand-driven processes and lack of formal titling. While these reform characteristics may appear puzzling, they represent additional mechanisms for political elites under autocracy who distribute land to consolidate their rule. Given that land is a fixed resource and is difficult to re-redistribute under the same political regime, political elites often structure redistribution to meet the demands only of those groups whose support is necessary and who are most mobilized, and to develop subsequent dependencies among these groups on the state in order to retain their loyalty.

Demand-driven redistribution requires potential land beneficiaries to petition for land. This enables the state to address at lower cost the demands of those that have the greatest willingness and capacity to organize and helps relieve land pressure where it is most intense. Rather than expropriating many estates at once, the infrastructure of Bolivia's long-standing land reform program was set up so that organized groups of peasants could request the transfer of particular properties. The Movimiento Nacionalista Revolucionario (MNR) played a key role in organizing petitioning campesinos to obtain land and to partition it into family units (Thiesenhusen 1995, 61–62). Similarly in Mexico, Article 27 of the 1917 constitution stipulated that villages had to petition the government for land. This enabled the land reform to provide concessions to those organized peasants who posed the greatest threat to the government, leading Sanderson (1984, 38) to conclude that "[t]he entire history of Mexican land reform may be characterized as a pattern of pressure and government response." Decree 1551 of 1962 under Ydígoras Fuentes in Guatemala stipulated that individuals could petition for idle land and then turn to the land reform agency INTA for relocation if they received land. And in order to acquire land in Venezuela following the 1960 Agrarian Reform Law, peasants had to form provisional committees (Article 94) and fill out a land application to the local branch of the land reform agency (IAN). The formidable technical requirements of the petition demanded organization or connections with the national peasant federation (Albertus 2013).

Granting incomplete property rights through land redistribution is another typical tool used by governments that redistribute land to address pressure from below. By granting land but withholding land titles, property rights remain insecure and land cannot be used as collateral in order to access loans (de Janvry and Sadoulet 2011). One-time land transfers can therefore be transformed into a continuous reliance on state programs to access the inputs and services needed to cultivate land. Rather than peasants receiving land and then possibly organizing for other causes, they instead become dependent on the state for their livelihood and can be co-opted through clientelism. In Mexico, land beneficiaries only received usufruct rights over land and had to turn to the state for access to inputs and credit, which they received in exchange for voting for the PRI (Albertus et al. 2014). Similarly in Venezuela, land grants far outpaced titling, leaving more than 90 percent of land recipients without property title (Herman 1986, 357). Peasants had to turn to local union leaders and party operatives for credit and inputs, the delivery of which was conditional upon whether peasants provided electoral support to their patrons at the polls (Albertus 2013).

Model Extensions: Land Redistribution and the Rise of Industrialization

The formal model conceives of an economy in which productive assets are divided between land and control over institutions that yield rents. This captures the divide between the rural sector and ruling political elites. A large literature, however, focuses on the rise of industrialization in distributive conflicts between elites and the poor. Modernization has several consequences. The rise of factories located in cities leads to urbanization and therefore out-migration from the countryside. Demand for urban labor and larger urban wage dispersion relative to the agriculture sector leads to increased income inequality (Kuznets 1955). It also generates a growing bourgeoisie and middle class, which play a crucial role in democratization (Ansell and Samuels 2010; Lipset 1959; Moore 1966) and benefit disproportionately from public spending (Lizzeri and Persico 2004).

How could an industrial sector be incorporated into the model? And how might it change the predictions for land reform, if at all? One straightforward way to address this extension to the model is to conceive of a portion ϕ of the rents r held by the political elite as a rival sector to land. Suppose that industrial elites and political elites now have a combined population of λ, of which a proportion ψ are industrial elites. Industrial elites as a group will therefore have income $r\phi$, and individual members of the industrial elite will have income $y_{Ii} = \frac{r\phi}{\lambda\psi}$. Political elites now have net income $r(1 - \phi)$ and individual income $y_{Pi} = \frac{r(1-\phi)}{\lambda(1-\psi)}$.

In the nascent stages of industrialization, industrial elites often have ties to landed elites, especially if landed elite entrepreneurs move into the industrial sector early.[26] But as industrial elites become stronger, they become a more

---

[26] Some even hold land themselves as a hedge against risk in the urban sector. See, e.g., Gilbert (1977) for a discussion of this in the Peruvian case.

coherent set of elites with interests that are distinct from those of landed elites, even though certain circumstances – such as an overlap between the interests of agro-exporters and industrial exporters – can undermine the consistently deep divide between these groups. The income of industrial elites y_{Ii} also grows. If ruling political elites require some fixed set of rents to operate government, this implies that r increases at the expense of the agricultural sector.[27]

Industrialization therefore has multiple consequences that impact the likelihood of land reform. Several of these increase the prospects for land reform. As the industrial elite grows in size and economic clout, it is more likely that there will be coalitional overlap between the industrial elite and the ruling political elite. This pushes the ruling political elite to expropriate landed elites in order to demonstrate loyalty to the industrial interests that comprise their initial support coalition.[28] When higher income for political elites pushes r higher, the likelihood that landed elites will succeed in an attempted coup when faced with land reform also decreases because their income is lower.

On the other hand, industrialization will generally tend to decrease *demand* for land reform. Industrialization diminishes the threat of revolt by the rural poor for two reasons. First, urbanization reduces the number of rural poor that have an incentive to push for land reform. Decreasing numbers of rural workers simultaneously tends to place upward pressure on agricultural wages for those who remain in the countryside. As a result, the rural poor's share of agricultural income will increase vis-à-vis that of landed elites, reducing the expected payoffs of setting their own tax rate under democracy if they successfully revolt. There are, however, two potentially countervailing factors. If land concentration remains extreme for a sufficient portion of the population, there remains the possibility of rural unrest. Industrial elites will have incentives to pursue land reform if this unrest threatens to spill over into the urban labor pool. A related concern is if rural wages increase in absolute terms along with urbanization but nonetheless substantially decrease relative to the non-agricultural sector as urban wages increase. This again may cause unrest and encourage industrial elites to push for land reform.

This discussion yields the following prediction. In the very early stages of industrialization prior to the rise of an industrial elite, landed elites are more likely to overlap with ruling political elites and therefore land reform is unlikely, although far from impossible. As industrialization progresses amid political overturn, it is more likely that the ruling political elite's support coalition will

[27] A growing agricultural sector could also be modeled by increasing the size of the economy as a whole (see, e.g., Ansell and Samuels 2010). The important point here, however, is that the proportion of agriculture in the total economy becomes smaller.

[28] If landed elites are able to depress the share of industrial elite income when there is coalitional overlap between landed and political elites, a strengthened industrial elite also has incentives to destroy landed elites so it can set policies that will increase its share of the national income.

overlap with industrial elites. This increases the likelihood of land reform. In the later stages of industrialization when the agricultural sector has declined, there is no longer a strong demand for reform by the rural poor, and landed elites are weak relative to industrial elites. Winning the support of the rural poor is therefore less important because of the low likelihood of a successful rural revolt, and expropriating landed elites no longer has the same value in terms of demonstrating to the ruling political elite's initial support coalition that the political elite prefer the coalition's support over rival landed elite support. Land reform therefore drops from the agenda.

Landed elites, of course, *anticipate* that industrialization may bring land reform. Their calculation that democracy can better serve their interests therefore becomes stronger. As the formerly predominant landed elites become a smaller portion of the set of all economic elites with industrialization, the likelihood that they get cut out of the initial support coalition of a dictator increases. They risk losing the basis of their power – their land – if they are cut out of the coalition. Landed elites therefore have an incentive to push for democracy on their own terms (in which they disproportionately influence policy, i.e., when δ is large) when they anticipate this trajectory. A successful elite-biased transition enables them to replicate their strength under democracy.

Conclusion

This chapter has built a comprehensive theory of land reform. Redistributive land reform is most often the product of two concurrent circumstances: low institutional constraints to political rule and a coalitional split between ruling political elites and landed elites. Land reform is a veto gauntlet. Opposition from even one critical institutional actor can jeopardize reform. Land reform efforts frequently fail when the executive opposes reform, the legislature shuts off funding, the bureaucracy is captured by landed elites, or the judiciary strikes down the constitutionality of property redistribution. Under democracy, the probability of landed elites being represented in these forums is higher because of the nature of democratic institutions. With the rare exception of a majoritarian democracy characterized by few veto points, redistributive land reform is therefore typically implemented under autocracy. But for ruling political elites to implement land reform, there must be a coalitional split with landed elites. When landed elites form the cornerstone of the political elite's support coalition, land reform is politically self-defeating.

The theory and formal model in this chapter also advance several other testable predictions. First, land redistribution should be more likely as the threat of revolt by the rural poor increases. Second, while the probability of land redistribution increases as industrialization moves beyond nascent stages, it subsequently becomes less important and less likely once a country has largely industrialized.

The argument I advance challenges the received wisdom on redistribution and on the role of landowners in democratic transitions in several ways. First, I anticipate that redistributive land reform – arguably the most consequential type of redistribution in the developing world – is more likely under autocratic rule than it is under democracy. Although a majoritarian democracy instituted through a revolt by the masses may implement land redistribution, democratic transitions are more typically captured by elites that construct countermajoritarian safeguards against redistribution. Importantly, this implies that *even when asset specificity is extremely high*, the landed elite will not necessarily oppose democracy. This contrasts with the predictions of Acemoglu and Robinson (2006), Ansell and Samuels (2010), Boix (2003), Gerschenkron (1946), Moore (1966), and others that equate powerful landed elites with autocratic repression. I argue that this prediction only holds when the landed elite can consistently and reliably play the puppet master of the political elite. Yet as the coalitions of these two actors are more likely to diverge, landed elites will have incentives to push for democratic rule in which they can dominate policymaking. Contemporary Venezuela is one case among many that supports this intuition. As I demonstrate in Chapter 7, large landowners are among Hugo Chávez's and Nicolás Maduro's strongest opponents, and they consistently support opposition parties that promise greater property rights protection.

Land redistribution, of course, is not the only type of land reform. Less redistributive land reform in the guise of land negotiation and land colonization can also dramatically impact rural life. These types of land reform do not follow the same logic that land redistribution follows. Landed elite interests are less affected by negotiation and colonization, and landed elites may in some circumstances even support these types of reform. Furthermore, the number of institutions required to enact land colonization is lower than it is for either land redistribution or land negotiation. Chapter 4, delineates these other land reform policies in much greater detail and provides a picture of their incidence and temporal patterns relative to land redistribution. Chapter 5 provides further insight into when not only land redistribution but also land negotiation and land colonization will be implemented.

APPENDIX A: FORMAL MODEL PROOFS

Two-Group Model of Land Redistribution

Proposition 1. *An increase in the coalitional split α between the ruling political elite and the landed elite increases the likelihood that the political elite will implement land reform.*

Proof. Consider the case in which the political elite choose to redistribute land. The landed elite launch a coup if their expected payoffs for doing so exceed those for accepting land redistribution. The utility of members of the landed elite is as follows, where $U^L(\tau_L)$ is written as U^L_{Li} and $U^L(\tau_P)$ is written as $U^{P|R}_{Li}$ when the political elite redistribute land:[29]

$$U^L_{Li} = y_{Li} + (\tau^*_L - C(\tau^*_L)) \frac{y_P + y_R}{\mu(1-\lambda)} = \frac{\beta - \alpha r + (\tau^*_L - C(\tau^*_L))(1 - \beta + \alpha r)}{\mu(1-\lambda)}$$

$$U^{P|R}_{Li} = (1 - \tau^*_P) \cdot 0 = 0$$

The landed elite will attempt a coup when the following function is positive:

$$C_i = p_L U^L_{Li} + (1 - p_L)U^P_{Li} - c_{Li} - U^P_{Li}$$

$$= p_L \left(\frac{(\beta - \alpha r)(1 - \tau^*_L + C(\tau^*_L)) + (\tau^*_L - C(\tau^*_L))}{\mu(1-\lambda)} \right) - c_{Li}$$

If the costs are high relative to the probability that an attempted coup will succeed, landed elites are more likely to acquiesce to land redistribution.

We can see how C_i changes with an increase in the coalitional split α between the political elite and the landed elite by taking the derivative of C_i with respect to α:

$$\frac{\partial C_i}{\partial \alpha} = \frac{\partial p_L}{\partial \alpha} \left(\frac{(\beta - \alpha r)(1 - \tau^*_L + C(\tau^*_L)) + (\tau^*_L - C(\tau^*_L))}{\mu(1-\lambda)} \right)$$

$$- p_L \frac{r(1 - \tau^*_L + C(\tau^*_L))}{\mu(1-\lambda)}$$

Both terms on the right side of this equation are negative given that $\partial p_L / \partial \alpha < 0$.[30]

Given the landed elite strategy, how will political elites decide whether or not to redistribute land? Their choice depends on their utility under different outcomes. Their utility functions can be written as follows:

$$U^{P|R}_{Pi} = y_{Pi} + (\tau^*_P - C(\tau^*_P)) \frac{y_L + y_R}{\lambda} = \frac{r + (\tau^*_P - C(\tau^*_P))(1 - r)}{\lambda}$$

$$U^{P|\sim R}_{Pi} = U^{P|R}_{Pi} - c^{ISC}_{Pi} = \frac{r + (\tau^*_P - C(\tau^*_P))(1 - r)}{\lambda} - c^{ISC}_{Pi}$$

$$U^L_{Pi} = (1 - \tau^*_L)y_{Pi} = (1 - \tau^*_L) \frac{r}{\lambda}$$

---

[29] When the political elite does not redistribute land, the utility of members of the landed elite is $U^{P|\sim R}_{Li} = (1 - \tau^*_P)y_{Li} = (1 - \tau^*_P)\frac{\beta - \alpha r}{\mu(1-\lambda)}$.

[30] While $\partial C_i / \partial \alpha < 0$, an increase in the wealth of landed elites via an increase in β encourages landed elites to pursue a coup rather than to acquiesce to land redistribution (i.e., $\partial C_i / \partial \beta > 0$).

The political elite will choose to implement land redistribution when the following land redistribution function LR_i is positive:

$$LR_i = p_L U_{Pi}^L + (1 - p_L) U_{Pi}^{P|R} - c_{Pi} - \left(U_{Pi}^{P|R} - c_{Pi}^{ISC} \right)$$

$$= p_L \left(\frac{-r\tau_L^* - (\tau_P^* - C(\tau_P^*))(1 - r)}{\lambda} \right) + c_{Pi}^{ISC} - c_{Pi}$$

Taking the derivative of LR_i with respect to α yields the following:

$$\frac{\partial LR_i}{\partial \alpha} = \frac{\partial p_L}{\partial \alpha} \left(\frac{-r\tau_L^* - (\tau_P^* - C(\tau_P^*))(1 - r)}{\lambda} \right) + \frac{\partial c_{Pi}^{ISC}(\alpha)}{\partial \alpha}$$

An increase in α thus leads to an increase in the likelihood that the political elite will redistribute land from the landed elite (i.e., $\frac{\partial LR_i}{\partial \alpha} > 0$). This operates through (i) a lower likelihood that the landed elite will be capable of launching a successful coup to displace the political elite when faced with expropriation ($\partial p_L / \partial \alpha < 0$) and (ii) and a higher cost of having to coup proof against an internal threat from the political elite's initial support coalition. ∎

Three-Group Model of Land Redistribution

Lemma 1. *When the landed elite enjoys a higher level of political influence δ under democracy, it will be more likely to join the rural poor in a joint revolt against the ruling political elite.*

Proof. The utility of members of the landed elite under various regimes is as follows:

$$U_{Li}^P = (1 - \tau_P^*) y_{Li} = (1 - \tau_P^*) \frac{\beta - \alpha r}{\mu(1 - \lambda)}$$

$$U_{Li}^R = 0$$

$$U_{Li}^J = (1 - \tau_J^*) y_{Li} + (\tau_J^* - C(\tau_J^*)) \bar{y}$$

$$= (1 - \tau_J^*) \left(\frac{\beta - \alpha r}{\mu(1 - \lambda)} \right) + (\tau_J^* - C(\tau_J^*))$$

We have the following joint revolt function:

$$J_i = p_J U_{Li}^J + (p_R - p_J) U_{Li}^P - p_R U_{Li}^R - c_{Ji}$$

$$= p_J \left((1 - \tau_J^*) \left(\frac{\beta - \alpha r}{\mu(1 - \lambda)} \right) + (\tau_J^* - C(\tau_J^*)) \right)$$

$$+ (p_R - p_J)(1 - \tau_P^*) \left(\frac{\beta - \alpha r}{\mu(1 - \lambda)} \right) - c_{Ji}$$

Taking the derivative of J_i with respect to δ yields:

$$\frac{\partial J_i}{\partial \delta} = p_J \frac{\partial \tau_J^*}{\partial \delta} \left(\frac{(1-\delta)((1-\beta)-(1-\alpha)r) + \delta(\beta - \alpha r)}{(1-\delta)(1-\mu)(1-\lambda) + \delta\mu(1-\lambda)} - \frac{\beta - \alpha r}{\mu(1-\lambda)} \right)$$

We know that $\partial p_J/\partial \delta = 0$, $\partial p_R/\partial \delta = 0$, and $\partial U_{Li}^P/\partial \delta = 0$. The right side of this equation has $\partial \tau_J^*/\partial \delta < 0$, and the expression in the parentheses is negative when $\delta < 1$. Therefore, $\partial J_i/\partial \delta > 0$.   ∎

Proposition 2. *Land reform is more likely under autocracy with few institutional constraints than it is under democracy, provided that the rural poor are unorganized relative to landed elites.*

Proof. Consider the subgame between the landed elite and the rural poor absent land redistribution by the political elite. To determine whether the landed elite would join the rural poor in a potential revolt to establish a democracy with high veto points, we need to know how the landed elite fare under various political arrangements. We can define the utility of members of the landed elite as follows:[31]

$$U_{Li}^P = (1 - \tau_P^*)y_{Li} = (1 - \tau_P^*)\frac{\beta - \alpha r}{\mu(1-\lambda)}$$

$$U_{Li}^R = 0$$

$$U_{Li}^J = (1 - \tau_J^*)\, y_{Li} + (\tau_J^* - C(\tau_J^*))\, \bar{y}$$

$$= (1 - \tau_J^*)\left(\frac{\beta - \alpha r}{\mu(1-\lambda)}\right) + (\tau_J^* - C(\tau_J^*))$$

The landed elite will then choose to aid the rural poor in the attempt to push for democratization if the following joint revolt function J_i is positive:

$$J_i = p_J U_{Li}^J + (p_R - p_J)U_{Li}^P - p_R U_{Li}^R - c_{Ji}$$

$$= p_J \left((1 - \tau_J^*)\left(\frac{\beta - \alpha r}{\mu(1-\lambda)}\right) + (\tau_J^* - C(\tau_J^*))\right)$$

$$+ (p_R - p_J)(1 - \tau_P^*)\left(\frac{\beta - \alpha r}{\mu(1-\lambda)}\right) - c_{Ji}$$

There exist some p_J, p_R, δ, and c_{Ji} such that J_i will be positive. This becomes evident if we simply rewrite the previous equation as follows:

$$J_i = p_J(U_{Li}^J - U_{Li}^P) + p_R U_{Li}^P - c_{Ji}$$

---

[31] Because the political elite chooses not to redistribute land in this subgame, this section uses the notation U_{Li}^P to signify $U_{Li}^{P|\sim R}$ and U_{Ri}^P to signify $U_{Ri}^{P|\sim R}$.

Having examined the landed elite's choice of whether or not to aid the rural poor in revolt, we next turn to how the rural poor decide whether or not to revolt. The utility of members of the rural poor is as follows:

$$U_{Ri}^P = (1 - \tau_P^*)y_{Ri} = (1 - \tau_P^*)\frac{((1 - \beta) - (1 - \alpha)r)}{(1 - \mu)(1 - \lambda)}$$

$$U_{Ri}^J = (1 - \tau_J^*)y_{Ri} + (\tau_J^* - C(\tau_J^*))\bar{y}$$

$$= (1 - \tau_J^*)\left(\frac{((1 - \beta) - (1 - \alpha)r)}{(1 - \mu)(1 - \lambda)}\right) + (\tau_J^* - C(\tau_J^*))$$

$$U_{Ri}^R = (1 - \tau_R^*)(y_{RDi}) + (\tau_R^* - C(\tau_R^*))\bar{y}$$

$$= (1 - \tau_R^*)\left(\frac{1 - r}{(1 - \mu)(1 - \lambda)}\right) + (\tau_R^* - C(\tau_R^*))$$

Consider the case in which the landed elite will choose to aid the rural poor in the push for democratization if the rural poor decide to revolt. The rural poor will then choose to revolt if the revolt function R_i is positive:

$$R_i = p_J U_{Ri}^J + (1 - p_J)U_{Ri}^P - c_{Ji} - U_{Ri}^P$$

$$= p_J\left((1 - \tau_J^*)\left(\frac{((1 - \beta) - (1 - \alpha)r)}{(1 - \mu)(1 - \lambda)}\right) + (\tau_J^* - C(\tau_J^*))\right)$$

$$- p_J(1 - \tau_P^*)\left(\frac{((1 - \beta) - (1 - \alpha)r)}{(1 - \mu)(1 - \lambda)}\right) - c_{Ji} \quad \text{(A1)}$$

Now consider the case in which the expected utility of the landed elite is higher when it does not aid the rural poor in a revolt. The revolt function R_i for the rural poor is now redefined as follows:

$$R_i = p_R U_{Ri}^R + (1 - p_R)U_{Ri}^P - c_{Ri} - U_{Ri}^P$$

$$= p_R\left((1 - \tau_R^*)\left(\frac{1 - r}{(1 - \mu)(1 - \lambda)}\right) + (\tau_R^* - C(\tau_R^*))\right)$$

$$- p_R(1 - \tau_P^*)\left(\frac{((1 - \beta) - (1 - \alpha)r)}{(1 - \mu)(1 - \lambda)}\right) - c_{Ri} \quad \text{(A2)}$$

The rural poor are more likely to revolt against a political elite that does not redistribute land when they will be aided by the landed elite in their push for democratization. To see this, we can compare Equations A1 and A2. We know that $p_J > p_R$ and $c_{Ri} > c_{Ji}$. Given the typically steep barriers to collective action in the form of popular revolution, the increased likelihood of democracy when a revolt is joined by the landed elite can be preferable to a popular revolt, which is much more probable to fail. Simultaneously, the costs of revolt are smaller when the rural poor are aided by the landed elite. Only when the difference between these costs or the difference between the probabilities of revolt success are low and the payoff of a popular democracy is very high relative to a jointly established democracy would the poor prefer to revolt alone rather than jointly.

If $p_J \gg p_R$ or $c_{Ri} \gg c_{Ji}$, a revolt by the rural poor to establish a majoritarian democracy (with fewer institutional constraints) and redistribute land to themselves is unlikely. Although a higher level of δ under a joint democracy enhances the attractiveness of solo revolt, it simultaneously increases the likelihood that landed elites will hijack a revolt in an attempt to install an elite-biased democracy and block land redistribution. Land redistribution will consequently be more likely under autocracy than under democracy, provided that the rural poor are unorganized relative to landed elites and that there are significant incentives for land redistribution under autocracy. This is further supported by the fact that the likelihood of land redistribution under autocracy is greater in the three-group model than it is in the two-group model because of the threat of a challenge from below absent reform (see proofs for Proposition 3). ∎

Proposition 3A. *An increase in the coalitional split α between the ruling political elite and the landed elite has the following effects on the likelihood of land reform:*

(a) *When the rural poor will not revolt absent land reform, a larger coalitional split increases the likelihood that the ruling political elite will implement land reform.*

Proof. The political elite's utility under continued rule and its utility in the case of a successful landed elite coup is as follows:

$$U_{Pi}^{P|R} = y_{Pi} + (\tau_P^* - C(\tau_P^*))\frac{y_L + y_R}{\lambda} = \frac{r + (\tau_P^* - C(\tau_P^*))(1 - r)}{\lambda}$$

$$U_{Pi}^{P|\sim R} = U_{Pi}^{P|R} - c_{Pi}^{ISC} = \frac{r + (\tau_P^* - C(\tau_P^*))(1 - r)}{\lambda} - c_{Pi}^{ISC}$$

$$U_{Pi}^{L} = (1 - \tau_L^*)y_{Pi} = (1 - \tau_L^*)\frac{r}{\lambda}$$

The political elite's utility under jointly established democracy and under popular democracy is as follows:

$$U_{Pi}^{J} = (1 - \tau_J^*)y_{Pi} + (\tau_J^* - C(\tau_J^*))\bar{y} = (1 - \tau_J^*)\frac{r}{\lambda} + (\tau_J^* - C(\tau_J^*))$$

$$U_{Pi}^{R} = (1 - \tau_R^*)y_{Pi} + (\tau_R^* - C(\tau_R^*))\bar{y} = (1 - \tau_R^*)\frac{r}{\lambda} + (\tau_R^* - C(\tau_R^*))$$

When the rural poor are induced to acquiesce if faced with no land redistribution, the land redistribution function will be:

$$LR_i = p_L U_{Pi}^L + (1 - p_L)U_{Pi}^{P|R} - c_{Pi} - (U_{Pi}^{P|R} - c_{Pi}^{ISC})$$

$$= p_L \left(\frac{-r\tau_L^* - (\tau_P^* - C(\tau_P^*))(1 - r)}{\lambda} \right) + c_{Pi}^{ISC} - c_{Pi} \qquad (A3)$$

Taking the derivative of LR_i with respect to α yields the following:

$$\frac{\partial LR_i}{\partial \alpha} = \frac{\partial p_L}{\partial \alpha} \left(\frac{-r\tau_L^* - (\tau_P^* - C(\tau_P^*))(1 - r)}{\lambda} \right) + \frac{\partial c_{Pi}^{ISC}(\alpha)}{\partial \alpha}$$

An increase in α therefore leads to an increase in the likelihood that the political elite will redistribute land from the landed elite. This operates through (i) a decreased likelihood that the landed elite will be able to launch a successful coup to displace the political elite when faced with expropriation ($\partial p_L / \partial \alpha < 0$) and (ii) a higher cost of having to coup proof against an internal threat from the political elite's initial support coalition. ∎

Proposition 3B. *An increase in the coalitional split α between the ruling political elite and the landed elite has the following effects on the likelihood of land reform:*

  (b) When the rural poor will revolt alone absent land reform, a larger coalitional split increases the likelihood that the ruling political elite will implement land reform.

Proof. In this case, we can write the land redistribution function as follows:

$$LR_i = p_L U_{Pi}^L + (1 - p_L)U_{Pi}^{P|R} - c_{Pi} - \Big(p_R U_{Pi}^R$$

$$+ (1 - p_R)U_{Pi}^{P|R} - c_{PRi} - c_{Pi}^{ISC} \Big)$$

$$= p_L \left(\frac{r(1 - \tau_L^*)}{\lambda} \right) + (p_R - p_L) \left(\frac{r + (\tau_P^* - C(\tau_P^*))(1 - r)}{\lambda} \right) \qquad (A4)$$

$$- p_R \left((1 - \tau_R^*)\frac{r}{\lambda} + (\tau_R^* - C(\tau_R^*)) \right)$$

$$- c_{Pi} + c_{PRi} + c_{Pi}^{ISC}$$

There are several noteworthy differences between Equations A3 and A4. First, failure to redistribute in Equation A4 requires the political elite to incur an additional cost to fight off a revolution attempt by the rural poor. Second, if the political elite lose in that conflict, it will suffer a considerably higher tax rate under popular democracy. Consequently, if the rural poor pose a credible rebellion threat in the face of the political elite choosing not to redistribute land, then it is *more* likely that the political elite will redistribute land than it would be if the rural poor do not revolt.

The additional threat by the rural poor also manifests itself in how the land redistribution function varies with the coalitional split between the political elite and the landed elite. We can see this formally by taking the derivative of the land redistribution function with respect to α as follows:

$$\frac{\partial LR_i}{\partial \alpha} = \frac{\partial p_L}{\partial \alpha}\left(\frac{r(1-\tau_L^*)}{\lambda} - \frac{r+(\tau_P^*-C(\tau_P^*))(1-r)}{\lambda}\right)$$

$$+ \frac{\partial p_R}{\partial \alpha}\left(\frac{r+(\tau_P^*-C(\tau_P^*))(1-r)}{\lambda} - \left((1-\tau_R^*)\frac{r}{\lambda}+(\tau_R^*-C(\tau_R^*))\right)\right) \quad \text{(A5)}$$

$$+ \frac{\partial c_{Pi}^{ISC}(\alpha)}{\partial \alpha}$$

Equation A5 indicates that $\partial LR_i/\partial \alpha > 0$. The expression in the first set of parentheses on the right side of Equation A5 is negative because $U_{Pi}^L < U_{Pi}^P$. The expression in the second set of parentheses is positive because $U_{Pi}^P > U_{Pi}^R$. Given that $\partial p_L/\partial \alpha < 0$ and $\partial p_R/\partial \alpha > 0$, the entire expression in Equation A5 is positive. This demonstrates that a higher split between the political elite and the landed elite increases the political elite's incentives to pursue land redistribution. If we compare Equation A5 with $\partial LR_i/\partial \alpha$ in Proposition 3A, there is an additional factor pushing the political elite to redistribute: the revolutionary threat from the masses. A higher α diminishes the likelihood that the poor will win in a revolt because of the reduction in their income, but it nonetheless introduces the possibility that the political elite will have to pay taxes under democracy if a revolution is successful. ∎

Proposition 3C. *An increase in the coalitional split α between the ruling political elite and the landed elite has the following effects on the likelihood of land reform:*

(c) *When the rural poor will revolt absent land reform and the landed elite will aid them in a joint push for democracy, a larger coalitional split increases the likelihood that the ruling political elite will implement land reform.*

Proof. We can write the land redistribution function as follows:

$$LR_i = p_L U_{Pi}^L + (1-p_L)U_{Pi}^{P|R} - c_{pi} - \left(p_J U_{Pi}^J\right.$$

$$+(1-p_J)U_{Pi}^{P|R} - c_{Pji} - \left.c_{Pi}^{ISC}\right)$$

$$= p_L\left(\frac{r(1-\tau_L^*)}{\lambda}\right) + (p_J - p_L)\left(\frac{r+(\tau_P^*-C(\tau_P^*))(1-r)}{\lambda}\right) \quad \text{(A6)}$$

$$- p_J\left((1-\tau_J^*)\frac{r}{\lambda}+(\tau_J^*-C(\tau_J^*))\right) - c_{Pi} + c_{Pji} + c_{Pi}^{ISC}$$

The degree of the coalitional split between the political elite and the landed elite has potentially countervailing effects on the land redistribution function as the split varies. Taking the derivative of the land redistribution function with respect to α yields:

$$\frac{\partial LR_i}{\partial \alpha} = \frac{\partial p_L}{\partial \alpha}\left(\frac{r(1-\tau_L^*)}{\lambda} - \frac{r+(\tau_P^* - C(\tau_P^*))(1-r)}{\lambda}\right)$$

$$-p_J\frac{\partial \tau_J^*}{\partial \alpha}\left(\frac{(1-\delta)((1-\beta)-(1-\alpha)r)+\delta(\beta-\alpha r)}{(1-\delta)(1-\mu)(1-\lambda)+\delta\mu(1-\lambda)} - \frac{r}{\lambda}\right)$$

$$+\frac{\partial c_{Pi}^{ISC}(\alpha)}{\partial \alpha} \tag{A7}$$

The first and third terms of Equation A7 are identical to those in Equation A5 and are positive, indicating that a higher coalitional split increases the political elite's incentives to redistribute land.[32] The second term, however, is ambiguous. We know that $\partial \tau_J^*/\partial \alpha > 0$ when $\delta > 1/2$ and $\partial \tau_J^*/\partial \alpha < 0$ when $\delta < 1/2$. At the same time, the term in parentheses following $\partial \tau_J^*/\partial \alpha$ may be either positive or negative for a fixed δ, depending on whether the landed elite or the rural poor have greater political power and depending on the relative wealth of the political elite as compared to the other groups. When landed elites have more political power under a jointly established democracy but earn less as α increases, they will increase taxes. This is bad for political elites if they are wealthy relative to landed elites but good if they are poor relative to landed elites. When the landed elite have less political power under democracy and earn less as α increases, the rural poor will lower taxes because they are earning more. This benefits a relatively wealthy political elite but harms a political elite that is relatively poorer.

Irrespective of how a larger coalitional split affects the tax rate under a jointly established democracy, the net effect of a higher α on Equation A7 is almost certain to be positive under reasonable assumptions. This is because of how α influences the other two terms in Equation A7. A higher α reduces the odds of a successful coup attempt by the landed elite if the political elite redistributes, and it also increases the costs of internal coup proofing if the political elite fails to redistribute. Both factors encourage political elites to redistribute land. Moreover, they should operate more strongly than the potential enticement of a relatively lower tax rate under democracy. After all, political elites pay no taxes when they directly hold power. ∎

---

[32] Note that the likelihood of winning in a joint rebellion against the political elite p_J does not vary with α, so that $\partial p_J/\partial \alpha = 0$. This differs from the case of lone revolt by the rural poor, as in Equation A5.

4

Measuring Land Reform

One of the main practical challenges to understanding the politics of land reform is to gain an understanding of broad patterns of land reform over time. What precisely constitutes land reform? Have land reform policies changed over time and, if so, how? Where and when has land reform been implemented most intensely, and what consequences has it had?

There is a large body of literature on land reform that provides useful guidance regarding these questions. In addition to a host of case studies of land reform, there are a number of insightful compilations of reform analyses (e.g., Barraclough 1973; Binswanger-Mkhize, Bourguignon, and van den Brink 2009; Dorner 1992; Rosset, Patel, and Courville 2006; Thiesenhusen 1989). There is also a vein of research that attempts to make sense of the broad patterns of land reform as well as its efficacy in addressing a range of social issues such as poverty, inequality, and social inclusion (e.g., El-Ghonemy 2002; Herring 1983; Huntington 1968; Lapp 2004; Lipton 2009; Tai 1974; Thiesenhusen 1995; Tuma 1965).

The conclusions drawn from these studies are nearly as varied and numerous as the studies themselves. Some find that land reform has a largely successful record (Lipton 2009), whereas others lament its failures (Thiesenhusen 1995). Those that seek to explain the incidence and timing of reform conclude that land reform is most likely to occur under democracy as a consequence of political competition over rural votes (Lapp 2004), when single or hegemonic party structures dominate politics (Huntington 1968), or when "non-competitive" political systems with centralized power can overrun the resistance of landed interests (Tai 1974).

The widely varying findings on land reform in existing research are largely the result of differences in research design, data, and spatial and temporal scope. Many compilations of land reform select their cases based on the dependent variable, focusing on cases of significant reform at the expense of understanding why reforms took place in that set of cases in the first place. And although many of the case studies and works with broader scope provide key insights into land policies in selected states, it is hard to draw broader conclusions from them. This is partly because of the varied nature of land policies, which include programs of land expropriation and redistribution, negotiated transfers from the private market, colonization programs, land titling, and the generation of markets to buy and sell land. Indeed, there are few, if any, comprehensive studies of land reform in political science, economics, or sociology that have attempted to systematically code land policies and land transfers in a way that is cross-country comparable and which spans a sufficient time period to draw systematic inferences from the trends. Tai (1974, 10) acknowledges serious measurement problems in one of the more analytical studies of land reform: "Standards of measurement by which data are collected are widely different. Certain important data may be completely absent, or lacking in continuity, or incomparable for two or more countries."

One main goal of this book is to attempt to fill this important gap in the study of land reform. It does so by differentiating analytically distinct land reform policies and then classifying reforms according to these policies. I focus on three main policies of reform: land redistribution, land negotiation, and land colonization. Land reform through land titling and the generation or stimulation of private land markets are also discussed but are not included as separately coded land reform policies, primarily because titling does not involve actual land transfers and because the state plays a comparatively minimal role in transfers via private land markets.

The coding scheme for land reform policies developed here is not unique to the land tenure structure or to landholding patterns present in Latin America. It could therefore be applied to land reform in East and South Asia, the Middle East, Europe, and parts of postcolonial Africa. Doing so could enrich our understanding of the range of phenomena that constitute each type of reform. This exercise would reveal both the flexibility as well as the potential limits of the coding scheme. Boone (2013), for instance, highlights how most land in sub-Saharan Africa is not held as private property but rather under hierarchical or authority-based control in "neocustomary" land tenure systems. Although some changes in these land tenure systems may rest within the land reform typology here, others (e.g., shifts in rules regulating access to communal land) may fall beyond its scope.

A TYPOLOGY OF LAND REFORM

This section discusses and distinguishes four different types of land reform: land redistribution, land negotiation, land colonization, and land titling. In contrast to land redistribution, land negotiation, and land colonization, land titling as defined here does not include physically transferring either private or state-owned property to individuals. The remainder of the book therefore focuses on land redistribution, land negotiation, and land colonization.

Land Expropriation and Redistribution

The most consequential and controversial type of land reform is the expropriation of land from the private sector and its redistribution to the landless or the land-poor. Land redistribution from large landowners to laborers and the land-poor has the greatest potential for remedying rural inequalities and benefiting the rural poor. Land redistribution as defined here is measured as the area of private landholdings expropriated in a given year for the purposes of redistribution.[1] I only code land reform as expropriation and redistribution if compensation is below market value, such that large landowners do not simply receive full payment for their property that they can then invest in other sectors of the economy. This ensures that the poor are not simply "getting what they paid for": that taxes are not being used to compensate the wealthy and redistribute their assets to the poor.[2] As discussed in further detail later in this section, given the complex nature of coding the degree of compensation in environments of insecure and illiquid property rights, I do not code the degree of compensation in the case of land expropriation. However, in most cases land was expropriated at much less than market value or was wholesale confiscated.

Land expropriation and redistribution in Latin America has often been implemented through the establishment of land ceilings that set thresholds for the maximum size of property holdings. Additional land held in excess of the ceiling is subject to redistribution. The beneficiaries of expropriation are often rural inhabitants who either previously worked on large landed estates or who live nearby but have insufficient land. As Lipton (2009, 7) writes, "'classic' land reform – ceilings legislation and redistribution of above-ceiling landholdings to the farming poor – has spread much further, and with more success, than is widely believed ... [I]t is also a precondition for the success of other reforms, including much tenancy reform." Land ceilings played a key role in land reform in Cuba, Mexico, Peru, postcolonial India, and many other cases.

A second major mechanism through which land expropriation and redistribution can be implemented is through the requirement that property serve a "social function." By requiring that property be "efficiently" exploited for agricultural purposes according to production or utilization criteria or by making certain precapitalist tenure relations illegal, the state can subject land to expropriation for the purposes of redistribution. For instance, land tenure reforms that abolished feudalistic tenure arrangements such as *pongeaje* (Bolivia),

---

[1] I do not code how much land beneficiaries may pay for the land they receive, although they typically receive land for free or pay low rates with government subsidies (see, e.g., Thiesenhusen 1989).

[2] This scenario is similar to land negotiation, which is discussed in the next section.

huasipungaje (Ecuador), *yanaconaje* (Peru), *inquilinaje* (Chile), and *peonaje acasillado* (Mexico) eliminated many landlords that had been engaged in these practices by seizing their land.

The most high-profile land reforms have been those in which expropriation and redistribution played a central role. Following Mexico's revolution, a wide-ranging land reform was instituted based on Article 27 of the 1917 constitution. This provision was rooted in land reform legislation adopted by several revolutionary coalitions, particularly Pancho Villa's 1915 reform and Emiliano Zapata's Plan of Ayala (Thiesenhusen 1995, 34–35). Article 27 established eminent domain over all land and water within Mexico. It vested in the state the power to restore land to villages that could demonstrate that their land had been usurped (*restitución*) and the power to grant land to petitioning villages that needed it (*dotación*). The agrarian reform settlements were known as *ejidos*. President Álvaro Obregón in 1922 set a landholding limit at 150 hectares of irrigated land, 250 hectares of rain-fed land, or 400 hectares of land of lesser quality (Sanderson 1984, 46). Land reform increased under Obregón's successor, Plutarco Calles (1924–1928). Expropriated landowners were to be compensated with state agrarian bonds at an interest rate not exceeding 3 percent annually (Section 17). Beginning in 1921, land reform beneficiaries received expropriated land for free (Tai 1974, 204). The Agrarian Debt Law of 1920 authorized the issuance of twenty-year agrarian bonds to owners of expropriated property, but by 1933 only 170 landowners that had held 3 percent of the total expropriated land had received any compensation at all (Tai 1974, 205). The government defaulted in its payments for the rest of the expropriated land and did not issue new agrarian bonds after 1931. The vast majority of land was therefore simply confiscated from private owners. Peasants emerged as a major constituency in post-revolutionary politics, forming a central part of the Partido Revolucionario Institucional's (PRI) distributionist policy (Sanderson 1984, 36–37).

Land expropriation and redistribution was also at the core of Bolivia's land reform, which began in 1953. The primary objective of the land reform was to redistribute land away from hacienda landlords in favor of mobilized peasants in the highlands and valleys (Muñoz and Lavadenz 1997, 6). Article 2 of the Agrarian Reform Law stipulated that land ownership must fulfill its social function. The law defined the types and maximum sizes of private property consistent with their respective social functions. Large properties (*latifundios*) that were inefficiently exploited or operated under obsolete tenure or leasing arrangements (e.g., the feudal arrangements in the *altiplano*) were subject to expropriation. Preferential distribution rights were given to peasants who had been subjected to feudal exploitation, those who lived and worked on *latifundios* for two or more years prior to the law, and those who worked on medium-sized properties or agricultural enterprises as *colonos* (Thome 1970, 6). Land usurped from indigenous communities after 1900 was to be restituted to those communities. Grants of public lands that were not compliant with a 1905 law requiring owners to work and live on the land were to be revoked without compensation.

Bolivia's 1953 Agrarian Reform Law stipulated that landowners were to be compensated for their land based on the value that had been declared for tax purposes. But the vast majority of landlords were never compensated, because few landlords had either reported a value or paid land taxes and those that did had systematically reported lower values to reduce their tax burdens (Thiesenhusen 1995, 62). Indeed, agrarian bonds for compensation were never even printed (Thome 1970, 8). The legal provision that beneficiaries pay for their land through the Agricultural Bank was not enforced and few payments ever took place (Thome 1970, 8). Slower redistribution in the first few years of reform increased toward the end of the 1950s and during Victor Paz Estenssoro's second presidential term from 1960 to 1964. Redistribution again slowed in the late 1960s, but it increased under President Hugo Banzer and was only formally halted in 1996 before being reconstituted again. Reform efforts have recently gained some, albeit limited, strength under President Evo Morales.

Land reform conducted under military rule in El Salvador is another case of substantial land expropriation and redistribution. In the late 1970s, civic organizations radicalized in response to ongoing state repression, with rural and urban interests dovetailing in opposition to the regime. Land invasions increased despite facing state repression and threats from paramilitaries. A peaceful coup led by junior military officers ousted Carlos Humberto Romero's political movement (ARENA) in 1979. It formed the Revolutionary Junta and declared a land reform. Instability and turnover in the junta ended with the incorporation of Napoleon Duarte, a civilian and former presidential candidate who implemented Phase I of the land reform in 1980. A total of 472 estates in excess of 500 hectares were expropriated and owners were weakly compensated in the form of thirty-year bonds at low rates (McElhinny 2006, 283). Phase I expropriation was heaviest in 1980, with most properties having been expropriated by May 1980 (Thiesenhusen 1989). Although Phase II of the land reform was never implemented, the Phase III "land to the tiller" program converted a small number of peasants that had access to land as tenants into owners.

As mentioned earlier in this section, I do not code the degree of compensation in the case of land transfers through expropriation. There are insurmountable difficulties to doing so. From a practical standpoint, there are insufficient individual-level data to quantify compensation over time in these diverse cases. Those who were targeted for expropriation often did not collect any payment, either because compensation was not offered, because the amount offered was too low to be worthwhile bothering to collect, or because the threat of coercion or violence deterred them from collecting payment. Others collected limited payments many years later. Where there were national policies on compensation, the regulations were not always enforced, which short-changed property owners. In many cases, direct cash compensation was shunned in favor of long-term bonds that lost value against high rates of inflation, making them nearly worthless. In other cases, limited compensation was provided in the form of incentives in investing in other sectors of the economy such as industry.

Land Negotiations with the Private Sector

A second major type of land reform is the acquisition of land from the private sector with market-value compensation for subsequent redistribution to those with less land or no land at all. The main difference between "land negotiation" of this form and land expropriation and redistribution as discussed in the previous section resides in the level of compensation received by the affected landowners. Whereas land redistribution entails land acquisition at rates below market value, "negotiated" land transfers are those in which landowners are compensated at a value equal or greater to that which they would receive through sale in the private market and those in which landowners otherwise voluntarily sell their property to the state. Because market value may be difficult to assess when land is seized, the way in which land is transferred is key to coding land negotiation. Land negotiation can occur through willing sales by landowners to the state or through the creation of laws that require individuals to first offer their property to the state before putting it on the private market. Land negotiation may also occur through compulsory sales with market-value compensation as determined by courts. Negotiated transfers as coded here therefore need not occur through willing seller–willing buyer approaches (see, e.g., Binswanger-Mkhize et al. 2009, 21–23). Yet in order for compulsory transfers to be coded as land negotiation rather than expropriation, the courts must be able to credibly issue rulings that are deemed fair by landowners and therefore must not be unduly influenced by the executive.

It is important to underscore the difference between market-value compensation and compensation that is deemed fair, just, or appropriate by the state. "Just" compensation as defined by the state may fall well short of market-value compensation. As mentioned in the previous section, basing compensation on the value declared for tax purposes may dramatically undervalue land. Furthermore, "fair" or "just" compensation often takes into account the social function of land, thereby undervaluing property that is underexploited in the view of the law. Finally, forms of "fair" and "just" compensation are often interpreted differently by different agents of state, resulting in contestation over compensation rates.

Land willingly sold to the state through negotiated transfer is also distinct from the compulsory sales or seizures typical of land redistribution programs. Landowners may willingly sell to the state even if compensation rates are not equivalent to private market value rates because of the opportunity cost of holding land, because of a desire to sell in an illiquid land market, or because the transaction costs of selling in the private market make selling to the state an attractive option. Landowners who choose to dispose of their property in this manner engage in land negotiation because sales to the state in these cases are preferable to the private market. However, as noted earlier in this section, land need not be willingly sold to the state to be coded as land negotiation provided that compensation rates are at market value.

Several examples illustrate policies of land negotiation and how they differ from land redistribution. In Brazil since the 1960s, most settlement of rural inhabitants through land reform has occurred on formerly private land acquired by the state. Prices paid for land initially were typically below market value. Land expropriation proceedings changed considerably under Brazil's 1988 constitution. The constitution stipulated that land must be "unproductive" to be subject to expropriation and that the state must pay a "fair price." Land expropriation decreased, yet compensation remained below market value. A February 1993 amendment to the constitution stipulated that the government pay "market price" for the land (Assunção 2006, 8). As Assunção (2006, 11) writes, "the final cost stipulated by the judicial system in the end of a disappropriation process is, on average, five times the initial evaluation." The president begins an expropriation proceeding with a signature, and the process typically ends with a judicial decision that stipulates the level and form of compensation. Land acquired from the private sector after 1993 is consequently coded not as land redistribution from owners to beneficiaries but rather as land negotiation. Land expropriated prior to the 1993 amendment, however, is coded as land redistribution given that the "fair price" paid by the government to expropriated owners was considerably lower on average than the price that would have been paid in the market.

Costa Rica provides another example of how land negotiation and land redistribution differ. The agrarian reform debate of the 1950s resulted in a 1955 reform bill that was scuttled as well as several other draft laws that circulated in the assembly (Rowles 1985, 212). A land reform law (Law 2825) was finally passed in October 1961. The 1961 law placed a heavy emphasis on protecting private property, in part to deter land invasions that had increased in anticipation of the reform law. Yet compensation for expropriated land was based on the value of the property as declared by the owner for tax purposes (Seligson 1980, 126). Given that self-valuations were low in order to reduce taxes paid, many expropriations were blocked by landed elites in the Legislative Assembly, which was the only authority with the power to declare a property subject to expropriation (Seligson 1984, 30–31). Land reform therefore began primarily with the colonization of state-owned land. An important change in the part of the law regulating land expropriation was implemented in the late 1960s. The Supreme Court ruled in 1969 that owners had a legal right to insist on the fair market value of property targeted for expropriation (Seligson 1984, 31). Land negotiation has continued to the present under this principle, but it has been limited in scope because of the limited budget that has been allocated for purposes of private land acquisition.

Land reform in Colombia highlights a different way in which land negotiation can occur: voluntary sales to the state. The government began a small parcelization program in the early 1930s to purchase estates affected by property or work contract disputes and divide them between tenants and squatters (LeGrand 1986, 137–141). The government offered landowners full market value for their property. Many landlords of conflictive properties were unsurprisingly eager to sell to the government. The government tried to pass the high purchasing cost on to peasants by requiring them to pay market value for the land they received. Peasants typically refused: after receiving the land, they would then argue that it was public territory and therefore should be granted without cost.[3] From 1933 to 1940, the government purchased roughly 220,000 hectares of land for subsequent parcelization (LeGrand 1986, 157), in addition to several large haciendas it had purchased in 1933 that totaled 200,000 hectares (LeGrand 1986, 139). The parcelization program continued through the 1940s and 1950s until it was replaced by the Social Agrarian Reform Act of 1961 (Law 135). Although reform that was conducted under Law 135 allowed for both land redistribution and land negotiation, negotiation formed the bulk of transfers from the private market because landed interests dominated the Agrarian Reform Committee board (Zamosc 1986).

The distinction between land redistribution and land negotiation, while clear in theory, can be complicated in practice in certain cases. There may be explicit or implicit coercion of landowners to sell their property. There some are cases in which landowners were essentially forced to lease their land for free or at submarket rates (Dominican Republic), or were forced to allow squatters to produce on their land, effectively resulting in partial expropriation for which valuation is difficult and depends on the actual payments received by tenants or squatters as well as the value of the land were it otherwise to be used for production. Land invasions can similarly decrease property value and the liquidity of the land market. In the absence of clear determinants of property value, one metric that states often turn to is the reported value of the property for tax purposes. This is typically below market value, both because landowners can fraudulently avoid higher taxes by declaring lower property valuations and because land valuations are often only done intermittently, such as during ten-year cadastral surveys. Even if landowners contest their claims in local courts or special agrarian courts, judges may be pressured or politically allied with the government.

Distinguishing between land redistribution and land negotiation in these cases is done based on case details regarding the circumstances of land transfers. A transfer is classified as land redistribution when landowners are forced to sell at submarket rates or can only contest compensation through politically biased courts that owners widely deem as unfair.

---

[3] A similar situation occurred in the Philippines in the early 1900s when the US colonial administration tried to sell land acquired from Catholic religious orders to their former tenants.

In recent years, there have been an increasing number of "market-assisted" land reforms with programs funded by the World Bank that enable private individuals or collectives to purchase land from private landowners with state support in the form of loan subsidies or legal assistance (Binswanger-Mkhize et al. 2009, 21–22). Brazil, Colombia, and Mexico have all implemented such programs. This type of land reform is close in some ways to the notion of a "negotiated" reform in the sense that landowners are fully compensated and those who are relatively land-poor may become program beneficiaries, yet it differs from negotiated reforms in several key respects. First, the provision of subsidies to potential buyers often leads to the inflation of land prices by prospective sellers, which then depresses the demand for land through these programs (see, e.g., Machado 1998 on this in the case of Colombia in the late 1990s). Second, when land prices are inflated or state subsidies are small, market-assisted reforms operate much more similarly to private markets than they do to typical land reform, with the simple exception that the state or an external organization such as the World Bank acts as a "matchmaker" to help facilitate private transfers. The role of the state in these reforms is therefore often quite limited.

I do not classify these programs as land negotiation in most cases but rather treat them as private land markets that fall outside the major types of land reform. In the few cases where the state plays a major role in market-assisted reforms and beneficiaries pay very little or nothing for the land they receive because of state intervention, as under the Fondo de Tierras program in Guatemala (Granovsky-Larsen 2010), I code these as land negotiation. This coding decision is in any case not particularly consequential: market-assisted land reforms have not achieved wide-ranging results in Latin America due to a host of implementation problems (Deininger 1999).

Colonization of State-Owned Land

In addition to policies of land redistribution and land negotiation, land reform also often includes land colonization programs that involve land grants and settlement schemes. In contrast to land redistribution and land negotiation, in which land is transferred from some private individuals to others, land colonization programs distribute state-owned land. The important distinguishing feature of land colonization is therefore the origin of the land that is distributed. When colonization schemes that involve the settlement of rural migrants are implemented on private land that has been obtained either through forcible expropriation at below-market rates or through fully compensated transfers, I code these cases as land redistribution or land negotiation, respectively. Because colonization as coded here does not entail taking property from larger landowners to give it to the landless or land-poor but rather the more one-sided transfer of property from the state, it is more distributive than redistributive in nature.[4]

---

[4] To the extent that land colonization is funded by the state with little or no payment by settlers, with funds being generated through some form of progressive taxation, land colonization may be mildly redistributive in nature.

The state must play a role in the distribution of land in order for a colonization program to be coded as land colonization. The state's role may either be direct or indirect. Direct land colonization involves the opening up of specific tracts of land for colonization that are then granted as settlers occupy them. In some cases, land colonization involves an active state role in clearing virgin land, relocating settlers, and providing support for agricultural production. The state may also take an indirect role in colonization by legalizing certain forms of settlement and then providing administrative infrastructure to recognize land occupation. In contrast to these forms of state involvement in colonization, "spontaneous" settlement and squatting on unoccupied land are indicative of the absence of effective state policy for colonization. Because these actions are not sanctioned or catalyzed by the state, they are not coded as land colonization.

The distinction between private and state-owned land is typically quite clearcut. But as Turits (2003) demonstrates in detail in the case of the Dominican Republic, there are exceptions. Rafael Trujillo began a land distribution campaign in 1934 that sought to provide free access to idle land (*terrenos comuneros*, state land, and private land) on the basis of contracts. In most cases private land never had to be returned, resulting in de facto confiscation (Turits 2003, 97–98). At the same time, many de facto owners of *terrenos comuneros*, or communal land for which owners had failed to secure "prescription rights" to their (often illegal) enclosures, contested the state's claim that these were state-owned lands. Trujillo had also initiated a colonization program in which state-owned land, including former woodlands and pasture land, was distributed through land colonies (Augelli 1963). The incorporation of supposedly state-owned land was again contested in many cases by affected landowners. Contestation over ownership was not quickly or easily resolved. Together with the land distribution program, colonization was a "vast state program" that endured as one of the longest-lasting rural programs in the Dominican Republic in the twentieth century (Turits 2003, 182).

Ownership contestation is not unique to the Dominican Republic. LeGrand (1986) documents illicit land appropriation and enclosure by elites and land entrepreneurs in early twentieth-century Colombia. Much of this land was subsequently legalized into private property despite peasant pressure for the redistribution of what they viewed as vacant land (*baldíos*) for which there was no owner.

I address the question of private versus public ownership by coding as private property those holdings for which ownership is locally understood and consistently upheld in courts. State seizure of this property is therefore coded as land redistribution or land negotiation rather than colonization. Where ownership rights are widely locally contested or socially challenged and where properties under similar possession may yield different outcomes in court, I code these as state-owned lands. As mentioned earlier in this section, this coding issue only arises in a very small number of cases.

Land colonization may either complement or substitute for other land reform policies. In Bolivia, the military played an important role in developing early colonies in the late 1930s to create infrastructure in remote areas and populate frontier regions so that further territorial losses, such as those that occurred following the Chaco War with Paraguay would be prevented (Eastwood and Pollard 1985). Colonization of the eastern lowlands was encouraged following the 1952 revolution as a supplement to land redistribution in order to alleviate demographic pressure in the highlands and attract agricultural workers in an effort to increase national production, thereby offsetting any potential short-term productivity losses in the highlands that resulted from the reform (Eastwood and Pollard 1985; Stearman 1984). Most colonization was state-led or state-supported until 1977. The National Institute of Colonization (INC) and its predecessor, the National Council for Colonization (CNC), provided financial and technical support to colonists and in some cases cleared state-owned land for development and building infrastructure. As the road network expanded toward the end of the 1970s, colonization became driven by colonists settling on unoccupied state-owned land, often with subsequent recognition or even support from the state (INRA 2007, 48–52). Between 1961 and 1994, some 5 million hectares of land were colonized through the CNC and INC, benefiting approximately 150,000 families, particularly in Alto Beni, Chapare in Cochabamba, and Santa Cruz (INRA 2007, 51–52; Muñoz and Lavadenz 1997, 3). Roughly 25 million hectares of state-owned land (*tierras fiscales*) in non-hacienda regions (largely Santa Cruz and Beni) were also granted to individuals during this period (Muñoz and Lavadenz 1997, 3).

Land colonization also served as an important complement to land redistribution in Honduras from the late 1960s to the early 1990s. Following a series of government projects to homestead families in the 1950s that settled 2,300 families on approximately 33,000 hectares of land (COCOCH 2008, 15; INA 1965, 86), Villeda Morales approved a land reform law in 1962 that provided for the redistribution of public and idle private lands. Although land reform efforts in the early to mid-1960s consisted exclusively of colonization efforts due to the lack of funds that would have been necessary to incorporate private property into the reform sector (INA 1965, 2–5), President Oswaldo López Arellano increased land redistribution in tandem with land colonization in the late 1960s after seizing power in a coup. When López Arellano again seized power in 1972 following a short period of democracy, he issued two land reform decrees (Decree 8 and Decree 170) that affected both public and private lands. Subsequent governments continued these programs at differing levels of intensity into the early 1990s.

Early Chilean land policy from the late 1920s to the early 1960s demonstrates how land colonization can serve as a substitute for, rather than a complement to, other land reform policies. Article 10 of the 1925 constitution stipulated that "the state will promote the convenient division of land into private property" (Garrido 1988, 54). It simultaneously declared the "inviolability of all property," which was interpreted to mean that expropriated land had to be paid for in cash at the market value at sale, for which the government had few resources (Thiesenhusen 1995, 96). The Caja de Colonización Agrícola (CCA) was created by Law 4496 in 1928, and it was charged with forming colonies that were intended to organize and intensify production, providing loans to rural smallholders, subdividing *latifundios* in the central zone to found new colonies, and amending property titles in the southern part of the country. The CCA primarily parceled plots to colonists on state-owned land (Garrido 1988, 54). There were only eight properties expropriated prior to 1958. A 1962 land reform bill provided for the "social responsibility" of property ownership, enabling the expropriation of unproductive land (Lapp 2004, 66), yet in reality it was "designed to be an unimaginative and underfunded colonization program" similar to the CCA (Thiesenhusen 1995, 96). Significant land reform did not occur until Eduardo Frei won office in 1964 and began to purchase land from private landholders under Law 15020.

There are numerous other cases of countries that have used land colonization as an "escape valve" to push settlers to frontier regions and reduce demographic pressure on productive land in existing areas of agricultural production. In some cases, this was a result of state-led reform, as in Ecuador beginning with the 1929 constitution and the 1936 Law of Vacant Land and Colonization and continuing through various periods of land reform until the mid-1990s. In other cases, such as Colombia and Brazil, colonization programs coexisted with or were created as a response to widespread "spontaneous" settlement and land appropriation and squatting in relatively unoccupied frontier regions.

Land Titling

Beyond land redistribution, land negotiation, and land colonization, most states have implemented land titling programs as part of their broader efforts at land reform. This has been particularly true since the adoption of neoliberal economic policies. Land titling entails granting formal property rights to those with insecure tenure. The main targets of land titling programs are individuals who hold property with either a provisional title or de facto status that is undisputed. Of course, in practice, as property rights are redefined and institutions change, even established landowners may be required to update their ownership rights and receive new titles. By clearly delineating and formalizing property ownership, land titling efforts seek to establish widespread, transparent property rights that can attract investment and help spur growth by enabling beneficiaries to access services in the formal sector (e.g., by using their property as collateral for loans).

I do not code land titling as one of the chief measures of land reform. In contrast to land redistribution, land negotiation, and land colonization, land titling as defined here does not include the transfer of physical property to individuals either through the redistribution of private property from some individuals to others or through the distribution of state-owned land. Furthermore, the majority of land titling in Latin America occurred from the 1980s to the 2000s following the turn toward neoliberal policies and was therefore implemented as a separate reform from earlier land transfers. Coding both land titling and these other land reform policies could therefore result in "double counting" land reform if the transfers are coded first and then ownership rights over the same transfers are subsequently coded.[5]

What differentiates land titling from land redistribution or land negotiation when both policies are being implemented simultaneously? I code land reform as land redistribution or land negotiation if, using private land, the range of affected individuals is physically expanded, individuals relocate to newly granted land on which they had not previously worked, or there is a consequential change in land tenure relations that shifts ownership (e.g., share-croppers or wage laborers are converted into owners). Land titling, by contrast, is simply the conversion of de facto property rights into de jure property rights. Similarly, I distinguish land titling from land colonization by coding land colonization when individuals are granted state-owned land and land titling when individuals simply receive formal property rights over state-owned land that they have already occupied for some significant time or work in usufruct.[6]

In some cases, particularly in recent years as indigenous groups have made successful bids for recognition of their ownership of ancestral lands, communal or territorial land rights have been extended to indigenous or ethnic groups. Examples include the *resguardos indígenas* in Colombia and the *tierras comunitarias de origen* in Bolivia.[7] Consistent with the discussion earlier in this section, the territorial recognition of these groups is coded as land titling. In some cases, land rights are "amplified" to incorporate adjacent lands that were not previously recognized as pertaining to the group. These lands are typically state-owned lands and are often de facto used by these groups prior to the formal recognition of their ownership. Because amplifications do not entail migration, either to formerly private land or to colonization zones on formerly state-owned property, and because there is no change in tenure relations, these amplifications are coded along with land titling. Where amplifications do imply the extension of rights to areas that were previously unused by the group, these are coded as land redistribution, land negotiation, or land colonization depending on the origin of the land transferred and the rate of compensation to former owners.

---

[5] Land titling can nonetheless be redistributive in nature to the extent that the poor in the informal sector are the chief beneficiaries of it and if titling helps shift relative market power in their favor. Of course, powerful landowners can also attempt to dominate the titling process or use it to gain ownership rights over land that was dubiously held or for which they did not have de facto ownership.

[6] Land invasions or squatting on state-owned land for the purposes of receiving a grant are, if met with state-led land distribution, therefore coded as land colonization.

[7] A similar development has occurred with aboriginal groups in Australia under the 1993 Native Title Act in the wake of the landmark *Mabo v. Queensland* decision.

The coding rules detailed earlier in the chapter help distinguish between land titling and reforms such as land redistribution. Mexico provides an illustrative example. Much of Mexico's long-standing land reform following the Mexican Revolution was structured around the redistribution of privately held land to village-level agrarian reform settlements known as *ejidos*. *Ejidos* were designed to be usufructuary property, and their members were prohibited from renting, selling, or mortgaging their land, although this did occur in practice to a limited degree. *Ejido* communities typically created a governing council that would divide land according to rules that the council established. Although *ejido* membership was recorded, formal titles were rarely granted: nearly 90 percent of *ejidatarios* never received property titles (Thiesenhusen 1995, 38). In late 1991, President Carlos Salinas ended the PRI's long-standing land reform program. The Mexican government halted most land expropriation and redistribution in favor of privatization and titling of the *ejido* sector through the PROCEDE program. *Ejidatarios* were permitted to sell, rent, sharecrop, or mortgage their land plots as collateral for loans (Thiesenhusen 1995, 46–47). Through PROCEDE, roughly 28,800 *ejidos* were titled out of a total of 31,500 from 1993 to 2006 (SRA 2010). Although titling has contributed to more dynamic land markets within the *ejido* system, the new laws did not transfer property itself but rather altered rights regarding formal property ownership and use.

The Land Reform Typology

The discussion of different types of land reform and the coding rules pertaining to each type is distilled and summarized in Table 4.1. Land redistribution, land negotiation, land colonization, and land titling can be distinguished from one another by reform characteristics such as private versus public domain land, compensation levels, and legal procedures. The four types of land reform outlined here can also be differentiated by their modes of transfer, including whether and how land actually changes hands. The rightmost column of Table 4.1 provides illustrative examples of countries and time periods in which each type of land reform occurred.

LAND QUALITY

One potentially important omission from the discussion of land reform coding in the previous sections is the quality of the land that is transferred. In principle, it is possible to classify land transfers according to whether land was irrigated, rain-fed, pastureland, mountainous, desert, wooded, or otherwise. Although adjusting land reform policies for certain factors such as land improvements may distort incentives and undercut the intent of reform (Lipton 2009, 141), improvements or other characteristics of land quality may nonetheless be relevant in the coding of land reform. Losing or gaining a tract of irrigated land,

TABLE 4.1. *A Typology of Land Reform*

Type of Reform	Characteristics of Reform	Modes of Transfer	Examples
Land redistribution	Expropriation and redistribution of private land; compensation below market value	Compulsory seizures; compulsory sales	Bolivia 1953–1985; Cuba 1959–1963; Mexico 1917–1992; Peru 1968–1980
Land negotiation	Acquisition and redistribution of private land with market-value compensation or via willing sales	Willing sales; compulsory sales with market-value compensation enforced by courts; "market-assisted" reforms when state plays major role, beneficiaries heavily or fully subsidized	Brazil 1993–present; Colombia 1933–1940; Costa Rica 1969–present; Guatemala 1998–present; Paraguay 1936–present; Uruguay 1914–present
Land colonization	Distribution of state-owned land	Settlement programs; legalization and support of frontier settlement	Bolivia 1937–present; Chile 1929–1966; Ecuador 1930–1996; Honduras 1952–1990s
Land titling	Provision of formal land titles to those who have provisional titles or undisputed de facto land possession	No physical land transfers or change in land tenure	Ecuador 1995–present; Honduras 1983–present; Mexico 1993–present

for example, has different welfare and exploitation implications than losing or gaining an equivalently sized tract of hillside land with poorer soil.

Although it would be preferable to adjust for land quality according to soil quality, terrain, water access, or other salient characteristics, sufficient information to standardize land quality at the country-year level does not exist in the vast majority of land reforms that have occurred either in Latin America or elsewhere. Even if in the present one could trace what land was affected by reform, many land parcels would have changed significantly since reform due to development and infrastructure, and property has transferred hands. It is therefore difficult to know exactly how land would have been classified when it was transferred, even if complete cadastral information existed.

Adjusting for Land Quality

While it is not possible to standardize land transfers by land quality across space and time because of data constraints, it is possible to attempt to bound the potential biases that are introduced using the data on land quality that are available.

There are several cases of major land reform that incorporated marginal land into the reform sector. Perhaps the most notorious is Mexico. As time elapsed after the Mexican Revolution, it became increasingly common for marginal, low-quality land to be distributed (e.g., Sanderson 1984). This was particularly true in the more arid northern regions of the country. Gustavo Díaz Ordaz in particular, and Luis Echeverría to a lesser degree, became well known for such distribution (Sanderson 1984).

Related problems are present, albeit to a smaller degree, in the cases of Chile, Bolivia, and Peru. All of these countries redistributed non-negligible amounts of marginal land as part of their land reform programs. This is mainly because these countries intersect at the *altiplano*, a relatively arid, high plain atop the Andes. The *altiplano* has land of marginal quality (see, e.g., Caballero and Alvarez 1980). These countries also have substantial mountainous territory, of which less is agriculturally productive than the mountainous territory in their northern Andean neighbors that reside closer to the equator. It is important to emphasize, however, that although marginal land in these countries is less productive on a per hectare basis than heavily rain-fed zones, it is far from completely undesirable: the *altiplano*, for instance, is occupied by a reasonably dense population of agricultural laborers, particularly in Bolivia and Peru.

In an effort to bound the possible biases introduced in the empirical analysis by failing to directly account for land quality, I make use of data on the type and quality of land distributed in these countries in a set of empirical extensions presented in an online appendix to the book. In particular, I completely exclude redistributed land that is classified as mountainous or desert in Mexico (Sanderson 1984, 164–165; INEGI 1985, table 7.1) and land of marginal quality in Chile (Garrido 1988, 174), Bolivia (Urioste 1987, annex 10), and Peru (Caballero and Alvarez 1980, 16–17). In many cases this land was actually occupied and used by land reform beneficiaries. However, its productivity was relatively low. Excluding this land from the analysis implies that the modified results more closely measure high-quality land that was distributed. The modified coding is, if anything, likely to be a lower bound on the amount of redistributed land that was useful for land reform beneficiaries, given that it excludes the marginal land that was actually farmed. The results of this experiment nonetheless consistently confirm the main findings in Chapter 5 in which the measure of land redistribution is not adjusted for land quality.

Why might this be the case? The simple fact that land quality was not the chief consideration during land reforms is itself a mitigating factor in its omission from the coding. Landowners in Latin America that have larger holdings also tend to have lower average land quality (Lipton 2009, 139). Given that more powerful landowners own larger plots, large landowners are more likely to successfully distort the quality, and therefore the standardized size, of their plots in any land reform where information regarding soil quality or other property characteristics is imperfect. This would systematically down-weight the observed scale of reform in rough proportion to the degree of concentration of landholdings when land is standardized according to quality.

Several other factors may operate to address concerns with the lack of land quality data. First, social pressure for land redistribution is generally greater where land is more productive. When pressure plays a role in the distribution of land, it helps set a baseline threshold for average land quality. Second, and related to the previous point, much of the land in Latin America prior to land reform was held in dualistic *latifundia-minifundia* systems in which peasants worked on the estates of larger landowners and in many cases held additional small plots for family subsistence farming (Thiesenhusen 1995). The landlord's intent in these systems was to maximize production, and therefore peasants often labored on higher-quality tracts of land. When land redistribution or land negotiation granted the property of these large landowners to former laborers, early beneficiaries often received the relatively productive land on which they had worked.

This last consideration raises the point that there is heterogeneity in the quality of land transfers not only across space but also over time. It is conceivable that variation in land quality over time is equally or more important than spatial variation in quality in a fixed moment. Fortunately, temporal variation in land quality can be adjusted for statistically through the use of control variables and time trends. For instance, the amount of previous land redistributed in a state may impact the quality of further land that is redistributed. If pressure for redistribution is greater on more fertile or more productive land, this land may be redistributed first, followed by lower-quality land as time elapses and the supply of high-quality land becomes exhausted.

Similarly, land quality often changes during the process of land reform itself as a result of the role played by the state. This is true both because of how the security of property rights impacts the value of land and also because of development projects implemented by the state. In many land reforms, the state invests in irrigation projects, clears woodlands, creates roads and paths to increase accessibility to hills and mountainous areas, or provides access to machinery that makes previously difficult-to-work land manageable. Land quality and its use for agricultural purposes is therefore to some degree a function of development. Mechanization, frontier development, and an increased density of markets can all serve to open up previously unused or unusable land. Importantly, both of these possibilities – previous land redistribution and the level of development – can be controlled for in an empirical analysis of land reform policies.

Finally, the fact that there is not a clear-cut ordering in the value of land according to its soil quality or terrain also mitigates the lack of land quality data to a degree. Although it is reasonably straightforward that irrigated or rain-fed land is of a higher quality than desert land, the crops associated with these various land types may have considerably different yields per hectare. The way in which land is actually exploited is therefore important beyond land quality per se (Rajan and Ramcharan 2011). A cross-country comparison illustrates this point, although the same dynamic operates within countries. In contrast to much of Mexico, where mountainous land is frequently (but far from uniformly) rocky and relatively barren or wooded, mountainous land in tropical Colombia can be used to produce coffee and fruit that fetch high prices. Colombia's lowland eastern plains, by contrast, often have poor soils, even if they are rain-fed. And whereas stretches of Mexico's deserts are hot and parched (though often apt for agave), desert-like climates in the *altiplano* in Peru and Bolivia can yield large harvests of potatoes, corn, and quinoa.

SOURCES OF LAND REFORM DATA

The data used to code the land reform policies detailed in this chapter were gathered from primary and secondary materials. Every country in Latin America has had at least one, and in most cases several, agencies or other government entities dedicated to land reform. This is true even in countries such as Argentina, Costa Rica, and Uruguay, where land negotiation or land colonization have largely taken preference over land redistribution. Land reform agencies typically collect very detailed data on land transfers. And because many of these agencies were technical in nature, they frequently published yearly bulletins with disaggregated statistical information. In some cases – Bolivia, Colombia, Ecuador, Mexico, Peru, and Venezuela – I collected individual-level land transfer data or disaggregated data at the provincial or municipal level directly from land reform agencies through fieldwork. I obtained similarly detailed data for Brazil. For certain countries and time periods, I have simply collected national-level statistics or aggregated subnational statistics directly from land agencies or from land agency publications or other government publications. Data from countries where I have collected disaggregated statistics have enabled me to reconstruct national-level data and compare it to official figures in order to verify the fidelity of the aggregate data generation process.

For most countries, I used secondary sources such as the research findings of technical specialists and academic researchers to supplement land reform data for time periods that could not be found directly in government publications or obtained through land reform agencies. I also used secondary sources in all cases to investigate the validity of both government publications as well as other secondary data sources. Between primary and secondary sources, I was able to construct land reform measures for all countries with very little time-series missingness.

In many cases, I had to use several sources to be able to code land redistribution, land negotiation, and land colonization as defined earlier in this chapter. This is because any single publication may not have contained sufficient information to classify land reform in the appropriate category. For instance, some land reform agencies published collections of land colonization data without distinguishing in the same publication whether the source of land used for colonization was public or private. This required further research to determine the origin of the land transferred and the compensation that was paid in order to classify the type of reform.

The same issues apply with government or political rhetoric. Politicians often trumpet aggregate land reform statistics to demonstrate their credentials as reformers. For instance, in 2006 the Bolivian President Evo Morales vowed to redistribute some 20 million hectares of state-owned and private land, nearly 20 percent of the country's territory, within five years. Yet despite claims of considerable progress on land reform, the vast majority of reform has involved the land titling of de facto owners, with only 54,735 hectares redistributed and slightly more than 1 million hectares colonized by 2010 (INRA 2011). The important point is that although land reform may be discussed loosely in official rhetoric, land reform policies are typically clearly distinguishable in the statistics produced by land reform agencies using the coding rules detailed here.

The procedures I use to code land reform suffer from some of the same drawbacks as other government data. In particular, there may be corruption (e.g., illicit land transfers) or manipulation. Several factors help mitigate these concerns. First, there is widespread agreement within the literature about the relative level of land reform in these countries. Second, corruption in land distribution is relatively easier to detect than corruption in the form of bribery or financial pillaging. On the one hand, corrupt land transfers leave concrete physical evidence (land ownership) that increases with the severity of the corruption. On the other hand, local residents near illicitly transferred properties may have both the knowledge and incentives to denounce the corruption. When land reform resolutions affect specific property such that the government can claim credit for reform, the presence of local residents who know each other and their neighbors makes agency corruption more difficult. Finally, land transfers that are granted to regime cronies and not counted in official statistics are not particularly problematic for the measures here, given that such transfers are granted to powerful political or economic elites and would therefore not be redistributive in nature.

A complete description of the data sources used for each country can be found in the book's online appendix.

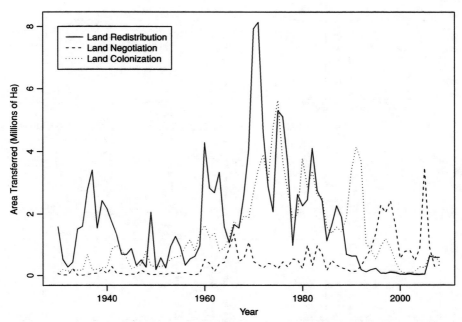

FIGURE 4.1. Land Reform in Latin America, 1930–2008. *Note:* Data compiled by the author. Solid line indicates land redistribution; dashed line indicates land negotiation; dotted line indicates land colonization.

TRENDS IN LAND REFORM, 1930–2008

Figure 4.1 is an aggregate plot of land reform for all of Latin America from 1930 to 2008. The plot depicts the amount of land transferred through land redistribution, land negotiation, and land colonization. There were a total of 128 million hectares, or 1.28 million km², of land expropriated and redistributed in Latin America from 1930 to 2008. There were 37 million hectares transferred through land negotiations and another 106 million hectares transferred through land colonization. A total of 14 percent of the entire landmass of Latin America transferred hands between 1930 and 2008 as a result of these three types of land reform. This represents an area nearly the size of all of Western and Northern Europe or the equivalent of roughly 1.5 times the land area of Mexico. More than 20 percent of the national territory of Bolivia, Colombia, Cuba, the Dominican Republic, Ecuador, El Salvador, Guatemala, Mexico, and Paraguay were affected by explicit state policies of land redistribution, land negotiation, and land colonization during the period.

Figure 4.2 displays a series of plots of land reform in all countries in Latin America from 1930 to 2008. The plots indicate the amount of land transferred through land redistribution, land negotiation, and land colonization. Land area transferred is divided by total cultivable land area to standardize

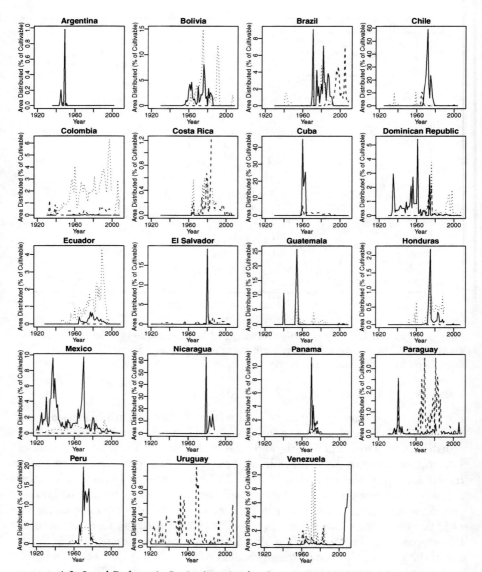

FIGURE 4.2. Land Reform in Latin America by Country, 1930–2008. *Note:* Data compiled by the author. Solid lines indicate land redistribution; dashed lines indicate land negotiation; dotted lines indicate land colonization.

the scope of reform. Mexico implemented the most land redistribution, at 51 million hectares since the promulgation of the 1917 constitution.[8] It also had the longest active program of land redistribution, spanning from the end of the Mexican Revolution until 1992. Mexico also continued processing petitions for land redistribution after 1992 that had been filed prior to that date as well as a number of claims in Chiapas in the wake of the Zapatista Uprising. Cuba's land redistribution was the largest relative to country size, expropriating 68 percent of the total land area. Bolivia, Brazil, Chile, Cuba, the Dominican Republic, El Salvador, Guatemala, Nicaragua, Panama, and Peru all redistributed more than 20 percent of their land relative to cultivable land area, and some of these redistributed considerably more. Argentina, Colombia, Costa Rica, and Uruguay all redistributed less than 5 percent of their cultivable land area. Uruguay was the only country that experienced no land redistribution through expropriation during the period.

Brazil conducted the most land negotiation during the period. Brazil transferred 19 million hectares of land through land negotiation from 1990 to 2008. Cuba and Paraguay implemented the most land negotiation relative to country size, at 28 percent and 20 percent, respectively. In addition to these three countries, Chile, Colombia, the Dominican Republic, El Salvador, and Venezuela all transferred at least 10 percent of their land as a proportion of cultivable land area through negotiations. Colombia had the greatest number of years of land negotiation at sixty-eight years. Argentina, Bolivia, Ecuador, Honduras, Mexico, Nicaragua, and Peru all transferred less than 1 percent of their total land area through negotiations.

The country with the largest amount of area transferred through land colonization during the period was Brazil, at 18 million hectares. Bolivia, Colombia, and Ecuador implemented the most land colonization relative to country size, with 29 percent, 20 percent, and 19 percent of their land area having been colonized, respectively. These countries all had active land colonization programs for at least fifty-five years during the period. Guatemala, Mexico, and Venezuela also granted more than 5 percent of their national territory through land colonization. Chile, Costa Rica, Cuba, and Honduras all had small land but non-negligible colonization programs.

Figure 4.2 demonstrates that there is significant variation in the timing and pace of land reform in the region. Early land redistribution began in Mexico following the 1917 constitution. Land negotiation began in Uruguay in the 1920s and continued in the 1930s, when Colombia began purchasing private land for redistribution in conflictive areas and Chile expanded land colonization. Paraguay began a land reform in the late 1930s under the military-led

---

[8] Redistribution is closer to 85 million hectares if one includes the recognition or confirmation of communities that already had de facto, relatively autonomous control of their property (*reconocimiento* or *confirmación y titulación de bienes comunales*), as does Sanderson (1984). Those grants are not included here for the reasons discussed earlier in the chapter.

Febristas, Mexico's land expropriations accelerated under Lázaro Cárdenas, and Trujillo began long-standing land redistribution and colonization policies in 1934. The 1940s witnessed a series of land expropriations under military rule and then under Juan Perón in Argentina, the seizure of property by General Jorge Ubico in Guatemala during World War II, land redistribution by General Higinio Morínigo in Paraguay, as well as more expansive land colonization in Colombia and Ecuador, continued land negotiation in Uruguay, and a series of land negotiations in Venezuela. Significant land reforms were initiated following the Bolivian Revolution in 1952, and in Guatemala under Jacobo Arbenz in 1953 and after the subsequent reversal by Carlos Castillo Armas. Trujillo continued his land redistribution program in the 1950s and began expropriating sugar plantations while Honduras began settling families in colonies on state-owned land. The decade ended with Cuba's large-scale expropriation after the 1959 revolution.

As Figure 4.2 indicates, land reform efforts increased in many countries in the 1960s. Venezuela passed an agrarian reform law in 1960, with land colonization and land negotiation taking preference over land expropriation and redistribution. Trujillo's extensive holdings in the Dominican Republic were expropriated in 1961 following his assassination, and a long-standing land reform began. Land reform laws were passed in the early 1960s in Colombia, Costa Rica, Honduras, and Guatemala following the 1961 Alliance for Progress, but all of these countries relied on land negotiation and land colonization over expropriation with the exception of Honduras, which was under military rule in the 1970s. Land reform laws were also passed in the mid-1960s in Brazil, Ecuador, and Paraguay. Brazil's military began land expropriation and expanded colonization, the Ecuadorian military increased expropriation and land colonization, and Paraguay's Alfredo Stroessner deepened what would become a major, long-time land negotiation program. The late 1960s witnessed increasing reformism in Chile and Mexico as well as under military generals in Bolivia, Panama, and Peru.

Land reform remained very active in the 1970s. Military rule again resulted in increased expropriation and colonization in Ecuador, and Bolivia, Chile, Mexico, Peru, and Panama all experienced large-scale land redistribution. Colombia and Venezuela had large land colonization programs. Costa Rica increased land negotiation and land colonization, and the Dominican Republic increased land negotiation, whereas Uruguay largely repressed strikes and union demands for redistribution. The decade ended with the overthrow and expropriation of the Somoza regime in Nicaragua in 1979.

Several trends in land reform began to change during the 1980s. Chile's reform under Salvador Allende had been substantially – although not completely – unraveled by Augusto Pinochet. Land redistribution declined in Ecuador as colonization increased. Redistribution effectively halted in Bolivia and Peru following their transitions to democracy, and it also ended in Panama. By contrast, a 1979 coup in El Salvador led to an agrarian reform in the early

1980s that started strong but quickly fizzled, whereas Nicaragua implemented a new agrarian reform in the mid-1980s after a hiatus. Land colonization increased in Colombia, held steady in Honduras, slowed in Brazil, and ended in Venezuela. Paraguay continued a considerable program of land negotiation.

Land reform persisted in the 1990s and 2000s despite considerable changes, and it reentered the political debate in the mid- to late 2000s in several countries. Land reform has increased in Brazil, although land negotiation replaced land redistribution following a 1993 constitutional amendment. Both Guatemala and El Salvador initiated small land negotiation and land colonization programs following an end to civil conflict in the 1990s. Costa Rica and Uruguay have continued their small-scale land negotiation programs, and the Dominican Republic and Paraguay continued both land redistribution and land negotiation, albeit on a smaller scale. After a shift to colonization in the 1990s, Bolivia again began land redistribution in 2007 following a new 2006 land reform law. A strengthened 2005 land reform law in Venezuela has led to Venezuela's largest land redistribution program, which continues to increase in scope. Increased land reform has also been promised in Ecuador, Honduras, and Paraguay, although there have been few results as of 2014.

Figure 4.3 displays how much each country's total land reform – redistribution, negotiation, and colonization – contributed to aggregate land reform in Latin America for every year from 1930 to 2008. The figure therefore indicates which countries did the bulk of land reform and when. It splits the countries in the region into four panels for ease of interpretation. The shaded region for each country in any given year indicates the proportion of total land reform attributed to that country (as a percentage of its cultivable land) relative to the net cultivable land transferred in all of Latin America in that year via redistribution, negotiation, and colonization. The white region in each panel is the proportion of land reform attributed to other countries in Latin America that are not included in that specific panel. The shaded regions across the four panels therefore add up to one in every year.

The figure confirms the earlier discussion of Figure 4.2 while also shedding additional light on the relative size of land reform programs. The first panel indicates that land reform in Argentina was only somewhat significant relative to other countries in the region around 1950. Chile's land reform in the late 1960s and 1970s was large in relative terms, whereas land reform in Latin America in the 1990s and 2000s was dominated by Bolivia, Brazil, Colombia, and, toward the end of the period, Venezuela. The second panel underscores the minor nature of land reform in Costa Rica throughout the period, and in Ecuador with the exception of the 1980s and 1990s. Cuba's reform is represented by the large spike in the early 1960s and El Salvador's by the spike in the early 1980s. The Dominican Republic's land reform was large for its time in the 1940s and 1950s.

The third panel in Figure 4.3 clearly signals the importance of Mexico's land reform in the region. Mexico accounted for roughly half of all reform until

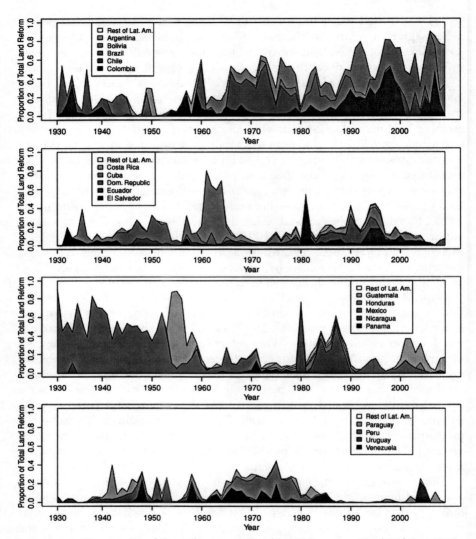

FIGURE 4.3. Country-Level Contributions to Total Latin American Land Reform, 1930–2008. *Note:* Data compiled by the author. Figures indicate the proportion of yearly land reform attributed to each country relative to net cultivable land transferred via redistribution, negotiation, and colonization.

the early 1950s. Guatemala came to dominate the land reform scene in the mid-1950s, and its postwar reform in the 2000s was also significant relative to most other land reforms at that time. Panama had an important, albeit measured, reform in the 1970s, and Nicaragua had large-scale reform in relative and absolute terms throughout the 1980s. The final panel in Figure 4.3 shows that the largest reforms in relative terms were Peru's reform in the 1960s and 1970s, Paraguay's early land reform in the 1940s, and Venezuela's land reforms in the middle of the overall time period and again in the 2000s.

THE FATE OF LAND BENEFICIARIES: WAS LAND REFORM REDISTRIBUTIVE?

The previous section demonstrates the widespread adoption of various land reform policies across Latin America since 1930. Yet how have rural beneficiaries been affected? Have their livelihoods benefited from access to land in the short and/or long term?

The land reform literature offers divergent conclusions. Some scholars argue that land reform – particularly the most redistributive types of reform – have had dramatic consequences. There are three main reasons why this is the case.[9] First, land reform that targets landed elites with expropriation may directly transfer land from large landowners to the land-poor, and it is therefore fundamentally redistributive in nature. Second, this type of reform creates incentives that further support its central redistributive aim. For instance, to avoid current or future land ceilings, large landowners may try to sell or rent out portions of their holdings. This pushes down land prices or rents and makes it easier for the poor to gain land access. Large landowners must also sell or yield land to individuals that have smaller landholdings. In support of this end, increased smallholder ownership drives up the price of rural labor. And land ceiling legislation can also create constituencies that lobby for implementation of the law through land invasions or other forms of pressure when progress stalls, as in the case of the Movimento dos Trabalhadores Rurais Sem Terra (MST) in Brazil. Third, and finally, by creating smaller and more equal farms, redistributive land reform tends to raise net farm output. This generates resources to help pay for the reform, whether by providing support to beneficiaries, compensating the losers, or effectively paying key constituencies that would otherwise not support the reform to do so.

Land reforms can also have redistributive effects by enabling the growth of human capital. A host of authors have long tied late development and a large lower class in Latin America to the pernicious effects of high land inequality in encouraging a small but powerful landed class to forestall the expansion of public education and other public goods (e.g., Engerman and Sokoloff 2002; Frankema 2010; Galor et al. 2009; Huber and Stephens 2012). By altering the distribution of land and eliminating actors that have incentives to restrict the supply of education, land reform can pave the way for growth in skilled labor and an associated increase in wages for the lower and middle classes.

---

[9] These reasons are largely drawn from Lipton (2009, 127, 146–147).

Even land tenure reforms that do not directly redistribute land can have redistributive effects. The prohibition of feudalistic tenure arrangements eliminated some of the most exploitative labor conditions that existed in the Western hemisphere in the mid-twentieth century and resulted in considerable improvements in the political and social independence of peasants. This was a dramatic shift in rural relations that enabled a new set of tools (e.g., the ability to organize more freely) that the rural poor could use to improve their welfare.

The Peruvian case demonstrates some of the wide-ranging redistributive consequences of land reform. From 1968 to 1980, Peru's military regime implemented a radical land reform program that redistributed roughly half of all agricultural land in favor of rural laborers. Despite widespread lingering rural and urban poverty, inequality was significantly reduced (by 1985, income inequality in Peru was lower than that in Costa Rica or Chile), education grew rapidly, and the middle class expanded significantly (McClintock 1999, 356).

Throughout the Sacred Valley, for instance, former haciendas have been transformed into a patchwork of smaller individual plots and communal holdings. Middle-class peasant agriculture has blossomed and much more land is under production now than prior to the reform. Labor mobility also enables peasants to supplement their income through other economic activity. The archetypal case of the cooperative José Zúñiga Letona on the former hacienda Huarán illustrates these patterns. Although the long-time agronomist Octavio Palma and peasants such as Justina López acknowledge that there were a host of problems with land policy after the return to democracy that undercut the cooperative's efficacy, they maintain that community members are undoubtedly better off now than they were when living under the punishing regimen of the former owner, Oscar Fernández.[10] Indeed, portraits of General Velasco still dot the community and administrative offices.

Of course, land reform can also be blocked or reduced in scope by landed interests, reducing its redistributive consequences. Thiesenhusen (1995) labels many of the cases of land reform in Latin America, when measured according to their stated goals, as little more than "broken promises." And Kay (1998) argues that although a host of Latin American countries implemented substantial land redistribution, most reforms ultimately favored the development of capitalist farming by the 1990s. Landed elites watered down reform in countries such as Colombia and Costa Rica, and almost entirely blocked it in Argentina and Uruguay.

Yet land reform has had far from negligible consequences for rural welfare. First, partial reforms may still result in substantial redistribution for a select set of the population. For instance, while land reform in Honduras under Decree 8 fell short of the rural demand for land, it nonetheless benefited nearly 24,000 families in the 1970s (Stringer 1989, 369). Similarly, partial land reform under Trujillo in the Dominican Republic resulted in land possession for many of

---

[10] Interviews by author, June 20–21, 2014.

the landless and land-poor, who then formed a foundation of regime support (Turits 2003). Accounts that treat these reforms as wholesale failures neglect the considerable achievements that were in fact made (Lipton 2009). The proper counterfactual to consider is how peasants would have fared had land never been redistributed at all.

Second, the fact that redistributive land reforms can be unraveled over time does not imply that these reforms were not redistributive when they were implemented. In many cases, giving peasants increased access to land via land reform was used as a quid pro quo to gain rural votes (Albertus 2013; Lapp 2004) or to build successful electoral coalitions (Gibson 1997). When votes were no longer needed from certain rural constituencies, support for land reform was withdrawn. The effects of some land reforms on rural welfare in Latin America were also undercut by economic crises in the late 1970s and 1980s. Peasants took another hit with the opening of markets in the 1990s accompanied by heavy subsidies to domestic agriculture in developed countries. Modern agribusinesses, like large landowners before them, can use market power to force smaller landholders out of business. Further complicating land reform gains is the fact that beneficiaries who are subsistence farmers often subdivide their plots among family members in subsequent generations, leading to progressively smaller and smaller holdings that lose their economic viability. Reversals in the welfare of some land reform beneficiaries, however, hardly imply that reform was not originally redistributive. Even the short- and medium-term redistributive gains can be translated into long-term redistribution if beneficiaries take advantage of their circumstances to invest in the future (e.g., by leveraging greater farm income in the short term to send their children to school).

Finally, the fact that the transformative impacts of land reform can be limited by other policies does not necessarily undercut the gains that are made. Land inequality may be reconstituted in the wake of land reform if new frontiers open up and are not distributed equitably, which exacerbates regional inequality, as was the case in the late twentieth-century and early twenty-first-century settlement of Bolivia's Santa Cruz department. And in many cases, land distribution was not followed by titling efforts that could have enabled land to serve as collateral to secure loans, or by investments in complementary reforms that could have aided land beneficiaries in improving their property and marketing their products (Thiesenhusen 1989, 1995). Some of these strategies were explicitly adopted to keep peasants dependent on government support and therefore easier to manipulate politically (Albertus 2013; de Janvry, Gonzalez-Navarro, and Sadoulet 2013). Land reform beneficiaries in these cases had difficulty extending small gains in prosperity, and intergenerational gains in rural welfare were at times elusive. Yet reform beneficiaries who could not use their land to improve their long-term welfare were typically able to at least sell their land in formal or informal markets and move to cities, earning at minimum a one-time payment for their land that they would not have received absent land reform. Others remained on their land and continue to exploit it, albeit with lower

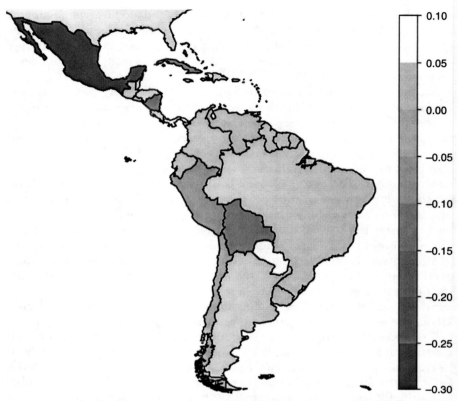

FIGURE 4.4. Change in Land Inequality in Latin America, 1950–1990. *Note:* Land inequality is measured using a Gini coefficient, with data taken from Crespo (1991), Eckstein (1986), and Frankema (2010).

levels of productivity than could have been achieved with greater government support.

Figure 4.4 demonstrates that those countries that had the most extensive land redistribution programs between 1950 and 1990 also witnessed the largest declines in landholding inequality during that period. The largest decreases in land inequality from 1950 to 1990 occurred in Bolivia, Cuba, Chile, Mexico, Nicaragua, and Peru – all countries that had large programs of land redistribution during the period, as Figures 4.2 and 4.3 indicate. By contrast, countries with a weaker record of land reform or with reforms that focused on colonization or land negotiation over land redistribution experienced little change in landholding inequality. This includes countries such as Argentina, Brazil, Costa Rica, Paraguay, and Uruguay. By the time that many countries had adopted neoliberal land policies in 1990, this latter set of countries, along with Guatemala and Venezuela, had some of the most unequal distributions of land in the region.

CONCLUSION

This chapter brings us a big step closer to being able to empirically test the theory developed in Chapter 3. It does so by systematically distinguishing and coding different types of land reform. Land reform is a broad term encompassing land confiscation and redistribution, negotiated transfers from the private market, the colonization of state-owned land, land titling, the generation of markets to buy and sell land, and even tenure reforms. Although this range points to the broad flexibility of land reform policies in addressing diverse problems in the rural sector, it poses a major challenge to comparative research that attempts to examine and draw inferences from similar policies that span time and space. This chapter outlines a coding scheme for four main types of land reform: land redistribution, land negotiation, land colonization, and land titling. Distinguishing these types of reform can enable scholars to code and systematically compare land reform programs in different countries at different times. Focusing on the first three types of land reform, this chapter then provides a broad overview of land reform in Latin America since 1930 using original data on land reform outcomes collected from land reform agencies and other sources.

I draw several important conclusions. First, land reform is more common than is widely understood. Every country in Latin America undertook land reform during this period. Land reform was so widespread that more than half of all the cultivable land in Latin America, a full 14 percent of the entire land area, was physically transferred between 1930 and 2008 as a result of land redistribution, land negotiation, or land colonization. Second, land reform has not been limited to any particular time period. Countries in the region implemented land reform in every single year during the period from 1930 to 2008. They were undertaking reform before and after this period as well. Some countries such as Colombia, the Dominican Republic, Ecuador, Mexico, Paraguay, Uruguay, and Venezuela conducted at least one type land reform in almost every year between 1930 and 2008. Third, land reform, and particularly land redistribution, has major redistributive implications. Countries that have had the most extensive land redistribution programs have also witnessed the largest declines in landholding inequality. This has had dramatic consequences for the rural sector.

5

A Cross-National Analysis of Land Reform
in Latin America

The theory and propositions in Chapter 3 anticipate land redistribution when two key circumstances are met: a coalitional split between ruling political elites and landed elites and low institutional barriers to reform. Rural pressure should also increase the likelihood of land redistribution. This chapter employs the data and coding scheme developed in Chapter 4 to empirically test this argument.

Land redistribution first requires a significant coalitional split between landed elites and ruling political elites. Ruling political elites will be motivated to target landed elites for redistribution when there is low coalitional overlap between these groups. The political elite's expropriation of landed elites in this case can preserve their ability to act independently in the future by eliminating powerful, potentially threatening rivals. The political elite's support coalition, which may harbor uncertainty about the intentions of the political elite, also benefits from this policy when its members are distinct from the landed elite. Redistribution away from current landed elites – even if land is not redistributed to the support coalition itself – reveals that ruling political elites favor the political support of the coalition that brought them to office over the support of landed elites. A political elite that fails to redistribute in these circumstances will therefore either be ousted or voted out by its support coalition, or it will pay steep costs to insulate itself from an internal coup. Conversely, political elites have few incentives to redistribute land when their coalition contains landed elites. Doing so would risk their political fate by upending the stability of their own governing coalition.

A coalitional divergence between ruling political elites and landed elites, however, is insufficient to yield land redistribution. Institutional constraints to policymaking must also be low enough to enable political elites to act decisively. Land reform efforts often fail when the executive opposes reform, the legislature cuts off funding, the bureaucracy is captured by landed elites, or the judiciary strikes down the constitutionality of property redistribution. Lower institutional constraints therefore increase the likelihood that land redistribution can be successfully implemented when the interests of political elites and landed elites diverge. This is most typically found under autocracy. Among democracies, majoritarian forms of democracy with fewer veto points face fewer institutional constraints to redistribution and therefore are more likely to redistribute than democracies that are characterized by heavy checks and balances.

I gain traction on these empirical implications using an original time-series, cross-section dataset on land redistribution, land negotiation, and land colonization that spans all of Latin America from 1930 to 2008. Most Latin American countries were long characterized by extreme social and economic inequality rooted in the skewed distribution and use of land. Against this backdrop, there was a turbulent political environment. Frequent political transitions in many states brought to power political elites that had widely divergent coalitions and agendas. Ruling political elites were at times allied with landed elites and at other times directly in conflict with them. Political regimes simultaneously varied widely in institutional constraints during the period and spanned from nearly unchecked executive power to diffuse and decentralized authority across a host of political institutions. This range of variation provides ideal circumstances for testing the theory in this region.

I find strong evidence in support of the theory that land redistribution is most likely when there are both coalitional splits between ruling political elites and landed elites as well as low institutional constraints to rule. Rural pressure from below is also linked to higher land redistribution. Granting land from former landed elites to rural laborers can help undercut the threat of instability from below in addition to satisfying the political elite's support coalition, thereby alleviating two major threats – one external and one internal – to political survival.

The results hold both in the descriptive statistics and in a host of regression models regardless of the estimation strategy. The findings are also robust to accounting for a series of alternative explanations, including country fixed effects to address unobserved country-specific time-invariant heterogeneity, and using instrumental variables estimation to account for potential endogeneity in elite splits and veto points. Furthermore, and as expected, less redistributive types of land reform such as land negotiation and land colonization occur under circumstances that are distinct from land redistribution.

RESEARCH DESIGN AND MEASUREMENT STRATEGY

To examine whether low institutional barriers to reform and a coalitional split between ruling political elites and landed elites are associated with land redistribution, it is necessary to create measures for the key independent variables in addition to the land reform measures constructed in Chapter 4. We must also identify other variables that may have an independent impact on land reform outcomes. In this section, I discuss the variables I use as part of an original panel dataset with coverage for all countries in Latin America from 1930 to 2008.

Dependent Variables: Land Reform Policy Outcomes

Land reform comes in a variety of forms: land expropriation and redistribution, negotiated transfers from the private market, colonization programs, tenure reforms, land titling, and the generation of markets to buy and sell land. I code land reform by differentiating between analytically distinct land reform policies and then classifying reforms according to these policies. I focus on the three main policies of land reform discussed in detail in Chapter 4, all of which are oriented at physically transferring the ownership of land: land redistribution, land negotiation, and land colonization. Data on these land reform policies were collected directly from land reform agencies as well as primary and secondary sources.[1]

Distinguishing between these three distinct land reform policies provides greater analytical leverage for testing the theory. Whereas land redistribution presents a clear threat to landed elites, consistent with the theoretical discussion, land negotiation poses at most a mild threat and land colonization poses no threat at all. Land redistribution should therefore be associated with lower veto points and a coalitional split between political elites and landed elites, but this is far less true of land negotiation or land colonization.

Each type of land reform is measured in the number of hectares transferred per country-year. Since countries have different sizes and geographical topographies, and therefore different endowments of land that may be used for agricultural purposes, the land reform variables are normalized by total cultivable land to generate comparable cross-country data. Cultivable land area data is taken from the Food and Agriculture Organization (FAO 2000). The land reform variables are therefore measured as the percentage of cultivable land transferred per year.

Table 5.1 contains descriptive statistics for the land reform variables and other variables used in the analysis. The Land Redistribution measure varies from 0 percent to 62.84 percent of cultivable land. The latter value corresponds to Nicaragua in 1979 when the Sandinistas expropriated the holdings of Anastasio Somoza and his cronies. Land Negotiation varies from 0 percent to 10.58 percent, and Land Colonization varies between 0 percent and 14.97 percent. Figure 4.2 in Chapter 4 displays detailed graphs of each of the three land reform variables for every country in Latin America from 1930 to 2008.

---

[1] See Chapter 4 and the online appendix for details.

TABLE 5.1. *Summary Statistics*

Variable	Mean	Std. Dev.	Min.	Max.	N
Land Redistribution (% of cultivable land)	0.70	3.58	0	62.84	1,467
Land Negotiation (% of cultivable land)	0.17	0.63	0	10.58	1,395
Land Colonization (% of cultivable land)	0.47	1.23	0	14.97	1,311
Veto Points	0.21	0.21	0	0.69	1,424
Elite Split	0.46	0.5	0	1	1,516
Log GDP	9.93	2.2	5.60	14.24	1,461
Rural Pressure	6.24	0.71	4.32	7.7	1,382
Percent Urban	24.18	15.1	0	65.37	1,482
Riots	0.55	1.24	0	15	1,386
Revolution	0.23	0.42	0	1	1,386
Prior Land Redistribution (% of cultivable land)	27.44	48.95	0	229.77	1,520
Civil Conflict	0.41	0.78	0	3	1,216
Veto Points (modified for military veto)	0.36	0.11	0	0.69	1,407
Left Ideology	0.19	0.39	0	1	1,120
Spatial Lag of Average Land Redistribution	0.69	2.14	0	44.72	1,457
Spatial Lag of Revolution	1.02	1.01	0	6	1,386
Foreign (US) Aid (2011 USD per capita)	14.97	24.91	0	261.42	1,178
Log Wheat/Sugar Ratio	− 0.37	2.27	− 3.59	4.45	1,520
Trade Openness (proportion of GDP)	0.54	0.33	0.05	2.15	1,078
Fuel Income (log, ths. of 2007 USD per capita)	− 4.82	2.39	− 6.91	1.7	1,444
Single-Party Regime	0.07	0.26	0	1	1,298
Military Regime	0.11	0.31	0	1	1,298
Personalist Regime	0.11	0.31	0	1	1,298
Hybrid Regime	0.18	0.38	0	1	1,298

Key Independent Variables: Institutional Constraints and Elite Splits

The two key independent variables in the analysis are institutional constraints to rule and coalitional splits between ruling political elites and landed elites. I capture institutional constraints using a measure of Veto Points (POLCONIII) from Henisz (2002), with data updated to 2007.[2] This measure captures the

---

[2] I filled in several missing values as 0 for observations under dictatorship when there was no legislature and were therefore no veto points, with regime data taken from Cheibub, Gandhi and

feasibility of policy change by identifying the number of independent branches of government (i.e., executive, lower, and upper legislative chambers) with veto power over policy change. It is then modified to take into account the distribution of preferences of the actors that inhabit them. The Veto Points measure varies from 0 to 0.69, with higher values indicating more veto points. The 25th percentile of Veto Points is 0, and the 75th percentile is 0.4. Examples of leaders facing a very high number of veto points include Brazil under Fernando Henrique Cardoso and Chile under Eduardo Frei from 1994 to 2000. Cases of leaders facing no veto points include Fulgencio Batista and Fidel Castro in Cuba and Rafael Trujillo in the Dominican Republic.

It bears emphasizing that the Veto Points variable is not simply tapping democracy. There is substantial variation in the Veto Points measure among democratic regimes *and* among autocratic regimes. Figure 5.1 illustrates this point. The figure plots the mean of Veto Points by political regime episode, with a regime episode defined as an uninterrupted period of either democracy or autocracy. Some episodes of democracy are characterized by few or no veto points, such as Cuba in the 1940s and Peru under José Bustamante. Others such as Brazil and Uruguay since 1985 face high institutional constraints. The right-hand side of Figure 5.1 demonstrates that autocratic regimes are much more likely than democracies to have no veto points. Yet half of the autocratic regime episodes have a positive number of veto points for at least some years. A quarter have higher than the average number of veto points across the entire dataset. Take Mexico as an example: Veto Points grew in number over the course of the PRI's rule, varying from 0 in the early years to 0.39 before its democratic transition. This tracks well with how Mexico scholars conceive of constraints to the PRI's rule (e.g., Magaloni 2006), and it directly accounts for the constraining role that legislatures can indeed play in autocratic regimes (e.g., Wright 2008).

Although Veto Points should be a good proxy for institutional constraints, it represents a lower bound given the possibility that other actors, such as the military or judiciary, can constrain reform initiatives. The military is perhaps a particularly important potential veto player to consider from an empirical perspective. If the military plays a more important constraining role under dictatorship than it does under democracy, this raises the question of whether the Veto Points measure is strictly comparable across democracies and dictatorships.

I test two modified versions of the Veto Points measure to address these potential concerns. The first, discussed in greater detail later in this chapter, is a measure of Veto Points that I modify in order to take into consideration the role of the military as a potential de facto veto player. This modified measure also varies between 0 and 0.69, but the 25th percentile is now 0.33 and the 75th percentile is 0.404. The results presented later in the chapter primarily employ

Vreeland (2010) and legislature data taken from Wright (2008). The results are very similar if these observations are left as missing.

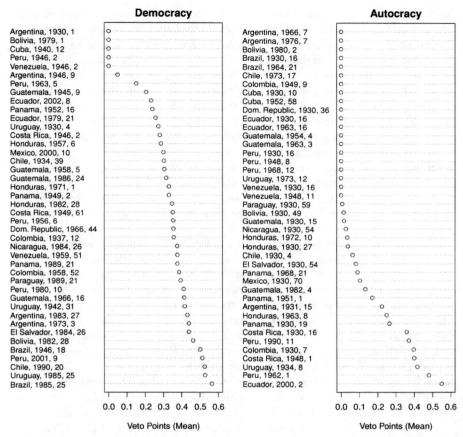

FIGURE 5.1. Veto Points across Political Regimes in Latin America, 1930–2008. *Note:* This figure plots the mean of Veto Points over a particular political regime episode, calculated as an uninterrupted period of either democracy or autocracy. Regime episodes are listed according to the country, the year the particular regime episode began, and the number of years the regime lasted. A regime episode is listed as beginning in 1930 if it began on or before this year, and the duration of these regime episodes is calculated since 1930. Data on Veto Points are from Henisz (2002), with data updated to 2007. Political regimes are coded according to Cheibub, Gandhi, and Vreeland (2010).

the unadjusted Veto Points measure, although I also present a specification with the modified measure that takes into account the military as a veto player. The main results are nonetheless similar using the modified measure.

The second alternative Veto Points measure is an additional measure of Veto Points (POLCONV) from Henisz (2000), with data updated to 2007. This measure accounts for the judiciary as another independent branch of government (alongside the executive, lower, and upper legislative chambers) that has veto power over policy change.[3] Like POLCONIII, this measure takes into account the distribution of preferences of the actors that inhabit various veto points. The measure varies between 0 and 0.89. The 25th percentile is 0 and the 75th percentile is 0.56. This measure, however, has a serious drawback: data on the judiciary are only coded back to 1960. It therefore provides much less coverage than the POLCONIII measure. Unfortunately, there are no other systematic and reliable data on judicial independence in Latin America in the pre-1960 period that could be used to extend this variable. I consequently used this measure in a series of robustness tests but focus on the results using POLCONIII in the analyses in this chapter because there is much better temporal coverage for the latter variable. The main results, however, are again similar in both statistical and substantive terms using the POLCONV measure.[4] This is not particularly surprising: these measures are correlated at 0.84. Governments characterized by effective legislative veto players are also more likely to have independent judiciaries.

The second key independent variable is the coalitional split between ruling political elites and landed elites. Chapter 2 provides a detailed discussion of these elite groups. I code coalitional splits between landed elites and political elites using a host of country-level primary and secondary sources. When ruling political elites are landed elites, when they are appointed by landed elites, or when their rule is fundamentally materially supported by landed elites, I code Elite Split as a 0. It is otherwise coded as 1. In this latter case, the ruling political elite is often actively avoiding alliances or significant material support from landed groups. Table 5.1 indicates that slightly less than half of all country-years during the period were characterized by elite splits. Democracies account for 48 percent of all country-years in which there was an elite split. Sources and details of the coding decisions in each case are located in the appendix online.

To understand how elite splits are coded in practice, recall that Chapter 2 defines the ruling political elite as being comprised of key military players and civilian politicians and important political appointees, and it is typically headed by an elected executive under democracy and a dictator or junta under autocracy. I restrict the focus on civilian politicians to the executive branch given its primacy in land reform initiatives. Key political appointees include those that occupy cabinet positions and the appointed leadership of the main agencies, if indeed these individuals are appointed. Top military officers may also constitute political elites – most often, although not exclusively, under dictatorship – if they are critical political players that have considerable policy influence. To code elite splits, I first examine whether ruling political elites are themselves

---

[3] POLCONV also accounts for independent sub-federal entities as a veto player when those entities impose substantive constraints on national fiscal policy. Brazil is the only country coded as such in Latin America during this period. Sub-federal entities therefore had very little impact on the analysis.

[4] The full results can be found in the book's online appendix.

landed elites or whether they are appointed by landed elites (e.g., if the head of state is indirectly elected by a legislature dominated by landowning interests). If this condition is satisfied, I code an elite split as being absent. If the first condition is not satisfied, I next determine whether landed elites provide substantial financial, logistical, repressive, or other material support that fundamentally bolsters the ability of political elites to rule in office. If this second condition is satisfied, I code an elite split as being absent regardless of the first condition. By contrast, an elite split is present if neither the first nor the second condition is satisfied. Evidence that the ruling political elite actively avoided alliances or significant material support from landed groups aids in coding the presence of an elite split.

One particularly useful piece of information in constructing the elite split variable aside from whether the executive is a member of the landed elite is the composition of the cabinet. A strong landed elite presence in the cabinet, where landed elites take on the role of ruling political elites, signals the lack of an elite split. One illustrative example is Argentina from 1910 to 1940, during which 40 percent of all cabinet appointments went to members of the Rural Society, the most prominent organization of large landowners (Teichman 2002, 509). Powerful landed interests also held key government posts under Pedro Aramburu, Arturo Frondizi, and José Maria Guido during the 1955–1970 period. Another example is Arturo Alessandri's presidency in Chile. Alessandri won office in 1932 with support from the Radicals, who, despite their rhetoric supporting workers, nonetheless followed their *latifundista* and capitalist leadership that frequently allied with traditional elites (Petras 1969, 121). Indeed, they joined Alessandri's oligarchic cabinet.

Although cabinet composition often helps with coding elite splits, the classification is not as mechanical as this. On the one hand, large landowners can gain status as political elites if they are appointed to important agencies that lack cabinet portfolios or are simultaneously powerful military players that intervene directly in governing. Landed elites may also ally with political elites in more informal ways. Recall the example of the Aspillaga family in Peru from Chapter 2. This powerful planter family brazenly supported the dictator Luis Miguel Sánchez Cerro through massive financial contributions and even offered the use of their private railway to the military to counter disparate uprisings. Yet they did so outside of the public limelight in order to avoid retribution from future leaders (Gilbert 1977). Many other landed oligarchs collaborated with the Aspillagas in supporting Sánchez Cerro. This case is therefore not coded as an elite split.

One example of an elite split, by contrast, is General Juan Velasco's rule in Peru. Discussed in detail in Chapter 6, Velasco and a small group military officers (the Earthquake Group) seized power in 1968 and ruled with the support of the military to the exclusion of landed elites. Most officers in Velasco's inner circle came from Peru's outlying provinces and were born to largely impoverished families. Similarly in Paraguay, long-time ruler and Colorado Party leader

Alfredo Stroessner (1954–1989) constructed a narrow cabinet composed primarily of military figures that had few regional interests or coherent substantive economic interests (Lewis 1980, 115). They were selected on the basis of loyalty.

Elite splits, however, are not simply concentrated in military regimes – a point I return to in greater depth later in this chapter. Among military regimes, 42 percent of military regime country-years had elite splits, which is slightly less than the 47 percent of country-years for autocracies overall. Elite splits were also present in regimes where leaders that were split from landed elites consolidated personal power to the exclusion of other elites (e.g., Trujillo in the Dominican Republic) and in regimes that built dominant political parties that drew from outside of traditional landowning elites (e.g., Castro in Cuba and the PRI in Mexico).[5] At the same time, elite splits occurred in many democratic regimes where leaders were elected from political parties that excluded landed elites and then appointed ministers and agency heads within the executive largely to the exclusion of powerful landowners (e.g., Evo Morales in Bolivia, Juan José Arévalo and Jacobo Árbenz in Guatemala, Daniel Ortega in Nicaragua, and Luiz Inácio Lula da Silva in Brazil). Chapters 6 and 7 elaborate on the coding of elite splits across periods of dictatorship and democracy throughout most of the twentieth century and into the twenty-first century in Peru and Venezuela, and Chapter 8 discusses the coding of elite splits in Egypt, Hungary, Taiwan, and Zimbabwe.

It is important to note that information about land reform was not used in the coding of the Elite Split variable. The reason is obvious: inferring an elite split from the implementation of a land reform program would induce bias in favor of my hypothesis.[6] Cases can and do go against the grain of the argument, both when there is land redistribution absent an elite split and when there is no land redistribution in the presence of both an elite split and low institutional constraints. Examples of the former include trailing redistribution in the Dominican Republic after 1966 and Mexico after its 2000 transition,

[5] Notwithstanding the PRI's efforts to develop peasant dependency on the state in Mexico, peasants were a major cornerstone of the PRI's political coalition in post-revolutionary politics (e.g., Sanderson 1984). Landowners as a class did not have a completely solid or consistent position in the coalition throughout the PRI's rule. Among northern, central, and southern pre-revolutionary landed elites, only selected ascendant northern landowners were able to forge an alliance with the governing coalition for a period following Cárdenas, but even this alliance was not sufficient to prevent large-scale land redistribution in the north by Díaz Ordaz and Echeverría in the late 1960s to early 1970s (Albertus et al. 2014).

[6] One consequence is that I code elite splits forward in time when a ruling coalition that is split from landed elites and has entirely destroyed landed elites as a class persists in office. Doing so ensures that land reform is not influencing the elite split variable in these cases by eliminating the possibility of a split, and biases against finding results in favor of the theory. Although the wholesale destruction of all landed elites in a country for any substantial time is absent in Latin America with the exception of Cuba, it has occurred in a handful of cases outside the region such as in the Soviet Union, China, and South Korea.

Peru in the 1980s, Brazil in the 1990s, and low-level redistribution in Colombia for much of the period from the early 1960s until 2000. Examples of a lack of land redistribution despite an elite split and low institutional constraints include Peru and Venezuela in the late 1940s and Ecuador in the 1950s. Chapter 8 provides additional examples of disconfirming cases outside of Latin America. Yet as the analysis indicates, these cases are the exception rather than the rule.

Control Variables

The models include a series of other time-varying determinants of redistribution whose omission may confound the results. The log of real GDP, measured in thousands of constant 1970 dollars and taken from the Oxford Latin American Economic History Database (OXLAD), is included because higher levels of wealth may capture the capacity of a state to implement land redistribution.[7]

I include a control for rural pressure from below since this may increase land reform (Barraclough 1973; Thiesenhusen 1995). In particular, governments may use land redistribution to court the lower classes as a base of regime support (Levine 1998; Turits 2003). Rural Pressure is measured by value added agriculture per dweller in the agricultural sector. The size of the agricultural sector, measured in millions of constant 1970 dollars and taken from OXLAD, relative to the size of the agricultural population, taken from Vanhanen (2009), taps land pressure and should be lower when the amount of land and the value of agriculture are high relative to the size of the rural labor force. I invert this measure for ease of interpretation so that higher values indicate higher land pressure and log it to normalize its distribution. As expected, Argentina and Uruguay score at the bottom end of the land pressure measure within Latin America. These countries have historically had low population densities and relatively fertile land, leading to less labor-repressive institutions in the rural sector, the absence of a traditional peasantry, and low land pressure (Engerman and Sokoloff 2002; Lapp 2004). By contrast, consider the example of the Bolivia, which takes some of the highest values on the land pressure measure. The overwhelming majority of Bolivia's population prior to 1952 lived in the highlands and most peasants worked on haciendas under *colonato* (Thiesenhusen 1995). Population density and land pressure were high whereas agricultural productivity was low, because large landowners left portions of their estates uncultivated and exploited cheap peasant labor over mechanization for the purposes of production (Turovsky 1980).

The models also include Percent Urban, from the Correlates of War data, to proxy for the importance of agrarian reformation and the demand for land

---

[7] Results are similar using log real GDP per capita. I also tested a measure of the debt ratio to capture circumstances in which governments are not able to fund redistribution because of fiscal constraints. The coefficient on this variable was negative, as expected, but it was never statistically significant.

reform (Huntington 1968). Demand for land reform may decline with rising urbanization and make land reform less politically salient.

The models sequentially add several further controls to this basic set. Riots, taken from Banks's CNTS Data Archive, proxy for the threat of rural insurrection that is sometimes supported by an urban alliance. As Acemoglu and Robinson (2006) indicate, popular unrest may yield concessions in the form of redistribution. The Banks measure, unfortunately, is far from perfect due to potential urban bias. I therefore substitute this measure for Civil Conflict in some model specifications. This variable, with data taken from UCDP-PRIO (Themnér and Wallensteen 2013), picks up fine-grained gradations of conflict and in particular helps tap rural insurgency. I code this variable on an ordinal scale from 0 to 3, with 0 for no civil conflict, 1 for conflict short of 25 battle-related deaths, 2 for more than 25 but fewer than 1,000 battle-related deaths, and 3 for 1,000 or more battle-related deaths.[8] Because these data are only available for years after 1946, however, I rely principally on Banks's riots measure despite its imperfections.[9] I also include a measure of revolution to tap active, popular threats. Revolution, taken from Banks's CNTS Data Archive, may result in large-scale redistribution and also reduce institutional constraints to rule (Boix 2003).

Lastly, I include Percent Prior Land Redistribution, measured as the cumulative percentage of total land redistributed since 1930. This variable captures the idea that the likelihood of major land redistribution may be influenced by the amount of past redistribution in a country. A government with higher institutional constraints that follows a redistributionist dictatorship may be less likely to implement its own redistribution program.

POLITICAL INSTITUTIONS, ELITE SPLITS, AND LAND REDISTRIBUTION

I begin investigating the link between land reform on the one hand and political institutions and elite splits on the other hand by examining bivariate relationships. This section focuses on land redistribution in order to engage most directly with the main theoretical argument.

Figure 5.2 plots the data for land redistribution, elite splits, and veto points for every country in Latin America over the 1930–2008 period. There is substantial variation in all three of these variables. Consistent with the theory, nearly all of the spikes in land redistribution across the region coincide with splits between political and economic elites, which are indicated by the shaded regions of the graphs. But the theory is not limited to the effect of elite splits on land redistribution. Elite splits must arise amid low institutional constraints

---

[8] Results are similar using a dichotomous measure of civil conflict based on a threshold of twenty-five battle-related deaths.

[9] See Chapter 6 for more fine-grained measures of rural unrest in the case of Peru.

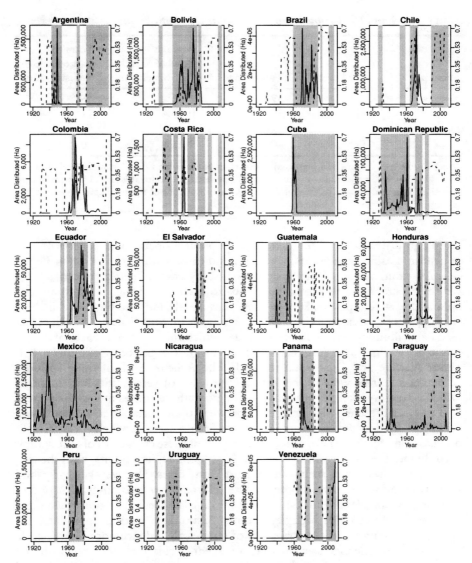

FIGURE 5.2. Land Redistribution, Elite Splits, and Veto Points in Latin America, 1930–2008. *Note:* Solid lines indicate land redistribution. Dashed lines indicate veto points, taken from Henisz (2002), with data updated to 2007 and the right-hand-side y-axes indicating scale. Years of elite splits are shaded in gray. Data on land redistribution and elite splits was compiled by the author.

TABLE 5.2. *Land Redistribution by Elite Splits and Veto Points*

Elite Split	Veto Points	Total Years	Average Yearly Land Redistribution	Years of Large-Scale Redistribution
Yes	Low	374	2.16%	56
	High	300	0.47%	11
No	Low	388	0.17%	6
	High	404	0.02%	0

Note: Cutoff between low and high veto points is set at the mean value during the period (0.21). Average yearly land redistribution is expressed as a percentage of cultivable land. Large-scale redistribution is defined as land redistribution greater than 3 percent of the total cultivable land in a given year.

to rule in order for land redistribution to occur. I operationalize institutional constraints using veto points, which are indicated with dashed lines in Figure 5.2. An examination of the basic data case by case indicates strong support for the theory. Land redistribution tends to occur when there is both an elite split and low veto points. Several cases that clearly indicate this trend include Bolivia, Brazil, Mexico, Nicaragua, Panama, Peru, and Venezuela. Figure 5.2 also helps illuminate the conditions under which the two major cases of democratic reform in Latin America occurred during the period: Chile under Salvador Allende and Guatemala under Jacobo Arbenz. Both of these episodes of democratic rule were characterized by a value of veto points less than 0.2, which is roughly the 15th percentile for democratic countries during the period.

Table 5.2 presents the relationship between these variables in tabular form. The table divides country-years in the dataset into cases in which elites are split and cases in which they are not split. For each of these categories of elite split, it then divides the data again by low and high levels of veto points, with the cutoff between these set at the mean value of Veto Points. The average yearly land redistribution when there is both an elite split and low veto points is 2.16 percent of cultivable land. This far exceeds average land redistribution when there is either no elite split or high veto points. A similar pattern is apparent if we examine the number of country-years of large-scale redistribution. Large-scale redistribution is defined as more than 3 percent of cultivable land redistributed in a given country-year. This threshold captures cases that are generally referred to in the literature as major land reforms.[10] There were fifty-six years of large-scale redistribution under conditions of an elite split and low veto points. High veto points and the lack of an elite split yields far fewer episodes of major land redistribution.

---

[10] Shifting the threshold up or down does not substantially change the distribution of episodes of large-scale redistribution.

Although these bivariate relationships support the theoretical argument, a host of other variables may also influence land redistribution. Failing to control for these variables may confound the observed patterns. Other factors, such as secular trends in land redistribution or unobserved time-invariant heterogeneity across countries, may also impact these bivariate associations. I therefore turn to a series of regressions that address these issues in a rigorous manner.

STATISTICAL ANALYSES OF LAND REFORM

I report a series of panel regression models using tobit and Ordinary Least Squares (OLS) specifications. I primarily model land reform using tobit models, which take into account the censored nature of the data. This is important because there are a significant number of country-years in which there was no land reform. Roughly one-fourth of all country-years had no land reform at all. In this case, using OLS models will yield biased coefficients. Yet because tobit models have some shortcomings, such as bias when using unit-level fixed effects, I also use OLS models for robustness tests. I cluster standard errors by country across the tobit models in order to adjust estimated errors for any arbitrary patterns of correlation within countries, such as serial correlation and correlation resulting from country-specific components. The OLS models address heteroskedasticity, serial correlation, and contemporaneous correlation using Driscoll-Kraay standard errors with a Newey West adjustment with a one-order lag length.

The dependent variable across the Table 5.3 models is Land Redistribution, which is measured as the percentage of cultivable land redistributed per country-year. The theory developed in the previous chapters holds that the two key factors that determine whether land redistribution will occur are the institutional concentration of political power and elite splits. Because land redistribution is predicted to occur when veto points are low and there is an elite split, the models include Veto Points, Elite Split, and an interaction of these two terms. If the theory is correct, the effect of elite splits on land redistribution should be greater when the number of veto points is lower.

Model 1 of Table 5.3 presents the results of a tobit model that includes the main control variables, Veto Points, Elite Split, and an interaction term between Elite Split and Veto Points.[11] As expected, the coefficient on Elite Split is positive and strongly statistically significant, and the coefficient on the interaction term is negative and highly significant. The results are similar in Model 2, which includes year dummies to control for common shocks and secular trends in land reform. Perhaps the most prominent example is President John F. Kennedy's

[11] The Table 5.3 results are very similar if the independent variables are all lagged by one year. However, since the theory suggests that the key independent variables should operate quickly on land redistribution rather than with a lag, the main results are presented with unlagged independent variables.

TABLE 5.3. *Land Redistribution, Political Institutions, and Elite Splits in Latin America, 1930–2008*

	Tobit							OLS	
	Model 1	Model 2	Model 3	Model 4	Model 5	Model 6	Model 7	Model 8	Model 9
Veto Points	4.423	6.281**	6.490**	7.737**	5.079	10.473**	7.296**	0.183	1.438
	(3.319)	(3.151)	(3.279)	(3.615)	(3.307)	(4.444)	(3.517)	(0.550)	(0.857)
Elite Split	8.987***	8.590***	8.142***	7.988***	7.386***	9.433***	7.515***	1.707***	2.808***
	(2.418)	(2.294)	(2.223)	(2.207)	(2.345)	(2.387)	(2.177)	(0.424)	(0.704)
Elite Split* Veto Points	−14.198***	−14.443***	−13.378***	−13.390***	−10.398***	−16.466***	−11.794***	−1.924*	−4.791***
	(4.409)	(4.773)	(4.945)	(4.807)	(4.789)	(4.978)	(4.562)	(1.019)	(1.498)
log(GDP)	0.347	0.505	0.493	0.474	0.348	0.069	0.714**	−0.114	0.818
	(0.356)	(0.332)	(0.340)	(0.354)	(0.353)	(0.267)	(0.290)	(0.095)	(0.566)
Rural Pressure	3.692*	3.152*	2.967*	2.761*	3.227**	3.102*	3.007*	0.074	0.794
	(1.883)	(1.661)	(1.615)	(1.531)	(1.574)	(1.651)	(1.592)	(0.210)	(0.533)
Percent Urban	0.163*	0.096	0.084	0.054	0.084	0.121*	0.039	0.019*	−0.006
	(0.084)	(0.071)	(0.068)	(0.065)	(0.072)	(0.073)	(0.070)	(0.010)	(0.015)
Riots			0.710*	0.679*		0.666*	0.671*	0.431	0.491*
			(0.395)	(0.384)		(0.363)	(0.387)	(0.250)	(0.259)
Revolution			2.344	2.304		2.290	2.471*	0.973**	1.057**
			(1.478)	(1.466)		(1.514)	(1.461)	(0.409)	(0.391)
Percent Prior Land Redistribution				0.018*	0.019*	0.031**	0.016	0.014**	−0.000
				(0.010)	(0.010)	(0.015)	(0.014)	(0.006)	(0.008)
Civil Conflict					1.504*				
					(0.855)				
Year Effects	NO	YES	YES	YES	YES	YES	YES	YES	YES
Region Fixed Effects	NO	NO	NO	NO	NO	NO	YES	YES	NO
Country Fixed Effects	NO	NO	NO	NO	NO	NO	NO	NO	YES
Observations	1,283	1,283	1,201	1,201	1,097	932	1,201	1,201	1,201

Note: $* p < 0.10$; $** p < 0.05$; $*** p < 0.01$ (two-tailed)
Dependent Variable: Percent Land Redistribution. Standard errors clustered by country in parentheses in Models 1–7. Models 8–9 use Driscoll-Kraay standard errors. Model 6 limits the sample to 1930–1992. Constants and time dummies are not shown. Country fixed effects are controlled for via within transformation in Model 9.

156

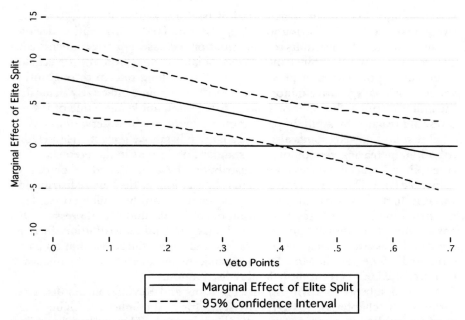

FIGURE 5.3. Marginal Effects of Elite Split on Land Redistribution as Veto Points Vary.

initiation of the Alliance for Progress in 1961 following the Cuban Revolution (see, e.g., Montgomery 1984), which provided US aid to "attack archaic tax and land-tenure structures." Cold War pressures and global conditions during the 1960s and 1970s were more conducive to autocratic rule and ISI strategies that favored industrial elites, whereas by the 1980s and 1990s conditions had shifted toward support of democratization and economic orthodoxy that benefited landed elites as well. At the same time, both peasants and elites in and out of government were aware of land reform (or the lack thereof) in the region, which influenced pressure for land reform and affected government decisions about whether and when to address it (Tai 1974; Thiesenhusen 1989).

The results hold after controlling for Riots and Revolution in Model 3 and for Prior Land Redistribution in Model 4. Both Rural Pressure and Riots are positive and statistically significant in Model 4, as expected. Revolution is positive but just short of statistical significance ($p < 0.12$). Prior redistribution is positive and statistically significant, although its substantive significance is very low.

To ease interpretation of the interaction terms, Figure 5.3 plots the marginal effect of an elite split on land redistribution as the number of veto points varies. Using the Model 4 coefficients, the marginal effect of an elite split on land redistribution is positive until Veto Points is 0.6, which is close to the maximum for this variable. It is only statistically distinguishable from 0 at the 95 percent level,

however, until Veto Points reaches 0.4. Therefore, while elite splits are positively linked to land redistribution, their effect on land redistribution declines
as the institutional constraints to redistribution increase. For governments with
a large number of veto points, the absence of landed elites from the top echelon
of executive power cannot prevent them from stalling reform through other
venues, such as legislative minorities. Indeed, veto points effectively neutralize
the influence of an elite split on land redistribution above the value of 0.4 – a
threshold reached by a full 26 percent of the country-year observations.

Elite splits and veto points also have a large substantive impact on land redistribution. Increasing veto points two standard deviations in the presence of an
elite split in Model 4 reduces land redistribution by an estimated 5.6 percent of
cultivable land. This is nearly two standard deviations of the land redistribution
variable. In the absence of any veto points, the rise of an elite split increases land
redistribution by a predicted 8.0 percent of cultivable land. Rural pressure also
has an important, though more muted, impact on land redistribution. Increasing Rural Pressure two standard deviations increases land redistribution by an
estimated 3.9 percent in Model 4. Increasing the number of riots by one leads
to a predicted 0.7 percent more land redistribution.

Model 5 substitutes Civil Conflict for Riots and Revolution. As discussed
earlier in the chapter, the UCDP-PRIO data for civil conflict are higher quality than for the other measures, particularly for riots. The results are similar:
Civil Conflict is positively and statistically significantly linked to land redistribution at the 10 percent level. Because the results are similar and the post-1945
data availability for the UCDP-PRIO Civil Conflict variable truncates all earlier
observations in the sample, I return to using the Riots and Revolution variables
in the remaining models. None of the results are sensitive to this decision.

Model 6 returns to the Model 4 specification but restricts the sample to
country-years up until 1992. Mexico announced the end of its seventy-five years
of land redistribution in 1992, which some interpreted as the death knell of
land reform in Latin America (e.g., Kay 1998). Most countries in the region
were predominantly urban by the 1990s, and open borders and other neoliberal reforms that deepened in the 1990s put downward pressure on land redistribution. Because this period also coincides with the spread of democracy in
the region, it may be driving a spurious association between veto points and
land redistribution. Model 6 gauges whether the temporal period is driving the
results in previous models. The results are nonetheless similar. The interaction
term between Elite Split and Veto Points remains highly statistically significant
and actually increases slightly in magnitude.

Model 7 returns to the full sample but now introduces region fixed effects
for Central America, the Caribbean, the Andes, and the Southern Cone.[12] The
inclusion of region fixed effects controls for region-specific and time-invariant
heterogeneity (e.g., geography or history), which may jointly influence a

---

[12] See the appendix online for details on how these regions are coded.

country's elite splits and veto points as well as its level of land redistribution. The Model 7 results are very similar to those in Model 4. Revolution now reaches statistical significance, and the presence of a revolution increases land redistribution by an estimated 2.5 percent of cultivable land. Although it would be ideal to include country fixed effects, conditional fixed effects tobit models unfortunately cannot be estimated, and unconditional fixed effects tobit models are biased.[13]

Models 8–9 shift to an OLS framework to examine the robustness of the previous findings to an alternative distributional assumption and the inclusion of country fixed effects. Model 8 is specified similarly to Model 7 and includes region fixed effects. The results are largely similar to those in Model 7. The interaction of Elite Split and Veto Points is statistically significant, although it declines in magnitude. Indeed, every coefficient declines in magnitude. This is not surprising. It is well known that under the assumptions of a left-censored data generation process, OLS parameter estimates are downward biased while Tobit estimates are consistent and asymptotically normal (Amemiya 1973).

Model 9 includes country fixed effects in the regressions to account for country-specific and time-invariant heterogeneity that might influence both a country's elite splits and veto points and its amount of land redistribution. The main results again hold. The interaction term is negative and highly statistically significant, whereas Elite Split is positive and significant. Rural Pressure is positive but short of statistical significance ($p = .15$). Riots are again positive and statistically significant, as is Revolution. Consistent with the model predictions outlined earlier in the book, this indicates that the rural threat from below encourages land redistribution. The coefficient on Percent Prior Land Redistribution loses statistical significance.

Alternative Explanations for Land Redistribution

There are several prominent alternative explanations for redistributive policies such as land redistribution as well as a potential measurement concern with Veto Points. Table 5.4 first addresses the measurement issue and subsequently examines each of the alternative explanations empirically to test the robustness of the results in Table 5.3. All of the Table 5.4 regressions use tobit models. The results are nonetheless similar using OLS.

Including the Military as a Potential Veto Player

Although Veto Points should be a good measure of institutional constraints, it captures a lower bound since other actors such as the military or judiciary can constrain the executive's capacity to implement land reform. The military is one potentially critical veto player that is not coded in the commonly used

---

[13] A set of unconditional fixed effects tobit models nonetheless yields similar results.

TABLE 5.4. *Alternative Explanations for Land Redistribution, 1930–2008*

	Military Veto in Autocracy	Partisan Orientation	Contagion	Foreign Aid	Geographic Endowment	Economic Openness	Declining Land Value	Non-Revol. Regimes	Autocratic Regime Types
	Model 1	Model 2	Model 3	Model 4	Model 5	Model 6	Model 7	Model 8	Model 9
Veto Points	4.419	6.437*	7.686**	7.238*	7.113*	6.923*	8.428**	1.371	4.869
	(5.735)	(3.895)	(3.679)	(3.711)	(3.758)	(3.783)	(3.997)	(0.927)	(3.618)
Elite Split	10.063***	7.353***	7.882***	7.478***	7.761***	6.134***	8.533***	2.910***	7.855***
	(3.785)	(2.516)	(2.243)	(2.278)	(2.160)	(2.418)	(2.363)	(0.897)	(2.300)
Elite Split* Veto Points	−14.661*	−14.035**	−13.218***	−12.269**	−12.534***	−9.931*	−14.973***	−5.135**	−13.398***
	(7.941)	(5.904)	(4.882)	(4.893)	(4.826)	(5.164)	(5.227)	(1.902)	(4.994)
log(GDP)	0.486	0.337	0.487	0.363	0.581	0.708*	0.410	0.415	0.507
	(0.356)	(0.343)	(0.339)	(0.371)	(0.389)	(0.430)	(0.388)	(0.418)	(0.374)
Rural Pressure	3.036*	1.761	2.873*	2.786*	2.706*	3.414**	2.219	0.882	2.695*
	(1.568)	(1.289)	(1.578)	(1.549)	(1.547)	(1.729)	(1.398)	(0.536)	(1.591)
Percent Urban	0.064	0.037	0.053	0.062	0.047	0.062	0.044	−0.017	0.046
	(0.063)	(0.061)	(0.065)	(0.070)	(0.067)	(0.060)	(0.066)	(0.018)	(0.073)
Riots	0.665*	0.440	0.634	0.557	0.696*	0.472	0.650*	0.398	0.614
	(0.376)	(0.339)	(0.410)	(0.383)	(0.381)	(0.372)	(0.375)	(0.313)	(0.382)
Revolution	2.244	1.706	2.376	2.577*	2.360	2.112	2.264	0.874*	2.485
	(1.439)	(1.201)	(1.525)	(1.548)	(1.450)	(1.362)	(1.431)	(0.437)	(1.562)
Percent Prior Land Red.	0.017**	0.025***	0.018*	0.017*	0.020*	0.017*	0.022**	0.002	0.020*
	(0.008)	(0.009)	(0.010)	(0.010)	(0.011)	(0.010)	(0.010)	(0.008)	(0.010)
Left Ideology		1.598							
		(1.343)							

Spatial Lag of Land Redist.			−0.013						
			(0.116)						
Spatial Lag of Revolution			−0.295						
			(0.454)						
Foreign Aid				−0.015					
				(0.016)					
Log Wheat/Sugar Ratio					−0.198				
					(0.306)				
Trade Openness						2.663			
						(1.989)			
Fuel Income							0.031		
							(0.291)		
Single-Party									−1.203
									(2.212)
Military									−3.362
									(2.435)
Personalist									−0.115
									(1.789)
Hybrid Regime									−2.240
									(1.388)
Year Effects	YES	YES	YES	YES	YES	YES	YES	YES	YES
Observations	1,192	1,010	1,169	1,095	1,201	1,018	1,174	1,011	1,125

Note: * $p < 0.10$; ** $p < 0.05$; *** $p < 0.01$ (two-tailed)
Dependent Variable: Percent Land Redistribution. All models are estimated with a tobit specification. Standard errors are clustered by country in parentheses. Model 8 drops Bolivia, Cuba, Mexico, and Nicaragua. Constants and time dummies are not shown.

Veto Points measure.[14] In addition, ignoring the military as a veto player could bias the results if autocratic regimes that score low on the Veto Points measure face greater policy constraints because of the role of the military than those of regimes that score high on the Veto Points measure. Of course, it is not a priori clear that the Veto Points measure used earlier is systematically underestimating constraints under dictatorship: half of autocratic regime episodes have a positive number of veto points for at least some years, and a quarter have more than the average number of veto points across the entire dataset (see Figure 5.1). The military also plays a key role in generating many autocratic regimes and consequently often has a direct voice in critical policy affairs rather than standing alongside as a potential constraint. Nonetheless, in order to more rigorously examine this measurement concern I generate a second, modified version of the Veto Points measure that takes into account the military as a potential de facto veto player.

In constructing this modified Veto Points measure, it is important to recognize that militaries may act as veto players under democracy as well as dictatorship. Mainwaring and Pérez-Liñán (2014) fortunately provide a coding of all cases of democratic regimes in Latin America since 1900 wherein "military leaders or the military as an institution are able to veto important policies in … areas not related to the armed forces." They code major and partial violations of civilian control on the part of the military for each government administration. I treat both of these as indicating the presence of an independent military that serves as a veto player. I also code the military as a veto player in all instances where these authors coded a regime as being autocratic. Finally, I code the fractionalization of the military (relative to the executive's preferences) as one-half.[15] This indicates that at least half of the military supports the executive when it has veto player status. A regime is unlikely to stand with majority opposition from a politically involved and powerful military. This is a rather weak assumption; Acemoglu and Robinson (2006), for instance, assume that the military is completely aligned with the ruling elite. This assumption also biases against the main findings in two ways. First, to the extent that the military is aligned with the executive under dictatorship, the true measure of institutional constraints should approach the main measure employed, whereas this measure would make constraints under dictatorship appear artificially high. Second, it is conceivable that the military may act as a veto player under democracy but not need to explicitly violate civilian control if it is sufficiently power to deter any civilian action that would elicit a response. Adjusting the constraints measure in the way outlined earlier would underestimate the true number of veto points under democracy in these cases.

---

[14] See the section on Key Independent Variables earlier in this chapter for further discussion of the judiciary.

[15] See the online appendix for further coding details on this measure.

Model 1 of Table 5.4 substitutes the modified Veto Points measure in the Model 4 specification of Table 5.3. As anticipated, the uninteracted Veto Points term is now smaller in magnitude than it is when using the original Veto Points measure. The interaction between the modified Veto Points measure and Elite Split nonetheless remains statistically significant, as does the uninteracted Elite Split coefficient. Because this alternative measure is likely a substantial overestimate of institutional constraints in some regimes, I return to the original Veto Points measure in further model specifications.

Ideology

The first alternative explanation for the main findings is ideology. In particular, it could be that left-wing governments are those that are most motivated to redistribute. Left-wing governments may also be most likely to split from landed elites and cut the latter out of their cabinets and ruling coalitions. Indeed, a number of authors find that ideology matters for redistribution, particularly in the context of advanced democracies (Boix 1998; Bradley et al. 2003; Korpi 1983). Yet these results seem to be less robust outside of developed, postindustrial democracies.[16] Huber, Mustillo, and Stephens (2008), for instance, fail to find a relationship between redistribution and left-wing government in the context of social spending in Latin America. This finding, however, may be driven in part by the temporal scope of their study, which falls predominantly within the neoliberal era. As the authors note, "left and right were extremely constrained in finding resources for social policy" during this period (Huber et al. 2008, 423).

Model 2 of Table 5.4 includes a dummy variable for left-wing executives in order to test whether the omission of a control for left-wing government may be driving the findings. Data are taken from Huber et al. (2012), who build on the comprehensive work of Coppedge (1997). Huber et al. (2012) code executive ideology for the 1945–2001 period. I extend the data up to 2008 under the same coding rules.[17]

Whereas Left Ideology is positive in Model 2, it fails to reach conventional levels of statistical significance. Its magnitude is also relatively small in substantive terms. The main results hold: the interaction term between Elite Split and Veto Points is negative and statistically significant, and its magnitude is very similar to that in the tobit models of Table 5.3. In short, examining land redistribution over a longer period than that for which Huber et al. (2008) examine social spending yields a similar result: ideology does not have a measurable impact on redistribution.

A host of examples support both the empirical finding that many non-left leaders have implemented land redistribution and the finding that many left

---

[16] One notable exception is Verdery (1991), who highlights redistribution as a central legitimating principle in the socialist economies of the former Soviet Union and Eastern Europe.

[17] I also filled in missing observations when there was no clear left executive.

leaders have not implemented it. Take Gustavo Díaz Ordaz in Mexico. He carried out massive land reform in northern Mexico that, while different in many respects, paralleled Lázaro Cárdenas's large-scale redistribution in southern Mexico in the 1930s. Yet by virtually every account, Díaz Ordaz was as an example of a heavy-handed "law and order" conservative politician. His successor, Luis Echeverría, who by all accounts was a leftist and populist leader, did not distribute land more intensely than other presidents or even than Díaz Ordaz.

Díaz Ordaz is far from the only leader who implemented land redistribution absent a leftist ideology. The military leaders Emílio Garrastazu Médici and Ernesto Geisel implemented a land reform program in Brazil that shared a number of important characteristics with that proposed by the populist president João Goulart whom they had overthrown. The military dictator Hugo Banzer, almost uniformly characterized as right-wing, colonized large swathes of land in Bolivia's east but also continued land redistribution, because peasants remained a key cornerstone of Bolivia's governing coalitions to the exclusion of traditional landed elites (Klein 1992). Eduardo Frei, a Christian Democratic president in Chile from 1964 to 1970, accelerated the conservative Jorge Alessandri's land reform and began a large-scale program of land redistribution that Salvador Allende subsequently deepened. Joaquín Balaguer in the Dominican Republic, José Napoleón Duarte in El Salvador, and Oswaldo López Arellano in Honduras, not leftists by any account, also initiated and implemented substantial programs of land redistribution. The absence of a strong link between ideology and land redistribution seems to extend beyond Latin America as well. The Shah of Iran and the Hashemite King Hussein of Jordan implemented land redistribution programs despite having few ideological motivations for doing so. Land redistribution under most of these leaders instead followed the theoretical logic laid out in previous chapters and supported here empirically: it occurred in the presence of elite splits when veto points were relatively low.

There are also a host of leftist executives who have either not pursued land redistribution or have not been successful in doing so in the face of political opposition. Several examples include José Figueres in Costa Rica, Juan José Arevalo in Guatemala, Bustamante in Peru, Gabriel González Videla in Chile, and several left executives in Uruguay, such as Luis Batlle Berres, although he did increase land negotiations. Again, the evidence is not limited to Latin America. Bardhan and Mookherjee (2010), for instance, demonstrate a tenuous link between Left Front rule and land reform in West Bengal.

Development Trends and Contagion

Development trends and contagion spillovers in land redistribution are another set of alternative explanations for the findings. Cold War competition between US capitalism and Soviet communism, for instance, substantially influenced theories and strategies of development in Latin America and in developing countries in other regions (e.g., Haggard and Kaufman 2008; Hirschman 1968;

Montgomery 1984). Import substitution industrialization and a heavy state hand in the economy, including in land reform programs, replaced liberal policies in many countries. These policies were often, though not exclusively, implemented by autocratic governments. The debt crisis and the fall of the USSR then ushered in neoliberalism, which favored privatization and the establishment of individual property rights (e.g., De Soto 2003). Land redistribution began to fall from the agenda (Thiesenhusen 1995), although it never entirely died (Lipton 2009). Indeed, the rise of the New Left has brought a return to statist and interventionist economic policies in countries such as Argentina, Bolivia, Ecuador, and Venezuela (Roberts 2007; Weyland 2009). Several of these countries have new land reform programs.

Most of the models in Table 5.3 and all of the models in Table 5.4 account for secular trends and exogenous shocks influencing land redistribution through the inclusion of year fixed effects. The regressions therefore examine variation in land redistribution that is not explained by broader development trends and external pressures to the region.

In addition to broader secular trends in land redistribution resulting from external pressure and development trends, land redistribution may also have been subject to contagion effects, wherein redistribution tends to spill over or cluster in certain neighborhoods. Take for instance the Cuban Revolution. Countries such as Colombia (Tai 1974), the Dominican Republic (Stanfield 1989), and Honduras (Stringer 1989) responded to the Cuban Revolution via land reform efforts aimed at undercutting similarly threatening domestic social and economic conditions that seemed conducive to revolution. Cuba tried to directly increase the likelihood that nearby countries would follow its path by aiding left-wing insurgencies in countries such as Venezuela (Powell 1971). Indeed, Wright (2001) traces much of the social conflict, development of militaries, and interventions in Latin America during the Cold War to the Cuban Revolution.

In order to address the possibility that the results are driven by contagion effects, Model 3 includes a spatial lag of land redistribution that captures the one-year lagged average of the percent of land redistributed in the other states within a country's neighborhood.[18] Model 3 also introduces a spatial lag of the count of revolutions in the other states within a country's neighborhood, given that fears about conditions being ripe for social unrest and spillover effects in collective action may induce reform even absent substantial neighboring land redistribution.[19] Both of these variables are statistically insignificant, and the main results are similar to previous models. The interaction term between Elite Split and Veto Points remains highly statistically significant and negative. The statistical significance of the other coefficients is similar to Model 4 of

---

[18] A three-year running average yielded similar results.
[19] I also tested a variable that captured the latitudinal distance from Cuba, with similar results. Furthermore, a three-year running sum of revolution in the region yielded comparable results.

Table 5.3. These results are also consistent with OLS Models 8 and 9 in Table 5.3 that account for contemporaneous correlation using Driscoll-Kraay standard errors.

A closer look at the data displayed in Figure 5.2 suggests that broad development trends and local contagion effects cannot explain the findings. Land redistribution occurred in many countries prior to the rise of ISI and the Cuban Revolution, and it persisted in many countries despite neoliberal reforms. The Mexican Revolution ushered in major land redistribution well before the Cold War. Paraguay implemented small-scale land redistribution following the Chaco War in the late 1930s–early 1940s. Bolivia and Guatemala initiated major reforms in the early 1950s. In Costa Rica, initial efforts at agrarian reform began in the 1940s as a result of economic dislocations caused by World War II (Seligson 1980). The debate over land reform in the 1950s spurred the passage of a reform law in 1961 shortly after the Punta del Este Conference and the creation of the US-sponsored Alliance for Progress. However, as Rowles (1985, 212) emphasizes, a 1955 bill and the agrarian reform debate of the 1950s underscores "the erroneous belief that the issue of agrarian reform arose, and that the 1961 agrarian reform was passed in Costa Rica, primarily in response to the Charter of Punta del Este."

Similarly, the adoption of neoliberal policies did not immediately or unilaterally spell death for land redistribution, although it did place downward pressure on reform. Land redistribution in Mexico continued for a decade after the debt crisis and then only slowly tapered off after the declared end of reform in 1992 as pending applications and the Zapatista Uprising led to the continuation of limited reform. In Paraguay after Stroessner's fall, the expropriation of unproductive land was reaffirmed in the 1992 constitution, and campesinos "continued to articulate their demands in policy language laid out in the 1960s" well into the 2000s (Hetherington 2009, 226). Furthermore, some countries that wholesale adopted Washington Consensus policies, such as Bolivia and Ecuador, initiated or proposed new land reform programs that carved out space for land redistribution while maintaining many neoliberal macroeconomic policies.

Foreign Aid and Foreign Influence
Foreign influence, particularly via foreign aid, may also have impacted where and when governments in Latin America pursued land redistribution. Foreign influence could have operated in a manner distinct from secular development trends or contagion effects. In particular, foreign aid increasingly supported land reform in the 1960s while simultaneously placing pressure on political institutions.

The most prominent expression of foreign influence was Kennedy's 1961 Alliance for Progress. Announced in March of 1961 shortly after the Cuban Revolution, the Alliance for Progress required that Latin American countries undertake land reform in order to be eligible for foreign aid (Thiesenhusen

1989). Foreign aid then helped finance the operation of land reform offices, studies regarding the viability and need for land reform, and loans and grants that were used for land improvement and rural infrastructure improvement. Further elaboration of the Alliance for Progress goals as well as implementation strategies were agreed upon at the Punta del Este Conference in August that same year. US aid made up the bulk of foreign aid to Latin America during this period (Lapp 2004, 32).

Yet several aspects of land redistribution suggest that foreign aid cannot explain the variation in land redistribution or its link with fewer veto points in the political system. First, as Lapp (2004) aptly demonstrates and the discussion about development trends in the previous section confirms, land redistribution and land reform more generally began well *before* the Alliance for Progress. Furthermore, the Alliance for Progress was not simply a US-sponsored idea. It built in part on Operation Pan America, which stemmed from Brazilian President Juscelino Kubitschek's 1958 initiative that proposed economic and social policy changes to address problems of underdevelopment in the region.

Second, the United States explicitly stipulated that it would not provide foreign aid for redistributive land reform. Land reform efforts had to respect private property in order to be eligible for assistance. Aid could not be used to fund the expropriation of land. Domestic actors in many Latin American countries nonetheless constructed stronger redistributive land reforms despite the reservations of US officials (Levinson and de Onís 1970).

Third, only a small amount of foreign aid actually went to land reform. Between 1962 and 1968, only 10 percent of US aid was dedicated to promoting land reform (Lapp 2004, 32). Half of that went to commercial farmers, and only 15 percent of it targeted land reform or reform beneficiaries.

Although relatively little foreign aid was used for land reform efforts, and although aid could not be used for land redistribution per se, it is conceivable that via a "substitution effect," countries that pursued land negotiation or colonization with foreign assistance may have faced less domestic pressure for redistributive reform. Alternatively, countries that received aid may have reallocated part of their domestic budgets to fund land redistribution and used foreign aid to cover other development expenditures. In order to more rigorously examine the effect of foreign aid on land redistribution, Model 4 of Table 5.4 therefore introduces a control variable that measures US foreign aid.[20] I use data on aid transfers from the US Agency for International Development's (USAID) "Greenbook" dataset, US Overseas Loans and Grants, Obligations and Loan Authorizations. Data on aid transfers are available beginning in 1945. I code the variable Foreign Aid using both economic and military aid, although the results are the same for each of these measures if disaggregated. Foreign Aid is calculated on a per capita basis in constant 2011 dollars.

---

[20] Results were similar using data on all foreign aid in the form of official development assistance (ODA) from the World Bank's World Development Indicators.

The coefficient for Foreign Aid is statistically insignificant in Model 4. Its magnitude is also relatively small. As with Models 2 and 3, the main results are robust to testing this alternative explanation.

This result is perhaps not surprising given that US aid supporting land reform also tended to emphasize democracy (Lapp 2004, 29). Yet at the same time, the United States supported the ousting of democratically elected leaders that had either implemented or attempted to implement major land reforms in countries such as Chile and Guatemala.[21] This is an alternative channel of foreign influence. This channel also, however, fails to explain the link between land redistribution and the presence of elite splits amid few veto points.[22] Nondemocratic leaders that seized power in these cases following military coups were allied with elites and had few incentives to engage in large-scale land redistribution. This works against the main hypothesis. An analysis of the bulk of evidence instead supports Lapp's (2004, 35) conclusion that "[d]omestic political concerns outweighed the influence of international actors."

Geographical Endowments

Another potential alternative explanation for the findings resides in countries' differing geographical endowments. Gallup, Sachs, and Mellinger (1999), for instance, emphasize how geography and factor endowments impact countries' paths of development by influencing how their institutions evolve. More specific to Latin America, Engerman and Sokoloff (2002) argue that initial geographic conditions in the New World colonies led to different labor and land tenure relations that influenced the long-term structure of institutions as well as inequality. This may influence the results if countries with different endowments had differing levels of demand for land reform that are not captured by the controls and if the response in the form of land redistribution varied with these endowments (e.g., because of institutions) in a way that differed from the region as a whole.

Engerman and Sokoloff (2002) highlight three distinct types of New World colonies. The first encompasses those colonies with climates and soils that were well suited for the production of sugar and other highly valued crops characterized by extensive scale economies associated with the use of slaves (e.g., Brazil and Cuba). This created a large, poor, disenfranchised segment of population. The second category includes colonies with a substantial native population that survived European contact and in which land and native labor was possessed by a small number of colonists, which led to large-scale estates and mining

---

[21] The military leaders that took power, Augusto Pinochet in Chile and Carlos Castillo Armas in Guatemala, returned some of the expropriated land back to the original owners. These cases are the only instances of upward redistribution. They are included in the analysis, although excluding them does not materially change the results.

[22] An explicit control for US foreign influence in favor of democracy, taken from Mainwaring and Pérez-Liñán (2014), was statistically insignificant while the main results were otherwise similar.

characterized by tribute (e.g., Mexico and Peru). The third category spans colonies with populations of European descent who had similar levels of human capital where land was abundant and capital requirements were low. Native populations were insubstantial, and climates and soils were suited to wheat and other grains for small-scale farming rather than slave labor (e.g., Argentina and Uruguay). In contrast to this last category, colonies based on large-scale extraction became characterized soon after initial settlement by extreme inequality in wealth, human capital, and political influence. These colonies tended to adopt institutions that were significantly less progressive and more extractive, and were less likely to fund local public investments and services. These patterns became self-reinforcing and persisted well into the twentieth century and even up to the present day (Engerman and Sokoloff 2002, 84).

Several of the models in Table 5.3 help address the impact of geographical endowments on land redistribution outcomes. Region fixed effects control for variation in fixed endowments in the colonial period to some degree in the tobit specification in Model 7 of Table 5.3 and in the OLS specification in Model 8 of Table 5.3. But there still may be unexplained country-level variation in endowments in the region fixed effects models. Country fixed effects in Model 9 of Table 5.3 control in a more fine-grained manner for variation in geographical endowments and initial levels of landholding inequality or land tenure patterns.

In order to directly control for geographical endowments in a tobit model, I follow Easterly (2007) and control for persistent structural inequality resulting from geographical endowments as the log of the percent of land suitable for wheat to the percent of land suitable for sugar cane. Those places with a history of wheat being grown on family farms have had persistent egalitarian institutions, and places with a history of sugar cane being grown on large plantations have had persistent inegalitarian institutions and policies.

Model 5 in Table 5.4 presents the results. The coefficient for the Log Wheat/Sugar Ratio is statistically insignificant. Although geographical endowments may have influenced other public policy outcomes, they had little impact on land redistribution adopted in the period of analysis here.

Economic Openness

There is a large and sophisticated literature on the influence of economic openness on redistribution and the welfare state (e.g., Avelino, Brown, and Hunter 2005; Kaufman and Segura-Ubiergo 2001), which provides the foundation for a fifth rival explanation for the findings. One of the key questions in this literature is whether governments respond to increased economic integration with policy choices that are oriented toward cutting social programs in order to maintain competitiveness (the efficiency hypothesis) or whether they increase social insurance to protect citizens from the fluctuations of global capitalism (the compensation hypothesis). It is also possible that economic openness and globalization more generally have increased social atomization and undermined collective action, thereby enabling governments to implement policies contrary to the interests of the poor (Kurtz 2004). Economic openness may provide a rival explanation for the findings if openness both encourages democracy and discourages redistribution (Acemoglu and Robinson 2006; Boix 2003; Freeman and Quinn 2012). Although this explanation is linked to some degree with the development trends discussed previously in this chapter, it nonetheless varies more on a yearly basis and may operate through different causal pathways.

Following much of the literature (e.g., Albertus and Menaldo 2014), I use trade openness as a measure of economic openness. Trade Openness is measured as exports plus imports as a share of GDP and is taken from the Penn World Tables 6.2. Data are available beginning in 1950. Model 6 of Table 5.4 includes the Trade Openness measure. The coefficient on Trade Openness is positive but far from statistically significant. As in Models 1–5 of Table 5.4, the main results also hold. Openness is therefore not driving the results.

Declining Land Value

An additional alternative explanation of the findings resides in the possibility that land redistribution is easier to implement when land values are declining. This argument suggests that economic opportunity either plays a more important role in reform than political opportunity or that economic opportunity impacts the political conditions relevant for reform. When the value of land is declining, landed elites will be weaker. They may also be less willing or capable of resisting below-market compensation for their land if they fear a long-term negative price trend. Consider the falling land prices and agricultural output in Ireland that sparked the Land War and the Plan of Campaign in the 1870s and 1880s. Amid the agricultural crisis, poor tenant members of the Irish Land League and Irish National League refused to pay rents and physically intimidated their Anglo-Irish landlords. The stance of recalcitrant landlords caused William Gladstone to turn on the traditional landed aristocracy, which led him "down the path to land reform," a path that included the Land Acts (Cannadine 1999, 111–112).

Declining land prices could explain the observed results if they encourage an elite split or weaken checks on authority so that the state has a greater incentive and capacity to expropriate these landowners. Unfortunately, there are no widely available historical data on the prices of agricultural land, especially given incomplete tax registries in the region. It is nonetheless possible to create a proxy for declining land values using natural resources revenues. A large literature indicates that natural resource wealth induces so-called Dutch Disease, wherein a strengthening currency makes exports more expensive abroad and therefore reduces the competitiveness of exporting firms in international markets (e.g., Corden 1984; Roemer 1983). Increasing oil production in Venezuela beginning in the 1930s, for instance, led to an overvalued exchange rate that squeezed agro-exporters and shrank the agricultural sector (Karl 1990, 7). The relative value of land in Venezuela declined concomitantly: many landowners sold their property to pursue commercial ventures in urban areas (Karl 1990).

I use Fuel Income in Model 7 of Table 5.4 to capture natural resource dependence, with data taken from Haber and Menaldo (2011). Fuel Income is measured as income per capita earned from oil, natural gas, and coal, expressed in thousands of constant 2007 dollars.[23] I log this measure to normalize its distribution. The coefficient on fuel income is positive, as expected, but far from statistical or substantive significance. The main results again hold. Declining land values thus do not undermine the association between land redistribution, elite splits, and institutional constraints.

Revolutionary Regimes

Another potential critique of the regressions rests with the potentially disproportionate influence of "revolutionary regimes" on the findings. Prior to the creation and widespread use of data from the Polity Project, the Przeworski et al. (2000) dichotomous regime type measure, and the classification of "semidemocracies" (Mainwaring, Brinks, and Pérez-Liñán 2001) and "competitive authoritarianism" (Levitsky and Way 2010), some Latin America scholars considered revolutionary regimes to be a distinct type of political regime. One of the early and influential contributions on revolutionary regimes is Anderson's (1967) work. Anderson distinguishes between traditional, reformist, and revolutionary regimes, and examines how these regime types influenced policy outcomes.

The clearest cases of revolutionary regimes are those that took power in Bolivia, Cuba, Nicaragua, and Mexico. One might argue that guerilla and popular movements that seized power in these countries yielded stable, highly progressive dictatorships that were committed to implementing large land reforms. Model 8 of Table 5.4 excludes all of these countries from the analysis. The Revolution control predictably drops in substantive and statistical significance. The main results for Elite Split and Veto Points nonetheless remain strong. The interaction term between these variables maintains its statistical and substantive significance. Revolutionary regimes are therefore not driving the results – indeed, the results of a modified jackknife analysis indicate that no single country is driving the findings. One could also argue that the land redistribution outcomes under the revolutionary regimes examined are consistent with the theory: landed elites were cut out of ruling coalitions in these cases and institutional constraints to rule were low, thereby enabling land redistribution.

Autocratic Regime Types

The omission of autocratic regime types may also be biasing the results. Geddes (2003) argues that military, single-party, and personalist regimes have characteristically different support coalitions and incentives for seizing and retaining

---

[23] An alternative measure of natural resource dependence that also includes precious and industrial metals was positive and borderline statistically significant ($p = 0.10$). The substantive significance was relatively small, however, and it only strengthened the main results.

power. These distinct autocratic regime types may impact land reform policies in several ways. First, they differ in the extent to which they rely on broad-based coalitions that reach deep into society and distribute goods to the population. Wright (2009) demonstrates that single-party regimes have larger coalition sizes, necessitating either public goods provision or the widespread distribution of particularistic goods to broad-based social groups in order to maintain regime stability. In rural societies with a large peasantry, this may make policies such as land redistribution attractive given that it can broaden the regime's rural base of support. Second, because autocratic regimes differ in their support coalition sizes, elite splits may be more likely in some circumstances than in others. More narrowly based regimes – military and personalist regimes – may more often cut landed elites out of their coalitions, thereby enabling reform. This could be particularly true of military regimes if these regimes come about as the result of a moral hazard problem between authoritarian elites and their repressive agents, giving the latter a wide-ranging ability to implement radical policies when they seize power from those they are supposed to serve.

Several descriptive patterns in the data cast initial doubt on the hypothesis that autocratic regime types are driving the findings. First, average yearly land distribution across the dataset is 1.25 percent of cultivable land for autocratic regimes with a personalist component, 1.17 percent for regimes with a military component, and 1.42 percent for regimes with a single-party component – not a particularly large difference.[24] With respect to elite splits under military regimes, it is not the case that most dictatorships with elite splits in the region were military regimes. To the contrary, of the 317 country-years of elite splits under dictatorship in Latin America for which data on autocratic regime type are available, only 58 (18 percent) were military regimes. Among military regimes, 42 percent of country-years had elite splits, which is slightly less than the 47 percent of country-years for autocracies overall and also less than the 44 percent of democratic country-years with elite splits. In short, elite splits are far from simply being shorthand for military dictatorship.

In order to more systematically test the impact of autocratic regime type on land redistribution, I include dummy variables for single-party, military, and personalist regimes along with a dummy for hybrids of these distinct types. Data are taken from Wright (2009). Wright's data span the period from 1946 to 2002. I extend these data back in time and up to 2008 when the same regime was in power before or after the period covered by Wright's data.

Model 9 of Table 5.4 presents the empirical results examining the effects of autocratic regime types. The baseline omitted category is democratic regimes. The coefficients for single-party, military, personalist, and hybrid regimes are all statistically insignificant. An F-test of the joint significance of the autocratic regime type variables indicates that we cannot reject the hypothesis that these

---

[24] The single-party average is also driven disproportionately by Mexico, which makes it difficult to distinguish a "single-party effect" from a Mexico effect.

coefficients are all equal to zero ($p = 0.15$). Autocratic regime types therefore have no discernable impact on land redistribution once we account for elite splits and institutional constraints to rule.

Economic Inequality

Another set of omitted variables that may potentially be driving the findings is related to economic inequality. It is possible, for instance, that the empirical findings are in fact consistent with social conflict theory. Boix (2003) offers one circumstance in which redistribution can occur when there are few institutional constraints: when inequality is high and revolutionary movements seize power and expropriate assets for redistribution among the masses. Acemoglu and Robinson (2006) offer another scenario: when inequality is in a middling range and the masses pose a current and future credible threat of revolt. In contrast to cases where the masses pose a transitory threat to the regime and therefore demand democracy as a credible commitment to future redistribution, an autocratic regime may be able to pacify the masses with redistribution when they are well organized and will continue to be so in the future.

I tested these arguments in several ways, although I do not present the results in Table 5.4 for reasons of space. To capture inequality, I used the Gini coefficient from the Standardized Income Distribution Database (SIDD). This Gini coefficient, constructed by Babones and Alvarez-Rivadulla (2007), reflects an adjustment to the raw UN WIID data that standardizes differences in scope of coverage, income definition, and reference unit across countries. A second measure of inequality, which yielded similar results, was taken from Boix (2003), who uses "high-quality" observations from Deininger and Squire (1996) and then averages them over five-year periods to increase coverage and reduce measurement error. I also create squared terms for these inequality measures to test the Acemoglu and Robinson (2006) hypothesis.

Inequality either alone or with a squared term was consistently statistically insignificant, and the main results hold. Land redistribution does not simply occur because there is a high, or medium, level of inequality. A more direct test of these authors' hypotheses, however, may be an interaction between inequality and collective action. To tap collective action, I return to the measure of Civil Conflict from UCDP-PRIO. I separately tested both an ordinal measure of Civil Conflict, as detailed earlier in this chapter, and a dichotomous measure that captures the yearly threshold of twenty-five battle-related deaths. The results were similar in both cases.

I included Inequality, Civil Conflict, and the interaction between these variables as a preliminary test of Boix's (2003) hypothesis. The interaction term and the Inequality term were statistically insignificant, which indicates that rebellion amid high inequality does not necessarily give way to land redistribution. This test, however, could include incumbent elites fighting off rebellions in addition to revolutionary regimes sweeping to power under conditions of high inequality. As a separate test, I therefore threw out the observations of above-average inequality for the clearest cases of revolutionary regimes that were discussed in the context of Model 8 of Table 5.4: Bolivia, Cuba, Mexico, and Nicaragua. The results were similar to those in Model 8. Although the coefficient on the interaction between Elite Split and Veto Points declined somewhat, it remained highly statistically significant and its magnitude remained substantively large.

To test Acemoglu and Robinson's (2006) hypothesis, I included linear and quadratic terms for Inequality, Civil Conflict, and the interaction between Civil Conflict and each Inequality term. The main results again hold. Furthermore, the interaction terms between the inequality variables and Civil Conflict did not support Acemoglu and Robinson's (2006) hypothesis. None of these variables were statistically significant using the Boix inequality data. And the findings ran *opposite* to those hypothesized by Acemoglu and Robinson using the SIDD data: the interaction of Civil Conflict with the linear term for Inequality was negative, whereas the interaction of Civil Conflict with the squared term for Inequality was positive.

"Upward" Land Redistribution and Indirect or Market-Based Redistribution

A final possible explanation for the findings is that they do not explicitly consider policies or laws that may have the effect of increasing land concentration. Mexico's Ley Lerdo is a classic example of a law that was used as legal cover for the enclosure of lands held by smallholders and indigenous communities (often through customary law) by large landowners. If this type of law is disproportionately implemented under the same political conditions that yield land redistribution – an elite split alongside low institutional constraints – then the estimated effects of these conditions on redistribution in the regression models may be upward biased. The empirical analyses also do not take into account policies and laws (e.g., land titling or market-based incentives) that may lead to redistribution or concentration by influencing land transfers in the private market.

To capture the effects of these other policies, I used a first-difference of Van-hanen's (2009) family farms measure as a dependent variable to pick up changes in the distribution of landholdings. The family farms measure is calculated as the area of family farms as a percentage of the total area of holdings. Changes in this measure tend to pick up the sum of the other policy tools that can influence land redistribution mentioned earlier in this chapter, but they do not effectively proxy for land redistribution itself, in part because many redistributive land reforms redistributed land to collectives, cooperatives, and communities rather than in family farm–sized plots.[25]

None of the results, which are reported in an appendix online, suggest that indirect forms of land redistribution occur under conditions opposite of those hypothesized in the theory. Policies other than land redistribution that have a progressive impact on the distribution of landholdings are, if anything,

---

[25] See the online appendix for further discussion.

weakly linked to the same political conditions under which redistributive land reforms occur: low veto points and elite splits.

Political Institutions, Elite Splits, and Land Redistribution "Substitutes"

Table 5.4 rejects a host of alternative explanations for the main finding that most land redistribution occurs in the presence of both elite splits and few veto points. The control variables introduced to test many of these alternatives are consistently statistically insignificant. The restricted temporal span of data available to test the rival hypotheses also reduces the number of overall observations in the analyses. As a result, I drop these additional controls in further specifications. I now turn instead to additional land reform data that can aid in testing the observable implications of the theory.

Although land redistribution presents a clear threat to landed elites, land negotiation and land colonization do not. In the case of land negotiation, landed elites lose their land but receive full market-value compensation. Landed elites may resist this loss when their identity is tied to the land – especially if valuable social and political networks are linked to landholding – or if they oppose the idea of peasants receiving it. Despite market-value compensation to private owners in Brazil's ongoing massive land reform, for instance, large landowners often attempt to organize to avoid the land invasions that can trigger expropriation by the state (Albertus, Brambor, and Ceneviva 2015). Yet landed elites in the case of land negotiation face at most a minor direct material loss. In the case of land colonization, landed elites do not lose any of their property, or the social ties that go with it, at all. If the theoretical mechanisms are correct, the interaction between Elite Split and Veto Points should therefore be much less important for land negotiation. It should be irrelevant for land colonization. Indeed, landed elites may at times support land colonization as a way to relieve pressure from the landless on the property of large landowners.

Table 5.5 examines these empirical implications. Models 1 and 2 are specified in the same way as Models 4 and 7 of Table 5.3, but now employ Land Negotiation as the dependent variable. Several differences from the Table 5.3 models are worth noting. First, the interaction terms between Elite Split and Veto Points in these models are much smaller in magnitude than they were for Land Redistribution: 6.4 times smaller in Model 1 and 6.7 times smaller in Model 2, which includes region fixed effects. A two standard deviation increase in veto points in the presence of an elite split in Model 1 only reduces land negotiation by 0.88 percent. The Elite Split variable that is not interacted is statistically significant in Models 1 and 2, which indicates that elite splits are linked to land negotiation in the absence of veto points. Yet as with the interaction term, the substantive significance is much smaller than it is for the Table 5.3 models of land redistribution. An elite split absent veto points leads to an estimated 0.70 percent increase in land negotiation. The Veto Points variable is positive and statistically significant in Models 1 and 2. A greater number of veto points

TABLE 5.5. *Land Negotiation, Land Colonization, and Aggregate Land Reform, 1930–2008*

Dependent Variable	Land Negotiation			Land Colonization			All Land Reform		
	Model 1	Model 2	Model 3	Model 4	Model 5	Model 6	Model 7	Model 8	Model 9
Veto Points	2.050**	2.062***	2.347***	1.880*	1.044	0.707	4.770**	4.560**	4.594*
	(0.848)	(0.792)	(0.860)	(1.054)	(0.901)	(1.022)	(2.334)	(2.282)	(2.405)
Elite Split	0.695*	0.508*	0.570*	0.282	0.552	0.336	4.058***	3.927***	3.669***
	(0.380)	(0.301)	(0.332)	(0.497)	(0.392)	(0.386)	(1.092)	(1.115)	(1.126)
Elite Split* Veto Points	-2.086**	-1.754**	-2.102**	-2.005	-1.745	-1.185	-7.985***	-7.348**	-6.951**
	(0.931)	(0.720)	(0.847)	(1.562)	(1.083)	(1.128)	(2.916)	(2.991)	(3.065)
log(GDP)	0.032	-0.006	0.012	0.180	0.192*	0.224*	0.173	0.199	0.235
	(0.095)	(0.111)	(0.128)	(0.136)	(0.106)	(0.125)	(0.242)	(0.315)	(0.325)
Rural Pressure	-0.470	-0.379	-0.502*	1.600***	1.179***	1.224***	1.291**	1.264*	1.162*
	(0.313)	(0.261)	(0.261)	(0.453)	(0.365)	(0.382)	(0.638)	(0.696)	(0.656)
Percent Urban	-0.009	-0.020	-0.025**	0.022	0.033	0.027	0.021	0.008	-0.007
	(0.016)	(0.013)	(0.013)	(0.027)	(0.030)	(0.029)	(0.034)	(0.035)	(0.036)
Riots	-0.033	-0.037	-0.039	0.080	0.074	0.079	0.450	0.452	0.414
	(0.044)	(0.043)	(0.041)	(0.086)	(0.082)	(0.081)	(0.312)	(0.319)	(0.334)
Revolution	-0.175	-0.122	-0.141	0.472	0.166	0.117	1.512*	1.454*	1.654*
	(0.165)	(0.147)	(0.141)	(0.327)	(0.264)	(0.299)	(0.837)	(0.857)	(0.968)
Percent Prior Land Reform	-0.000	0.000	0.001	-0.001	-0.003	-0.002	0.017***	0.017***	0.018***
	(0.003)	(0.002)	(0.002)	(0.005)	(0.004)	(0.004)	(0.006)	(0.006)	(0.006)
Foreign Aid			0.008**			0.003			0.005
			(0.004)			(0.005)			(0.011)
Year Effects	YES	YES	YES	YES	YES	YES	YES	YES	YES
Region Fixed Effects	NO	YES	YES	NO	YES	YES	NO	YES	YES
Observations	1,142	1,142	1,044	1,080	1,080	1,010	1,042	1,042	972

Note: * $p < 0.10$; ** $p < 0.05$; *** $p < 0.01$ (two-tailed)
Dependent variables are in percentages. All models are estimated with a tobit specification. Standard errors are clustered by country in parentheses. Constants and time dummies are not shown.

is therefore linked to greater land negotiation in the absence of an elite split. Finally, and in contrast to Table 5.3, Rural Pressure, Riots, and Revolution are not linked to more land negotiation.

Other factors may influence land negotiation beyond those included in Models 1–2. Foreign aid might be particularly relevant. As I discuss in the context of Model 4 in Table 5.4, the timing of foreign aid and the fact that US aid was explicitly barred from being used for land redistribution per se undercuts this as an alternative explanation for the observed patterns of land redistribution. Yet foreign aid could be – and was – used for land negotiation. US aid via the Alliance for Progress went to financing land reform offices, studying reform possibilities, and providing grants for critical complements to reform such as rural infrastructure (Lapp 2004). This aided countries such as Venezuela and Colombia in conducting land reform via land negotiation while simultaneously freeing resources to be used to compensate landowners. The magnitude of the effect of foreign aid on land negotiation, however, is likely to be minor. On the one hand, the United States did not provide consistent support for land reform throughout the period. And on the other hand, only a very small portion of US aid went to land reform, even when land reform implementation was at its peak (Lapp 2004, 32).

Model 3 of Table 5.5 introduces Foreign Aid to the Model 2 specification. Foreign Aid is measured on a per capita basis in the same way as it is for Model 4 of Table 5.4. Its coefficient is positive and statistically significant. The magnitude of the effect, however, is relatively small. An increase in US aid per capita by $50, two standard deviations of this variable, yields a 0.4 percent increase in Land Negotiation. The main results in Models 1–2 hold. I also tested the robustness of the results on Land Negotiation to the addition of other variables from Table 5.4. The results continue to hold, and none of these other variables entered as robustly statistically significant.

Models 4–6 of Table 5.5 are specified in the same way as Models 1–3 but use Land Colonization as the dependent variable. As expected, the interaction term between Elite Split and Veto Points is no longer statistically significant in these models. The constituent term for Veto Points is positive in Model 4, suggesting that veto points are linked to greater land colonization in the absence of an elite split, but this finding is not robust to using region fixed effects in Models 5 and 6. In short, elite splits and veto points do not have a sizeable or consistent impact on land colonization outcomes. The key predictor of Land Colonization across Models 4–6 is Rural Pressure. Latent popular pressure from the rural sector for reform is strongly positive and statistically significant across these models. A two standard deviation increase in this variable increases Land Colonization by an estimated 2.3 percent in Model 4 and an estimated 1.7 percent in Model 5. Other types of pressure as captured by Riots and Revolution are consistently positive, but they never reach conventional levels of statistical significance. GDP is also positively linked to colonization. Wealthier states are more likely to dedicate some resources to resettling rural dwellers.

Model 6 includes Foreign Aid. In contrast to Model 3, Foreign Aid is not a robust predictor of Land Colonization.[26]

The null finding for the effect of elite splits and veto points on land colonization is not surprising if we consider the conditions under which colonization occurs. In some cases such as Guatemala in the 1930s, land colonization is repressed in order to restrict the movement of rural labor and increase its supply for large landowners (Wittman and Saldivar-Tanaka 2006). In other cases, like Venezuela under the dictator Pérez Jiménez or Honduras in the 1950s, limited land colonization is encouraged to expand the agricultural base and make more efficient use of public lands. Finally, and speaking more directly to findings for rural pressure, land colonization can also be used as a "safety valve" to reduce pressure from the landless on the property of landed elites. In Colombia, Brazil, and Panama, to name but a few examples, large landowners supported state-led efforts to move potentially volatile landless or land-poor farmers to sparsely populated areas as a way of reducing popular pressure for the redistribution of large estates. In some of these cases, although not always as a part of state-led colonization programs, land colonizers were also used as a cheap way to clear frontier land with poor soil. Colonizers would use slash and burn techniques, farm the land for a year or two, and then move on as elites or land entrepreneurs moved in (e.g., LeGrand 1986).

Given the disparate findings for Land Redistribution, Land Negotiation, and Land Colonization, what conclusions can we draw about the overall determinants of land reform? Do land negotiation and colonization, which represent alternative paths to a more equitable distribution of land, dominate in importance relative to land redistribution during this period? Models 7–9 of Table 5.5 mirror Models 1–3 but use Land Reform – the sum of Land Redistribution, Land Negotiation, and Land Colonization – as the dependent variable. These models therefore provide a complete picture of the determinants of land reform as a whole. The results are similar to those in Table 5.3. This is not particularly surprising given that more land redistribution has occurred than land negotiation or land colonization (see Table 5.1). The association between land reform more generally and the presence of both an elite split and low institutional constraints in Models 7–9 is driven primarily by land redistribution. Revolution is again positive and statistically significant in Models 7–9, as is Rural Pressure. These latter findings indicate that land reform is also more likely when the rural poor form a more credible threat of revolt.

Table 5.5 provides scope conditions for the promises and pitfalls of reform alternatives to land redistribution that hold lessons for contemporary land

---

[26] As with Land Negotiation, I also tested the robustness of the Land Colonization results to the addition of other Table 5.4 variables. The main results consistently hold, and the only variable with some explanatory power was Fuel Income. Land colonization is somewhat more likely amid declining land prices.

reform efforts. I return to this point in greater depth in the conclusion to the book in Chapter 9.

Robustness to Endogeneity Bias

Tables 5.2 to 5.4 provide strong evidence that elite splits amid low veto points provide the most fertile ground for land redistribution. Table 5.5 demonstrates that these conditions have a much smaller effect on land negotiation and no consistent measureable effect on land colonization. But is it possible that the results are affected by endogeneity bias running from land redistribution to coalitional splits between political and economic elites? Perhaps elite splits do not in fact provide incentives for land redistribution. Rather, it may be the case that land redistribution itself, by weakening or destroying landed elites, sets the stage for political elites to form coalitions excluding landed elites. Furthermore, it may be the case that elite splits are collinear with unobserved variables that also impact land redistribution such as the strength or shrewdness of a particular leader. Such an omission could potentially confound the results.

I use an instrumental variable (IV) approach designed to capture the exogenous variation in splits between political and economic elites to address these potential concerns. A valid instrumental variable must satisfy the exclusion restriction. Its effect on the dependent variable should operate exclusively through the potentially endogenous independent variable. In this case, the instrument must be correlated with the dependent variable of Elite Split in a first-stage regression but not correlated with the error term of a second-stage regression where Land Redistribution is the dependent variable.

Two instrumental variables that, from a theoretical perspective, should only influence land redistribution in this indirect manner are a leader's age at the time of assuming power as well as its squared term. I use the variable Leader Age at Entry from the Archigos dataset (Goemens, Gleditsch, and Chiozza 2009) to construct these variables and expect the linear term to be negative and the squared term to be positive, indicating that the likelihood of an elite split decreases as a leader takes office at a higher age and then reverses course and increases once a leader's age at the time of assuming office passes a critical threshold. These instruments satisfy the exclusion restriction from a statistical perspective and are therefore valid ways of capturing the exogenous variation in elite splits. Statistical tests of the overidentifying restrictions never fail to reject the hypothesis that the instruments are valid – orthogonal to the error term in the second-stage equation.

Consider first why relatively younger leaders are more likely to exclude landed elites from their political coalitions. It is useful to draw in part from the discussion in Chapter 2 on the origins of elite splits and the role of the military in society. The internal dynamics of the military change as the demands for warfare increase and militaries are forced to recruit outside the ranks of landed elites. The officer corps becomes socially differentiated as middle- and lower-class recruitment increases. This places pressure on the military's internal hierarchy (Huntington 1968). High-ranking officers with ties to traditional elites may be reluctant to promote junior officers or to modify training curricula. If they accommodate these new officers, they risk changing the role the military plays in politics as its affinity to traditional elites declines (Stepan 1978). But if high-ranking officers fail to accommodate this ascendant new class, they run the risk that alienated junior officers may attempt to overturn the status quo through a coup. Diversity in military recruitment therefore empowers younger officers that have few ties to traditional landed elites. These officers may either directly seize office or place pressure on civilian leaders to shun coalitions with landed elites.

Omar Torrijos in Panama and Rafael Franco in Paraguay are two illustrative examples. Take the case of Torrijos. Born to a large family in a small town in the countryside, Torrijos entered the military academy in San Salvador on a scholarship. The Panamanian bureaucracy grew substantially in the aftermath of World War II as the state took on new development functions and elites attempted to use these functions to their own benefit. State growth also generated a modernizing military/police organization that gained increasing autonomy (Ropp 1992). The police force transformed into a national guard in the 1950s, leading to an influx of academy-trained officers such as Torrijos. In contrast to much of the military leadership, which had ties to business and landed elites, the new officer class had "few personal and family ties to the civilian commercial elite" (Ropp 1992, 223), including large landowners and agro-exporters. When the conservative Arnulfo Arias won the 1968 election with the support of traditional elites, several young National Guard leaders including Torrijos launched a coup to preserve the rising power and autonomy of the National Guard.

Younger non-military leaders are also more likely to split from landed elites even absent military pressure. This is apparent both with rebel leaders that successfully seize power and with nascent political party leaders. Many successful rebel leaders in Latin America began as student organizers or protestors aligned against status quo leaders. Some of the most prominent examples include Castro in Cuba and Ortega in Nicaragua. Rebel movements in the region, with the exceptions of Colombia's festering civil war and Guatemala's civil war, have generally been relatively short-lived, either because they were successful like Castro's and Ortega's, or because they were quickly crushed like Hugo Blanco's movement in the Peruvian highlands and the communist insurgency in Venezuela in the early 1960s (Weitz 1986). Victorious rebel movements therefore typically swept to power young leaders that had few ties to landed elites.

Many nascent mass-based political party leaders were also young when they ascended to power. These leaders tended to have social roots in urban areas where organizational efforts were more fruitful because of population density. Rómulo Betancourt in Venezuela and Arbenz in Guatemala, for instance, were young urban intellectuals that were born in urban centers rather than on large rural estates. These political entrepreneurs built mass-based parties with strong support from urban and rural laborers rather than traditional elites.

Young political elites are not the only ones that are more likely to split from landed elites. Leaders that enter office when they are older are also more likely to exclude landed elites from their ruling coalitions. Older leaders entering office have shorter time horizons and are therefore more likely to pursue myopic coalitions rather than be bound to predominant economic interests (Olson 1993). These leaders are consequently more likely to pursue parochial interests, even if it means circumventing or alienating powerful elites. Take for example Brazil in the 1960s and 1970s under a series of older military rulers that had long been in the military establishment. The first leader, Castelo Branco, began in office by systematically harassing and imprisoning former elite allies (Stepan 1971). Artur da Costa e Silva, Médici, and Geisel sought to bolster the military's strength and autonomy and ruled with a narrow coalition of military allies while also building a broad bureaucracy.

Older leaders are more likely to be elected or brought into government because of a reputation for independence or sustained charisma rather than allegiance to a sector of elites such as landed elites. Long-time charismatic politicians Velasco Ibarra in Ecuador and Juan Perón in Argentina were elected when they were well into their seventies. Balaguer of the Dominican Republic cultivated his reputation as a relative independent across a long series of dramatic shifts in Dominican politics, which aided his repeated election in the 1960s and 1970s.

This discussion suggests that leader age should be related to elite splits in a U-shaped manner. Political leaders that are either young or old at the time they assume office are more likely to split from landed elites than those who are middle-aged when they gain power. I construct the variables Leader Age at Entry and Leader Age at Entry Squared to capture this. Because Elite Split is interacted with Veto Points, the interaction term is possibly endogenous as well. It is therefore necessary to estimate another first-stage regression across the IV models in which the interaction term is instrumented. Following common practice, I instrument the interaction term with interactions between Veto Points and the instruments for Elite Split: Leader Age at Entry and Leader Age at Entry Squared (see, e.g., Ozer-Balli and Sorensen 2010). I include all four instruments in both first-stage regressions per standard procedure.

I conduct a series of IV estimations via the Generalized Method of Moments (GMM). The two first-stage models for each IV regression estimate, respectively, the determinants of Elite Split and the interaction between Elite Split and Veto points. The second-stage model in each IV regression estimates whether the predicted values of Elite Split and Elite Split*Veto Points calculated from the first stages explain variation in Land Redistribution.

Table 5.6 reports the IV regressions. Model 1 includes region fixed effects, similarly to Model 8 of Table 5.3. Model 1a reports the coefficients calculated from the first-stage regression where the dependent variable is Elite Split and

TABLE 5.6. IV and Heckman Estimates of Land Redistribution, 1930–2008

	IV-GMM			IV-GMM			Heckman Elite Split	IV-GMM Split = 1	IV-GMM Split = 0
	Stage 1	Stage 1	Stage 2	Stage 1	Stage 1	Stage 2	Selection Eq.	Stage 2	Stage 2
	Model 1a	Model 1b	Model 1c	Model 2a	Model 2b	Model 2c	Model 3	Model 4b	Model 5b
Veto Points	−6.788***	−0.334	7.819*	−7.076***	−0.184	6.244*		−6.965*	−0.476
	(1.576)	(0.589)	(4.647)	(1.784)	(0.604)	(3.551)		(3.718)	(0.501)
Elite Split			3.686*			4.820**			
			(2.179)			(2.104)			
Elite Split* Veto Points			−18.951*			−15.346**			
			(10.319)			(7.653)			
log(GDP)	0.059***	0.004	−0.157	−0.016	0.048**	1.496**	−0.254	4.136***	0.322
	(0.011)	(0.003)	(0.133)	(0.063)	(0.022)	(0.720)	(0.204)	(1.304)	(0.206)
Rural Pressure	0.011	−0.055***	−0.849	−0.054	−0.028	0.556	−0.369*	1.282	0.442*
	(0.028)	(0.010)	(0.638)	(0.065)	(0.023)	(0.458)	(0.201)	(2.751)	(0.239)
Percent Urban	−0.008***	−0.002***	−0.002	−0.004	−0.004***	−0.043	−0.010	0.003	−0.020**
	(0.002)	(0.001)	(0.024)	(0.003)	(0.001)	(0.033)	(0.009)	(0.063)	(0.009)
Riots	0.007	0.000	0.433*	−0.012	−0.004	0.484**	−0.039	1.074**	−0.103**
	(0.012)	(0.003)	(0.247)	(0.011)	(0.003)	(0.245)	(0.037)	(0.499)	(0.049)
Revolution	0.006	0.008	1.116**	0.027	0.017	1.196***	0.063	1.670**	0.116
	(0.036)	(0.011)	(0.450)	(0.034)	(0.010)	(0.419)	(0.106)	(0.739)	(0.074)

Percent Prior Land Redistribution	0.000 (0.000)	0.000 (0.000)	0.014*** (0.005)	−0.000 (0.000)	−0.002 (0.006)	−0.001 (0.001)	−0.031 (0.021)	0.010*** (0.004)
Leader Age at Entry	−0.071*** (0.017)	0.005 (0.003)		−0.094*** (0.019)	0.004 (0.004)	−0.158*** (0.038)		
Leader Age at Entry Squared	0.001*** (0.000)	−0.000* (0.000)		0.001*** (0.000)	−0.000 (0.000)	0.001*** (0.000)		
Leader Age at Entry* Veto Points	0.234*** (0.059)	0.024 (0.021)		0.260*** (0.066)	0.021 (0.022)			
Leader Age at Entry Squared*Veto Points	−0.002*** (0.001)	−0.000 (0.000)		−0.002*** (0.001)	−0.000 (0.000)			
Inverse Mills Ratio							−0.216 (1.462)	0.256 (0.240)
Year Effects	YES	YES	YES	YES	YES	YES	YES	YES
Region Fixed Effects	YES	YES	YES	NO	NO	NO	NO	YES
Country Fixed Effects	NO	NO	NO	YES	YES	YES	YES	NO
Observations	1,201	1,201	1,201	1,201	1,201	1,288	489	467

Note: * $p < 0.10$; ** $p < 0.05$; *** $p < 0.01$ (two-tailed)

Dependent Variable: Percent Land Redistribution. 2SLS = two-stage least squares. Robust standard errors are in parentheses in IV-GMM models. Models 4–5 are robust to bootstrapping errors in IV-2SLS framework. Country fixed effects are controlled for via a within transformation. The Heckman selection equation for elite splits in Model 3 uses a probit specification. Instruments for Veto Points in second-stage equations in Models 4–5 are Bueno de Mesquita et al.'s (2003) winning coalition size and the lagged three-year average of polity score in a country's region. First-stage equations for Models 4–5 are not shown because of space limitations. Constants and time dummies are not shown.

the independent variables of interest are Leader Age at Entry and Leader Age at Entry Squared. Model 1b reports the coefficients from the first-stage regression where the dependent variable is the interaction between Elite Split and Veto Points. The results suggest that these are good instruments. The first-stage F-statistics are 23.12 and 26.38, which are above the common threshold of 10 that is used to separate strong from weak instruments (Staiger and Stock 1997). Model 1c reports the coefficients calculated from the second stage. Elite Split and its interaction with Veto Points are now the predicted values estimated from the first-stage regressions. As in most of the previous tables, Veto Points and Elite Split are both positive and statistically significant. The sign on the interaction term in Model 1c is negative, as expected, and the estimated coefficient is statistically significant at the 10 percent level. Importantly, a Hansen J-test of the overidentifying restrictions returns a chi-square of 0.548 with a p-value of 0.76. We therefore cannot reject the hypothesis that the instrumental variables are exogenous.

Model 2 tests the robustness of the Model 1 results by using country fixed effects rather than region fixed effects, as in Model 9 of Table 5.3. The results strengthen in both the first- and second-stage regressions. Veto Points, Elite Split, and the interaction of these variables are all statistically significant. The interaction term is negative and statistically significant at the 5 percent level, and its magnitude is similar to that in the tobit models in Tables 5.3 and 5.4. A two standard deviation increase in Veto Points amid an elite split reduces land redistribution by an estimated 6.4 percent of cultivable land. Although the instruments in Model 2b are not individually statistically significant, they remain highly jointly significant in that first stage model ($p < 0.01$).

The IV coefficients in Models 1c and 2c of Table 5.6 for Elite Split and the interaction of Elite Split and Veto Points are notably larger than the OLS coefficients in Models 8 and 9 of Table 5.3. Because the Hansen J-tests indicate that the instruments are valid in Models 1 and 2, the measure of elite splits is most likely endogenous and the direction of bias is apparently against the hypothesis. One possible omitted factor in the non-IV models that may confound the association between elite splits and land redistribution and lead to an underestimate of the true effect is political party strength. Weak political parties may be positively correlated with elite splits, making it more likely that political elites can exclude landed elites from their coalition while the latter cannot effectively organize through a party to capture politics. At the same time, weak parties may be negatively correlated with land redistribution since they tend to be less responsive to citizen preferences.[27] Another factor that would act similarly is whether there is foreign intervention or the threat of foreign intervention to replace leaders. This may put into power parochial leaders that

---

[27] On party competition and redistributive land policy, see, e.g., Bardhan and Mookherjee (2010) and Boone (2009).

have narrow interests or military leaders that have few social ties while simultaneously placing pressure on governments to avoid undertaking land redistribution. Accounting for these and other potential sources of endogeneity implicitly in the IV framework therefore yields a more accurate estimate of the effect of Elite Split and the interaction of Veto Points and Elite Split on land redistribution.

Treating Both Elite Splits and Veto Points as Potentially Endogenous

Models 1 and 2 of Table 5.6 provide evidence that possible endogeneity in the measure of elite splits is not driving the findings. But what if there is also endogeneity bias in the Veto Points measure? It is possible, for instance, that land redistribution or the threat of land redistribution provides incentives for landed elites and other key actors to push for greater institutional constraints to rule via a negotiated pact that protects their interests.

This section addresses this concern. Because the previous section provides some evidence of endogeneity in elite splits, it is important to account for possible endogeneity in both measures simultaneously. One way of doing this is to use a Heckman selection model and an IV approach sequentially.[28] I first use a Heckman selection model to estimate when elite splits are observed. Consistent with Models 1 and 2, I use the variables Leader Age at Entry and Leader Age at Entry Squared to predict Elite Split in the selection equation only. This first stage probit selection equation generates a new variable that contains the non-selection hazard known as the Inverse Mills Ratio. I then split the sample between observations in which Elite Split is coded as 0 and observations where Elite Split is coded as 1. Next I estimate two second-stage equations, one on each subsample of the Elite Split dummy variable. This enables an examination of the conditional effect of Veto Points in the presence or absence of elite splits. Importantly, each of the second-stage equations includes the Inverse Mills Ratio on the right-hand side to adjust for endogenous selection into elite splits. In other words, the adjusted second-stage equations examine the conditional effect of Veto Points based on an estimation of exogenous selection into elite splits.

Each second-stage equation must account for the possibility of endogeneity in Veto Points. To do so, I turn to an IV-GMM approach in each of the second-stage equations. This requires finding an instrument for Veto Points. I identify two instrumental variables for Veto Points. These variables should only influence land redistribution indirectly through Veto Points.

The first way I capture the exogenous variation in Veto Points is with the lagged three-year average of the Polity score in a country's region. This follows

---

[28] It would also be possible to instrument Elite Splits and Veto Points simultaneously in an IV framework. Yet this would require at least six instruments to conduct statistical tests on the overidentifying restrictions to examine the validity of the instruments. It also becomes difficult to interpret the results in a two-step framework (Angrist and Pischke 2008).

empirical research on the diffusion of institutions. Gleditsch and Ward (2006), for instance, find that democracies are more likely to emerge and survive in a friendly environment where there are a greater number of democracies. Diffusion of the institutional components that constitute democracy and contribute to veto points should therefore also be more likely to spread to geographically proximate countries. At the same time, this lagged measure of Polity score in a country's region should not directly induce land redistribution in that country. This logic is further bolstered by the earlier finding in Model 3 of Table 5.4 that regional land redistribution and regional social conditions conducive to revolution do not directly influence land redistribution in a country. Foreign aid is also not a significant predictor of land redistribution in Table 5.4. This suggests that land redistribution is driven primarily by internal country dynamics.

The second way in which I capture the exogenous variation in Veto Points is with the size of the support coalition that is necessary to sustain a leader's rule. Leaders that require broad societal support are more likely to structure this support in the form of legislatures and parties. Leaders that rely on a small number of supporters to maintain power such as military regimes, by contrast, should face fewer institutional constraints – although they still face coalitional constraints. Support coalition size should not directly affect land redistribution if the exclusion restriction is to be satisfied. Several cases of incongruence between support coalition size and veto points help illustrate this point. Consider the Dominican Republic under Balaguer in the early 1970s and Honduras under Ramón Villeda Morales from the late 1950s to the early 1960s. In both of these cases, support coalition size was small and there were elite splits, yet no land redistribution resulted. Redistribution was blocked by the relatively high institutional constraints under democracy.

I capture support coalition size using Bueno de Mesquita et al.'s (2003) measure of the size of the winning coalition (W). W is constructed based on meeting threshold values of three Polity variables (XROPEN, XRCOMP, and PARCOMP) along with a regime being civilian in nature, as coded by Banks's CNTS dataset. Bueno de Mesquita et al. (2003) add one point to W for each of these criteria and then divide by four to scale the measure between 0 and 1. It is worth underscoring their point that W is not simply a proxy for democracy; it incorporates elements of the Polity index that are not highly correlated with the Polity democracy score.[29]

Model 3 of Table 5.6 presents the results of the Heckman selection equation for Elite Split. This model includes country fixed effects. As with Models 1 and 2, Leader Age at Entry and Leader Age at Entry Squared are robustly linked to Elite Split. The linear term is again negative and the squared term positive, as expected. Models 4b and 5b present the second-stage IV regressions on the split

---

[29] Extending the data for W beyond 1999 and using Wright's (2009) data on military regimes to increase coverage because of some missingness in Banks's coding of military versus civilian regimes yields similar, and somewhat stronger, results.

subsamples. Model 4 is run on the subsample where Elite Split is coded as 1, and Model 5 is run on the subsample in which Elite Split is coded as 0. I do not present the first-stage results of the Model 4 and Model 5 IV estimations for reasons of space. As expected, the lagged three-year average of Polity score in a country's region and the size of the support coalition are positively related to Veto Points in the first stages of Models 4 and 5. First-stage F-statistics indicate strong instruments in both Models 4 and 5, and they are jointly significant in both models. Furthermore, from a statistical perspective, the instruments satisfy the exclusion restriction in both subsamples.

The results of the Model 4 and Model 5 second-stage IV regressions confirm the earlier results. Despite the reduced sample size, Veto Points is negative and statistically significant in the presence of elite splits in Model 4b. This suggests that land redistribution is more likely when there is an elite split if institutional constraints to rule are lower. Veto Points is much smaller in magnitude and no longer statistically significant in the absence of elite splits in Model 5b.[30]

The difference between the Veto Points coefficients across Model 4b and Model 5b provides additional evidence that the effect of Veto Points on land redistribution is conditioned by elite splits. Comparing these coefficients is a direct test of this "interaction hypothesis." The difference in the Veto Points coefficients across these models is −6.49, a difference that is statistically significant ($p < 0.1$). This confirms the conditional effect of veto points found in previous tables.

The Case of Paraguay: An Exogenous Elite Split amid Low Institutional Constraints

To complement Table 5.6, this section provides an example – Paraguay in the 1940s – of a plausibly exogenous elite split yielding land redistribution in an environment of institutional constraints that were low for reasons that were clearly unrelated to land redistribution. The source of exogeneity in the elite split draws from the identification strategy used by Jones and Olken (2005), who exploit exogenous leader deaths – due to natural causes and accidents – to examine how leaders impact subsequent economic growth. The death of the Liberal President José Estigarribia in an accidental plane crash when he was touring the country's interior led to an effectively random transition to an elite split that was determined by Estigarribia's accidental death rather than land reform or the threat of reform.

Land concentration in Paraguay was extreme at the outset of the twentieth century. Initially minimal rural pressure resulting from low population density rose by the 1930s with population growth (Carter and Galeano 1995). Large

---

[30] The Model 4 and Model 5 results are also robust to bootstrapping the standard errors to adjust for the fact that the Inverse Mills Ratio in these models is an estimate based on the Model 3 Heckman selection equation predictions.

landowners resisted reform during this period via the ruling Liberal Party: agro-exporters were key players among ruling Liberal Party elites.

Following an interim Liberal government from 1937 to 1939, the Liberal Party chose Estigarribia, a celebrated General in Paraguay's Chaco War with Bolivia (1932–1935), as their candidate in the 1939 elections. Estigarribia won office in an uncontested election despite a growing fissure within the Liberal Party (Lewis 1991, 241). In September 1940, less than a month after promulgating a new, more authoritarian constitution, Estigarribia died in a plane crash while touring near his country residence.

Since the 1940 constitution had eliminated the vice president and elections for the Chamber of Representatives had not yet been held, the top military brass immediately met and selected General Higinio Morínigo, Estigarribia's Minister of War, as interim president for two months until elections could be held. The two most influential figures, Colonels Ramón Paredes and Damaso Sosa Valdes, supported Morínigo and thereby respected the military chain of command because he was "a seemingly genial and unambitious officer. ... Paredes and Sosa Valdes thought Morínigo could be easily controlled, and for a while he encouraged this belief" (Lewis 1991, 243). Morínigo confirmed all of Estigarribia's cabinet ministers. Yet as a military nationalist and the son of peasants, his allegiance was with the military over the Liberal elite, and within a few weeks, he excised the Liberals that Estigarribia had in his cabinet. Morínigo then took an unexpected step to further solidify his power and eliminate even his powerful military rivals: he cancelled upcoming elections, banned political parties, purged Paredes and Sosa Valdes, and turned to a narrow military coalition for political support. The split with Liberals, and consequently with landed elites, was complete.

Unencumbered by landed elites in his cabinet, Morínigo began expropriating land and granting it to peasants in order to attack his political rivals and build an alternate support base. He expropriated 950,000 hectares of land from large landowners from 1940 to 1947 with compensation that was either absent or insufficient (Carter and Galeano 1995, 57). This was the largest episode of land redistribution in Paraguay's history, rivaled only in scale by Stroessner's land negotiation program.

Low institutional constraints to rule during Morínigo's tenure were also exogenous to his decision to redistribute land. Using Haggard and Kaufman's (2012) coding rules for determining whether a regime transition is motivated by distributive conflict, the decline in institutional constraints in Paraguay in 1931 that endured until Morínigo's rule can be clearly classified as nondistributive in origin. The absence of institutional constraints that had lingered since the early 1930s was primarily a result of political turmoil linked to the Chaco War and then to a political tussle over a United States versus Germany World War II alliance decision that spilled on to the streets (Lewis 1991, 233–242).

CONCLUSION

This chapter empirically tests the theoretical argument developed in previous chapters. It does so using an original dataset on three types of land reform – land redistribution, land negotiation, and land colonization – over the 1930–2008 period in Latin America. The long time period of the analysis is advantageous in that it spans wide variation in elite splits and shifts in political institutions. It also extends over broad developments trends and changes in international pressures resulting from factors such as the Cold War. This enables the testing of a host of potential alternative explanations to the main argument that land redistribution is most likely when there are both coalitional splits between ruling political elites and landed elites as well as low institutional constraints to rule.

I find substantial evidence in favor of the theory. The findings hold in the descriptive statistics and in a series of regression models, and they hold when accounting for alternative explanations, including country fixed effects to address unobserved country-specific time-invariant heterogeneity, and using instrumental variables estimation to account for potential endogeneity in elite splits and veto points. Furthermore, and as expected, less redistributive types of land reform such as land negotiation and land colonization occur under circumstances that are distinct from land redistribution.

6

Elite Splits and Redistribution under Autocracy

Peru's "Revolution from Above"

Chapter 5 provides broad confirmatory evidence for the theory linking elite splits and institutional constraints to rule to land redistribution using large statistical tests at the country level. Chapters 6 and 7 focus on Peru and Venezuela and take a different, but complementary, approach. Each chapter first begins by examining whether the timing and type of land reform corresponds with the theoretical predictions from Chapter 3. But the principal aims of these chapters are to probe the theory's causal mechanisms and to test observable implications, thereby demonstrating the internal validity of the theory. In addition, these chapters show the usefulness of the theory in generating an understanding of the spatial and temporal variation in land reform within countries.

The conditions under which land reform occurred in Peru and Venezuela, along with the subnational data I employ to analyze these programs, also help develop further observable implications of the theory and illuminate the relevance of the land reform typology outlined in Chapter 4. Land reform in Peru occurred mainly as land redistribution under military rule. Land reform in Venezuela took place largely through land negotiation and land colonization under democracy, and then more recently under Hugo Chávez and Nicolás Maduro as land redistribution under an increasingly autocratic regime. The Peru case demonstrates social differentiation in the peasant groups that received land through the military's land redistribution program from 1968 to 1980. This sheds light on the organizational capacity necessary for members of the rural poor to become land reform beneficiaries. The Venezuela case provides further insights into the logic of land negotiation and land colonization and how these programs are structured to become politically popular under democracy even though they are less redistributive than land redistribution programs.

CASE SELECTION FOR SUBNATIONAL ANALYSES

Several reasons support the decision to examine Peru and Venezuela in greater detail. First, both countries varied substantially over time in elite splits and institutional constraints, which enables careful tracing of the causal mechanisms driving land redistribution. The variation in elite splits provides a chance to investigate in depth the coalitional dynamics between ruling political elites and landed elites and how and why key insiders of the political elite's initial support coalition push for land redistribution policies when there is a split from landed elites. The variation in institutional constraints presents an opportunity to demonstrate the nuts and bolts of how high institutional constraints block land redistribution efforts while allowing other types of land reform, such as land negotiation and land colonization, to filter through. In this manner, these chapters contribute internal validity to the theory and to the econometric tests in Chapter 5.

Second, and in part because of to their topographic and climatic diversity, Peru and Venezuela both had wide spatial variation in the presence of landed elites and rural laborers. This provides fruitful ground for conducting subnational analyses on the targets and beneficiaries of land reform programs.

Third, neither Peru nor Venezuela faced foreign-sponsored coups or forced democratic transitions from 1930 to 2008.[1] Unlike Chile, Cuba, and Guatemala, which experienced varying degrees of foreign meddling (mostly from the United States), and notwithstanding the shrill Venezuelan rhetoric against the United States under Chávez and Maduro, Peru and Venezuela charted relatively independent political paths and enjoyed the autonomy to largely develop their own political institutions and class structures. We can therefore clearly attribute land reform outcomes to domestic political conditions without significant concerns about complicating outside factors.

Finally, land reform in these countries has received substantial scholarly attention, and competing arguments have been advanced to explain each reform. Applying the theoretical framework developed in previous chapters sheds new light on these cases and thus demonstrates the usefulness of the theory for explaining the mechanisms at work.

Beyond these reasons, Peru and Venezuela both have high-quality subnational data on land reform available throughout the period, facilitating empirical analysis.

PERU AND THE "MOMENTOUS SHIFT" IN THE ANDES

This chapter examines in depth the historically prominent case of Peru. Peru long had an agrarian economy in which landed elites were powerful economic

---

[1] Although the United States sided with the group that launched the 2002 coup in Venezuela, there is little evidence that the coup was a direct result of US intervention.

and political players. The case helps shed greater light on four key points linked to the theory. First, it provides detailed background on the economic and political conditions that gave rise to land reform at a particular point in time. Second, it unpacks the coalitional politics that led to a split between the landed elite and the ruling political elite. Whereas the theory indicates that such a split in the context of low institutional constraints to rule provides both the incentives and capacity to implement reform, this chapter fleshes out how landed elites and the military jockeyed for power both within and between their respective groups. Third, if the theory in Chapter 3 is valid, a subnational analysis of Peru's land reform should reveal that the program was indeed used to target powerful landed elites and thereby eliminate them as rivals in a manner consistent with the theory. The data I have gathered from Peru enable just such a test. Finally, the Peru case illuminates which groups of peasants received land and why. It therefore speaks to the point of how the threat of peasant organization from below directly factors into the decision about how to redistribute land and which groups should be beneficiaries.

From 1968 to 1980, Generals Juan Velasco Alvarado and Francisco Morales Bermúdez implemented a set of radical reform projects known as the "revolution from above." One of the most significant and high-profile projects was a land reform program that destroyed the landholding elite in favor of rural laborers. Roughly 15,000 properties were expropriated and redistributed, constituting 45 percent of all agricultural land in the country. Although the reform left out some sectors of the rural poor, many peasants materially benefited from it, and it drastically changed land tenure relations in Peru. According to the prominent Peruvian anthropologist Enrique Mayer (2009, 3), "it was the first government ever to execute significant income distribution in a society of great inequalities. It completed the abolition of all forms of servitude in rural estates, a momentous shift in the history of the Andes, akin to the abolition of slavery in the Americas."

Why did Peru's military regime pursue a massive land reform, and how was the reform targeted? The literature on Peru's agrarian reform provides a host of explanations: a self-interested autonomous military that sought to reduce the threat from landed elites, ideological orientation, a "father of the poor" strategy, and an attempt to stave off revolution. This chapter outlines the theoretical bases for these alternative explanations and then empirically examines support for each of them.

If the theory in Chapter 3 holds, we should find evidence consistent with the first explanation: a pragmatic autocratic regime that pursued its own autonomous interests in order to undercut its rivals and solidify its support base. Using original data on the universe of more than 15,000 land expropriations in Peru from 1968 to 1980 along with data on land tenure and landholdings, I find that the regime targeted the largest, most influential landowners for expropriation, redistributing to peasant workers but leaving out the poorest, least-organized rural inhabitants – landless workers and indigenous communities. Furthermore, expropriation and redistribution was not simply focused on the areas that had previously formed the greatest threat of revolution; nor did the adoption and implementation of land reform indicate a clearly ideological motivation.

The Peruvian military had long been manipulated by powerful landed elites. These elites had acted to regulate the military's budget and training curriculum, called on the military to overthrow threatening democratic regimes, and then used their ownership of the press and lucrative export sector to coordinate opposition and to pressure military rulers who deviated from their desired policies (Gilbert 1977). The military dictators Velasco and Morales Bermúdez and their political coalitions consequently sought to "break the back of the oligarchy" with the land reform program in order to diminish landed elite influence over the military's institutions, budget, and actions: the key concerns of their military support coalition. Land was redistributed to "middle-class" peasants that had worked on expropriated estates and had the greatest potential to organize against the regime had the reform excluded them or been broadened to include the landless poor. This dual-pronged strategy, which benefited both the military support coalition and the most organized rural threat from below, was politically effective: Velasco ruled for seven years and Morales Bermúdez for five years, compared to the majority of dictators in Latin America from 1935 to 2008 who survived in office for less than two years. In fact, Velasco was Peru's longest-lived leader between Augusto Leguía's rule in the 1920s and Alberto Fujimori's in the 1990s. This was no small feat given that seventeen executives passed through office between 1930 and Velasco's coup in 1968.

LAND REFORM IN PERU, 1930–2006

The economy in Peru until the 1960s largely revolved around land: according to census calculations, half of the economically active population in 1965 was involved in agriculture. But there was long-standing pressure for land reform. The 1961 census demonstrates the severe inequality in landholdings in the country. The largest 1 percent of landowners held 80 percent of private land, whereas 83 percent of farmers held properties of five hectares or less, representing only 6 percent of total private land. Peru lagged its peers on a number of social and economic dimensions in the 1960s despite its level of income per capita (Palmer 1973), and many professional Peruvians attributed this to the lopsided and archaic agrarian structure. In addition to the massive sugar and cotton enterprises on the northern coast, sprawling haciendas such as Runatullo (Junín), Yanahuara (Urubamba), and Lauramarca (Quispicanchi) dotted the landscape. The haciendas had their roots in colonial land grants that had frequently been passed down through hereditary succession.

Figure 6.1 is a map that displays the extremely skewed distribution of land ownership in the Ollantaytambo district in the department of Cusco in the mid-1960s. Large haciendas ran up and down the valley in a fashion typical of

FIGURE 6.1. Haciendas, Indigenous Communities, and Small Properties in Ollantay-tambo District, Cusco, 1960s. *Note:* Map produced by the Oficina de Ingeniería y Catastro, Ministerio de Agricultura. Accessed in the Centro Bartolomé de las Casas, Cusco, June 2014.

the time, flanking the railroad that bisected them. Narrowly squeezed between these haciendas were disparate indigenous communities and smaller properties. Members of these communities and smaller properties were part and parcel of the hacienda economy – their livelihoods, security, and freedom of movement were impacted by the hacienda owners. Other communities were physically encircled by or incorporated within hacienda land, lending landowners a tight grasp over the mobility and labor of residents.

Land tenure relations varied widely but were archaic in much of the country, the most notorious being in the feudal haciendas of the highland Sierras. In the Sierra haciendas, indigenous campesinos cultivated small plots for family consumption on the owner's land in exchange for (often unpaid) labor on the hacienda, typically during seeding and harvesting times when campesinos most needed to tend to their own plots. Furthermore, these *colonos* were not free to move, and the owner could rotate or take away the land at his discretion.

One illustrative example was the hacienda Huarán, located in the Calca district of Cusco. Laborers tied to Oscar Fernández Oblitas's hacienda complained of a host of abuses, which were not limited to being pushed to smaller and smaller parcels while paying exorbitant fees for access to their plots, having animals stolen or killed by Fernández, contracting illnesses from unknown agrochemicals, being denied educational opportunities, suffering arbitrary arrest and incarceration in a prison that Fernández himself ran, being denied social benefits when they could no longer work, and having personal property stolen by Fernández.[2] As one group of resident *colonos* put it after Fernández's property was targeted for expropriation: "These abuses and the permanent submission we were subjected to by the powerful owner of the hacienda, who himself has been Department Prefect [of Cusco], prevented us from denouncing him and forced us to live under a permanent threat of reprisals if we were to go to any authorities to claim unpaid salaries or appeal against abuses."[3]

Table 6.1 provides a summary of the leaders in Peru from 1939 to 2006 and the regime types under which they ruled. Tracing the key variables from the theory in Chapter 3, the table also includes leaders' incentives for pursuing land reform on the basis of whether their initial support coalition excluded landed elites, the institutional constraints they faced in implementing land reform, and the reform outcomes. Table 6.1 guides the discussion in the remainder of this section.

Failed Land Reform, 1930–1968

The mantle of agrarian reform was first taken up in the 1930s by the political party APRA. But the military largely protected the wealth and power of the preexisting landowning elite until the 1960s. Its status quo orientation was derived from an officer class composed largely of elites and restricted recruitment among the poor (Lowenthal 1974, 121). Civilian politicians operated within, and often reinforced, this counter-reform stance.

Lieutenant-Colonel Luis Miguel Sánchez Cerro overthrew the dictatorship of Augusto Leguía in 1930 and was subsequently elected in 1931. He quickly allied himself with conservative elite interests, including the powerful agro-export industry on the northern coast (Bertram 1991, 412). A constituent assembly named the decorated military man Óscar Benavides president in 1933 when Sánchez Cerro was assassinated. Benavides's cabinets were dominated by traditional elites with landed and other economic interests (Bertram 1991, 418). As the theory in Chapter 3 suggests, there were consequently few incentives for implementing land reform. Like Sánchez Cerro, Benavides repressed the opposition, outlawing APRA and suppressing the Communist Party. Benavides

---

[2] All of this was documented in sworn declarations to the regional director of Zone XI of the agrarian reform.

[3] This statement was filed on January 15, 1970, to the regional director of Zone XI of the agrarian reform. Many peasant beneficiaries of the expropriated hacienda later participated as actors in a film titled *Kuntur Wachana* about hacienda life and the arrival of agrarian reform.

TABLE 6.1. *Land Reform in Peru, 1939–2006*

President	Years	Regime Type	Reform Incentive	Reform Capacity	Land Reform Outcome
Manuel Prado	1939–1945	Civilian Dictatorship	Low	High	None
José Bustamante	1945–1948	Democracy	High	Low	None; allowed unionization on sugar estates
Manuel Odría	1948–1956	Military Dictatorship	Low	High	None
Manuel Prado	1956–1962	Democracy	Low	Low	Presidential Commission proposed agrarian reform law; designed by large landowners but never passed
Ricardo Pérez Godoy	1962–1963	Military Dictatorship	Limited	High	Limited reform in Cusco region
Nicolás Lindley López	1963	Military Dictatorship	Low	High	None
Fernando Belaúnde	1963–1968	Democracy	High	Low	1964 Agrarian Reform Law passed but weakened by Congress; 380,000 ha. from 1964 to 1968
Juan Velasco Alvarado	1968–1975	Military Dictatorship	High	High	1969 land reform Decree Law 17716; 4.6 million ha. from 1968 to 1975
Francisco Morales Bermúdez	1975–1980	Military Dictatorship	High	High	Continued implementation of Decree 17716; 3.3 million ha. from 1975 to 1980
Fernando Belaúnde	1980–1985	Democracy	Low	Low	420,000 ha. under previous laws; laws passed to enable parcelation of collectives but none for redistribution
Alan García	1985–1990	Democracy	Low	Low	Continued parcelation but no redistribution; 1987 Law of Demarcation and Titling of Communal Territory
Alberto Fujimori	1990–2000	Democracy/Dictatorship	Low	Low/High	Laws aimed at investment and individual titling; 1992 Special Land Titling Project (PETT)
Alejandro Toledo	2001–2006	Democracy	Low	Low	Individual land titling via PETT continues

Sources: Albertus (2015a); Ballantyne et al. (2000); Carter and Alvarez (1989); Cleaves and Scurrah (1980); COFOPRI (2008); Gilbert (1977); Lastarria-Cornhiel (1989); Mayer (2009); McClintock (1981).

called elections in 1936 but then annulled the unfavorable results. He dissolved the National Assembly and appointed a conservative, all-military cabinet with backing from traditional elites.

Manuel Prado was elected president after Benavides's term ended in 1939 within a restricted electoral field in which APRA remained banned. He was the president of one of Peru's largest banks and had substantial holdings in other financial insurance institutions (Masterson 1991, 67). The oligarchic Prado family also had a strong resource base in coastal export agriculture (McClintock 1981, 67). This made him a natural ally of the large agribusinesses that fueled the export sector, particularly the sugar enterprises on the northern coast. Indeed, his vice president was the wealthy *hacendado* Rafael Larco. Prado therefore had no personal or coalitional incentives to pursue land reform and did not propose any changes to the structure of landholding in Peru.

President José Bustamante came to power in 1945 through democratic elections, leaning heavily on Prado's constituency, the newly legalized support of APRA, and elements of the growing urban middle class and organized labor (Bertram 1991, 425). He had a rather vague platform as a candidate that included tax and social welfare reforms along with a proposal to expropriate uncultivated land with compensation and to redistribute it among smallholders (Masterson 1991, 82). Upon coming to office, Bustamante's first cabinet excluded APRA (Masterson 1991, 93), the political group most vocal about reform at the time. His cabinet also excluded established elites (Bertram 1991, 426), rendering an elite split. Bustamante embarked on a program of economic liberalization and expansion of political participation. APRA's influence grew over time within the National Congress and within Bustamante's cabinet. APRA repealed a 1939 constitutional amendment expanding presidential powers as well as emergency laws passed by Benavides and Prado. Its legislative majority brought down Bustamante's first cabinet and won posts in the newly formed cabinet. Rather than initiate an agrarian reform proposal that congressional landowning interests could kill, Bustamante attempted decentralization reforms aimed at marginalizing the powerful coastal landholders. He also expanded political participation to undermine the role of the military in political and economic life. This antagonized the coastal oligarchs and their military allies, who shared similar social and economic interests. APRA's harassment of political opponents and alleged support of the assassination of the *La Prensa* director led to another cabinet change in which *apristas* were ousted and the hard-line General Manuel Odría was brought in. Odría bolstered the state's repressive apparatus.

An economic and parliamentary crisis led to the regime's overthrow in 1948 by General Manuel Odría. Odría's coup was financed by key business circles and strongly supported by Peru's oligarchic "forty families" (McClintock 1981, 68–69), which counted the largest landowners in the country among their ranks. Peru appeared on the cover of *Fortune* magazine, which lauded its "scrupulous respect for private property" and praised it as a "standard in international economic conduct."[4] Any hint of land reform was buried.

The democratic successor to Odría's rule was again Manuel Prado. Prado legalized APRA in exchange for the moderation of its leftist positions, including agrarian reform, in its 1956 platform (McClintock 1981, 69). Prado established the Comisión para la Reforma Agraria y Vivienda in 1956 to create an agrarian reform law. Yet land redistribution was hardly the goal: his cabinet and Congress were populated with landed elites. Pedro Beltrán, a landowner and the president of the powerful landed elite–dominated National Agrarian Society (SNA), was named as the commission chair. Prado elevated Beltrán to the post of prime minister in 1959. Four years transpired before a mild law was even proposed. Conservative landowners and lawmakers then predictably stymied the law's passage in Congress (Lastarria-Cornhiel 1989, 136; Masterson 1991, 168). Nonetheless, a land colonization agency named the Instituto de Reforma Agraria y Colonización (IRAC) was created in 1960 (Mejía and Matos Mar 1980, 90), and it quickly began several colonization and irrigation projects to relieve land pressure. Chief among these were Proyecto San Lorenzo, Proyecto La Morada, and more diffuse colonization via petitioning in both the Selva and Sierra regions (Cleaves and Scurrah 1980, 142; Mejía and Matos Mar 1980, 90; Prado 1962, 114–115). Consistent with the Chapter 5 findings, the lack of an elite split and higher institutional constraints did not block land colonization.

Although the industrial bourgeoisie were gaining increasing influence within the broader elite by the 1960s, the coastal oligarchy composed of sugar and cotton growers remained strong until the eve of Velasco's rule in the late 1960s (Stepan 1978, 119). It was against this backdrop that the hectic and indeterminate elections of 1962, which raised the prospect of putting Odría back in office, were cancelled in a coup and immediately rescheduled for the following year. Meanwhile, the head of the narrow military junta that seized power, General Ricardo Pérez Godoy, pursued several limited reformist policies that had been circulating around the Center for Higher Military Studies (CAEM). Despite the attempt of elites to modify the military's changing progressive curriculum during the 1960s (Gilbert 1977; McClintock 1981, 49), the military was gradually growing more autonomous, in part as a result of wider recruitment from the middle class.

Pérez Godoy's junta gave permanent legal status to IRAC in November 1962 (Masterson 1991, 186). It also unilaterally declared an agrarian reform law known as the Ley de Bases de la Reforma Agraria (Decree Law 14328). Although the law put forth a relatively complete agrarian reform, the junta focused its agrarian efforts almost exclusively in the La Convención and Lares valleys in the Cusco region, where peasants had taken over *hacendado* lands and instituted a labor boycott. The junta expropriated and purchased at low

---

[4] John Davenport, "Why Peru Pulls Dollars," *Fortune* 54 (Nov. 1956), 131–132.

rates a number of hacienda lands for redistribution to the campesinos who had invaded them (Masterson 1991, 187). They also continued parcelation programs begun by the Comisión para la Reforma Agraria y Vivienda. In addition, the government declared Decree Law 14197, which, even though it was never applied, stipulated the reversion of *tierras eriazas* (defined in the law as unexploited lands, typically due to a lack or an excess of water) to the state (Mejía and Matos Mar 1980, 92).

As Pérez Godoy began showing signs of wanting to extend his time in office, his original co-conspirator General Lindley López overthrew him in another coup. Fernando Belaúnde, a young architect who headed the new reformist party Acción Popular, was democratically elected as president in the 1963 elections that followed quickly after Lindley's coup. The military supported Belaúnde as an alternative to APRA, which had nonetheless begun to seriously betray its original reformist spirit (McClintock 1981, 69–70), and because of the military's anticipated role in his proposed development program in the eastern jungle highlands. Belaúnde had promised vigorous agrarian reform during his campaign. His initial political coalition was nonetheless heterogeneous, and it included both pro-reform ministers and a substantial number of ministers from landed families. Landowners could never quite gain a stable foothold in Belaúnde's administration, however. The first cabinet was quickly censured; the extreme cabinet volatility that ensued over the subsequent years undermined any significant or sustained landowner presence. Landed elites fared better in the legislature. Although a reform law passed through Congress in 1964, landholding interests successfully added so many modifications to it that the law became nearly useless. Even a smooth expropriation required fifty-one steps and at least twenty-two months to implement (Cleaves and Scurrah 1980, 41). Institutional constraints effectively strangled reform.

Belaúnde's term was frustrated by crises. Land invasions and leftist rebellions cropped up in the Andes from 1963 to 1965. Hugo Blanco's farmers' union movement in the La Convención and Lares valleys in the late 1950s resulted in land invasions that ultimately required army intervention in the early 1960s. Peasants again launched large-scale land invasions in the Andes in 1963–1964 in anticipation of expanded land reform under Belaúnde. A rural guerrilla movement in the Andes in 1965 yet again required a military response. The increasingly professional military crushed the rebels and virtually eliminated the leadership of the Movement of the Revolutionary Left (Einaudi 1973). But the military became increasingly wary of potential instability catalyzed by organizing peasants, and many officers were appalled by seeing first-hand the archaic land tenure relations in the Sierra and the conditions of the poor (Lastarria-Cornhiel 1989, 136). This deepened military support for agrarian reform and helped solidify the idea within the military that landed elites must be eliminated.

Loans from foreign creditors during an economic crisis generated public turmoil toward the end of Belaúnde's term. Belaúnde was nonetheless able to continue colonization programs through IRAC, distribute *tierras eriazas*, and redistribute several hundred thousand hectares of land (Mejía and Matos Mar 1980; Ministerio de Agricultura 1991, 170).

Land Reform under Military Rule, 1968–1980

General Juan Velasco Alvarado seized power from Belaúnde in October 1968 with the help of a military coalition of middle-class officers that was not tied in with the exclusive social circles of the landed elite. Velasco's coup began the *Docenio*, a period of centralized autocratic rule that lasted until 1980. A clean elite split alongside low institutional constraints paved the way for heavy land redistribution.

Velasco's Support Coalition

Velasco relied on a core coalition (the "Earthquake Group") with whom he had plotted the coup to construct and guide major policies. The four key colonels comprising this group were Leonidas Rodríguez Figueroa, Jorge Fernández Maldonado, Enrique Gallegos, and Rafael Hoyos (Cleaves and Scurrah 1980, 43). Civilians at times were drawn close to this inner circle, but typically only for advising on specific issues. The broader set of political elites comprising Velasco's government included army, air force, and navy officers who were charged with implementing the regime's policies. Key members included José Graham Hurtado, Arturo Valdez Palacio, Rolando Gilardi, Anibal Meza Cuadra, Miguel Angel de la Flor, Jorge Barandiarán, Luis Barandiarán, Pedro Richter, Javier Tantaleán, Enrique Valdez Angulo, and Luis Vargas Caballero (Cleaves and Scurrah 1980, 43–44; Kruijt 1994; Masterson 1991, 248). Several of these individuals became closer to Velasco over time whereas others were excluded. In addition, several committed civilians were brought into this group, including Carlos Delgado, Augusto Zimmerman, and Guillermo Figallo. Most key officers came from Peru's provinces and had been born to largely impoverished families (Kruijt 1994, 46). This was true of the entire Earthquake Group. Rodríguez Figueroa and Gallegos had humble Cusco roots, Fernández Maldonado was born in a small town in remote Moquegua, and Hoyos was from Cajamarca, initially joining the army as a volunteer soldier.

All of Velasco's main supporters were expected to secure the support and cooperation of the broader launching organization – the rest of the armed forces – in exchange for their positions in Velasco's government. Their views were diverse on a range of issues. Henry Pease García (1977) divides these individuals into three loose, shifting "tendencies": bourgeois liberals, progressives, and "La Misión." Philip (1978) categorizes them as revolutionaries, developmentalists, and conservatives. McClintock (1983, 280) emphasizes that these were tendencies and not clear factions or ideologies, underscoring the Chapter 5 finding that ideology fails in explaining reform outcomes. Divergent opinions required Velasco to maneuver politically at times to achieve his preferred outcomes. Velasco's key supporters were nonetheless united (particularly the Earthquake Group) against the landed elite and in favor of agrarian reform. They were also united against elites in the industry, finance, and export sectors and favored early redistributive initiatives in these areas.

Expropriation and Redistribution under Velasco

The military regime under Velasco forged a more interventionist, statist economic policy as it built "state capitalism." The military quickly seized the International Petroleum Company's Talara installations upon taking power. It subsequently expropriated foreign mining companies and privately owned Peruvian companies that it deemed to be in the national interests, including banks, utilities, fishing enterprises, and major newspapers. The regime created state enterprises with monopoly privileges that hobbled private businesses in the export sectors of cotton, sugar, minerals, coca, and petroleum marketing (Saulniers 1988). Furthermore, it created manufacturing laws (e.g., the Industrial Community Law) that specified worker participation in profit distributions, worker shareholding, and participation in company management in all industries.

One of Velasco's most prominent initiatives, the agrarian reform Decree Law 17716 of 1969, was aimed squarely at preexisting landed elites. His support coalition's split from powerful landed elites was at the root of the reform. Velasco himself underscored this point on the first anniversary of the coup: "Some people expected very different things and were confident, as had been the custom, that we came to power for the sole purpose of calling elections and returning to them all their privileges. The people who thought that way were and are mistaken" (Velasco Alvarado 1969, 189). The agrarian reform law stipulated that all landholdings larger than 150 hectares on the coast and 15–55 hectares in the Sierra (depending on the location) were subject to expropriation without exception. Landholding limits were lowered to fifty hectares on the coast and thirty hectares in the highlands in a 1975 revision to the law. Those in violation of labor laws were subject to expropriation regardless of property size, and capital assets on expropriated landholdings, such as mills, agricultural equipment, and even animals, were also to be expropriated. Compensation was based on the property value previously declared by the landowner for tax purposes, which was often well below market value, and reimbursement was primarily paid in long-term government bonds that became next to worthless against very high inflation at the end of the 1970s.[5] Only in early 2014 did the government take the first definitive steps toward compensating remaining bondholders in response to a 2013 Constitutional Court ruling, which set compensation at a small fraction of the originally low valuations.

Unlike land reform efforts under previous governments, Law 17716 drastically altered land tenure relationships and property ownership. To deepen

---

[5] According to Mayer (2009), land was compensated at roughly 10 percent of its 1967 market value, and 73 percent of the total compensation was in government bonds.

the political support of agrarian reform beneficiaries and to harness this support to bolster the regime, Velasco created the Confederación Nacional Agraria (CNA), an agricultural sector organization that beneficiaries were pushed to join in order to defend the regime's progress. The CNA was given access to the Parliament building and television coverage for their inaugural meeting.

Velasco's Failure to Consolidate Power and the Morales Coup

Despite Velasco's massive land reform, he was ultimately ousted by an internal coup in 1975. Opposition to land reform as it was designed, and to the CNA, grew from groups that did not benefit from the agrarian reform. Some of these individuals joined the Confederación Campesina Peruana (CCP), which at times grew faster and more effectively than the government-sponsored CNA. Furthermore, Velasco implemented several policies in the agrarian cooperatives that diminished rural support, such as attempting to require the admission of more *comuneros* and *eventuales* as enterprise members, and his regime redistributed less to the urban poor. In the face of this discontent, mounting economic problems, a festering territorial dispute with Chile, and Velasco's increasingly severe illness, the military became more factionalized. Then Prime Minister General Francisco Morales Bermúdez pushed the ailing Velasco out of office in 1975 with the tacit support of many insiders (McClintock 1983).

Though Velasco proved to be one of Peru's longest-lasting leaders in the twentieth century, why did his policies not generate even greater regime stability and continue well beyond his downfall? Why is there no Velasquismo analogous to Cardenismo, Peronismo, or Chavismo? The chief reason is that Velasco did not found a popularly based political party to entrench his reforms and legacy. He chose to remain above the fray of formal political organizations, arguing that they were divisive and that a direct link between citizens and the military was the most effective mode of advancing the revolution (Kruijt 1994, 307). The closest the regime came to creating a party was the founding of the National Social Mobilization Support System (SINAMOS) in 1972. Yet SINAMOS sought to channel social participation in the implementation of regime policies rather than elicit support in policymaking itself – one of several factors that condemned it to failure (McClintock 1983). The only other organized political effort came a few weeks before Velasco's ousting in the form of a provisional committee for the new Political Organization of the Peruvian Revolution (OPRP). Although there were many pro-Velasco peasant demonstrations prior to his overthrow (Mayer 2009, 37), there was no strong and coordinated popular opposition to the Morales coup.

Morales's tactics contributed to the muted popular response to Velasco's overthrow. Following the coup, Morales at first continued Peru's agrarian transformation, promising not to vary "one millimeter" from Velasco's reforms and initially keeping many key Velasco advisers such as Rodríguez, Fernández Maldonado, Gallegos, and Graham. He simultaneously promised greater citizen participation in policymaking and ideological pluralism. Many even thought that Morales might be more progressive than Velasco had been (Kruijt 1994, 294). This notion was furthered by Morales's support of the radical Plan Túpac Amaru, which went further than Velasco's Law of Social Property and promised severe decentralization and local organization in support of many of Velasco's policies (Kruijt 1994, 294–295). Many progressives, however, left government because Morales eventually veered right in the face of economic turmoil. Only then did many of them meet to form a Velasquista party, the Socialist Revolutionary Party (PSR), which was built in part from the OPRP. The PSR met with Velasco in 1977. Although he expressed his sympathies, Velasco nonetheless declined to join a political party, as he had always done (Kruijt 1994, 307). Amid changing policies and slower redistribution by 1977, the CNA and other groups forced the government to declare a national holiday upon Velasco's death in December 1977. Some 700,000 people descended on Lima for the funeral – the largest gathering Peru had ever witnessed (Kruijt 1994, 308). Yet there was insufficient popular support to pressure Morales to return to Velasco's path of reform.

Redistribution under Morales
The Morales government tacked right in the midst of economic turmoil in 1976–1977. Yet despite changes in his cabinet and in his set of close advisors, the support coalition still did not overlap substantially with landed elites (Kruijt 1994). The new minister of agriculture after Gallegos, General Luis Arbulú Ibáñez (July 1976–July 1979), was a long-time military man who declared the agrarian reform "irreversible." Arbulú accused the modernized cooperatives of "excessive consumption which contrasts with the deprived areas surrounding them," and he even promised to favor labor- over capital-intensive agricultural firms with tax cuts. Morales therefore never reversed the reform (McClintock 1981), but he did taper its intensity substantially in his later years in office as he "consolidated" the revolution (Gorman 1997, 324), leading the CNA and the CCP to join in two strikes against the military government's agrarian policies.

Morales also changed the industries law, deemphasized social property, devaluated the *sol*, and entered into negotiations with the IMF to stabilize the economy in the face of economic crisis and increasing coalitional overlap with remaining urban economic elites that forged tacit alliances with newly powerful cabinet members such as Parodi and Cisneros. These policies favored economic elites and put pressure on Morales from the remaining progressive members of his military support coalition. Morales then quickly announced in July 1977 upcoming elections to maintain unity within the fractionalized military.

Under Velasco and Morales, roughly 15,000 properties were expropriated through agrarian reform – a total of more than 8 million hectares. This represents an incredible 45 percent of all agricultural land in the country. By 1979, more than 400,000 families were spread among 1,800 new agricultural units, mostly cooperatives, averaging more than 5,000 hectares each (Cleaves and Scurrah 1980, 263). Although many peasants did not prefer cooperatives, their creation enabled the regime to closely monitor production and administration and to attempt to subvert politically active cooperative members (e.g., former union leaders) by empowering technicians (McClintock 1981).

In addition to redistributing land, Velasco and Morales Bermúdez distributed state-owned land to extend the agricultural frontier and settle campesinos that lacked land. These lands were primarily *tierras eriazas*, which were declared state property: from 1962 to 1991, slightly more than 2 million hectares of *eriazas* were distributed (Ministerio de Agricultura 1991, 169). Land from public agencies, abandoned lands, and donated lands were also incorporated and redistributed by the Dirección General de Reforma Agraria, the agency charged with implementing the reform. These lands constituted almost 1 million hectares during the 1962–1991 period (Ministerio de Agricultura 1991, 169).

The Death of Land Reform and the Turn to Individual Property Rights, 1980–2006

The fact that Morales dramatically slowed redistribution by 1977 resulted in widespread protests and increasing popular pressure for democracy. The debilitated remaining economic elites also supported a turn to democracy in the face of continually uncertain prospects under military rule. The democratic successors to these twelve long years of military reform, Fernando Belaúnde (1980–1985) and Alan García Pérez (1985–1990), granted concessions to the now well-organized left. Yet remaining elites blocked the most serious redistributive threats by gaining positions and influence in the legislature, bureaucracy, and judiciary. Belaúnde and García tended to tread relatively lightly on redistributionist policies as compared to their military predecessors, with tax revenues declining sharply and land redistribution trickling along at a very small fraction of what it had been under military rule. Article 158 of the 1979 constitution, which returned Peru to democracy in 1980, called for the state to support the colonization of previously unoccupied lands as well as to construct irrigation works and to rehabilitate fallow agricultural lands. The government also passed an agrarian reform law upon democratization that enabled the parcelation of the large coastal collective enterprises. Both of these laws shifted the emphasis of agrarian reform away from redistribution. Between 1981 and 1986, about three-fourths of the large coastal collective enterprises had been parceled up into individual titled holdings, with members typically receiving four to six hectares (Carter and Alvarez 1989). Parcelation continued into the 1990s.

In 1991, after Fujimori's election, Peru's Congress passed the Law of Promotion of Investment in the Agrarian Sector, formally ending the agrarian reform by eliminating the restrictions placed on the sale, rental, and mortgaging of agricultural land. Land expropriation and redistribution halted completely. The law also recognized the private rights over land occupied by former cooperative members (Ballantyne et al. 2000). Fujimori's neoliberal economic policies brought him into an alliance with large agricultural producers and agro-exporters, and many of his policies reflected this alliance (Crabtree 2002). His first minister of agriculture, Carlos Amat y León, was a leftist economist who quickly resigned after being undercut by the neoliberal Prime Minister Juan Carlos Hurtado Miller, especially on the issue of agricultural credits that went to agro-exporters.

Fujimori disbanded the Congress in April 1992 in an auto-coup. He had been facing staunch political opposition in both houses of Congress that blocked his attempts to implement an austerity program in an effort to win international aid and clean up the macroeconomic wreckage that had been left in the wake of Alan García's disastrous attempt to nationalize the banking sector. He then created a new constitution in 1993, which was approved in a nationwide referendum. The 1993 constitution attempted to increase land tenure security by guaranteeing individual and collective property rights. This built on Fujimori's 1992 decree establishing the Special Land Titling Project (PETT), which enabled titling and registration for privately held land. PETT granted approximately 930,000 rural titles from 1996 to 2000 and another 790,000 from 2001 to 2006 (COFOPRI 2008). Law 26505 of 1995 enacted additional land tenure reform. The law stipulated that the collectively farmed *comunidades campesinas* could receive private property rights by allowing them to be titled individually (Ballantyne et al. 2000, 699).

Given Fujimori's relative autonomy, why was there no land redistribution under his administration? There are several reasons. First, although Fujimori faced relatively few institutional constraints for a democratically elected leader after he disbanded Congress, the constraints he did face throughout the 1990s were high for an autocrat. Figure 5.1 in Chapter 5 indicates that Fujimori faced some of the most restrictive veto points of any autocratic regime spell in Latin America since 1930. Second, his support coalition did not clearly exclude landed interests. His coterie of neoliberal economic advisors shared a close affinity to large agricultural producers and the export sector; indeed, one of his final ministers of agriculture was the large agribusiness owner José Chlimper. Finally, the demand for land reform under Fujimori was much lower than that encountered in the 1960s. This was in part due to the massive land redistribution program that the military had already implemented and in part due to the later efforts of Belaúnde and García to unravel the reform and cast it in a negative light (Mayer 2009). Fujimori therefore did not implement a land redistribution program, but he did attempt to gain some support in the countryside through titling programs such as PETT.

Land titling continued to be the focus of land reform in the 2000s under Alejandro Toledo and Alan García (2006–2011). There was no active program of expropriation and redistribution. PETT was merged with the Organization for the Formalization of Informal Property (COFOPRI) in 2007. Among other objectives, COFOPRI is charged with formalizing ownership of *tierras*

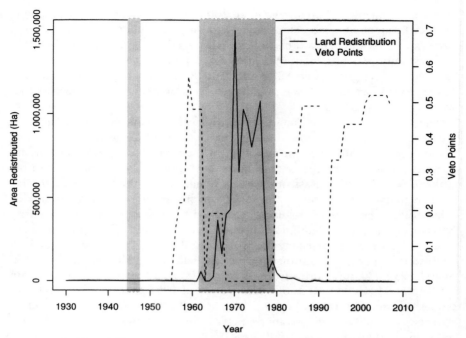

FIGURE 6.2. Elite Splits, Institutional Constraints, and Land Redistribution in Peru, 1930–2008. *Note:* Shaded regions indicate years of an elite split.

eriazas, with the primary goal of spurring private-sector investment in irrigation projects.

ELITE SPLITS, INSTITUTIONAL CONSTRAINTS, AND LAND REFORM IN PERU

The previous section details the background conditions under which redistributive land reform was either blocked or implemented in Peru. To what extent is this variation in land redistribution explained by the two key factors highlighted in the theory in Chapter 3: elite splits and institutional constraints to rule?

Figure 6.2 plots veto points and elite splits against land redistribution.[6] The vast majority of redistribution occurred when there was a split between political elites and landed elites in the presence of low institutional constraints (1968–1980). Elite splits amid higher institutional constraints (1964–1968) yielded substantially less land redistribution. Land redistribution under Belaúnde from

---

[6] Land colonization in Peru began earlier than land redistribution did and was much smaller in scale. See Figure 4.2 for patterns of land colonization and negotiation in Peru.

1964 to 1968 was largely blocked by landed elites who occupied key veto points that were critical to the reform process, particularly the Congress. A lack of elite splits amid low institutional constraints (1930–1945; 1948–1956) similarly yielded little land redistribution. Military and civilian rule during these periods was characterized by alliances with landed elites and other traditional elites. Although the executive could have acted to implement reform during these periods without the risk of facing opposing veto players, there were few coalitional incentives to implement reform. A lack of elite splits alongside high institutional constraints (1980–1991; 1993–2008) also largely foreclosed land redistribution. In this case, both incentives and a capacity for land redistribution were absent.

There was one other period during which political elites and landed elites were split in the presence of relatively low institutional constraints: during Bustamante's rule from 1945 to 1948. Although Bustamante's cabinets from 1945 to 1947 largely excluded landed elite interests, he faced little pressure for land redistribution from the rural sector along the lines discussed in Chapters 3 and 5. APRA had not yet made significant electoral inroads to the peasantry (Bertram 1991, 425), and most peasants were still excluded from voting. Furthermore, rural unions would not develop into effective vehicles for action until the late 1950s. Lastly, Bustamante could hardly implement the policies he desired without resistance. Bustamante won office under the National Democratic Front (FDN). Yet many of the legislators that won seats via the FDN in the Chamber of Deputies and the Senate were in fact APRA members. When Bustamante excluded APRA from his first cabinet, APRA took charge in Congress. It quickly engineered Congress's ability to grant itself the authority to override presidential vetoes with a majority vote and then began an ambitious legislative agenda of its own (Bertram 1991, 427). Within a year, APRA had brought down Bustamante's first cabinet. Yet because APRA lacked a peasant base of support at the time, it too failed to propose agrarian reform and was itself ousted from the cabinet within a year.

HYPOTHESES FOR THE PERUVIAN LAND REFORM

Figure 6.2 demonstrates that the theory largely explains the *timing* of major land redistribution in Peru. Yet it does not indicate whether redistribution occurred for the reasons anticipated by the theory. Was land redistribution implemented because ruling political elites sought to eliminate landed elites, thereby eliminating a strategic enemy and elongating their tenure in office? Or was it carried out for other reasons such as a radical ideology or to undercut the threat of revolution?

There is considerable debate among Peru scholars over the political motives and intentions for the land reform program. One important explanation that is consistent with the theory of land reform detailed in Chapter 3 is rooted in the corporate interests of the military coalition that brought these political elites to power. This argument cites the military's indignation with being manipulated by landed and other economic elites.

The oligarchy had long relied on the military to overthrow governments that threatened their interests and to lead repressive autocratic regimes, as was the case with Sánchez Cerro, Benavides, and Odría (Gilbert 1977, 145–146). Oligarchs took up collections to bribe military figures and support the Odría coup, and they explicitly funded the military repression of uprisings by collecting funds for improved armaments after the APRA revolt under Sánchez Cerro and buying up bonds to finance the brutal repression of guerrilla activities in the Andes in the 1960s (Gilbert 1977, 150–151). Yet they had also used their ownership of the press and dominance in the lucrative banking and export sectors to punish military rulers that deviated from their desired policies by rallying popular opposition and restricting the flow of government credit. Meanwhile, elites intervened in the military's changing progressive curriculum and regulated its budget (McClintock 1981, 49; Gilbert 1977). Both the Center for Advanced Military Studies (CAEM) and military intelligence introduced changes toward more merit-based promotion and emphasized the military's role in economic and social development (including agrarian reform) as the key to fostering stability and national autonomy beginning in the 1950s. This threat was not lost on entrenched elites. Belaúnde's Prime Minister, Pedro Beltrán, the president of the powerful landowners' National Agrarian Society, ordered CAEM to cut non-military matters from its curriculum (Kruijt 1994, 39).

This wide range of elite manipulation made Velasco and Morales Bermúdez and their military coalitions wary of these powerful elite families. Velasco and Morales Bermúdez also recognized the importance of empowering the military officers that supported their rule to avoid disaffected officers from conspiring against them, perhaps with the support of targeted elites.

Although this explanation provides a clear prediction that the most powerful landed elites would be the chief targets of reform, it has less specific predictions about land reform beneficiaries. The theory developed in Chapter 3 suggests that for the military coalition to gain popular support and reduce rural resistance, military rulers had to redistribute land to those peasants that had the greatest capacity to organize. Strengthening regional and national peasant unions and experiences with repressing rural uprisings in the 1960s made it clear that organized peasants had to be included in the land reform to ease the task of ruling (Malloy 1974). Because expropriated estates were generally adjudicated to those who had previously worked on those properties, this anticipates more expropriation in regions that had greater land pressure: more peasants living in labor-dense areas more conducive to collective action.

The main hypothesis therefore anticipates that the military dictators explicitly targeted the oligarchy with its land reform in order to empower its military initial support coalition, and then it redistributed land to the peasants that had the greatest organizational capacity. I demonstrate later in this chapter that this hypothesis, which flows from Chapter 3, is the most consistent with the reform structure and implementation.

Alternative explanations for the military's reform program can be grouped into four different hypotheses. Three of these have parallels in the broader literature on redistribution under dictatorship: ideological orientation, a "father of the poor" strategy, and staving off revolution. Along similar lines to the literature on the role of ideology in the implementation of redistributive policies discussed in Chapter 5 (e.g., Bradley et al. 2003), one argument attributes the military's reform to its progressive ideology, citing the presence of radical high-level colonels in Velasco's regime. Upon obtaining power, these actors pushed to "raise mass living standards" to redress historical injustices (Masterson 1991, 231; Philip 1978). This explanation finds a more generalized form in Laclau (1977) and Canovan (1981), who associate the redistributive emphasis of traditional populist policies with an ideological discourse underscoring the gulf between "the people" and the elite as justification for providing material benefits to the former. Similarly, Verdery (1991) highlights redistribution as a central legitimating principle in the socialist economies of the former Soviet Union and Eastern Europe. The Soviets during this period of Peru's history, in competition with US capitalism, substantially influenced theories and strategies of development in developing Latin American countries and beyond.

A second, somewhat related argument holds that the military regime adopted a "father of the poor" strategy, distributing land to the poor in order to cultivate the support of the lower classes (Cotler 1970). Redistribution to the poor in this view is pursued for instrumental reasons: a host of authors in the broader literature argue that it can be used to court the lower classes as a base of support for the regime (e.g., Levine 1998; Turits 2003). Indeed, some saw the creation of SINAMOS in exactly this light. And to the extent that poorer constituents are easier to please than rich ones given the diminishing marginal utility of income, a dynamic documented in the clientelism literature (e.g., Dixit and Londregan 1996), the poorest individuals should be the chief benefactors.

The ideological orientation and "father of the poor" hypotheses both imply similar observed patterns of land redistribution from wealthier landowners to the mass of the poorest rural inhabitants: those who were landless, living in indigenous communities, or sharecropping (Handelman 1975). Yet while these explanations shed light on the potential benefactors of redistribution, they have less specific predictions regarding the targets of expropriation.

A third explanation of the military's land reform points to its concerns over leftist rebellions in the 1960s, which may have led politicians and military leaders to fear recurrent peasant protest and implement change simply to avoid revolution (Malloy 1974). This explanation is consistent with the work outlined in Chapter 5 that anticipates redistribution under dictatorship as a result of revolutionary pressure. Acemoglu and Robinson (2006) and Boix (2003) argue that because democracy is a greater redistributive threat to elites than dictatorship under this alternative logic, elites will enter into a coalition with the military aimed at repressing the masses and maintaining dictatorship that is favorable to elite interests. Only when the threat of revolution is high – perhaps as in mid-1960s Peru – will elites accede to some redistribution in an attempt to avoid a worse revolutionary outcome. This literature assumes, contrary to the theoretical argument in this book, that dictators act as faithful agents of a unified economic elite (Acemoglu and Robinson 2001). The most important revolutionary movement in Peru during this period was a guerrilla campaign launched from a series of bases in the Andes in 1965, although attacks extended beyond these areas. Viewed by some as a direct threat to national stability and to the military itself, the armed forces explicitly forced Belaúnde to cede total control over anti-guerrilla operations, which had strong support among the landed elite (Masterson 1991, 215). The second movement was a series of land invasions from 1963 to 1964. Under the slogan "land or death," roughly 300,000 peasants organized land invasions and occupations in the highlands, many of which were eventually repressed violently by the police. According to this account of the reform, the military may have targeted land in restive regions rather than in poor or unequal regions regardless of whether they were visibly unstable.

A fourth and final hypothesis for the land reform, which is unique to the Peruvian case, is that redistribution was aimed at undermining political opposition and support for opposition leaders, particularly those in the political party APRA (Cotler 1970). The Peruvian military was perennially skeptical of APRA's unpredictable political shifts, and it had a well-known antipathy for APRA dating back to the 1930s. The military also feared APRA would steal their mantle of reform if elected, appealing to the significant populist support APRA still held (Masterson 1991, 233). Consequently, the military may have crafted the reform to strike at traditional APRA strongholds. Indeed, major sugar plantations on the northern coast were some of the first properties to be affected, which coincided with Aprista labor strongholds that had successfully fought for exemption from Belaúnde's agrarian reform.

These explanations for the agrarian reform continue to be debated among Peru scholars. Consistent with the main hypothesis in this book, McClintock (1983) and Mayer (2009, 103) argue that Peru's military selectively targeted the landed oligarchy to eliminate a strategic enemy. Although it is not his focus, Philip (2013, 280) concurs with this point, arguing that after Velasco leveraged economic nationalism to bolster his position, he moved with core supporters to "selective confrontation" against the landed oligarchy. Philip nonetheless attributes some of this to the radical orientation of core officers. Cant (2012), by contrast, argues that the regime implemented the agrarian reform to undercut the threat of insurgency through economic development, and then it deployed sophisticated propaganda to articulate aspirations for a more equal, integrated society. Seligmann (1995) contends that the regime had an "ideology of national integration and development" and designed the agrarian reform to integrate indigenous groups into the nation while simultaneously spurring development.

It is important to note that other major alternative explanations for the observed patterns of land redistribution offered in Chapter 5 such as foreign aid, geographical endowments, economic openness, declining land values, and autocratic regime type fail to explain the timing of major land redistribution in Peru as it is displayed in Figure 6.2. Furthermore, most of these could not possibly explain the spatial variation in land reform since they operate at the national rather than the subnational level. Perhaps unsurprisingly, therefore, these factors are not offered in the Peru literature as explanations of the military's land reform program. All of the alternative explanations that operate over time at the national level are controlled for in the subsequent analyses through the use of year dummy variables.

RESEARCH DESIGN AND DATA

In order to test competing hypotheses regarding the military regime's land redistribution program, each of which has different implications for expected patterns of distribution, I conduct an empirical analysis using data on the targeting and timing of redistribution to determine who the chief targets of expropriation were and who the beneficiaries were.

An analysis of the determinants of land redistribution within Peru is advantageous for several reasons. First, the military dictators in Peru from 1968 to 1980 kept scrupulous and verifiable accounts of their expropriations. Landholding and tenure data is also available in great detail from the national agricultural census. Second, there was significant subnational variation in Peru in land inequality, landholding and tenure patterns, political party preferences, and agricultural activity, enhancing the ability to empirically identify the determinants of expropriation. Because of the unique disaggregated data available during this period of dictatorship, the analysis here represents one of the first empirical studies of a major program of redistribution under autocracy that exploits subnational variation in redistribution to investigate its determinants.

Measuring Land Reform

I use a rich, original dataset on land expropriation to examine variation in land redistribution during this period. Direct expropriation and redistribution to rural peasants in the form of collectives and cooperatives was heavily prioritized over other types of land reform such as land colonization, land negotiation, and land titling. In collaboration with the government agency COFOPRI in Lima, Peru, I reconstructed a list of expropriation decrees in Peru during the years 1969 to 1980.[7] This information was documented contemporaneously by the Ministry of Agriculture, which kept records of every government resolution

---

[7] There was, unfortunately, considerable missing data for the area expropriated. Nonetheless, the number of properties expropriated is a valid indicator of the key concept here, which focuses on

emitted to enact an expropriation and simultaneously published the decrees in newspapers with national circulation in order to make the information public. There are two main reasons why expropriation information was handled in this manner. First, as is not uncommon in military regimes (Nordlinger 1977), Velasco placed a high premium on order and procedure, which prioritized the creation of clear metrics for the progress of the reform. Second, property expropriations were published in order to gain popular support for the regime's actions. The public was informed of the pace and degree of the reform and how it affected their own districts. This policy had the additional benefit of reducing corruption in land redistribution, of which there were very few accusations by peasants or officials. Hacienda workers knew each other and their neighbors and what properties were targeted for expropriation and redistribution, which made corruption by the otherwise technical Ministry of Agriculture staff even more difficult.

After property inspection by a local land reform official who reported to Lima, the Ministry of Agriculture could decree a property in violation of Law 17716 and affect its expropriation. Following the expropriation was a study of the property and its value, which was necessary for later reimbursement in the form of cash and bonds.[8] It is important to note, however, that few landowners ever recuperated their reimbursement, in large part because runaway inflation in the mid- to late 1970s made the bonds nearly worthless and because the redemption of the bonds often required a prohibitively complicated set of paperwork. This served to reinforce the redistributive nature of the land reform. The case of Edgar Pajares is illustrative. Although he had been an employee of the Ministry of Agriculture since 1958, his family's estate in Trujillo was expropriated by the Velasco government. After forty years of collecting relevant documents to claim payment for his property, he has yet to receive compensation.[9] This is despite his uninterrupted employment in the Ministry of Agriculture and then PETT/COFOPRI, which gave him unparalleled access to land reform documents and knowledge of the claims process.

Following expropriation, properties were adjudicated as cooperatives or to communities (and in very rare cases, to individuals), typically to those who had previously labored on the estate (see, e.g., Cleaves and Scurrah 1980; Mayer 2009; McClintock 1981). An Agrarian Tribunal was created to deal with litigation associated with the reform, but the tribunals did not adjudicate litigation regarding expropriation, having ruled expropriation to be an executive administrative decision to which a judicial opinion did not apply (Cleaves and Scurrah

---

landed elites and inequality. This is supported by Peru's relatively bimodal landholding distribution.

[8] While separate data on property evaluations linked to expropriation decrees was used to verify expropriations, many of the records stating valuations themselves are missing.

[9] Edgar Pajares, in discussion with the author, Lima, Peru, July 2008.

1980, 154).[10] From 1969 to 1980, roughly 15,000 properties constituting more than 8 million hectares were expropriated throughout Peru.

The geographical distribution of properties targeted for expropriation is displayed in Figure 6.3A. Expropriation varied widely. The areas most affected by the reform were Peru's northern coastal departments, such as La Libertad and Ancash, and the southern highlands of Cusco and Puno, as is described in the literature (Mayer 2009; McClintock 1983). The highland and lowland jungle departments in eastern Peru were largely untouched by the reform after the failure of Belaúnde's famous road-building and colonization master plan in the Ceja de Montaña.

The timing of the reform also varied significantly. Figure 6.4 displays the number of expropriation decrees per year from 1969 to 1980. The reform began in 1969 with a series of high-profile expropriations of the lucrative and sprawling sugar agro-industry on the northern coast. That same year, expropriation began to affect some of the enormous southern highland *latifundios* such as Runatullo in Junín. The pace of expropriation increased in 1972 and remained high throughout Velasco's tenure. Landholding limits were decreased, and the government applied other clauses of the land reform law, such as illegal labor practices, more vigorously. Expropriation reached its height under the first year of Morales's rule in 1976, after which it tapered off. By the time expropriation declined, almost all coastal landholdings of more than fifty hectares and highland holdings of more than thirty hectares had been expropriated (McClintock 1983). The measure of expropriations varies from 0 to 610 per department-year, with a mean of 50.88 and a standard deviation of 92.37.

Key Explanatory Variables: Land Inequality and Landholding Elite Presence

I argue that the presence of landholding elites was a crucial factor that drove the within-country spatial targeting of the Peruvian land reform under military rule. This hypothesis suggests that higher local land inequality, which captures the presence and power of large landholders through land concentration, should be positively associated with land redistribution. To test this, I make use of information on the distribution of agricultural landholdings from the 1961 national census of Peruvian agriculture, which surveyed more than 850,000 properties. For each department, the number of farms and their total land area was recorded for each of sixteen different size classifications. A full 70 percent of farms were less than 3 hectares, whereas there were 3,600 farms of more than 500 hectares. I use the distribution and land area of farms in each size category to create a Gini index of land inequality by department, which captures deviation from an equitable distribution, reflecting the degree to which land in a given

---

[10] This was later revised in 1974, but of the 501 adjudicated expropriation cases, 80 percent were ruled against the litigant.

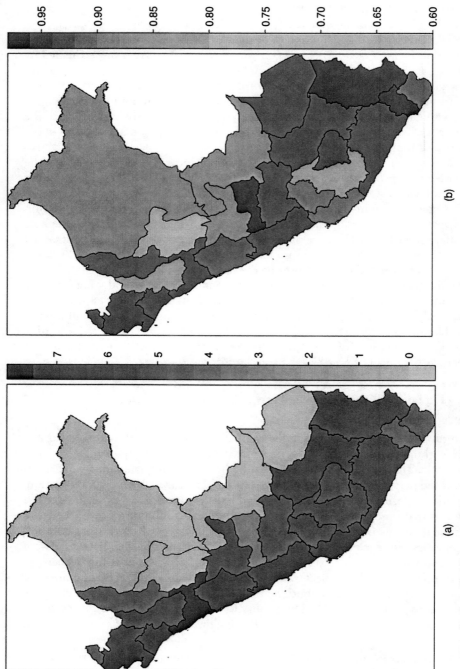

(a)

(b)

FIGURE 6.3. Landholding Inequality and Expropriation in Peru. (a) Log Properties Affected by Expropriation, 1969–1980. (b) Land-holding Inequality (Gini), 1961.

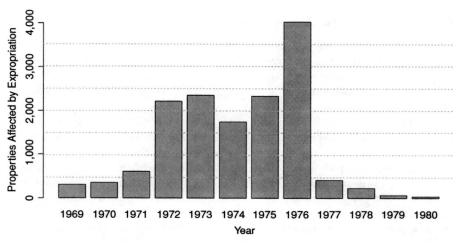

FIGURE 6.4. Number of Properties Affected by Expropriation in Peru by Year, 1969–1980.

department is concentrated in the hands of a few wealthy owners. That this measure captures elite influence is supported by the fact that larger landowners came from wealthier, more prominent elite families (Gilbert 1977, ch. 6). That land inequality is measured prior to land redistribution eliminates the possibility of endogeneity running from expropriation under the military regime to the distribution of land. Furthermore, the distribution of land in 1961 closely represents that at the beginning of military rule in 1968. The only attempt at land reform between these years was by Belaúnde, who only redistributed 380,000 hectares to fewer than 15,000 peasants (Thiesenhusen 1989, 138). Figure 6.3B displays the distribution of the land Gini coefficient by department. Inequality was most heavily concentrated in the coastal regions and southern highlands. The measure of the Gini coefficient varies from 0.60 to 0.97 across departments, with a mean of 0.91 and a standard deviation of 0.09.

I create two other variables to capture inequality and elite presence, since two departments with equivalent Gini coefficients may have different elite presence. These two additional variables directly measure the total number of large landholdings (*latifundios*) in a department. The first variable is a count of the properties greater than 200 hectares, and the second is a count of properties larger than 100 hectares. These indicators measure elite power and presence in a department, and their relevance is bolstered by the fact that the government used landholding ceilings as one of the chief criteria for expropriation. Like inequality, both are constructed from the 1961 agricultural census. The count of properties larger than 200 hectares ranges from 2 to 1,645 and has a mean of 293.25 and a standard deviation of 348.3.

Other Independent Variables and Controls

The analysis includes a set of measures to test the four main alternative hypotheses for the military's motivations for land reform and a series of control variables typically hypothesized to affect land redistribution. It also includes a proxy for latent pressure from below by rural workers with a capacity to organize.

The first two alternative hypotheses are ideological orientation and the adoption of a "father of the poor" strategy, wherein the regime redistributed land to poor peasants in order to cultivate their support for the military's rule. These explanations anticipate land redistribution from wealthier landowners to the mass of the poorest rural inhabitants. I measure the presence of the rural poor using the 1961 agricultural census, which recorded the distribution of land tenure institutions in each department. As described in the Peru literature, the poorest peasants were those who were landless, living in indigenous communities, or sharecropping (Handelman 1975; McClintock 1981). I create an indicator of the presence of rural poor by calculating the percentage of total land under an indigenous or sharecropping tenure regime. Land under these regimes did indeed qualify for reform. This measure ranges from 0 to 0.55 with a mean of 0.15. The areas with greater rural poor presence should have experienced greater land reform if one of these hypotheses is correct. Other characteristics of the regime help further distinguish between these hypotheses, a point discussed in the next section.

The third alternative account of the land reform in Peru holds that the military tried to redress grievances in unstable regions in order to prevent disorder, violence, and even a revolution in which the armed forces could be dissolved and the elites stripped of their assets. The two movements in the 1960s that most concerned elites and the military were a guerrilla campaign in the Andes in 1965 and a series of land invasions from 1963 to 1964. Because the number of guerrillas killed was never published, I use a dichotomous measure of the presence of guerrilla violence based on military and guerrilla accounts and the secondary literature (Béjar 1969; Masterson 1991; Ministerio de Guerra 1966). One-third of departments witnessed guerrilla violence: Arequipa, Ayacucho, Cusco, Junin, La Libertad, Lima, Pasco, and Piura. I also construct two measures of land invasions to test the robustness of the results for guerrilla violence. The first is an ordinal measure of the intensity of land invasions based on accounts in the literature, and the second is a dichotomous measure (Béjar 1969; Handelman 1975). Both yield results similar to those for guerrilla violence.[11]

---

[11] As in Chapter 5, I also tested an interaction between inequality and collective action, which is here measured as guerrilla violence. Consistent with the Chapter 5 results, rebellion amid high inequality does not necessarily give way to land redistribution.

The final alternative explanation of the Peruvian land reform holds that redistribution was aimed at undermining support for the political party APRA. To tap whether the regime was trying to undercut a political foe, I measure APRA support using its vote share in the 1966 municipal election, the last election before the military coup.[12] I aggregate the municipal vote share up to the department level. APRA vote share ranged from 14 percent to 69 percent, with a mean of 46 percent and a standard deviation of 10 percent.

Beyond these alternative hypotheses and consistent with the theoretical argument and main hypothesis advanced earlier, another major factor that might have impacted the pattern of redistribution was latent pressure from below by rural workers that had a capacity to organize if they were excluded from the reform. I create a proxy for the influence of popular pressure by value added agriculture per agricultural worker. This parallels the Chapter 5 measure of rural land pressure. Land pressure should be lower when the amount of land and the value of agriculture are high relative to the size of the labor force in agriculture. I invert this measure of rural pressure for ease of interpretation so that higher values indicate higher land pressure. I then log it to normalize its distribution. Because peasant pressure and organization can provide problematic resistance to autocratic rule in many ways other than outright revolution (e.g., strikes, road blockades, or work stoppages that inflate urban food prices), this measure captures pressure differently from the guerrilla violence variable. Yearly agricultural production data are measured in constant 1979 *nuevos soles* and are taken from the National Statistics Institute (INEI). The number of economically active workers in agriculture, also from INEI, is measured for 1965. The measure of latent pressure from below has a mean of 1.57 with a range of 0.18 to 2.71 and a standard deviation of 0.51. When this measure is included along with the measure of the presence of the rural poor discussed earlier, it should tap a greater presence of workers on haciendas, which formed the basis of peasant unions that became increasingly strong and active throughout the 1960s (Handelman 1975).

The relative ordering of land pressure by department accords well with intuition and the literature on land reform in Peru. Land pressure at the outset of the reform registered highest in southern Sierra departments such as Puno, Ayacucho, Huancavelica, Apurímac, and Cusco. Several of these departments were rent by large-scale land invasions in the mid-1960s. They were also characterized by some of the most abusive land tenure relations in the country, which were propped up by an exploitative and in many cases underproductive hacienda system despite a considerable peasant population. Some of the regions with the lowest rates of rural pressure were jungle departments such as Madre de Dios and Amazonas.

[12] APRA vote share in the 1962 and 1963 presidential elections yielded similar results, although the former failed to reach statistical significance in the fully specified model.

As in other cases of land reform beyond Peru, I include a measure of the percentage of the population that is urban (taken from census data) to proxy for the importance of agrarian reformation, which may vary across regions in accordance with their level of modernization. Land ownership patterns are less problematic in areas where agriculture plays a relatively small role in the economy and where modernizing elites can therefore challenge or displace landowning interests (Huntington 1968).

I include the log of GDP as an indicator of development. GDP is measured in constant 1979 *nuevos soles* and taken from INEI. Levels of wealth may capture demand for land reform (Huntington 1968) and may also tap the ability of the state to implement land redistribution in a given region.

To control for the possibility that the level of land expropriation in a given district and year may be influenced by the amount of past redistribution in that district, I include a measure of prior expropriation. A history of heavy expropriation may reduce future redistribution or alternatively signal the administrative infrastructure necessary to carry out further reform. Prior expropriation is measured as the cumulative sum of expropriated properties in a department prior to the current year.[13]

EMPIRICAL ANALYSIS

To investigate the political logic of the Peruvian land reform and its material achievements, I utilize a panel dataset of expropriation for the twenty-three Peruvian departments from 1969 to 1980. With the dependent variable being the number of properties expropriated in a given department-year, I use a negative binomial estimator to model cases of land expropriation as event counts.[14] The results are not sensitive to the choice of estimator, however. Tobit models yield similar results, as do OLS models. All models include year dummies to control for contemporaneous shocks and exogenous trends in land reform, of which Figure 6.4 is indicative. All models also estimate robust standard errors.[15] I first estimate a set of regression models to test each explanation of land reform individually, followed by a set of encompassing models that jointly test these theories to determine which has the most support. The results are shown in Table 6.2.

[13] Including a control for the number of agricultural units, since departments with more parcels may have experienced greater expropriation, does not affect the main results.

[14] I use a negative binomial estimator rather than a Poisson estimator because a goodness-of-fit test of the Poisson model indicates overdispersion ($p < .001$).

[15] Because there may be spatial dependence, in that land expropriation and inequality/elite presence may be susceptible to geographically clustered common shocks or trends, I also estimated the models using OLS with Driscoll-Kraay standard errors. Results are similar. Results are also similar using OLS with panel-corrected standard errors to control for contemporaneous correlation and panel-level heteroskedasticity and an AR(1) error structure to address serial correlation.

TABLE 6.2. *Determinants of Land Expropriation in Peru, 1969–1980*

	Model 1	Model 2	Model 3	Model 4	Model 5	Model 6	Model 7	Model 8
log(GDP)	0.724***	0.815***	0.700***	0.715***	0.737***	0.593***	0.752***	0.435***
	(0.142)	(0.115)	(0.157)	(0.144)	(0.147)	(0.146)	(0.156)	(0.163)
Rural Pressure	1.035***	1.476***	1.012***	0.954***	0.934***	0.791***	1.511***	0.202
	(0.272)	(0.297)	(0.281)	(0.316)	(0.294)	(0.301)	(0.360)	(0.376)
Percent Urban	0.007	0.011**	0.007	0.006	0.001	0.008	0.012*	−0.008
	(0.005)	(0.005)	(0.005)	(0.005)	(0.006)	(0.005)	(0.007)	(0.006)
Prior Expropriation	0.001***	0.001***	0.001***	0.001***	0.001***	0.001***	0.001**	0.000
	(0.000)	(0.000)	(0.000)	(0.000)	(0.000)	(0.000)	(0.000)	(0.000)
Rural Poor		−2.107***					−1.999***	−0.907*
		(0.544)					(0.579)	(0.545)
Guerrilla Violence			0.077				−0.110	0.062
			(0.184)				(0.190)	(0.180)
APRA Vote 1966				−0.005			0.026*	0.009
				(0.007)			(0.014)	(0.011)
Land Inequality (Gini)					7.153***		6.388**	5.247**
					(2.246)		(2.599)	(2.516)
Latifundios						0.001**	0.001*	0.001**
						(0.000)	(0.001)	(0.001)
Year Dummies	YES	YES	YES	YES	YES	YES	YES	YES
Region Fixed Effects	NO	NO	NO	NO	NO	NO	NO	YES
Observations	253	253	253	253	253	253	253	253
Departments	23	23	23	23	23	23	23	23
R-Squared	0.315	0.428	0.323	0.303	0.324	0.316	0.406	0.498

Note: * p < 0.10; ** p < 0.05; *** p < 0.01 (two-tailed)
Dependent Variable: Number of Expropriations. All models use a negative binomial specification. Robust standard errors are in parentheses. Constants, year dummies, and region fixed effects are not shown.

Model 1 of Table 6.2 provides a baseline specification with the control variables, which track the main controls in the Chapter 5 tables. GDP, Rural Pressure, and Prior Expropriation are all positive and statistically significant. The latter two resonate closely with the findings in Table 5.3. In departments with a higher agricultural value per worker, a proxy for lower land pressure by rural workers that have a capacity to organize, fewer properties were seized. Percent Urban is positive but short of statistical significance, which is again similar to Table 5.3.

Model 2 includes the rural poor along with the control variables. In contrast to the ideology or "father of the poor" hypotheses, the coefficient for rural poor is negative and statistically significant, which indicates that expropriation was not simply targeted at areas where poverty was higher. This is consistent with much of the literature that notes that some of the poorest segments of the population – many in indigenous communities, those working *minifundios*, and most of the landless – did not benefit from the reform (Mayer 2009; McClintock 1983); nor did the military want to cultivate active popular support among the very poor (Pease García 1977). Furthermore, there is little evidence that Velasco had a radical political perspective prior to becoming president that might have motivated him to redistribute to the poor for ideological reasons. As with most of the Peruvian military, he had an explicitly anticommunist strain (McClintock 1981, 52–54). The diverse and shifting tendencies in top military circles were far from constituting ideologies (Pease García 1977).

Could the Model 2 results be the artifact of a relative lack of available land to expropriate in highland areas where the poorest communities were concentrated, as suggested by the prominent economist José María Caballero? Several pieces of evidence suggest this is not the case. First, rural pressure is strongly positively associated with expropriation. Net of accounting for the presence of the rural poor, departments where the agricultural value per worker was higher witnessed fewer seized properties. Second, although more land was distributed in the highlands than on the coast, the "intensity" of highlands reform relative to productive land was lower (Caballero and Alvarez 1980; Mason 1998). This indicates that the regime could have gone even farther in the highlands.[16]

Model 3 tests the revolution hypothesis by introducing a variable for guerrilla violence. Its coefficient is positive but statistically insignificant, implying that the military governments did not redistribute property just to redress peasant unrest or in areas where land was scarce and peasant invasions occurred. As McClintock (1983, 288) argues, the pattern of expropriation is not consistent with narrowly countering "communism" or fostering "social peace." Although junior officers who fought guerrillas in the 1960s were strongly impacted by witnessing the appalling conditions of the poor (e.g., Kruijt 1994), after their successful counterinsurgency campaign the military did not appear to be as

---

[16] See Gorman (1997, 324) for a further discussion of this point.

intensely concerned with areas of radical peasant protest and guerrilla agitation; many of these areas were affected last by the agrarian reform.

In fact, in one of history's powerful examples of the unintended consequences of social policy, the military regime's land reform ultimately contributed to Shining Path's rise. With some parallel to Colombia's patchwork titling efforts that backfired (Albertus and Kaplan 2013), subsequent guerrilla activity was concentrated in regions with less comprehensive reforms, like Ayacucho and Apurímac, and often in poorer, indigenous peasant communities that had been left out of the reform (Hunefeldt 1997). In contrast to the substantial number of peasants from marginalized communities neglected by land reform who joined or supported Shining Path, very few members of the coastal cooperatives – major beneficiaries of land reform – joined. Peasants from more organized communities (e.g., in Puno and the *rondas* in Cajamarca) also tended to resist rather than join Shining Path.

Model 4 includes a measure of APRA vote share in 1966. The coefficient is negative and insignificant, suggesting that the military did not simply target the reform at eliminating a long-time political foe. Although many of the initial large-scale expropriations took place in northern coastal departments where APRA had strong support (known as *el sólido norte*), further expropriation occurred in the central coast and southern highlands where APRA had little support. There are also cases such as the adjacent departments of Cajamarca and Piura, where the former had 25 percent more APRA support but a landholding Gini 10 points lower than that of Piura and experienced less expropriation.

Model 5 introduces a measure for landholding inequality to test the main hypothesis of whether reform was targeted at areas where inequality was highest and the landed oligarchy was strongest in order to reduce its influence over the military. Inequality is positive and statistically significant. Yet one could argue that inequality is perhaps a proxy for latent revolutionary potential associated with grievance and that the military acted as an agent of the elite to undercut this threat by redistributing from the middle class or weaker elites to poorer peasants. Model 6 rejects this possibility. A greater presence of large landholders, directly measured as the total number of *latifundios* in a district, is positively and significantly associated with greater land expropriation.

Redistribution was therefore aimed squarely at the most privileged landed elite. As Mayer (2009, 92) writes, "Landowners unanimously claim that the reform cheated them." Indeed, Velasco acknowledged that the military's policies surprised and angered the elite. Landlords themselves perhaps capture elite sentiment best. Lucho Alcázar, a landowner in Junín, recounted his expropriation vividly: "The agrarian reform came on November 28, 1973 ... It hit us like a bucket of cold water. I will never forget it because it was most unpleasant ... With that paper I ceased to be an owner of what had been mine for so many years, something that had belonged to my grandparents" (Mayer 2009, 90). Rafael Seminario owned several haciendas in Piura that were expropriated, and he then was continually harassed even several years later:

"Everywhere I went I was hounded and cornered. My non-agricultural properties were embargoed, my bank accounts were frozen, and I could not write nor cash checks. I was pushed to last resorts. I had stolen three or four truckloads of cattle from my expropriated hacienda. I stole my own cattle and sold it. The buyer wanted to pay me with a check but it could not be in my name. So I told him to make it out to an employee and loyal friend of mine. At nine o'clock in the morning this employee swore that he would rather chew on his fingernails than take something from me, at eleven o'clock of the same day he disappeared with my $25000" (Mayer 2009, 92).

In order to more effectively target the elite while reducing their collective resistance, the regime adopted a policy of stealth by creating landholding ceilings that became gradually stricter over time, winnowing elites by setting those under the limits against those above them, then later redefining the rules (McClintock 1983). The result was the destruction of landed elites and their long-standing ability to manipulate the military by calling on them to topple threatening democratic regimes, by leveraging resources to regulate its behavior once in office, and by acting to control its budget and training doctrine. A long period of military rule ensued that elites had little capacity to sanction. The military was modernized, and it doubled in size and more than quintupled its funding (Kruijt 1994). This legacy extended beyond Peru's 1980 democratic transition.

Could the findings in Models 5–6 be explained by an "anti-oligarchy" ideology held by Velasco? This explanation would be observationally equivalent to the statistical results, but two pieces of evidence cast doubt on it. First, although top military circles sought to eliminate the oligarchy, their views were not consistent ideologies but rather shifting tendencies (Pease García 1977). Second, the results for the landholding Gini and the *latifundios* measure are similar when the sample is truncated to the post-1975 period when Morales Bermúdez ruled, despite the fact that few scholars would describe him as being as anti-oligarchy as Velasco.

Columns 7–8 of Table 6.2 present a set of encompassing models. The Model 7 results are largely similar to those in Models 1–6. Land Inequality and *Latifundios* remain statistically significant and are similar in magnitude. Even controlling for land inequality, expropriation was more heavily targeted where there were more large landholders. This is strong confirmation of the main hypothesis. The substantive effects of these variables are large. Using Model 7 coefficients, shifting Land Inequality from its mean to one standard deviation above its mean while holding other variables at their means yields an 80 percent increase in expropriation. For the average department, the total difference in expropriation over the twelve-year course of the reform would be about 500 properties, or an estimated 250,000 hectares of land. The substantive effect of elite presence is similarly large. An increase in *Latifundios* by 700 properties (two standard deviations) results in an estimated 10 percent increase in properties expropriated per year, or 610 over the course of the reform for the average department.

Rural Pressure remains statistically significant in Model 7, and its magnitude is higher than in those models that do not include a measure of rural poor, indicating that expropriation and redistribution was greater where there was greater potential for organized rural resistance to the regime. Guerrilla Violence is not statistically significant in Model 7, and Rural Poor is significant but still negative; the hypotheses linked to these variables therefore find little support. The one difference is that APRA vote share in 1966 is now positive and statistically significant at the 10 percent level. We cannot therefore reject the hypothesis that the reform was targeted at least in part at APRA strongholds, such as where the profitable sugar agribusinesses were located on the northern coast. The substantive significance of APRA vote share is nonetheless small relative to Land Inequality and *Latifundios*. A 10 percent increase in APRA vote share in the 1966 elections, one standard deviation for this variable, yields an estimated 29 percent increase in land expropriation.

Model 8 of Table 6.2 is specified similarly to Model 7 but includes region fixed effects for the coast, the Andes, and the Selva. These fixed effects control for region-specific, time-invariant factors such as geography and the ratio of potentially exploitable land that could be expropriated to the number of poor and landless peasants. Given the small number of departments per region and the fact that Land Inequality and *Latifundios* are measured prior to the land reform, this sets a high empirical bar for testing the theory. Static and slow-moving variables are less likely register their effects if they are collinear with the region fixed effects.

The main results nonetheless hold in Model 8. The coefficient on Land Inequality declines only slightly relative to Model 7, and the coefficient on *Latifundios* is nearly identical. Both are strongly statistically significant. Land was therefore expropriated in more unequal departments that had a greater presence of landed elites *even within the same geographical region*. The log of GDP remains positive and significant, and Rural Poor remains negative and statistically significant. The coefficients for Rural Pressure and Prior Expropriation retain their signs but lose statistical significance. This is likely a result of the fact that these variables do not exhibit wide variance in the few departments of the sparsely populated Selva region and therefore do not contribute much to the estimated coefficients. Indeed, dropping the Selva dummy returns both of these variables to similar magnitudes and significance as those in Model 7. APRA vote share drops in magnitude and is no longer statistically significant in Model 8.

In sum, Table 6.2 provides little support for hypotheses that the military was ideologically or strategically motivated to help the poor above all else, and there is also no evidence that it focused the reform in areas of guerrilla violence that posed a greater revolutionary threat to elites. The hypothesis that the reform was aimed at undercutting APRA only gains tenuous support in Model 7, but not otherwise. By contrast, elite presence is positively and strongly associated with land expropriation, whether measured by a land Gini coefficient or by the presence of *latifundios*.

CONCLUSION

Peru's history of land redistribution largely conforms to the theoretical expectations laid out in Chapter 3. The main episode of land redistribution in Peru occurred when there was simultaneously a clean split between ruling political elites and landed elites and few institutional constraints to rule. When either of these conditions was absent, attempts at significant land redistribution failed. This chapter also demonstrates how expropriating powerful preexisting landed elites can serve to demonstrate a dictator's loyalty to an initial support coalition while destroying elite rivals outside of government that nonetheless have the capacity to threaten the dictator's survival. Expropriating preexisting elites also serves the complementary function of providing resources to buy the support of key non-elite groups that could otherwise organize destabilizing opposition.

An analysis of original data on the universe of land expropriations under military rule in Peru from 1968 to 1980 reveals that redistribution was a dual-pronged strategy to undercut the military's rivals and solidify its own support base. Prior to 1968, the military had long been pressured by powerful elites that sought to exercise oversight of its budget and training curriculum, turned to it to overthrow threatening democratic regimes, and then used their influence to coordinate popular opposition and pressure military rulers to abandon policies to which elites objected. Consequently, rather than operating on behalf of economic elites, the military aimed a massive land redistribution program squarely at the most privileged landed elites and thereby destroyed their long-standing influence over the institution of the military. Upon leveling landed elites, Generals Velasco and Morales Bermúdez doubled the military's size and more than quintupled its funding. Land was then redistributed to "middle-class" peasants that had the greatest potential to organize against the regime to the exclusion of the poorest rural inhabitants.

7

Land Reform Transformed to Redistribution

Venezuela's Punto Fijo Democracy and Chávez's Bolivarian Revolution

This chapter investigates land reform in Venezuela, one of the first countries in Latin America to establish a stable and long-standing democratic regime. The Venezuelan case illustrates four points. First, like the case of Peru, it illuminates the economic and political conditions that gave rise to land reform at a particular point in time. Second, it demonstrates how the institutional constraints that characterize democracy can obstruct redistributive land reform regardless of elite splits. Third, it demonstrates how potentially redistributive land reform is transformed in the presence of high institutional constraints into distributive politics. Whereas high institutional constraints frequently block redistributive land reform, other types of land reform such as land negotiation and land colonization nonetheless occur often under democracy. This chapter takes an additional step beyond the main theory by examining why these types of land reform persist even if they are not directly redistributive as defined in Chapter 4. Finally, the chapter demonstrates the transformation of land reform into land redistribution under Hugo Chávez's "Bolivarian Revolution."

With the exception of a brief period of reformist military rule from 1945 to 1948, land reform in Venezuela was largely inactive prior to 1958 despite a large rural population and high landholding inequality. Democratization swept to power Venezuela's most popular political party, Acción Democrática (AD). AD convened a broad coalition to pass a sweeping land reform that endured until Chávez's rise to office. From 1958 to 1998, a total of 8.2 million hectares of property were distributed for the purposes of agrarian reform, constituting more than half of the cultivable land in the state. The bulk of the land was distributed through the Peasant Federation of Venezuela (FCV), the most organized and effective rural union working on land petitioning. Yet in contrast to Peru's massive land reform under military rule from 1968 to 1980, the overwhelming majority of land transferred during Venezuela's land reform occurred via land colonization and land negotiation rather than land redistribution. Landed elites helped craft the legal basis of the reform and were also paid handsomely when their land was acquired for the purposes of reform.

Why did Venezuela's democratic leaders pursue a land reform program that tabled land redistribution? And how was the land that was distributed targeted at peasants? Scholarship on Venezuela's land reform provides several explanations: that the land reform was designed to advance the material well-being of peasants by transferring land to them from large landowners who exploited their land inefficiently; that the reform was intended to boost agricultural productivity, which sagged under the weight of Dutch Disease; and that incumbent politicians targeted land reform at groups of voters in a way that directly maximized their electoral prospects via clientelistic exchanges that cultivated voter dependency.

An analysis of all land transfers in Venezuela from 1958 until the 1990s indicates that incumbent political parties used land reform as a tool to build electoral support by targeting land at the peasant groups that would be most electorally responsive. From before the time of democratization, political parties realized that land distribution was a very effective tool of patronage that could be used to generate votes in rural areas by connecting concrete benefits with a political party. Despite increasing urbanization and natural resource wealth after democratization, political parties had to construct broad coalitions with the rural sector to win elections. They did so by taking partisan advantage over the distribution of land to rural families in order to bolster their electoral support. The reform agency also withheld land titles in most cases, which deprived peasants of the necessary collateral to acquire loans and therefore made them dependent on other government programs controlled by politicians. Elites whose land was taken for the purposes of reform were overcompensated to ensure their willingness to participate in the new democracy and not instead work to overthrow it. Indeed, these elites strongly contributed to building institutional constraints to executive authority upon Venezuela's democratization. These findings are consistent with the theory in this book and also help enhance it. Furthermore, the findings serve to illustrate in greater depth how redistribution can be undercut under democracy. In Venezuela's case, a potentially redistributive land reform was transformed into a case of large-scale distributive politics that relied heavily on doling out public land and well-compensated private land.

Land reform as distributive politics was a great political success. It helped build and solidify electoral constituencies while stabilizing democratic rule. Land distribution nonetheless had long-term consequences. Because land is a finite resource, it eventually became difficult to continue land distribution. This is true even though land was "rationed" in order to make the most use of it rather than distributed quickly, as in Peru, in an effort to break opponents and rapidly consolidate a support coalition.

The decline and stagnation of land distribution coincided with the collapse of Venezuela's party system and the rise of a populist candidate – Hugo Chávez – who promised to empower the poor and free them from the corrupt, clientelistic grasp of the older parties. As Chávez progressively dismantled a host of institutional constraints in Venezuela's democracy, he paved the way for the passage of a new, radical reform law that represents the largest current redistributive land reform program in the Western Hemisphere.[1] This reform strikes at large landowners and redistributes property to rural smallholders and the landless. It therefore shares more similarities with land reform under Peru's "revolution from above" than it does with Venezuela's earlier phase of land reform under democracy.

LAND REFORM IN VENEZUELA, 1930–2013

As in most Latin American states, Venezuela had a traditional agriculture-based economy and repressive military rule until the early twentieth century. The commercial agricultural sector was based on cattle, cacao, sugar, and coffee, and was organized in export-oriented plantations (Powell 1971). Export growth since the 1920s was dominated by oil, and even though agricultural exports did not decline, the agricultural sector stagnated. This was problematic for the 40 percent of the economically active population that worked in agriculture as of 1950. As the International Bank for Reconstruction and Development (IBRD 1961, 141–142) noted:

[T]here were in 1960 about 200,000 farm families living close to the subsistence level. Most of these farmers have had no education and little contact with modern agriculture. They produce primarily for their own consumption...They mainly work as shifting cultivators using only a machete and a planting stick...The remaining 200,000 farm families operate large extensive cattle ranches, large commercial farms, small family-sized mixed farms and small specialized farms producing for the market.

The 1961 agricultural census reflected this disparity in the agricultural sector, despite the fact that traditional elites from the colonial era had been largely destroyed during the internal Federal War from 1859 to 1863. The largest 1.3 percent of landowners held 72 percent of all land in farms that were greater than 1,000 hectares in size. A considerable number of these large holdings were cattle ranches in the plains states of southern Venezuela. The smallest 79.7 percent of landholders held a mere 5 percent of all land. Most small farmers labored under insecure tenancy arrangements. In 1950, 34 percent of agricultural units were worked by squatters, 6 percent by sharecroppers, and 15 percent by renters (Powell 1964, 15). Most of the remaining owned units employed landless day

---

[1] Brazil's current land reform program is larger in terms of land area but is composed mainly of land negotiation and land colonization (see Albertus, Brambor, and Ceneviva 2015).

laborers, who comprised slightly more than one-third of the agricultural labor force in 1950.

This backdrop of rural life was at times stable and at other times in flux as political changes, urbanization, and land reform policies shifted. The remainder of this section of the chapter details these developments. Table 7.1 provides a summary of Venezuela's political leaders from 1908 to 2013 and the regime types over which they presided. The table also applies the theoretical lens developed in Chapter 3 by coding leaders' coalitional incentives for pursuing land reform, the institutional constraints they faced in policymaking, and land reform outcomes. Table 7.1 helps guide the following discussion.

Land Reform Suppressed, 1908–1945

The military strongman Juan Vicente Gómez seized power in Venezuela in 1908 and ruled until 1935. Rapidly growing oil revenues bolstered his rule and enabled him to reduce the tax burden for elites (Karl 1987, 67–68), particularly those from his favored home state of Táchira. He acquired tracts of land throughout the country while building a massive personal fortune, and he favored powerful caudillo allies from the 1899 Restoring Revolution.

Power remained with the same set of military elites after Gómez's death in 1935. Gómez's successors, Generals Eleazer López Contreras and Isaías Medina Angarita, gradually allowed political parties to form over the next decade both because an ascending set of political entrepreneurs had the ability to credibly threaten to mobilize violent opposition in urban centers and because the highly exclusive electoral system ensured their inability to win sufficient representation to overturn the status quo. Seizing on less repressive authoritarian rule after 1935, political entrepreneurs, the foremost of whom was Rómulo Betancourt, began to mobilize a peasant union movement with the goal of agrarian reform. Betancourt helped form the Partido Democrático Nacional in 1936 by cultivating a national cadre of leaders who in turn recruited local peasant leaders and helped them form peasant unions. The intent was to win urban and rural working-class representation on municipal councils and in the state legislative assemblies, ultimately forming a base for a national political party that would implement socioeconomic reform. This movement, later renamed Acción Democrática (AD), became the most popular political party by 1945. Landowners loathed AD from the start given that its party platform called for the dissolution of large landholdings (Myers 2004, 15).

Land reform was largely stifled under López and Medina because of their alliances with wealthy military elites and business elites in export agriculture. There were no coalitional incentives for reform. Besides the limited nationalization of some of Gómez's landholdings, official policy focused on colonization schemes. Congress passed the Law of Colonization and Immigration in 1936, and the newly created Ministry of Agriculture (MAC) began settling migrants. By 1938, the growing colonization program within the MAC became

TABLE 7.1. *Land Reform in Venezuela, 1908–2013*

President	Years	Regime Type	Reform Incentive	Reform Capacity	Land Reform Outcome
Juan Vicente Gómez	1908–1935	Dictatorship	Low	High	None; Gómez himself acquired large tracts of land
Eleazer López Contreras	1935–1941	Dictatorship	Low	High	Limited colonization under the 1936 Law of Colonization and Immigration
Isaías Medina Angarita	1941–1945	Dictatorship	Low	High	Limited colonization; adoption of reform law in 1945 never put into effect
Junta Revolucionaria de Gobierno	1945–1948	Dictatorship	High	High	Agrarian reform decrees in 1945, 1946, and 1947; mostly land negotiation
Rómulo Gallegos	1948	Democracy	High	High[b]	Passed broad 1948 Agrarian Reform Law; never implemented because of coup
Carlos Delgado Chalbaud	1948–1950	Dictatorship	Low	High	Passed 1949 Agrarian Statute emphasizing commercial production
Marcos Pérez Jiménez	1950–1958	Dictatorship	Low	High	Retained 1949 Agrarian Statute; small-scale colonization projects
Wolfgang Larrazábal[a]	1958–1959	Dictatorship	High	High	Convoked Agrarian Reform Commission to draft reform law
Rómulo Betancourt	1959–1964	Democracy	Medium	Low	Passed 1960 Agrarian Reform Law; 800,000 ha. during term
Raúl Leoni	1964–1969	Democracy	High	Low	Continued implementation of 1960 law; 1.7 million ha. during term
Rafael Caldera	1969–1974	Democracy	Low	Low	Continued implementation of 1960 law; 2.7 million ha. during term, heavy emphasis on colonization
Carlos Andrés Pérez	1974–1979	Democracy	High	Low	Continued implementation of 1960 law; 1.9 million ha. during term
Luis Herrera	1979–1984	Democracy	Low	Low	Continued implementation of 1960 law; 700,000 ha. during term, substantial land titling
Jaime Lusinichi	1984–1989	Democracy	High	Low	Continued implementation of 1960 law; 400,000 ha. during term
Carlos Andrés Pérez[a]	1989–1994	Democracy	High	Low	Continued implementation of 1960 law; minimal transfers
Rafael Caldera	1994–1999	Democracy	Low	Low	Continued implementation of 1960 law; minimal transfers, substantial land titling
Hugo Chávez	1999–2013	Democracy	High	Low/High	Passed 2001 Law of Land and Agrarian Development, which was strengthened in 2005; 2.5 million ha. private land from 2005 to 2009

[a] These leaders had their terms completed by interim replacements. Larrazábal stepped down early to contest elections, and Pérez was impeached in 1993.

[b] High reform capacity under these democratically elected leaders was a result of low institutional constraints.

Sources: Albertus (2013); Albertus (2015b); Alexander (1982); Coppedge (1994; 2000); Crisp, Levine, and Molina (2003); Herman (1986); Lynch (1993); Myers (2004); Powell (1964); Soto (2006).

the autonomous Technical Institute of Immigration and Colonization (ITIC). The emphasis on colonization was in part to stem the rural exodus that began after Gómez's death, in which individuals sought to take advantage of growing urban opportunities. Colonization was also intended, consistent with the discussion in Chapters 4 and 5, to alleviate increasing land conflicts and land invasions that stemmed from peasant syndicates that were more militantly backing peasant claims to land rights (Powell 1964, 18–19). Colonization programs were ultimately unsuccessful in addressing these problems. Despite its generous budget, ITIC only put 2,730 hectares of new land into production between 1938 and 1945 (Powell 1964, 31).

Stagnating agricultural production and an attempt to consolidate a shifting support base following the more hard-line former president López's announced candidacy for the 1945 election – which split Medina's support – spurred Medina to push for an agrarian reform beginning in 1944. A law was drafted and presented to the Chamber of Deputies in 1945. It called for the transfer of public and underutilized private land to qualified petitioning peasants. If insufficient public land was present in an area, the National Agrarian Institute (IAN) would attempt to purchase underutilized private land to transfer and would expropriate land with compensation in the event that a negotiated transfer could not be arranged (Powell 1964, 38). Size and utilization exemptions to expropriation were substantial. But Medina at this point was a dead man walking, stuck between popular pressure for reform and resistance from long-standing elites in his support coalition. He was overthrown less than a month later.

First Steps toward Land Reform Cut Short, 1945–1958

The professionalizing younger officer class chafed at López's candidacy for another presidential term and the possibility of a return to the old system of patronage to conservative generals. The younger officers sought a political partner with popular support that could undergird a coup attempt. They found it in AD. AD judged that they had few other avenues for turning their support into political power and became a partner in the coup immediately after it was executed. AD also likely judged that the base of support for Medina's reform was too narrow to achieve a true transformation amid sizable political obstacles (Powell 1964, 44).

The successful October 1945 coup conspirators subsequently formed a seven-member ruling junta, which was staffed by four civilians from AD (Rómulo Betancourt, Gonzalo Barrios, Luis Beltrán Prieto, and Raúl Leoni), an independent civilian (Edmundo Fernández), and two military officers from the self-fashioned Union Patriótica Militar, or UPM (Carlos Delgado Chalbaud and Mario Vargas). AD leader Rómulo Betancourt presided over the junta. Many of the civilians were former student leaders from the Generation of '28, and they included a doctor, a political organizer, a teacher's union leader, a formerly exiled politician, and a lawyer. None was from a family of large landowners.

The two military officers were a French-educated engineer (Delgado Chalbaud) and a captain who had attended the Escuela Militar de Venezuela (Vargas). The two military officers were part of the larger UPM, which itself was led by thirteen members who opposed Medina's rule and wanted increased pay, better equipment, and more predictable promotions. The junta appointed a set of military and civilian cabinet officials that were equally socially varied. These individuals represented the two chief groups that comprised the initial support coalition of the regime: the UPM and Betancourt's ascendant political party AD. Table 2.2 in Chapter 2 provides a summary of the key players involved.

Policies under the Junta Revolucionaria de Gobierno reflected the coalitional split from traditional elites alongside low institutional constraints, consistent with the theory in Chapter 3. The military delivered benefits to the officers: salaries to junior officers were increased by up to 30 percent, and there were greater fringe benefits and better equipment and training (Powell 1971, 85). For its part, AD reformed the electoral rules and extended the franchise to all Venezuelans over eighteen years old. Betancourt decreed several de facto agrarian reform guidelines in 1945 (Powell 1971, 69–70). These were deepened by successive decrees in 1946 and 1947. In the meantime, the peasant union movement formed the Peasant Federation of Venezuela (FCV) at the national level. The junta created the Land Commission within ITIC in 1945, which enabled organized peasant groups to petition for land access. Broader in scope was the 1947 Decree of Rural Property Rentals, which required all private landowners with land that was not actively being exploited to lease that land to the government for subsequent rental to peasants. It created a series of state-level Agrarian Commissions to implement the decree. The commissions also gained jurisdiction to lease any government land to petitioning peasants.

In 1946, the junta convoked a constituent assembly, which promulgated a new constitution in 1947 that enshrined changes to the electoral system. Secret, direct elections in December of that year consolidated AD's political power. The writer Rómulo Gallegos, AD's presidential candidate, won the election with 74 percent of the vote. AD also won supermajorities of 38 of 46 seats in the Senate and 83 of 109 seats in the Chamber of Deputies. Congress then passed a more comprehensive agrarian reform law in October 1948 that was largely similar to the 1945 law, with the exception that it integrated peasant union organizations into the administration process (Powell 1971, 80).

Although AD dominated the scene among political parties during this period, three other key parties formed in 1946: the Catholic-based Comité de Organización Electoral Independiente (COPEI), the Unión Republicana Democrática (URD), and the Communist Party (PCV). COPEI was founded as a Christian Democratic party and adversary to AD's leftist and anticlerical tendencies (Crisp, Levine, and Molina 2003, 275). It was a traditionally conservative party founded by Rafael Caldera that originally represented Catholics, the middle-class right in rural areas, and landed elites (Crisp et al. 2003, 283–284; Lynch 1993, 97), and it had particularly strong support in the Andes. URD was a less programmatic party that depended strongly on its charismatic founder, Jóvito Villalba (Myers 2004, 14–15). The PCV had strong Marxist roots.

The political opening under AD's popular democracy did not last long. AD's policies were quickly cut short as the other major parties charged AD with partisan favoritism in its selection of peasant recipient groups of the land reform, and factions in the military junta became wary of an AD proposal to arm its militant trade union loyalists. A military faction led by Pérez Jiménez and Delgado Chalbaud paired with opposition political leaders to overthrow the AD government in November 1948. Supported by the old landed elite, the new junta severely cracked down on AD and reversed the land reform, evicting former beneficiaries. It also outlawed the FCV. Pérez Jiménez consolidated power after Delgado Chalbaud was assassinated in 1950 and dominated the political scene until 1958. Besides the emphasis on large-scale commercial production in the 1949 Agrarian Statute, the limited land reform that occurred during the period focused on a series of small-scale colonization projects.

Land Reform under Democracy, 1958–1998

Serious agrarian reform did not resume until a military faction ousted Pérez Jiménez's repressive dictatorship in 1958. The air force and navy were discontented with Pérez Jiménez's ongoing favoritism of army officers from the state of Táchira. The air force attempted a coup on New Year's Day in 1958. Although it failed, the coup attempt precipitated popular rebellion and widespread strikes. Political party leaders from COPEI, URD, and the PCV joined with AD in opposition strikes against the regime to establish a competitive electoral process.

Amid the political instability, leaders from AD, COPEI, and URD met secretly to discuss power sharing when Pérez Jiménez fell (Karl 1987, 79). These parties, in the Pact of Punto Fijo, pledged to respect future elections and to fairly consider incorporating members of each party in governments of national unity following elections. They committed to a Common Minimum Program that included not only land reform but also respect for private property (Coppedge 1994, 41). They also agreed to exclude the Communists from government. For landowners, such an arrangement was preferable to the prospect of returning to the rough-and-tumble years of the mid-1940s and the risks such political instability carried. Shortly thereafter, in late January, Admiral Larrazábal organized a set of military elites to overthrow Pérez Jiménez. Larrazábal announced elections only four days after coming to office under withering popular pressure.

Peasants and Landowners: The Support Coalitions of AD and COPEI

The December 1958 elections resulted in a victory for AD's Betancourt and ushered in a long period of democratic rule in Venezuela. Betancourt included COPEI and URD representatives in his cabinet in adherence to the Punto

Fijo pact, although URD quit within two years (Neuhouser 1992, 124). Betancourt's inclusive cabinet reined in AD's otherwise strong incentives to implement land redistribution. Newfound institutional constraints further served to check Betancourt.

Party politics in Venezuela slowly evolved into two-party competition over the following decade after 1958. AD again won the presidency in 1964 under Leoni. This time, COPEI chose not to accept ministerial posts in his government, widening the coalitional split between the executive and large landowners (Neuhouser 1992, 194). Splits within AD then enabled COPEI's Rafael Caldera to capture the presidency in 1968. Caldera chose to govern without a coalition cabinet, which changed the institutional incentives to support third parties and helped consolidate political competition between AD and COPEI (Crisp 2000, 236). His first cabinet members contained COPEI adherents, independents, and businessmen (Crisp 2000, 31). The presidency then rotated between AD and COPEI for the next twenty years until Caldera split from COPEI and won office again in 1994 with the support of an amalgamation of smaller parties, though his positions were still representative of COPEI constituents (Coppedge 2000, 114).

The social bases of AD and COPEI were distinct at their founding. The early beginnings of what would eventually become AD stemmed from student organizers opposed to the Gómez regime (Alexander 1973, 197–198). These individuals seized on the somewhat less repressive post-Gómez political environment to form a nascent political party that targeted the urban and rural working class. They had a strongly redistributive land reform platform that elicited concerted opposition from landed elites (Myers 2004, 15). Yet AD learned from its ultimate failure to implement their progressive platform from 1945 to 1948 (Karl 1987) and therefore broadened its base of support in the lead-up to the 1958 elections. Over the ensuing few decades AD became a catchall party, but with particular support from the rural poor, workers, the center left, and states in the east (Coppedge 1994, 40).

COPEI, by contrast, was founded as a Christian Democratic party with roots in the student movement in the late 1930s. It had the support of traditional conservatives such as landed and other business elites (Lynch 1993, 86–87), and it attracted many of the most right-wing elements in national politics (Alexander 1973, 340). It simultaneously had a social base in the middle-class right in rural areas (Crisp et al. 2003, 283–284) and strong support in the Andean states of Táchira, Mérida, and Trujillo (Alexander 1973, 340). By the 1970s, COPEI substantially broadened its base and became a catchall party that reached into student organizations, professional organizations, trade and labor unions, and the peasantry, although it was overshadowed in most social and labor organizations by AD (Crisp et al. 2003, 283–284). Relative to AD, COPEI received greater support from the middle class, the right, and residents of metropolitan Caracas (Coppedge 1994, 41). It continued to garner support from voters to the right of its platform (Myers 1986, 118). The differences between AD and

COPEI were nonetheless mostly a matter of degree by this time; they often tried to avoid taking clear positions in order to not offend constituents.

The role of landed elites in the two main political parties during this period is tied to social divisions associated with urbanization. With the growth of the petroleum industry beginning in the 1920s, a new set of urban elites slowly developed and higher paying jobs attracted peasants to the cities, driving up the cost of rural labor. AD built early support among urban workers and then tried to link this constituency with poorer rural peasants in a cross-sectoral coalition. COPEI, by contrast, drew its initial support from political powerbrokers in the countryside, particularly in the rural Andean states that had dominated the political scene since Gómez. As Lynch (1993, 86) writes, "Landowners depended upon COPEI to protect them from the Social Democratic policies of Acción Democrática." While COPEI did promise land reform in its early political platforms, it nonetheless emphasized that reform should be done while respecting private property and private initiative (Lynch 1993, 86), which in part reflected dependence on financing from pro-clerical conservatives sympathetic to the Caracas and Andean elites (Martz and Myers 1986, 459). Rafael Caldera reiterated respect for private property in 1960, the same year the Agrarian Reform Law passed, as did the COPEI leaders Borregales in 1968 and Herrera in 1978 (Lynch 1993, 86–87). COPEI's inclusion of landed elites and their role in government throughout the 1958–1998 period helped blunt what would have likely been more redistributive AD land policy in the absence of organized opposition.

Although landed elites found a relatively reliable partner in COPEI after 1958, this relationship decoupled over time. The distinction between the programmatic policies of AD and COPEI weakened as these parties evolved into the 1970s and broadened the ideological and social diversity of their constituencies. Elite families then began to protect their interests through more informal ties with individual politicians in an effort to hedge against the risk of future policy exclusion (Coppedge 2000, 111, 120).

Land Reform under Punto Fijo Democracy

An agrarian reform draft law was quickly approved with only minor modifications by Betancourt's coalition cabinet in 1959. The draft was the product of a series of conversations between a distinguished and wide-ranging group of administrators, economists, lawyers, ex-cabinet members, and officials in the IAN and the Ministry of Agriculture (Powell 1971, 107). By the recommendation of the minister of agriculture, Larrazábal's junta authorized the group to form the Agrarian Reform Commission in September 1958. The commission was composed of representatives of all political parties and a wide range of interest groups concerned with agriculture (Powell 1971, 108). It continued this way after AD formed its coalition government in December 1958. The new minister of agriculture, COPEI member Giménez Landínez, began attending commission sessions and presenting COPEI's views on agrarian reform. Even large landowners played an important role in drafting the legal basis of the reform in cooperation with the major political parties (Powell 1964, 84).

The Agrarian Reform Law was ultimately passed in 1960. Only the Communists opposed its final passage.[2] The IAN managed the vast majority of land reform in Venezuela from 1960 until the 1990s in accordance with the law. The 1960 reform law called for the redistribution of land that was not being exploited according to its social function as well as the distribution of state-owned land. In addition, the law called for the provision of credit, assistance, and public services such as roads and irrigation to facilitate agricultural production (Article 112). In the case of an agrarian problem of "evident seriousness" that could not otherwise be solved, efficiently used land could be expropriated (Article 27). There was no explicit ceiling set on the size of landholdings that could be expropriated.

The lack of a clear elite split during the law's construction and passage weighed heavily on its content. Landowners were to be compensated in either bonds or cash according to the market value of their property (Article 178). Given that expropriation also afforded landowners the opportunity to invest in more profitable sectors of the economy, thereby improving their economic position (Neuhouser 1992, 128), many landowners "rushed to offer their lands for expropriation" (Derham 2010, 178). Figure 7.1A indicates that although a small number of landowners suffered forced expropriations and turned to the courts to increase compensation, most private landowners did not avail themselves of the option to use the courts to achieve a fair price for their land. This latter set of landowners negotiated the price of their land with the government and in many cases won compensation above market rates.

Because landlords who received a low rate of compensation may have judged that a court appeal would not improve their settlement and therefore simply accepted the government's offer, perhaps a more appropriate metric of fair compensation is the difference between government reimbursement rates and the contemporary market value of land in a given region. Figure 7.1B displays land prices paid to private landowners by the government relative to the market value of land in four selected municipalities that are representative of different property rights structures and modes of agricultural production.[3] The median

---

[2] The radical AD peasant union leader Ramón Quijada was able to force a bill into Congress in 1961 to modify the relatively moderate Agrarian Reform Law, but opposition from conservative interests and landowners led the government to drop the bill.

[3] Colón and Turén were districts at the agricultural frontier during this period. In the former, on the border of Colombia, banana cultivation and cattle raising were dominant, and in the latter, on the plains at the foot of the Andes, mechanized agro-industry became important starting in the 1950s. Zamora and Zaraza were districts with a history of property ownership and agriculture beginning in the early nineteenth century. Zamora was a more urban district in central Venezuela with a history of haciendas, and Zaraza a more rural plains district where cattle herding was important. Data on market land prices are from Delahaye 2001, constructed from *El registro de la propiedad inmobiliaria*.

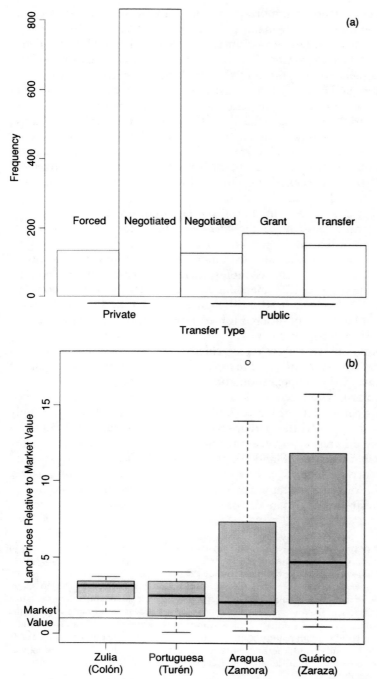

FIGURE 7.1. Land Transfer Types and Compensation under Venezuela's 1960 Agrarian Reform Law.

rate of government reimbursement for private lands in these districts, indicated by the bold lines, is between two and five times market value. Landowners were willing to give up their holdings at these favorable rates to pursue more lucrative opportunities in the urban sector.

The peasant union movement, and the FCV in particular, played a key role in the distribution of agrarian reform benefits. Although AD had a stronger presence in the FCV in its early years, executive power in the organization was shared with COPEI starting in 1962 (Powell 1971), which built significant peasant support through the FCV and equally took partisan advantage of it when in government (Lapp 2004). The FCV developed expertise in the law's technical requirements, which were otherwise formidable to peasant groups, and it typically handled these groups' petitions. More than 90 percent of petitions for land submitted to the IAN under Betancourt (1959–1964) were processed by the FCV (Powell 1964, 89). The IAN relied on the FCV both to increase land applications and to oversee land distribution (Lapp 2004).

From the reforms in 1946 until 1991, a total of 8.6 million hectares of property passed through the hands of the government for the purposes of agrarian reform (Albertus 2013). Over 8 million of these hectares were transferred after 1958. The majority of land transferred – 6.2 million hectares – was state-owned, and the remainder was private property. Given that the total land area of Venezuela is 91 million hectares, roughly 10 percent of all land in the state changed hands. But only 11 million hectares in Venezuela are cultivable. Because most of the land transfers took place in these areas, in the end more than half of the cultivable land in the state was transferred through land reform programs.

The 1960 reform also affected a significant portion of the electorate. Given the roughly 200,000 families that received land and the average electorate size from 1958 to 1988, the land reform directly affected an estimated 3 percent of the voting population in each election cycle during this period. This translates to an estimated 12 percent of the rural voting population having been affected by the reform per election since the reform was targeted at rural areas. This is a substantial figure given that two of the seven presidential elections during the period were decided by vote margins of 3 percent or less.

The amount and type of land distributed varied across AD and COPEI administrations. Impelled by both AD supporters and a serious rural guerrilla movement, Betancourt emphasized expropriation of the private sector and redistribution during his term (Herman 1986, 354). The Leoni administration (AD, 1964–1969) continued with redistribution and also began to emphasize economic objectives. Caldera (COPEI, 1969–1974) continued this shift. Compensated redistribution from the private sector slowed in favor of state-owned land, and the government decreased credits for small-scale agriculture in favor of commercial producers (Herman 1986, 354). Carlos Andrés Pérez (AD, 1974–1979) returned the emphasis somewhat to the social component of agrarian reform by continuing private-sector expropriation and cancelling peasant debts. The Herrera administration (COPEI, 1979–1984) focused more on granting land titles and lessening the state's role in agricultural production. His administration also de facto ended the already tepid undercompensated expropriations from the private sector. The distribution of state-owned land and compensated private sector transfers then foundered and tapered off in the late 1980s and 1990s.

Land Reform Accelerates under Chávez, 1999–2013

Venezuela's political system changed dramatically in the 1990s. Economic crisis and a decline in living conditions bolstered the appeal of anti-system candidates. The charismatic Hugo Chávez was elected president in the 1998 presidential election on an anti-corruption and anti-poverty populist platform, promising to end the long-term domination of Venezuela's entrenched political parties that had presided over the extended economic decline. The traditional party system collapsed as Chávez was swept to power with 56.2 percent of the vote for his Fifth Republic Movement candidacy.

Chávez remade the Venezuelan political system over the next fourteen years, whittling away institutional constraints. Venezuela consequently tilted first toward a popular democracy and then toward dictatorship. Chávez first convened a constituent assembly to draft a new constitution that was approved by popular referendum in 1999. The constitution strengthened executive powers and abolished the upper house of Congress, creating a unicameral legislature (Corrales and Penfold 2007). Chávez won passage of the Organic Law of the Supreme Tribunal of Justice in 2004. The law increased the number of justices, and Chávez used it to pack the court with partisan allies. The law also rendered the court less independent by making it easier to impeach justices. Chávez forged a new political party in 2007, the Partido Socialista Unido de Venezuela (PSUV), from an array of existing supportive parties. The PSUV quickly dominated both the National Assembly and state-level politics. A 2009 referendum eliminated presidential term limits. Severe gerrymandering prior to the 2010 legislative elections and a partisan electoral council reinforced Chávez's political advantages. Nicolás Maduro, Chávez's PSUV successor, availed these political advantages during his controversial election in April 2013.

Chavez's Support Coalition
Chávez built much of his electoral support from poor voters (e.g., Canache 2004; Handlin 2013; Roberts 2003).[4] A former lieutenant colonel, Chávez also empowered the military by enhancing its resources and domestic role and by appointing officers to his cabinet (Trinkunas 2004). By contrast, Chávez largely excluded traditional elites from his political coalition (Handlin 2013; Zúquete 2008). Roberts (2003, 66) writes that "Chávez's mobilization of lower-class

[4] For a dissenting view, see Lupu (2010).

support overwhelmed the capacity of elite sectors and the political establishment to craft a less threatening alternative."

Landed elites found themselves excluded from policy access and vilified as obstacles to Chávez's Bolivarian Revolution, generating an elite split. Chávez's antipathy toward large landowners was evident in his speech declaring the initiation of a new land reform program. On December 10, 2001, at the historic battlefield of Santa Inés where the famous general and advocate for peasant rights Ezequiel Zamora had triumphed over the powerful conservative landed oligarchy in a battle on the same day in 1859, Chávez addressed a crowd of peasants and government functionaries: "[T]he revolution goes to the counterattack, against the reaction of [sic] the oligarchy that threatens, conspires, and undermines it ... From Santa Inés de Barinas and shouting 'Long Live Zamora!,' beginning today, I declare the revolutionary Land and Agrarian Development Law to be in effect."[5]

Land Reform under Chávez and the PSUV

As part of a package of forty-nine laws passed by presidential decree in 2001, Chávez initiated a new land reform program under the Law of Land and Agrarian Development. The law set forth a number of ambitious goals. The main provisions called for land distribution to the poor, a tax on unexploited land, and a landholding ceiling. Although an elite split paved the way for land reform, institutional constraints were initially an obstacle: controversial provisions that enabled the preemptive occupation of property by peasants (Article 89) and the confiscation of farm improvements where landowners could not prove legal title (Article 90) were struck down in 2002 by the Supreme Tribunal of Justice. The National Lands Institute (INTi) was created to administer the land reform. Begun as a decentralized process with regional INTi offices registering and distributing land, the reform only affected state-owned property until 2005. The Land Law was strengthened and amended in that year to overcome the previous Supreme Tribunal annulments (Duque Corredor 2009); the newly packed tribunal was more pliable. The revised law allows peasants to legally occupy private land if they hold *cartas agrarias*, or usufruct certificates that are valid until legal disputes over ownership are settled. In 2007, INTi's organizational structure also changed under the new Land Law, transferring final decisions on property registration and land distribution to its central offices in Caracas.

The 2005 Land Law stipulates that land must fulfill its social function and that *latifundios* are subject to expropriation and redistribution. *Latifundios* are defined as properties larger than the regional average and with a yield that is less than 80 percent of that suitable to its extent (Article 7). Applying this provision, however, is complicated by the fact that complete cadastral data by region do not exist (Delahaye 2006). Owners are required by law to register their property

---

[5] *Aló Presidente* 202, August 29, 2004.

with INTi to rectify the lack of a property registry. But to receive a definitive title, owners must prove a consistent line of property ownership from 1848 (when the Law of Public Lands was passed) until the present (Duque Corredor 2009). Very few owners are capable of doing so, which dramatically increases the pool of land for potential redistribution. Not only is there a large informal market for land, but most land titles dating before 1848 are vague in terms of property limits. Much of the subsequent titling and transfers have referred to and built on these original vague titles. Furthermore, of the more than 8 million hectares of land that passed through the IAN in the thirty-five years following the 1960 Agrarian Reform, only 27 percent of the grants were definitively titled (MAC, IAN, and IICA 1995).

The two chief actors that are pushing the land reform forward are peasants and the government. Peasants seeking a plot of land can "denounce" seemingly unproductive properties to INTi, thereby requiring owners to prove both ownership and productivity. Anyone can challenge the ownership of a given property (Article 35). If the owner either cannot prove title or can only prove title to part of the land, then the land ownership reverts to INTi, even though an owner may retain partial or full use if the land is being exploited efficiently. Successful claimants of a challenge receive a plot from INTi, and if their proposed plan of its use is incomplete upon a two-year INTi review, the land can revert back to the state. The government may also target unproductive or illegal landholdings for redistribution absent peasant denouncements. It has done so in a number of cases, the most high profile of which was the army's seizure of the property of Manuel Rosales, a former governor and chief opposition candidate to Chávez in the 2006 presidential election.

Data from the National Federation of Cattle Ranchers indicates that from 2005 to 2009, 2.5 million hectares of private land were redistributed under the Land Law. A substantial amount of state-owned land has also been distributed or used to create state farms that employ peasants. These expropriations have generally either undercompensated or failed to compensate former owners.

ELITE SPLITS, INSTITUTIONAL CONSTRAINTS, AND LAND REFORM IN VENEZUELA

The previous section describes the conditions and circumstances that led to either land reform progress or failure in Venezuela. How well are these trends in land reform accounted for by the two key factors – elite splits and institutional constraints to rule – highlighted in the theory in Chapter 3?

Figure 7.2 plots veto points and elite splits against land redistribution, land negotiation, and land colonization. With the exception of a brief elite split during the 1945–1948 period, landed elites and ruling political elites were unified against redistribution from 1930 until 1958. Despite low institutional constraints that would have enabled reform, there were few political incentives for reform.

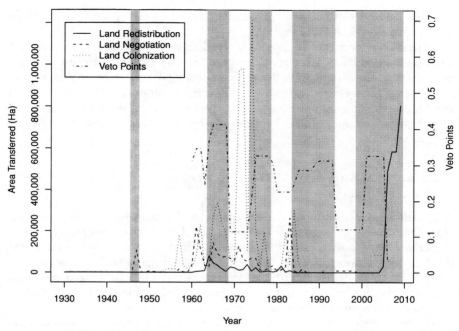

FIGURE 7.2. Elite Splits, Institutional Constraints, and Land Reform in Venezuela, 1930–2009.

Elite splits were much more common after Venezuela's 1958 democratic transition as AD and COPEI rotated in office until the 1990s. Although Betancourt had an inclusive first cabinet, which tamed AD's incentives to redistribute land when Betancourt was president, subsequent AD rule largely excluded most landed elites. Yet the institutional constraints under democracy were substantial, which undermined any transformative efforts at redistribution until Chávez's term. Presidents during this period had significant policymaking influence, but the nature of Congress and the courts made it difficult for executives to pursue policies without substantial support. From 1958 through the 1993 elections, no party ever won an absolute majority of the legislative votes (Molina 2004, 157). And with the exception of 1958, when Betancourt chose a unity coalition for his cabinet, no party ever held an absolute majority of the seats in both the Chamber of Deputies and the Senate (Crisp 2000). These constraints required executives to compromise on their preferred policies. Legislative and executive rules further militated toward compromise. Presidents could not pursue programs through decrees without the consent of Congress, nor could they reject legislation with a veto that required more than a simple plurality to override it (Crisp 2000, 227). Although the courts were politicized and generally composed of AD affiliates, they nonetheless acted as a check at times, and the increasing number of independents on the Supreme Court played a key role in impeaching President Pérez in 1993.

Institutional constraints to ruling eroded substantially under President Chávez. Landed elites were simultaneously largely excluded from his political coalition. Consistent with the theory developed in previous chapters, this set the stage for more redistributive land reform beginning in the late 2000s. A large land reform program is now under way despite Venezuela's high rate of urbanization and agricultural imports. Maduro has pushed forward with this campaign.

LAND REFORM AND DISTRIBUTIVE POLITICS UNDER DEMOCRACY

Although high institutional constraints under Venezuelan democracy foreclosed the chance of large-scale redistribution, land reform was far from inactive: more than half of the cultivable land in the country was distributed through land reform programs. Why did the less redistributive land reform policies persist under democracy? How were these programs structured? Answers to these questions help shed light on the political logic of land reform and other potentially redistributive programs under new democracies.

The answer to the first question of why land reform persisted under democracy is well documented: land reform was politically quite profitable (Albertus 2013; Lapp 2004; Powell 1971). Political parties under Venezuela's Punto Fijo democracy recognized that agrarian reform was a very effective tool of patronage that could be used to generate votes in rural areas by connecting concrete benefits with a political party. These votes were important for building national electoral coalitions capable of winning the presidency. The result was that the most popular parties constructed a large agrarian reform program through which they distributed land and agricultural inputs to rural areas. But this does not tell us *how* land reform was politically profitable. Given the sizeable rural population that was landless or land-poor, what was the ideal way to distribute land in order to maximize votes?

Alternative Land Reform Logics in Punto Fijo–Era Venezuela

There are three dominant narratives that seek to explain how land was distributed under Punto Fijo democracy in Venezuela. The first holds that land reform was designed to advance the material well-being of peasants by transferring land from large landowners who exploited their land inefficiently. Landholding inequality was very high upon democratization in 1958 with a Gini coefficient of 0.86 (Frankema 2010), and roughly half of agricultural workers labored as subsistence farmers (IBRD 1961, 141–142). As a result, Article 1 of the Agrarian Reform Law of 1960 called for "the substitution of the *latifundio* system for a just system of property, tenancy, and exploitation of the land, based on the equitable distribution of the same." Betancourt himself emphasized this in his March 5, 1960 speech inaugurating the reform at the historic battlefield of Carabobo. Soto (2006) argues that the law ushered in the expropriation of *latifundios* and the growth of medium-sized producers. Powell (1964, 86) calls the result a "sweeping program of progressive land reform."

This explanation is consistent with recent work that argues that redistribution following democratization will target elite interests (Acemoglu and Robinson 2006; Boix 2003), particularly those with fixed assets such as land (Ansell and Samuels 2010; Boix 2003). Even if landed elites in the Venezuelan case were well compensated because of the fortuitous presence of oil (Karl 1987), this explanation still holds that reform was structured to meet the most serious land reform demands by transferring large holdings to those with less land. This explanation would also be consistent in this case with a progressive ideology guiding reform, as was outlined in Chapter 5, at least when AD was in power. Betancourt clearly outlined such a vision in his speech inaugurating the agrarian reform, arguing that a "democratization of wealth" was the required antidote to the "marginalization of the rural masses" that suffered from "subhuman living conditions." Betancourt even proposed dubbing the reform "Operation Rescue the Peasantry." This line of argument suggests that the reform was targeted principally at unequal areas where large landholdings could be transferred to poor and landless peasants.

The second explanation for Venezuela's reform argues that efficiency concerns outweighed equity concerns. The discovery of oil in Venezuela dramatically changed the economy by reducing the competitiveness of other sectors. Oil exports and the resultant influx of foreign currency made imported products in both agriculture and industry cheaper than domestic products (so-called Dutch Disease), which put heavy pressure on the agricultural sector. By the end of Gómez's dictatorship in 1935, agriculture comprised only 22 percent of Venezuela's GDP, though it employed 60 percent of the labor force (Wilpert 2006, 250). Venezuela was a net importer of food by the time the 1960 Agrarian Reform Law was in swing. This placed downward pressure on land prices and productivity, as discussed in Chapter 5. Increasing agricultural productivity therefore became a major concern of many subsequent administrations under both AD and COPEI (Herman 1986). Indeed, the Agrarian Reform Law of 1960 specifically targeted potentially productive land that was not being exploited according to its "social function" to be redistributed to peasants. At the same time, bolstering commercial agriculture and agroindustry held the promise not only of increasing domestic food production but also of creating jobs and improving the livelihood of those who remained in the rural sector (Herman 1986, 356).

The third and final main account that seeks to explain how land was distributed focuses explicitly on the role of land distribution in garnering the support of critical voters. Rather than focusing on the most unequal regions or those where production lagged, this explanation holds that incumbent politicians targeted land reform at groups of voters in a way that directly maximized their electoral prospects via clientelistic exchanges that cultivated voter dependency (Albertus 2013; Lapp 2004; Powell 1971). This explanation draws from the broad literature on distributive politics and patronage politics (e.g., Cox and McCubbins 1986; Dixit and Londregan 1996; Stokes 2005). As one agrarian reform official stated, "Vote-buying is good politics. There is no better kind."[6]

There was a massive pool of previously disenfranchised rural voters upon democratic transition in 1958. Although Venezuela was much more urbanized upon democratization than it had been when Betancourt first began organizing a peasant movement in the 1930s, the rural vote remained critical in building national electoral coalitions capable of winning the presidency. The two most popular parties in the 1963 election, AD and COPEI, "were solidly based in rural areas, yet the Venezuelan population was highly urbanized" (Powell 1971, 139). Similar to Gibson's (1997) description of the PRI in Mexico and Peronism in Argentina, AD and COPEI had both urban and peripheral coalitions, the latter of which played an important role in generating electoral victories. The most popular parties in urban areas upon democratization, the URD and the Fuerza Democrática Popular (FDP), failed to build national coalitions, which contributed to the muted importance of the metropolitan vote to governing parties despite high rates of urbanization (Canache 2004). Although urban voters later shifted their support toward AD and COPEI, the fact that they were divided between these parties meant that neither party could rely solely on urban constituencies.

This chapter finds that this last account – maximizing votes via clientelistic exchanges – best explains why land distribution under Punto Fijo democracy followed the pattern it did. Land reform did not occur in the most unequal places. It also tended to occur in regions that had greater agricultural productivity rather than in regions where productivity lagged. Vote share was a stronger, more consistent predictor of land reform than these other two measures. The two main political parties from 1958 until the 1990s, AD and COPEI, engaged in the particularistic targeting of land grants to peasants in order to maximize their electoral payoffs.

What targeting strategy was most attractive for a distributive good such as land in a political context similar to that of Venezuela's? The most effective electoral strategy was swing voter targeting given the limited ideological differences between AD and COPEI and the sufficiently large number of swing voters who could play a deciding role in elections between these parties (Coppedge 1994; Myers and O'Connor 1983). As indicated in the clientelism literature (e.g., Cox 2009; Stokes 2005), these conditions are conducive to swing voter targeting.[7]

---

[6] Quoted in Huntington (1968, 391).
[7] This strategy was further bolstered by the nature of land as a distributive good during this period. See Albertus (2013).

The provision of land to rural voters then gave parties future leverage over beneficiaries using tools such as the provision of credit or fertilizer, which multiply a rural owner's income and reduce the price at which such voters can be bought in the future. Once land was received from the IAN, its productivity could be enhanced by agricultural credits, which primarily had to be obtained through the government (in particular, the Banco Agrícola y Pecuario), because peasants rarely received land titles and therefore lacked collateral to obtain loans.

As with the analysis of Peru in Chapter 6, other major alternative explanations for the observed patterns of land reform offered in Chapter 5 such as foreign aid, geographical endowments, economic openness, and declining land values cannot explain the spatial variation in Venezuela's land reform since they operate at the national rather than the subnational level. These factors are therefore not offered in the Venezuela literature as explanations of the pattern of land reform in the Punto Fijo era. Furthermore, I implicitly control for the alternative explanations that operate at the national level in the statistical analyses by using period dummies.

Figure 7.3A demonstrates that the timing of land reform corresponds closely with the election cycle. This figure sums land redistribution, land negotiation, and land colonization together for a clear picture of the timing of net transfers. Most land transfers, as Figure 7.3B shows, took place in an arc from southern Lake Maracaibo in the northwest to Sucre on the northeast coast and in the municipalities bordering the Orinoco River, which runs through the center of the country from west to east. The greatest intensity of reform was in the same northern arc from Lake Maracaibo to Sucre, where land is more fertile and productive and population density is higher.

RESEARCH DESIGN AND DATA ON LAND REFORM
UNDER DEMOCRACY

The analysis makes use of a dataset on the universe of land transfers in Venezuela from 1958 to 1990 (Soto 2006). These data are used to analyze land distribution through the IAN. The data cover the range of transfer types displayed in Figure 7.1A, and thus primarily consist of land negotiation and land colonization.

I estimate a set of regressions that test each of the main reform logics detailed earlier in the chapter against each other: equity, efficiency, and distributive politics. For the political variables, I first estimate a set of regression models, including political variables that tap whether benefits were provided to swing voters, as argued by Lindbeck and Weibull (1993) and Dixit and Londregan (1996). I then estimate models that test the Cox and McCubbins (1986) theory that parties will target core constituencies with particularistic benefits. Finally, a set of encompassing models are estimated to test both theories in an effort to determine which has more support for each dependent variable. The results are also

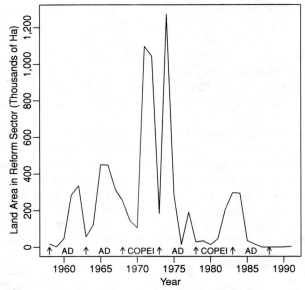

(a) Aggregate Land Transfers and Elections. Note: Arrows indicate elections. Incumbent party listed between arrows.

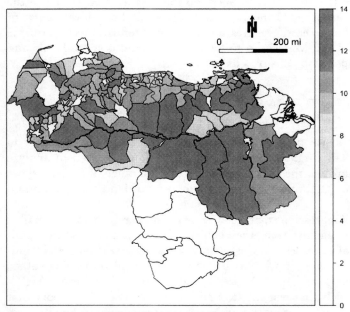

(b) Log Land Transfer Area by Municipality

FIGURE 7.3. Land Reform in Venezuela, 1958–1990.

subjected to robustness tests to examine their sensitivity to both model specification and the level of data aggregation.

Following a host of authors (e.g., Albertus 2013; Calvo and Murillo 2004; Dahlberg and Johansson 2002; Magaloni 2006; Schady 2000), I use aggregate vote returns to empirically identify swing and core groups.[8] Building from Lindbeck and Weibull (1993) and Dixit and Londregan (1996), who derive conditions under which district electoral returns are linked to the presence of swing and core groups of voters, Dahlberg and Johansson (2002, 30) indicate that "under some assumptions about the distribution functions (i.e., symmetry and single peakedness) and parties' objective functions, there will be a one-to-one correspondence between the density at the cutpoint and the closeness of the last election." The presence of swing voters is therefore associated with the margin of victory in a district.

I conduct the first part of the empirical analysis at the statewide district level at which congressional legislative candidates were elected.[9] State-level support for legislative candidates was important because presidents who held majorities in Congress were much more effective than those with minority support (Carey 1996, 53). Second, party control over candidate nominations enabled parties to use congressional nominations strategically by granting seats as both rewards and co-optation devices to forge inroads into organizations that could aid them in implementing policy and expanding their constituencies (Coppedge 1994, 29). For example, a number of FCV officials served in Congress and as political party leaders during periods of AD rule (Martz and Myers 1986, 336).

The second part of the analysis extends to the municipal level, focusing on rural municipalities that were the chief potential beneficiaries of reform. An analysis of these smaller localities within state electoral districts enables better identification of the groups of voters targeted with benefits. Furthermore, similarities between the municipal- and state-level analyses enhance confidence that the statewide district results are indicative of underlying voter group targeting rather than strictly district targeting. This is important given that parties could possibly concentrate benefits to core voters within swing districts and vice versa (Cox 2009).

Dependent Variable

The dependent variable in the analysis is land reform. Land reform is primarily measured as the physical area of land transferred in a given state- or municipality-year in log hectares.[10] This enables a fine-grained analysis that

---

[8] Another strategy to measure swing and core groups is to use surveys (e.g., Stokes 2005).

[9] The term "district" as it is used here for state-level congressional elections should not be confused with *distritos*, the term for municipalities within which local-level government operated during that era.

[10] Land transfer area is logged in order to normalize its distribution.

can assess the marginal effect of the independent variables on each hectare transferred by the government. There were 1,403 land transfers from 1958 to 1990. Given the roughly 200,000 beneficiaries and their families who received parcels of land within the large properties transferred in this period, each family received forty-two hectares of land on average. At the state level, Land Reform has a mean of 10,083 hectares, a standard deviation of 50,197 hectares, a minimum of 0 hectares and a maximum of 955,600 hectares. At the municipal level, Land Reform has a mean of 1,289 hectares, a standard deviation of 13,861 hectares, a minimum of 0 hectares and a maximum of 697,681 hectares.

For robustness, I also measure land reform as the number of properties transferred in a given state- or municipality-year. This measure focuses on the land petition and grant process, since land grants can vary substantially in their size as well as in the quality of land that is granted. At the state level, the count of transferred properties has a mean of 1.73 with a minimum of 0 and a maximum of 23. At the municipal level, the count of transferred properties has a mean of 0.23 with a minimum of 0 and a maximum of 13.

Key Independent Variables

The key independent variables in the analysis capture each of the three main reform logics described earlier in the chapter. The first key independent variable measures land inequality to determine whether reform was aimed at the most severely unequal places in an effort to enhance landholding equality. If this hypothesis is correct, land concentration should be positively linked to land reform. I make use of information on the distribution of agricultural landholdings from the 1961 national census of Venezuelan agriculture to test this hypothesis. For each state, the number of farms and their total land area was recorded for each of twenty-seven different size classifications. More than 320,000 farms were surveyed. A full 50 percent of farms were smaller than 5 hectares, whereas 4,200 landowners (1.3 percent) had holdings of more than 1,000 hectares, constituting over 18 million hectares and 72 percent of all landholdings. I used the distribution and land area of farms in each size category to create a Gini index of land inequality by state that reflects the degree to which land in a given state is concentrated in the hands of a few wealthy owners. The fact that Land Inequality is measured prior to land reform eliminates the possibility of endogeneity running from reform under democracy to the distribution of land. The measure of the Gini coefficient varies from 0.72 to 0.97 across states, with a mean of 0.88 and a standard deviation of 0.07. In order to examine the robustness of the results for inequality in several models in the analysis, I also construct a simple count of the number of large properties, or *latifundios*, in a state. I count large properties as those above the threshold value of 200 hectares, although the results are robust to changes in this threshold.

The second main independent variable measures agricultural production to test if land reform was aimed at increasing agricultural productivity. This could

TABLE 7.2. *Land Reform in Venezuela by State, 1958–1990*

	Negative Binomial								Tobit	
	Model 1	Model 2	Model 3	Model 4	Model 5	Model 6	Model 7	Model 8	Model 9	Model 10
Agricultural Unions	0.037**	0.024**	0.024**	0.021**	0.017	0.022**	0.023**	0.024**	0.003*	0.003*
	(0.015)	(0.011)	(0.010)	(0.010)	(0.011)	(0.011)	(0.010)	(0.010)	(0.002)	(0.002)
Percent Urban	0.027	−0.068**	−0.083***	−0.090***	−0.094***	−0.056*	−0.089***	−0.059**	−0.017	−0.017*
	(0.051)	(0.026)	(0.024)	(0.026)	(0.026)	(0.030)	(0.024)	(0.030)	(0.011)	(0.010)
Prior Land Reform[a]	0.244	−0.283	−0.184	−0.156	−0.075	−0.536	−0.178	−0.542	−0.013**	−0.013***
	(0.253)	(0.297)	(0.286)	(0.269)	(0.263)	(0.468)	(0.280)	(0.454)	(0.005)	(0.004)
Log Agricultural Prod.		3.838***	3.760***	4.199***	4.342***	5.063***	3.972***	4.819***	0.647**	0.657***
		(0.593)	(0.525)	(0.531)	(0.525)	(0.744)	(0.549)	(0.763)	(0.263)	(0.229)
Win Margin		−7.042**			3.986	−0.543			−0.542*	
		(2.856)			(3.166)	(2.571)			(0.308)	
Effective Number Comp. Parties (ENCP)			1.883***				1.088**	1.266***		0.258***
			(0.321)				(0.440)	(0.382)		(0.091)
Winning Party Support				−11.257***	−14.068***	−10.942***	−6.358**	−5.632**	−2.105***	−1.260**
				(2.457)	(2.928)	(2.832)	(3.344)	(3.277)	(0.381)	(0.642)
Landholding Inequality		13.493	15.550	18.617	21.761*		16.737		1.439	0.677
		(13.089)	(12.089)	(11.927)	(11.785)		(12.092)		(3.350)	(3.333)
Latifundios						−0.002**		−0.002**		
						(0.001)		(0.001)		
Period Dummies	YES	YES	YES	YES	YES	YES	YES	YES	YES	YES
Regional Fixed Effects	YES	YES	YES	YES	YES	YES	YES	YES	NO	NO
State Fixed Effects	NO	NO	NO	NO	NO	NO	NO	NO	YES	YES
Observations	736	736	736	736	736	736	736	736	672	672

Notes: * p < 0.10; ** p < 0.05; *** p < 0.01 (two-tailed)

The dependent variable is the log of land area transferred in Models 1–8 and the count of properties transferred in Models 9–10. Standard errors are in parentheses and are clustered by state in Models 1–8 and bootstrapped in Models 9–10. Period fixed effects are estimated but not reported.

[a] This is the lagged cumulative percentage of cultivable land transferred in Models 1–8 and the lagged cumulative count of properties transferred in Models 9–10.

The robustness tests in the encompassing models in columns 5–8 suggest a similar picture. Although Win Margin is no longer statistically significant in Models 5–6, Winning Party Support remains strongly negative. ENCP is positive and statistically significant in Models 7–8, and Winning Party Support retains statistical significance at the 10 percent level in Models 7 and 8. In sum, there is significant evidence that land was targeted at swing districts with a greater presence of swing groups but no evidence to suggest that parties targeted land at their core constituents.

Consistent with the theory laid out in Chapter 3 and the empirical findings in Chapter 5, land reform was greater where peasants were well organized. Peasant unions have a consistently strong, positive impact on land reform with the exception of Model 5, where it is just short of statistical significance. If Agricultural Unions in a state increase in number by thirty-five, the standard deviation of this variable, Land Reform is predicted to nearly double. A larger rural population relative to urban population is also associated with more land distribution. A 10 percent gain in Percent Urban decreases Land Reform by 60-90 percent in Models 7–8. This finding contrasts with those for Peru in Chapter 6, and it suggests that the Venezuelan reform was more focused on explicitly rural areas. Finally, Prior Land Reform is statistically insignificant and mostly negative across Models 1–8.

Models 9 and 10 are negative binomial estimates of the count of properties transferred in a given state-year. The results from the negative binomial models support the tobit models in columns 1–8 of Table 7.2. Models 9 and 10 mirror the specifications in Models 5 and 7. They indicate that a greater presence of swing voters is positively linked to land reform. This is true using both the Win Margin and the ENCP measures. Winning Party Support, by contrast, is negatively linked to land reform in these models. As with previous models, landholding inequality is statistically insignificant, and agricultural productivity is positive and statistically significant. Although I do not report them for reasons of space, negative binomial models that include the *Latifundios* measure rather than Landholding Inequality as in Models 6 and 8 indicate a negative relationship between *Latifundios* and the count of properties transferred. Prior Land Reform is again negative and now statistically insignificant, which suggests that in contrast to Peru or to the country-level findings in Chapter 5, land reform in Venezuela during this period reached some level of saturation that placed downward pressure on further reform.

In sum, Table 7.2 presents considerable evidence that land reform in Venezuela during this period was driven by maximizing votes via clientelistic exchanges rather than equity or efficiency considerations. Land reform did not occur in the most unequal places. It also tended to occur in regions that had greater agricultural productivity rather than in regions where productivity lagged. Vote share was a stronger, more consistent predictor of land reform than these other two measures. Furthermore, land seems to have been targeted at swing groups.

Municipal-Level Land Reform in Rural Municipalities

As discussed earlier in the chapter, there are some drawbacks to an analysis using state-level electoral districts because of the difficulties in attributing the targeting of benefits in politically competitive or incumbent-dominated states at swing and core voter groups, respectively. This section disaggregates the data to the municipal level in order to enable better identification of voting groups within districts. Furthermore, it restricts attention to rural municipalities, thereby focusing more explicitly on the populations eligible for land reform benefits.[17] There were 201 municipalities in Venezuela during the period. A total of twenty-two municipalities with larger cities had populations of more than 100,000 people on average during the period. In addition, there were four states comprised of eighteen municipalities that had particularly low levels of agricultural production and rural populations and were therefore less likely to be included in the reform. These states encompassed the federal capital district, the island of Nueva Esparta, and the remote states of Amazonas and Delta Amacuro; they are shaded darkly in Figure 7.3B. After excluding urban municipalities and those without significant agricultural production, the average municipality remaining had about 33,000 individuals, or roughly 5,000 families when taking into account average rural family size.

Table 7.3 displays the results, which are largely consistent with Table 7.2. The Table 7.3 models account for unit-specific unobserved heterogeneity using regional fixed effects for the tobit models and municipal fixed effects for the conditional logit and negative binomial models. Data on the percentage of the population that was urban, agricultural production, landholding inequality, and agricultural unions were unavailable at the municipal level, and are therefore included with state values. Because the landholding inequality measure is fixed over the period, it drops from the models that include municipal fixed effects. Given the sparser land transfers at the municipal-year level, I now include the cumulative count of properties transferred (Prior Land Transfers) as in Models 9–10 of Table 7.2 across the Table 7.3 models.

Models 1–5 are estimated with a tobit model, and mirror the specifications of Models 2–6 of Table 7.2. Landholding Inequality is consistently statistically insignificant, indicating that land reform was not targeted at the most unequal places. Log Agricultural Productivity is positive, as in Table 7.2, but it is statistically insignificant across all models except for Models 6–7. There is no evidence that land reform was targeted at less productive areas.

The political variables are similar in magnitude and statistical significance to those in Table 7.2. Municipalities with higher levels of political competitiveness, which is indicative of a greater presence of swing voters, were more likely to be targeted with land reform. Winning party support is again negative

---

[17] The Table 7.3 results are also robust to including all municipalities or to lowering the restriction threshold for urban population.

TABLE 7.3. *Land Reform in Venezuela by Municipality in Rural Municipalities, 1958–1988*

	Tobit					Logit		Negative Binomial	
	Model 1	Model 2	Model 3	Model 4	Model 5	Model 6	Model 7	Model 8	Model 9
Agricultural Unions	0.027***	0.030***	0.025***	0.026***	0.030***	0.009***	0.008***	0.006***	0.005***
	(0.008)	(0.008)	(0.008)	(0.008)	(0.008)	(0.002)	(0.002)	(0.001)	(0.001)
Percent Urban	−0.052	−0.060*	−0.063*	−0.063*	−0.061*	0.023	0.030	−0.004	−0.006
	(0.034)	(0.034)	(0.034)	(0.034)	(0.034)	(0.018)	(0.019)	(0.013)	(0.014)
Prior Land Transfers	0.449***	0.439***	0.449***	0.449***	0.441***	−0.167***	−0.161***	−0.067**	−0.060**
	(0.071)	(0.069)	(0.073)	(0.072)	(0.070)	(0.040)	(0.041)	(0.030)	(0.029)
Log Agricultural Prod.	0.941	0.871	1.138	1.123	0.912	1.056***	1.151***	0.293	0.327
	(0.832)	(0.829)	(0.798)	(0.837)	(0.832)	(0.302)	(0.313)	(0.276)	(0.264)
Win Margin	−4.817**			−0.237		−2.708***		−1.547***	
	(2.122)			(2.616)		(0.598)		(0.451)	
Effective Number Comp. Parties (ENCP)		1.971***			1.511**		0.605***		0.307***
		(0.446)			(0.668)		(0.160)		(0.111)
Winning Party Support			−7.198***	−7.066**	−2.644	−1.272**	−0.837	−1.171***	−1.017*
			(2.348)	(2.885)	(3.465)	(0.588)	(0.757)	(0.388)	(0.580)
Landholding Inequality	7.842	6.059	10.887	10.650	6.788				
	(9.813)	(9.718)	(9.314)	(9.865)	(9.773)				
Period Dummies	YES	YES	YES	YES	YES	YES	YES	YES	YES
Regional Fixed Effects	YES	YES	YES	YES	YES	NO	NO	NO	NO
Municipal Fixed Effects	NO	NO	NO	NO	NO	YES	YES	YES	YES
Observations	4,645	4,645	4,645	4,645	4,645	4,015	4,015	4,015	4,015

Notes: * p < 0.10; ** p < 0.05; *** p < 0.01 (two-tailed)
The dependent variable is the log of land area transferred for Models 1–5, a dummy for land transferred in Models 6–7, and a count of properties transferred in Models 8–9. Standard errors are in parentheses, and they are clustered by municipality in Models 1–7 and bootstrapped in Models 8–9. Constants, period dummies, and regional and municipal effects are not shown.

and statistically significant in Models 3 and 4 and negative but insignificant in Model 5, indicating little support for the core voter model for land reform.

Focusing on the municipality rather than the state as the unit of analysis, however, introduces significantly more zeros in the data. Models 6–9 address this feature of the data by treating land reform first as a binary outcome and then as an event count. Models 6 and 7 present municipal conditional fixed-effects logit estimations of the likelihood that a municipality experienced land reform in a given year. Landholding Inequality therefore now drops from these models. Agricultural Productivity is again positive but now gains statistical significance, similarly to Table 7.2. As in the tobit models, political competitiveness is associated with increased odds of land reform whether it is measured using the Win Margin or ENCP. A one standard deviation increase in Win Margin reduces the odds of land reform in a municipality by roughly 40 percent. By contrast, Winning Party Support is negative.

Models 8 and 9 use a negative binomial specification with the number of properties transferred as the dependent variable. The results of the encompassing Models 8 and 9 closely mirror other models in Tables 7.2 and 7.3: politically competitive municipalities with a greater presence of swing voters were more likely to be targeted with land reform than municipalities where core constituencies boosted incumbent support.

THE LONG-TERM POLITICAL EFFECTS OF LAND REFORM

Tables 7.2 and 7.3 demonstrate that land reform was driven by electoral considerations rather than equity or efficiency concerns. Furthermore, it was targeted at regions where political competitiveness and the concentration of swing voters was highest. But why did AD not push for greater reform upon transition to democracy in 1958 with the hopes of locking in political gains and eclipsing other parties in the longer term? After all, peasant unions had supported a more radical reform law in 1960 (Lapp 2004), as did certain factions within AD (Powell 1971). And even if high institutional constraints foreclosed the possibility of large-scale land redistribution, perhaps the scale of land negotiation and land colonization could have been increased.

AD president Betancourt recognized that a reform program that quickly distributed land to their peasant constituency would undercut the basis of AD's rural support by removing the issue on which the party platform had been founded. There is strong evidence to suggest that Betancourt's fears were well founded. Consider Figure 7.4, which displays the long-term electoral effects of land reform. The left panel displays AD vote share by state in the 1983 presidential elections – by which time land reform had nearly ceased (see Figure 7.2) – as a function of state-level land transfers during AD's first period of tenure in the presidency from 1958 to 1968. There is a strong negative relationship between these two, suggesting that once the land reform spigot was turned off, later

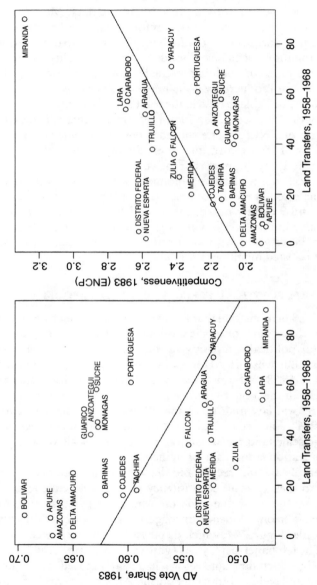

FIGURE 7.4. Long-Term Electoral Effects of Land Transfers by State.

electoral support for AD was lower in states that had received greater transfers in the early years. A similar story is true of political competition, which is displayed in the right panel of Figure 7.4. Political competitiveness in the 1983 elections, as measured by ENCP, was greater in regions that had received more land transfers under early AD administrations. The graphs look similar if one considers AD vote share or political competitiveness in the 1988 elections when all major episodes of land reform had ended, or if win margins are used as the measure of competitiveness rather than ENCP in the panel on the right.[18] The AD land transfer program was carefully structured not only with regard to the allocation of land transfers to districts where political returns would be highest but also with respect to timing in order to maximize the period during which land could be used to garner the support of rural voters.

It eventually became difficult to continue land distribution because of the finite supply of land. The decline and stagnation of land distribution coincided with the collapse of Venezuela's party system. The Black Friday economic crisis in February 1983 undermined the legitimacy of AD and COPEI, which failed to shield the population or right the economy effectively over the next decade (Molina 2004, 162). Clientelism and corruption became major political issues as the livelihoods of those in both the rural and urban sector deteriorated. There were two failed coups in 1992, and then Caldera broke from COPEI and won as an independent in 1993. Caldera's inability to alleviate economic crisis spelled the death and "deinstitutionalization" of Venezuela's party system (Molina 2004). It also created the opportunity for the rise of a populist candidate as voters psychologically grappled for a hopeful resolution to the country's ills (Weyland 2003).

HUGO CHÁVEZ AND THE TURN TO REDISTRIBUTIVE LAND REFORM

Chávez deftly sensed the opportunity presented by Venezuela's political and economic malaise in the 1990s. He campaigned in 1998 without AD or COPEI support and promised to empower the poor and free them from the corrupt, clientelistic grasp of these parties. Chávez's watershed victory paved the way for his progressive dismantling of a panoply of institutional constraints in Venezuela's democracy. With a ruling coalition that excluded landed elites, as discussed earlier in the chapter, Chávez remade Venezuela's political system and thus paved the way for the passage of a new, radical reform law that reordered property rights in the countryside and quickly ushered in more land redistribution than all of his Punto Fijo predecessors combined.

---

[18] A set of regressions demonstrates that this relationship remains after controlling for AD support/political competitiveness in 1958, and it is therefore not an artifact of state-specific factors that led to either low AD support or high political competitiveness throughout the entire period.

Chávez first won passage of a new constitution that strengthened executive power and abolished the upper house of Congress in 1999. He then won partisan control over the National Electoral Commission in 2000 through a favorable transition council that operated between the approval of the new constitution and the August 2000 election of a new Congress (Corrales and Penfold 2007, 20). The 2004 passage of the Organic Law of the Supreme Tribunal of Justice then increased the number of justices and enabled Chávez to place partisan allies on the bench. Venezuela's institutional constraints were now seriously deteriorated, as Figure 7.2 indicates. It was under these circumstances in 2005 that the Law of Land and Agrarian Development, which had been passed in 2001 by presidential decree, was strengthened and amended to overcome the 2002 Supreme Court annulment of its most redistributive provisions. The amended law quickly began targeting private property for redistribution. The scope of redistribution then expanded as institutional constraints eroded even further with a 2009 referendum eliminating presidential term limits.

In order to examine the logic of land redistribution under Chávez, Table 7.4 presents a series of tobit models that estimate land redistribution at the municipal level under Chávez from April 2007 until February 2009. This is the period after which INTi's offices were centralized and individual-level beneficiary data are available. Similar to Table 7.3, I limit the analysis to rural municipalities with a population of less than 100,000 people to focus on areas of most likely reform. Unlike in Table 7.3, however, I now include municipalities from Amazonas and Delta Amacuro. These municipalities are now better connected to national politics and have participated in the land reform.[19] The Table 7.4 models account for unit-specific unobserved heterogeneity using state fixed effects. The observations are pooled across the period to create a cross-section given data sparseness and the short time period.

Dependent Variable

The main dependent variable is the number of reform beneficiaries per 1,000 registered voters. This measure focuses on the land petition and grant process. The most credible and complete data on the expropriation side, that compiled by the National Cattle Ranchers' Federation (FEDENAGA), suffers from some data missingness. Of the 12 million registered voters in 2004, there were more than 115,000 that applied for at least one of INTi's programs between April 2007 and February 2009, when Chávez won a referendum for a constitutional amendment that removed presidential term limits. The land reform program is popular throughout the country's 334 municipalities and capital district, with an average of 345 applicants per municipality. All but one municipality had applicants. Of all land applicants, 6,000 successfully received land grants during this period. Land Beneficiaries has a mean of 0.79, with a minimum of 0

---

[19] Excluding these municipalities yields similar results.

and a maximum of 11.49. I also examine which individuals have reached the legal review stage, which is one step from becoming a beneficiary. Whereas the reform was still in its early stages at the beginning of 2009 and the number of assigned beneficiaries was relatively small, more than 21,000 individuals had reached legal review, and these applicants represent the most likely next round of beneficiaries. Legal Review has a mean of 2.37, with a minimum of 0 and a maximum of 28.90.

Independent Variables and Controls

Several key independent variables similar to those in Tables 7.2 and 7.3 are included: the poverty rate and average farm size, agricultural production, and electoral variables that capture win margin and winning party support. The poverty rate and average farm size are used in the absence of municipal-level data on landholding inequality. Poverty Rate, which is measured as the percentage of the population with unmet basic needs and is taken from the 2001 census, should capture the presence of the rural poor. Land redistributed in poorer areas is more likely aimed at benefiting farmers that have little or no land access over large landowners. Using a poverty measure from before the time land reform occurred eliminates the possibility of endogeneity running from land reform to levels of poverty. The mean of Poverty Rate is 33.8 percent, with a standard deviation of 11.2 percent. For robustness and to more directly tap threats to large landowners, I also include a measure of Average Farm Size based on the 2007 agricultural census. More land should be redistributed in municipalities that have larger farms on average if the regime is targeting the land of large landowners for redistribution to the rural poor. Average Farm Size is measured concurrently with the beginning of the April 2007–February 2009 period for which data on land beneficiaries are available. Fortunately, the relatively small number of land beneficiaries at the outset of this period is insufficient to materially change the Average Farm Size measure. The mean of this variable is 67.2 hectares, with a standard deviation of 99.9 hectares.

Like landholding inequality, net agricultural production data are not available at the municipal level. I use two proxies. The first is the Density of Agricultural Production, which is measured as the proportion of private municipal land held as farms, or "units of agricultural production," and is taken from the 2007 agricultural census. The second is Log Agricultural Production, which is used when Average Farm Size is employed as a proxy for landholding inequality. Average Farm Size is collinear with the Density of Agricultural Production because both utilize data on the area of farmland. Log Agricultural Production measures state-level agricultural production in 1990. The mean of Density of Agricultural Production is 0.30, and the mean of Log Agricultural Production is 12.22.

I construct electoral variables in a manner similar to that in Tables 7.2 and 7.3 using data from the 2004 recall referendum vote to remove Chávez from office. Data from the 2006 presidential election, which was still prior to the 2007 start of the land grant data, yields similar results. The two electoral variables are Win Margin and Winning Party Support. The latter captures vote share in support of Chávez. Reflecting Chávez's comfortable electoral victory, Win Margin has a mean of 0.51, and Winning Party Support has a mean of 0.76.

The Table 7.4 models also include several control variables. The first is Participation in Social Programs. This measures the rate of participation in one of the *misiones* social programs, and is a proxy for pressure for land reform. Data are taken from the leaked Maisanta database of the characteristics of all registered Venezuelan voters (see, e.g., Albertus 2015b). There is no national peasant union analogous to the Punto Fijo–era FCV. Peasant groups are instead formed as *asambleas, comunas, juntas,* and other ad hoc or small-scale groups. Although this proxy for rural pressure is certainly imperfect, it represents some degree of mobilization and interaction with government programs. Its validity is perhaps bolstered by the fact that the Table 7.4 models are restricted to rural municipalities. As in Table 7.3, I also include controls for Percent Urban and Prior Land Transfers. Prior Land Transfers now measures the cumulative number of properties transferred in the previous period of reform from 1958 to 1990.[20]

Empirical Results of Land Reform under Chávez

Table 7.4 displays the findings. In contrast to Tables 7.2 and 7.3, there is strong and consistent evidence that the reform favors the rural poor at the expense of large landowners. Poverty Rate is positive and consistently statistically significant across Models 1–4. A two standard deviation increase in Poverty Rate yields an estimated 0.45 per 1,000 more Land Beneficiaries, a sizeable increase relative to the 0.79 mean of Land Beneficiaries. The estimated impact of Poverty Rate on a land applicant who reaches the legal review stage is double that for Land Beneficiaries. Models 5–6 indicate that regions with larger average farm sizes are more likely to be targeted for land redistribution. This provides stronger evidence that the reform targets large landowners. A two standard deviation increase in Average Farm Size results in an estimated 0.8 per 1,000 more Land Beneficiaries, and 1 more case per 1,000 voters of Legal Review. A shift across the range of Average Farm Size yields a predicted 3.2 per 1,000 more Land Beneficiaries, nearly three standard deviations of that variable.

The electoral variables Win Margin and Winning Party Support, by contrast, are consistently statistically insignificant. Although it is possible that land was granted for individual political reasons (see Albertus 2015b), especially given

---

[20] Because a number of municipalities split between 1990 and 2007, bringing the total count to 335, I divided prior land transfers from antecedent municipalities equally among the subsequent municipal subdivision "heirs."

TABLE 7.4. *Land Distribution in Venezuela by Municipality in Rural Municipalities, 2007–2009*

Dependent Variable	Land Beneficiaries per 1,000 Registered Voters			Legal Review	Beneficiaries	Legal Review
	Model 1	Model 2	Model 3	Model 4	Model 5	Model 6
Participation in Social Programs	−0.361	−0.358	−0.351	1.978	−0.470	1.867
	(1.111)	(1.113)	(1.116)	(1.989)	(1.012)	(1.994)
Percent Urban	−0.773*	−0.772*	−0.778*	−2.066**	−1.335***	−3.314***
	(0.395)	(0.394)	(0.395)	(0.796)	(0.413)	(0.790)
Prior Land Transfers	−0.002	−0.002	−0.001	−0.008	0.008	0.006
	(0.019)	(0.019)	(0.019)	(0.028)	(0.019)	(0.030)
Density of Agricultural Production	0.863***	0.863***	0.863***	1.808***		
	(0.286)	(0.286)	(0.286)	(0.690)		
Log Agricultural Production					0.237*	0.322*
					(0.125)	(0.179)
Win Margin	−0.259		0.760	0.337	2.083	2.913
	(0.601)		(2.490)	(2.998)	(2.353)	(2.664)
Winning Party Support		−0.539	−1.964	−4.140	−3.325	−6.368
		(1.117)	(4.548)	(4.692)	(4.312)	(4.014)
Poverty Rate	0.020**	0.020**	0.020**	0.043**		
	(0.009)	(0.009)	(0.009)	(0.020)		
Average Farm Size					0.004**	0.005*
					(0.002)	(0.003)
State Fixed Effects	YES	YES	YES	YES	YES	YES
Observations	258	258	258	258	258	258

Notes: * p < 0.10; ** p < 0.05; *** p < 0.01 (two-tailed)

All models use a tobit specification. The dependent variables are the number of land reform beneficiaries per 1,000 registered voters in Models 1–3 and 5 and the number of individuals that reached the legal review stage of their applications in Models 4 and 6. Robust standard errors are in parentheses. Constants and state dummies are not shown.

the unique availability of individual data during this period through the leaked Maisanta database, there is no evidence of a strong electoral logic of land grants at the municipal level. The absence of swing targeting, at least, is unsurprising given the much more polarized political environment and fewer swing voters under Chávez, factors that are more conducive to core targeting (Cox 2009).

There is also little evidence that land reform initiated under Chávez has been aimed at improving economic efficiency in the agricultural sector. Beneficiaries have been disproportionately concentrated in agriculturally productive regions, as is indicated by Density of Agricultural Production and Log Agricultural Production. Furthermore, a number of observers highlight how the structure of the reform distorts producer incentives and has led to rural divestment (e.g., Quevedo 2007).

As in Table 7.2 and most of Table 7.3, Percent Urban is negative in the Table 7.4 models. Participation in Social Programs is unsurprisingly statistically insignificant given the lack of organization among Venezuela's rural agricultural producers. Prior Land Transfers is similarly statistically insignificant across models.

In short, land reform under Chávez looks more like redistribution during Peru's Docenio than like Punto Fijo–era reform in Venezuela. While Chávez ramped up land redistribution after 2009, the structure of the reform has remained the same. Furthermore, Chávez's successor, Francisco Maduro, has only promised to deepen land redistribution. The result has been an expansion of the most radical current land reform program in Latin America.

CONCLUSION

Venezuela's experience with land reform closely traces the theoretical expectations. The largest episode of land redistribution – that which is currently taking place under the PSUV – was initiated by Chávez when there was a major split between ruling political elites and landed elites and when Venezuela's long-standing institutional constraints had been eroded. Land redistribution was minimal when institutional constraints were high even among elite splits, and it was similarly low when elite splits were absent. But this is not to say that land reform was otherwise inactive. Large-scale land negotiation and land colonization took place following Venezuela's democratization in the late 1950s and lasted until the 1990s. Land redistribution during this period, by contrast, was stymied by the powerful landed elites that had helped create Venezuela's democratic institutions and then used those institutions to forestall significant redistribution.

This chapter also demonstrates how land reform is designed and targeted under democracy. In Venezuela's case, potentially redistributive land reform was transformed in the presence of high institutional constraints into a game of distributive politics wherein the main political parties competed over distributing land in order to win votes. An analysis of all land transfers from 1958 to 1990 indicates that incumbent parties did not distribute land for equity or efficiency reasons but rather to bolster their electoral support. They did so by targeting organized, rural swing constituencies that were critical to building national electoral coalitions capable of winning the presidency. This distributive strategy was a political success for nearly four decades.

8

Latin America in Comparative Perspective

This chapter moves away from Latin America to examine land reform in other regions of the world. The principal task is to investigate whether the main theoretical argument linking elite splits and institutional constraints to land redistribution holds beyond the specific geographical context of Latin America. I explore this point in three interlocking steps. Chapter 9 takes up alternatives to land redistribution in the form of land negotiation and land colonization.

First, I introduce an original and complete account of all cases of redistributive land reform that have occurred outside of Latin America since 1900 as well as the conditions under which these reforms have occurred. Redistributive land reform is far from limited to Latin America. There have been fifty-four episodes of land redistribution across forty-five countries outside of Latin America since 1900, spanning every region of the world. Including Latin America, more than one-third of all the countries in the world experienced redistributive land reform in the last century. Many more have implemented large-scale programs of land colonization and land negotiation. Still others – perhaps most notably France – delved into reform prior to the last century. The episodes of land redistribution outside of Latin America in the last century alone have resulted in the redistribution of hundreds of millions of hectares of land to hundreds of millions of rural inhabitants. The political determinants of these reforms largely mirror those that have been found in the context of Latin America to be most conducive to reform: a coalitional split between ruling political elites and landed elites alongside low institutional constraints to rule. More than 80 percent of redistributive land reforms beyond Latin America have occurred under these circumstances. Those that have not, typically as a result of higher institutional constraints, are overwhelmingly minor reforms.

A simple accounting of the cases and conditions of land redistribution, although suggestive, is nonetheless subject to potential bias due to selection on the dependent variable. I therefore double down on this exercise and conduct a global statistical analysis on this panel dataset of land redistribution since 1900. I find strong evidence in support of the theory that land redistribution occurs most frequently when there are both coalitional splits between ruling political elites and landed elites and low institutional constraints to rule. As in Chapter 5, rural pressure from below is also linked to higher land redistribution, though its substantive and statistical impact is relatively lower than that for elite splits and institutional constraints. The results hold in a host of regression models regardless of the estimation strategy and whether or not wholesale land nationalizations, such as those in many sub-Saharan African countries following independence, are included. The findings are also robust to including region or country fixed effects to address unobserved country-specific time-invariant heterogeneity and to accounting for a series of alternative explanations. The theory may therefore be transported to countries in other regions.

In addition to providing a global picture of land reform, I also examine in detail land reform within four countries outside of Latin America: Egypt, Hungary, Taiwan, and Zimbabwe. I embark on a process-tracing exercise to elucidate the causal mechanisms that link low institutional constraints and elite splits to land reform within these cases. There are several reasons why the choice of these countries is particularly illuminating. First, they contribute to the external validity of the statistical results, one important criteria of scientific research. The theory-testing cases in this chapter, despite wide variation in factors such as colonial legacies, culture, and historical experiences, support the statistical analyses by demonstrating that the inferences from Latin America are not restricted to that region.[1] Second, these cases exhibit considerable variation in both elite splits and institutional constraints to rule over time, and therefore contain within-case variation that is useful for process tracing. Third, these cases have garnered considerable scholarly attention, and competing arguments have been advanced to explain each case. Applying the theoretical framework developed here helps resolve existing contradictions and shed new light on these cases, thereby demonstrating the utility of the theory in explaining the mechanisms at work. Finally, examining these cases brings foreign occupation and ethnic difference into greater focus as origins of elite splits. These origins were discussed in Chapter 2, but they did not drive land redistribution in the Latin American cases. Hungary, Taiwan, and Zimbabwe are illustrative examples of these alternative paths to elite splits.

The countries examined in this chapter are "congruent" cases that, although differing substantially from the socioeconomic and cultural context of Latin America, largely trace the causal mechanisms of the Latin American cases. In Egypt, King Farouk and the landowner-dominated Parliament was abruptly

---

[1] These cases also support the country fixed effects statistical models in rejecting unobserved, time-invariant factors such as cultural or historical patrimony, or colonial legacies as explanations for the observed variation in land reform.

toppled by the 1952 Free Officers coup, leading to a devastating land redistribution that mirrors the Peruvian case. The subsequent regime under Anwar Sadat and Hosni Mubarak fostered a new landed elite and fused them into the political structure, thereby halting further reform. Land reform in Hungary came when the interwar alliance between Admiral Miklós Horthy and the aristocracy buckled under Red Army occupation at the close of World War II and a provisional Communist Party government was established. With many pre-war landowners being absent as a result of the wreckage and displacement induced by the war, the Communists declared a sweeping land reform. The Independent Smallholders then seized the reigns and implemented the reform rigorously, largely destroying landowning elites before the Communists reasserted power. Taiwan has parallels with the Hungary case. The Kuomintang (KMT) had no ties to indigenous Taiwanese elites and was eager to win peasant support when it retreated from mainland China to Taiwan in 1949. It subsequently executed a massive land-to-the-tiller reform. In Zimbabwe, the displacement of native blacks by British colonizers led to severe land concentration. Land expropriation was explicitly tabled for the ten years following Zimbabwe's 1980 independence via a negotiated constitution based out of Lancaster House. The constitution's expiration in 1990 led to increasing land redistribution that culminated in the large-scale expropriation of white farmers in the early 2000s.

LAND REDISTRIBUTION AROUND THE WORLD SINCE 1900

Land reform is hardly a phenomenon limited to Latin America. Countries in Africa, Asia, Europe, and the Middle East have also implemented redistributive land reform programs. Lipton (2009, 1) estimates that land reform has affected at least 1.5 billion people since 1945. A number of insightful compilations of case studies and works on agricultural development bear testament to the widespread nature of land reform policies (e.g., Binswanger-Mkhize, Bourguignon, and van den Brink 2009; Lipton 2009; Powelson and Stock 1990; Prosterman et al. 1990; Rosset, Patel, and Courville 2006; Tai 1974). None of these, however, has classified or coded the universe of all cases of redistributive land reform. Furthermore, because many of these studies examine a host of land reform policies that differ across cases such as land titling, tenure reforms, willing buyer–willing seller schemes, negotiated land reforms, and land colonization in addition to land redistribution, the inferences drawn and lessons learned are either not directly relevant to redistribution or are not necessarily generalizable.

The first step toward testing whether the theory in Chapter 3 helps explain land redistribution beyond Latin America is to systematically document cases of land redistribution across space and time. I collected and coded original data on all episodes of land redistribution as defined in Chapter 4 over the 1900–2010 period. The data distinguish between major and minor episodes of land redistribution. I define major episodes as the expropriation and redistribution of private land constituting at least 10 percent of total cultivable land over a continuous period, with at least one year in which more than 1 percent of cultivable land is expropriated. Landowners whose property is taken for redistribution must be compensated below market rates for land reform to be coded as redistribution. Major reforms of this nature send a chill down the spines of landowners and have the capacity to significantly reorder the countryside. Episodes of minor land redistribution are those where there was expropriation and redistribution as part of a land reform program but at a threshold short of major reform.

These coding criteria exclude several types of land reform (for further discussion, see Chapter 4). First, I do not include cases of land reform that qualify as land negotiation. Take the contemporary case of Namibia. After independence in 1990, a land reform program began in 1995 that targets foreign and predominantly white-owned land for redistribution to dispossessed and land-poor black farmers (De Villiers 2003). Yet this program is operated on a willing buyer–willing seller basis with market compensation often coming from foreign donors. South Africa's flagship Land Redistribution for Agricultural Development program is similarly structured as a willing buyer–willing seller reform (Lipton 2009). Second, I do not include policies for the colonization of public lands. In the Philippines, for instance, the ongoing large-scale CARP/CARPER land reform program founded in 1988 is dominated by the distribution of public lands alongside the more tepid redistribution of private land (Borras Jr. 2007). I code the land redistribution in the Philippines but do not include land colonization. Third, I omit land tenancy reforms that do not directly involve land transfers, such as Sri Lanka's 1958 Paddy Lands Bill (see, e.g., Gold 1977). Fourth, I do not include land titling or privatization that either do not involve land transfers or involve only state-owned lands, as in the ongoing titling of Australia's Aboriginal communities (De Villiers 2003) and the large-scale privatization in many countries of the former Soviet Union (Wegren 2003). Fifth, I do not include private property that was seized but kept for long or indefinite periods by the state, as in Tunisia's early reforms (Simmons 1970) and part of Iran's land reform (Lipton 2009), unless the property was quickly and purposefully populated by landless or land-poor peasants.[2]

There is also one final type of land reform that merits unique treatment: the wholesale nationalization of all property, as in Tanzania in 1963, Zambia in 1975, and Burkina Faso in 1984. This occurred in twenty countries in sub-Saharan Africa following independence (see Mabogunje 1992 for details).[3] In all of these cases, customary landholdings were far more extensive than

---

[2] Excluding these other land reform policies does not imply that they are not sometimes redistributive. Nonetheless, they do not capture the key focus here: land redistribution.

[3] Cases include Angola, Benin, Burkina Faso, Cameroon, the Central African Republic, Congo, Côte d'Ivoire, the Democratic Republic of Congo, Ethiopia, Guinea Bissau, Lesotho, Madagascar, Mali, Mozambique, Nigeria, Senegal, Somalia, Sudan, Tanzania, and Zambia.

privately held land (see, e.g., Boone 2013).[4] These customary land tenure structures, which have parallels in several countries outside of Africa such as Papua
New Guinea and the Solomon Islands, push the limits of the theory. Private
landowners in many instances of full nationalization were allowed to keep de
facto possession of their property. In other cases, some of the nationalized land
was allocated to a nascent domestic elite. Nonetheless, nationalization eliminated formal land markets and often made private possession less profitable,
which effectively encouraged transfers back to the state for reallocation. And
in some cases nationalization opened the door to gradually attack the de facto
rights of landowners in the small private sector. I therefore treat these nationalizations in two ways. I do not include them in the general discussion of cases of
land redistribution.[5] In the statistical analyses, I run both models that exclude
these cases and others that include them.

Table 8.1 displays all of the cases of major and minor land redistribution
from 1900 to 2010. It also lists the years of reform and the political circumstances under which redistribution was carried out. Land redistribution spans
this time period and is not circumscribed to eras of international pressure such
as the Cold War or to development trends such as import substitution industrialization. Neither is land redistribution a phenomenon of the past. In addition
to expanding contemporary redistribution programs in Venezuela and Bolivia,
land redistribution is ongoing in the Philippines, India, and Zimbabwe, and it
is frequently floated as a possibility by political leaders in Kenya, South Africa,
Ecuador, and Paraguay. Furthermore, many countries such as Brazil, Namibia,
and South Africa have large-scale land negotiation and land colonization programs. Burgeoning rural populations and increasing land scarcity have created
substantial pressure for further land reform in the developing world (Lipton
2009). In short, land reform is far from over.[6]

More than 80 percent of the episodes of land redistribution listed in Table
8.1 occurred in the midst of a coalitional split between ruling political elites
and landed elites along with low institutional constraints to rule. These conditions characterized all but three of the cases of major reform. This provides
supportive, albeit tentative, evidence that the geographical scope of the theory
is broad.

The trends in Table 8.1 contrast sharply with the expectations of social conflict theory, which views redistribution under autocracy as either implausible or
ineffectual (e.g., Acemoglu and Robinson 2006; Boix 2003). Boix, for instance,

---

[4] Although this is true in all of the cases of nationalization, it is not true for all of sub-Saharan
Africa. South Africa, Zimbabwe, and Namibia, for instance, all have substantial amounts of land
registered under private title.

[5] Ethiopia is one exception, because the Derg's reforms led to major and immediate changes in the
countryside. The large-scale creation of new peasant associations on former large commercial
farms paralleled other major land redistribution programs in key ways.

[6] Chapter 9 takes up this point in greater depth. See also Lipton (2009, ch. 7) for a discussion of
ongoing land reform and future reform prospects.

TABLE 8.1. *Major and Minor Cases of Land Redistribution Outside of Latin America, 1900–2010*

Country	Years	Major/ Minor Reform	Elite Split	Institutional Constraints	Details
Afghanistan	1979–1983	Major	Yes	Low	Amid Soviet invasion
Albania	1945–1967	Major	Yes	Low	Aftermath of World War II
Algeria	1971–1978	Minor	Yes	Low	Mostly French land; cooperatives formed
Algeria	1980–1985	Minor	Yes	Low	Mostly French land; to private farmers
Bangladesh	1972–1977	Minor	Yes	Low	1972 Land Holding Limitation Order
Bulgaria	1920–1923	Major	Yes	Low	Stamboliski; private and village lands
Bulgaria	1946–1958	Major	Yes	Low	Aftermath of World War II
China	1949–1952	Major	Yes	Low	Communist Party following civil war
Czechoslovakia	1918–1937	Major	Yes	Low/High	Czech-led reform; German discrimination
Czechoslovakia	1945–1948	Minor	Yes	Low	Aftermath of World War II
East Germany	1945–1960	Major	Yes	Low	Aftermath of World War II
Egypt	1952–1978	Major	Yes	Low	Following Free Officers coup
Estonia	1917–1926	Major	Yes	High	Baltic-German, church and state lands seized
Ethiopia	1975–1988	Major	Yes	Low	Derg reforms
Finland	1924–1939	Minor	No	High	Lex Kallio law; 1938 law
Greece	1918–1925	Major	Yes	Low	Venizelos; absentee and large lands to refugees
Hungary	1921–1938	Minor	No	Low	Pál Teleki; limited under Party of Unity
Hungary	1945–1962	Major	Yes	Low	Communists; Independent Smallholders
India	1947–	Minor	Yes*	Low/High	Landholding ceilings implemented by states
Indonesia	1962–1969	Minor	Yes	Low	Basic Agrarian Law under Sukarno
Iran	1962–1971	Major	Yes	Low	White Revolution under the Shah
Iraq	1958–1982	Minor	Yes	Low	Following Free Officers coup
Italy	1948–1953	Minor	Yes	High	Aftermath of World War II; undercut Communists
Japan	1946–1949	Major	Yes	Low	Under post–World War II US occupation
Jordan	1959–1971	Minor	Yes	Low	Part of East Ghor Canal Project

(continued)

TABLE 8.1 (*continued*)

Country	Years	Major/ Minor Reform	Elite Split	Institutional Constraints	Details
Latvia	1920–1937	Major	Yes	High/Low	Mainly targeted Baltic Germans
Libya	1969–1970	Minor	Yes	Low	Confiscated Italian property
Lithuania	1920–1930	Major	Yes	Low	Mainly targeted nobles' land from Russia
Mongolia	1929–1932	Major	Yes	Low	Targeted nobility and Buddhist church
Morocco	1956–1972	Minor	Yes	Low	Upon independence; French and state land
Myanmar	1953–1958	Minor	Yes	High	Pyidawtha Plan; Chettyar and large lands
North Korea	1946–1947	Major	Yes	Low	Aftermath of World War II
North Vietnam	1954–1956	Major	Yes	Low	Lao Dong Party; transfers and rent refunds
Pakistan	1959–1990	Minor	Yes	Low	Begun in West, 1959; new PPP law, 1972
Philippines	1956–1957	Minor	Yes	High	1955 Land Reform Law under Magsaysay
Philippines	1973–1979	Minor	Yes	Low	1972 Land Reform Law under Marcos
Philippines	1988–	Minor	No	High	CARP/CARPER
Poland	1918–1938	Minor	Yes	Low	Land Reform Bill in aftermath of World War I
Poland	1944–1948	Major	Yes	Low	Aftermath of World War II
Portugal	1975	Major	Yes	Low	Carnation Revolution under military
Romania	1921–1937	Major	Yes	Low	King Ferdinand after territorial expansion
Romania	1944–1948	Major	Yes	Low	Aftermath of World War II; communist pressure
Russia	1917–1927	Major	Yes	Low	Soviet Decree on Land and 1922 Code
South Korea	1948–1958	Major	Yes	Low	Japanese lands and large holdings
South Vietnam	1956–1973	Major	Yes	Low	Ordinance 57 and US-backed land-to-tiller
Spain	1932–1936	Minor	Yes	High	Prior to Spanish Civil War
Sri Lanka	1972–1990	Major	Yes	High/ Medium	1972 law following 1958 Paddy Lands Bill
Syria	1958–1974	Minor	Yes	Low	UAR followed by Ba'ath party
Taiwan	1949–1955	Major	Yes	Low	KMT after Chinese civil war
Thailand	1975–2003	Minor	Yes	Low/High	Following 1973 coup; mostly public lands
Tunisia	1964–1969	Minor	Yes	Low	Seizure of remaining French land

Country	Years	Major/Minor Reform	Elite Split	Institutional Constraints	Details
Yugoslavia	1921–1930	Major	Yes	Low	Mainly targeted Germans and Hungarians
Yugoslavia	1945–1954	Major	Yes	Low	Aftermath of World War II under Communists
Zimbabwe	1992–	Major	Yes	Low	White lands targeted by Mugabe

Notes: Major land reform is defined as the expropriation and redistribution of at least 10 percent of cultivable land over a continuous period with at least one year in which more than 1 percent of cultivable land is expropriated. Minor reforms are those where there was expropriation and redistribution as part of a land reform program but at a threshold short of major reform. Cultivable land area comes from the FAO. Earliest available agricultural land area is used where cultivable area is missing (primarily OECD countries).
* There was an elite split at the national level only during the first decade following independence. India is the one case in which land reform policy is set at the state level. There was considerable variation at the subnational level in elite splits and institutional constraints, although the national-level elite split following independence set the stage for state-level policies that often persisted.
Sources: Afghanistan: Amstutz (1986); Albania: Sabates-Wheeler and Waite (2003); Algeria: Smith (1975); Bangladesh: Alamgir (1981); Bulgaria: Howe (1998), Jörgensen (2006), Vaskela (1996); China: Kung, Wu, and Wu (2012), Moïse (1983); Czechoslovakia: Kotatko (1948), Vaskela (1996); East Germany: Naimak (1995); Egypt: Deininger (2003), Tai (1974); Estonia: Jörgensen (2006); Vaskela (1996); Ethiopia: Young (1997); Finland: Jörgensen (2006); Greece: Kontogiorgi (2006); Hungary: Mathijs (1997), Varga (2009); India: Binswanger-Mkhize, Bourguignon, and van den Brink (2009); Indonesia: Tjondronegoro (1972); Iran: Lipton (2009), Majd and Nowshirvani (1993), Tai (1974); Iraq: El-Ghonemy (2002); Italy: D'Aragona (1954), Ginsborg (1990); Japan: Deininger (2003), Kawagoe (1999); Jordan: Haddadin (2009), Hazleton (1979); Latvia: Vaskela (1996); Libya: Vandewalle (1998); Lithuania: Vaskela (1996); Mongolia: Bawden (1968); Morocco: Griffin (1975); Myanmar: Walinsky (1962); North Korea: Lee (1963); North Vietnam: Moïse (1983); Pakistan: Rashid (1985), Tai (1974); Philippines: Borras Jr. (2007), Kurkvliet (1983), Wurfel (1983); Poland: Pronin (1949), Vaskela (1996); Portugal: Pires de Almeida (2007); Romania: OECD (2000), Vaskela (1996); Russia: Atkinson (1983), Lipton (2009); South Korea: Deininger (2003); South Vietnam: Dacy (1986); Spain: Malefakis (1970); Sri Lanka: Gold (1977), Samaraweera (1982); Syria: Khader (1975), Tai (1974); Taiwan: Tai (1974); Thailand: Ramsay (1982), Suehiro (1981); Tunisia: Ashford (1969), Simmons (1970); Yugoslavia: Dovring (1970), Melmed-Sanjak, Bloch, and Hanson (1998), Vaskela (1996); Zimbabwe: Pazvakavambwa and Hungwe (2009).

argues that redistribution under autocracy can only occur under left-wing rule (most typically following revolution), but that it is naturally so riddled with corruption that it is ultimately inconsequential: "[R]apid domestic reforms, such as in the distribution of agrarian property, can hardly transform the underlying structure of unequal societies" (Boix 2003, 18). The only other time Boix mentions agrarian reform it is to cite Powelson and Stock (1990) as the most comprehensive evidence that agrarian reform under autocratic rule has never benefited peasants, with perhaps the exceptions of South Korea, Taiwan, and India's Kerala (Boix 2003, 216). Yet Powelson and Stock's conclusion is hardly in the mainstream. The scholarly consensus on the major land reforms in Table 8.1 is that, although they were in many ways imperfect, they have resulted in massive shifts in property ownership that typically paved the way for more egalitarian and robust growth (Alesina and Rodrik 1994; Binswanger, Deininger, and Feder 1995; El-Ghonemy 2002; Griffin, Khan, and Ickowitz 2002; Lipton 2009; Tai 1974).

The ways in which the redistributive land reform programs in Table 8.1 were generated map closely on to the theory in Chapter 3. Most reforms were implemented by above. Coups in Egypt, Ethiopia, Iraq, Pakistan, Portugal, Syria, and Thailand brought military rulers into office who attacked landed elites with whom they had few ties.[7] Portugal and Iraq are illustrative cases. The land reform in Portugal was spurred by a military coup that ousted the Estado Novo in April 1974. Incoming officers replaced national and local political elites and passed radical legislation aimed at "liquidating fascism and landowners" in "a general attack to private property" (Pires de Almeida 2007, 64). They quickly seized more than a million hectares of land in favor of workers and expelled traditional landowners. The Free Officers coup in Iraq in 1958 that toppled the Hashemite monarchy similarly introduced major reforms. Prior to the coup, the vast majority of land was held in the possession of politically influential tribal chiefs, although 78 percent was officially state property (El-Ghonemy 2002, 175). The successful 1958 coup quickly yielded substantial land redistribution. Estates exceeding 50 hectares in rain-fed areas of the north and 250 hectares in irrigated areas of central and southern Iraq were expropriated. Land belonging to the royal family and other "enemies of the revolution" was confiscated without any compensation. The land reform program remained in force despite political instability in the 1960s. The landholding inequality Gini dropped steeply from 0.902 in 1958 to 0.394 in 1982 as rural incomes rose (El-Ghonemy 2002, 180).

Autocratic leaders drawn from outside the ranks of landed elites who seek to consolidate their grip on power such as Sukarno in Indonesia, Alexander Stomboliski in Bulgaria, and Robert Mugabe in Zimbabwe are also capable of significant land reforms. Take for example Bulgaria. In the wake of World War I, the powerful Stamboliski led the Bulgarian Agricultural Union (BANU) to a 1919 electoral win with 31 percent of the vote. BANU shunned the Communists and instead formed a coalition with the Democrats. Stamboliski invalidated a host of communist mandates and formed an Agrarian Ministry in coalition with several smaller parties. He then pushed forward a radical land reform in 1920 that promised all cultivators at least four hectares of land and set a landholding ceiling at thirty hectares (Jörgensen 2006, 85).

Finally, land redistribution has also occurred in the wake of revolution when peasants are able to successfully overthrow the state (or aid in doing so) and implement "popular" government. The most prominent and consequential cases of such reform came in the wake of Russia's 1917 Bolshevik Revolution and China's 1949 Civil War.

Table 8.1 also indicates that, as detailed in Chapter 2, foreign occupation and ethnic difference have played an important role in generating elites splits that provided incentives for land redistribution. Large-scale land redistribution

[7] This phenomenon is not limited to land reform. For a discussion of "elite revolutions" in Meiji Japan, Turkey, and several other cases, see Trimberger (1978).

in Japan and South Korea was initiated by the United States as an occupying power (Deininger 2003). A similar scenario occurred in Taiwan when the retreating KMT occupied the island. And countries such as Yugoslavia and Romania implemented heavily redistributive land reform under Soviet pressure in the aftermath of World War II (Vaskela 1996). In these cases, foreign forces took the place of local political elites and operated according to their own interests distinct from those of landed elites.

The retraction of forces from occupied territories, most prominently with decolonization, also yielded elite splits between ethnic minority landowners and indigenous political elites. As foreign powers withdrew from their colonies under the pressure of independence movements and domestic political considerations, powerful landed and other economic elites that had long been influential under colonial rule saw their fortunes erode rapidly. Colonizers' dubious and forced land grabs, long sanctioned in colonial South Africa, Namibia, Algeria, Libya, Morocco, Tunisia, and Zimbabwe, were vulnerable to a new, hostile ruling political elite. Although institutional constraints and foreign pressure restrained land redistribution in some of these countries (South Africa and Namibia), colonizers' land was confiscated in others (Algeria, Libya, Morocco, Tunisia, and Zimbabwe). A similar outcome occurred with the Chettyars in post-independence Myanmar and former Ottoman estates in Greece in the 1920s.

There are ten instances of land redistribution in Table 8.1 that are not the result of elite splits amid low institutional constraints. These cases shed light on several other salient aspects of land reform. In seven of these cases, land redistribution occurred amid elite splits despite high institutional constraints. The theory developed in Chapter 3 suggests that the conditions for such reforms are rarely met: only when the rural poor have some organizational capacity and landed elites fail to fully capture key veto points do these reform efforts bear fruit. In four of these cases, land redistribution was predictably minor. Ramón Magsaysay in the Philippines is one example. Magsaysay was elected in 1953 with 68 percent of the vote and substantial rural support as a violent insurgency (the Huk Rebellion), which recruited landless farmers to fight against powerful landlords, simmered in the countryside. Congress was severely beholden to landowners (Tai 1974, 144), who had also previously been able to successfully defend local challenges to their property through courts (Wurfel 1983, 2). Magsaysay's proposed land reform bill was therefore watered down in Congress. Yet landowners lacked a unifying organization, enabling Magsaysay to achieve a very moderate land reform in 1955. The threat of peasant action also motivated reform efforts in Spain at the outset of the Great Depression (Malefakis 1970) and Italy (D'Aragona 1954) in the wake of World War II. In Spain's case, landowners and traditional conservatives provisionally supported democracy under the Second Republic beginning in 1931 (Alexander 2002, 103). Yet their weak electoral hold and popular pressure enabled minor land reform beginning in 1932. Spain is the one – and seemingly only – case of land redistribution that conforms to Acemoglu and Robinson's (2006) predictions that an organized popular threat leads elites to hand over power and suffer limited redistribution under middling levels of inequality.

In the cases of Estonia, Latvia, and Sri Lanka, major land reforms occurred amid elite splits and high institutional constraints. These three cases capture an empirically rare circumstance: landed elites were almost entirely excluded from power despite popular elections. They not only failed to entirely capture key veto points; they also failed to gain any significant representation at all. Why were they unable to marshal their resources to lobby against reform or use clientelism to their advantage at the polls? In Estonia and Latvia, Baltic German nobles held the bulk of large estates. Nationalist forces in Estonia defeated the Germans in 1918 and the Russians in 1919. They then formed a Constituent Assembly in 1919 that excluded Baltic Germans and paved the way for the redistribution of their land (Jörgensen 2006). A similar outcome transpired in Latvia. In Sri Lanka, Sirimavo Bandaranaike's United Front (UF) won the 1970 parliamentary elections by a landslide, capturing 116 of the 151 seats in Parliament. The UF brought together the two main leftist parties with the Sri Lanka Freedom Party, almost entirely excluding landowners from power and leading to expectations of "instant socialism" (Samaraweera 1982, 105). Major land reform was quickly thrust on the agenda in the wake of the insurrection of 1971 as the UF sought to "recover its socialist credentials" in the face of a threat to political stability (Samaraweera 1982, 105–106).

In three exceptional cases in Table 8.1, landed elites themselves adopted redistributive reforms when they held political power. These were all cases of minor reform in which the threat of peasant unrest spurred landed elites to act. Finland faced this situation in the 1920s. Jörgensen (2006, 88) writes that "the right-wing government's decision to adopt the Lex Kallio law in 1924 was nevertheless a truly radical solution since it weighed the compensation to former landowners against aspirations to political and social stability." Although voluntary sales, urbanization, and declining land prices ultimately blunted some of the redistributive impact of the law, it nonetheless focused on expropriation because of the remoteness of state-owned land for colonization and the insufficient number of voluntary transfers that could solve the stubborn "crofter issue."

Interwar Hungary and the Philippines after democratization also faced the threat of rural unrest. After a brief experiment with communism in 1919, Admiral Horthy was appointed regent and came to dominate interwar politics while depending on support from the aristocracy (Mathijs 1997). Horthy named Pál Teleki as prime minister, who in turn spearheaded a minor land redistribution program aimed at alleviating rural discontent by breaking up a few of the largest estates. The reform program was implemented as the major parties merged into the dominant and conservative but heterogeneous Party of Unity (Vardy 1983). In the Philippines, the 1986 People Power Revolution introduced democracy and raised Corazon Aquino, whose family held vast tracts of land, to power. The threat of peasant revolt was high in the countryside, and when

Aquino nonetheless declined to use her decree powers to pass reform, the Peasants' Movement of the Philippines marched on the Malacañang Palace. Peasant repression and stiff opposition from landowners in Congress, however, ultimately gave way to the mildly redistributive Comprehensive Agrarian Reform Policy (Wurfel 1989).[8]

In three cases in Table 8.1, Czechoslovakia, India, and Thailand, land redistribution was implemented in the presence of an elite split and low institutional constraints and then continued as institutional constraints increased. Although land redistribution did not end for bureaucratic and political reasons, it did decline substantially, as predicted by the theory. Take the case of Thailand. Although farmer discontent was growing in the 1970s, the government of Thanom Kittikachorn refused to implement land reform. Many middle- and high-level government officials were large landowners, including the powerful Praphat Charusathien (Ramsay 1982, 176). An uprising in late 1973 toppled Thanom and brought the more independent Sanya Thammasak to power. Sanya passed a redistributive land reform in 1975 amid mounting peasant pressure that targeted private property and set landholding ceilings on ownership. A series of ensuing civilian and military governments continued to allocate funds to land reform and the Agricultural Land Reform Office remained active. Yet landed elites were able to stall the pace of redistribution under civilian government, and although military leaders continued reform, they did so at a slower pace as peasant pressure waned (Ramsay 1982, 178). The land reform program subsequently shifted to the distribution of predominantly Crown and state lands (Suehiro 1981, 332).

India also began implementing land redistribution amid a national-level elite split and low institutional constraints, and continued redistribution even after the national split was eliminated and institutional constraints had increased. This is because of the singularly unique nature of India's land reform in that it is administered at the state rather than the federal level under the 1949 constitution. Landed elites were almost entirely excluded from the ruling Indian National Congress Party in the immediate aftermath of independence (Tai 1974, 93). Furthermore, the zamindars – despised intermediaries who worked under feudal lords to collect rent for the British – posed a political threat to the Congress Party. This motivated Congress to "break the back" of the zamindar system (Kohli 1987, 70). The Congress Party and several other parties galvanized by the zamandari alliance with the British catalyzed a host of reforms at the state level, including tenancy reform, the abolition of intermediaries, landholding ceilings, and landholding consolidation laws (Besley and Burgess 2000). Yet rural elites reemerged as politically significant within a decade and captured broad representation in national political parties (Kohli 1987, 70).

---

[8] In Jordan's minor reform, the split with landed elites came only in the Jordan Valley, where the government sought to implement a large-scale irrigation project and offer improved land to landless farmers. The resistance of local landed tribal and social leaders who faced expropriation was overcome by invoking Emergency Law (Haddadin 2009, 46).

Land redistribution stumbled in most states where parties and legislatures were captured by landed elites (Besley and Burgess 2000, 394). Consistent with the theory in this book, states in which there were sustained elite splits and weaker institutional constraints that could provide landowners an obstruction mechanism, such as Kerala and West Bengal, carried out more extensive redistribution in ensuing decades.

EMPIRICAL ANALYSIS OF LAND REDISTRIBUTION AROUND
THE WORLD

Table 8.1 and the discussion in the previous section demonstrate that the substantial majority of land redistribution across the world has occurred amid elite splits and low institutional constraints to rule. Of course, this conclusion is subject to a selection problem since it does not account for cases in which there are elite splits, low institutional constraints, and no land redistribution. A sufficient number of such cases may render any inferences from Table 8.1 misleading.

This section addresses this potential concern by conducting a formal statistical analysis of land redistribution around the world. The data included is therefore a global sample.[9] I measure the dependent variable, Land Redistribution, in several ways. I first create a binary indicator that captures both major and minor episodes of land redistribution. I also create an ordinal measure that codes major land redistribution as 2, minor land redistribution as 1, and the lack of land redistribution as 0. Finally, I return to a binary indicator of land redistribution and also include the episodes of wholesale land nationalization from sub-Saharan Africa discussed earlier in the chapter.

The key independent variables in the analysis build from those in Chapter 5. As in Chapter 5, I measure institutional barriers to redistribution using a measure of Veto Points from Henisz (2002), with data updated to 2007. The second main explanatory variable is the coalitional split between ruling political elites and landed elites. I code this variable across the world using a range of country-level primary and secondary sources and the coding rules laid out Chapter 5.[10] The control variables are also similar to those in Table 5.3 of Chapter 5. The log of real GDP per capita is taken from Haber and Menaldo (2011). Rural Pressure is again a logged and inverted measure of value-added agriculture per dweller in the agricultural sector. The size of the agricultural sector is taken from the World Bank's World Development Indicators (WDI), and the size of the agricultural population is from Vanhanen (2009). Higher values indicate higher land pressure. Because the historical agricultural data from the WDI start after 1960 and are much sparser than the OXLAD data for Latin America, this variable

---

[9] The results that follow are not simply driven by Latin America: results are robust to dropping countries in Latin America, and the magnitudes of the main coefficients of interest increase. See the online appendix for these findings.

[10] See the book's online appendix for details.

suffers from high data missingness. Percent Urban is constructed from the Correlates of War data. Riots and Revolution are again from Banks's CNTS Data Archive.[11] Prior Land Redistribution captures the number of previous years in which there was land redistribution. This includes years of land nationalization when the dependent variable includes land nationalization.

All of the regressions include either region fixed effects or country fixed effects to control for region- or country-specific and time-invariant heterogeneity (e.g., geography) that may jointly influence a country's elite splits and institutional constraints simultaneously with the likelihood of land redistribution. The models preference the use of region fixed effects because country fixed effects drop all observations for countries that do not vary in land redistribution over time. An outcome of no land redistribution may, however, be consistent with the theory if it is the result of consistently high institutional constraints or the lack of an elite split. All of the models also include linear, quadratic, and cubic terms for years in order to control for secular trends in land redistribution over time. I cluster standard errors by country to adjust estimated errors for any arbitrary patterns of correlation within countries, such as serial correlation and correlation resulting from country-specific components.

Because observations may be temporally dependent, I follow Carter and Signorino (2010) and include a cubic polynomial approximation to the hazard in all of the models. This entails including linear, quadratic, and cubic terms for the years since the last episode of land redistribution in order to adjust for temporal dependence.[12] A second issue is that episodes of land redistribution often take place over multiple years. Since it is implausible that second and subsequent event-years are generated identically to onset years, and as suggested by Beck, Katz, and Tucker (1998), ongoing years of multiyear periods of land redistribution are dropped. Results are similar if ongoing years are not dropped or if new leaders that come to power during land redistribution programs and continue these programs are counted as new onsets.

Table 8.2 presents the results of a set of panel regression models using probit, ordinal logit, and conditional logit specifications. Model 1 is a probit model that includes Veto Points, Elite Split, an interaction term between Elite Split and Veto Points, and all of the main controls except Rural Pressure. As anticipated, and consistent with both the theory and the results in Chapter 5, the coefficient on Elite Split is positive and strongly statistically significant, and the coefficient on the interaction term is negative and highly significant. Moving across the range of Veto Points in the presence of an elite split cancels out any impact that Elite

---

[11] Similar to Table 5.3, the results are similar when substituting a measure of civil conflict for Riots.

[12] This does not obviate the need for controls for secular trends in land redistribution over time; although results are robust to dropping time trends, Wald tests consistently reject the hypothesis that they are jointly insignificant. It also does not render extraneous the measure for prior land redistribution, although again results are robust to excluding that variable.

TABLE 8.2. Land Redistribution, Political Institutions, and Elite Splits around the World, 1900–2008

| | Probit | Probit | Ordered Logit | Includes Nat'lizations Probit | Majority Agricultural Population | | Includes Nat'lizations Probit | Includes Nat'lizations Conditional Logit | Includes Nat'lizations Conditional Logit |
| | | | | | Probit | Ordered Logit | | | |
	Model 1	Model 2	Model 3	Model 4	Model 5	Model 6	Model 7	Model 8	Model 9
Veto Points	2.014***	2.085**	4.601***	2.008***	2.996***	6.343***	2.896***	3.055	3.381
	(0.588)	(0.990)	(1.494)	(0.585)	(0.731)	(2.093)	(0.688)	(2.572)	(2.666)
Elite Split	1.560***	1.567***	3.437***	1.582***	2.136***	4.671***	2.110***	3.038***	3.180***
	(0.227)	(0.333)	(0.643)	(0.225)	(0.368)	(1.209)	(0.344)	(0.737)	(0.789)
Elite Split*Veto Points	−2.331**	−2.240**	−5.821***	−2.395***	−3.389***	−8.119***	−3.403***	−4.898**	−5.362**
	(0.726)	(1.070)	(1.744)	(0.718)	(1.012)	(2.358)	(0.994)	(2.294)	(2.185)
log(GDP)	0.073	0.973***	0.049	0.022	0.484***	0.864**	0.424***	−2.076	−0.544
	(0.141)	(0.341)	(0.323)	(0.134)	(0.177)	(0.366)	(0.163)	(1.328)	(1.596)
Percent Urban	−0.004	0.015	−0.003	−0.003	0.011	0.031	0.012	0.159**	0.156**
	(0.007)	(0.009)	(0.015)	(0.007)	(0.012)	(0.023)	(0.011)	(0.073)	(0.074)
Riots	0.025	−0.031	0.055*	0.023	−0.020	−0.029	−0.024	−0.253	−0.220
	(0.016)	(0.073)	(0.031)	(0.017)	(0.036)	(0.080)	(0.036)	(0.206)	(0.176)
Revolution	0.318*	0.011	0.820**	0.321**	0.388*	0.758	0.368*	0.807*	0.677
	(0.165)	(0.271)	(0.379)	(0.152)	(0.221)	(0.516)	(0.207)	(0.485)	(0.462)
Prior Land Redistribution	0.024**	0.013	0.043*	0.027**	0.014	0.004	0.017	−0.299**	−0.230**
	(0.011)	(0.009)	(0.022)	(0.011)	(0.018)	(0.039)	(0.018)	(0.117)	(0.099)
Rural Pressure		1.279***							
		(0.327)							
Time Trends	YES	YES	YES	YES	YES	YES	YES	YES	YES
Region Fixed Effects	YES	YES	YES	YES	YES	YES	YES	YES	YES
Country Fixed Effects	NO	NO	NO	NO	NO	NO	NO	YES	YES
Observations	4,453	2,206	4,453	4,447	1,761	1,761	1,757	631	728

Notes: * $p < 0.10$; ** $p < 0.05$; *** $p < 0.01$ (two-tailed)
Standard errors are clustered by country. A cubic polynomial approximation to the hazard is included in all models to address temporal dependence. Constants and time dummies are not shown.

Split has on land redistribution. Revolution and Prior Land Redistribution are positive and statistically significant, as in Chapter 5, and Riots is positive but short of statistical significance. The substantive significance of these variables is considerably lower than that for Elite Split.

Model 2 adds the Rural Pressure variable to the Model 1 specification. The main results hold, and Rural Pressure is positive and statistically significant. Latent pressure contributes to the likelihood of land redistribution but to a degree much smaller than elite splits and institutional constraints. Missing data on Rural Pressure, however, reduces the total number of observations by half. I therefore drop this variable in subsequent models, although including it yields similar results.

The dependent variable in Model 3 is the ordinal measure of land redistribution. I therefore run an ordered logit model otherwise specified similarly to Model 1. The results are similar. The odds of any land redistribution are an estimated thirty times greater with an elite split while holding other covariates constant. Similarly, the odds of major land redistribution are thirty times greater than either minor land redistribution or no land redistribution. Increasing Veto Points across its whole range when there is an elite split again eliminates any impact that Elite Split has on land redistribution. By contrast, the odds of land redistribution are only 1.1 times greater with a one standard deviation increase in Riots. The odds of redistribution are 2.3 times higher if there is a revolution.

Model 4 is a probit model where the dependent variable is dichotomous and coded as 1 when there is a major or minor instance of land redistribution or an instance of wholesale land nationalization of the variety discussed earlier in the chapter. It is coded as 0 otherwise. The results are very similar to those in Model 1.

The remaining models in Table 8.2 restrict the sample to country-years where the majority of the population is engaged in agriculture as coded by Vanhanen (2009). These represent the most agrarian societies where land reform is more likely a major political issue. A separate approach that restricts the analysis to country-years where landed elites had not previously been massively weakened or effectively destroyed as an actor (e.g., as in many formerly communist countries after collectivization) yields similar results. Models 5, 6, and 7 are specified in the same way as Models 1, 3, and 4, respectively. The results are similar and the magnitudes of Elite Split and the interaction of Elite Split with Veto Points now unsurprisingly increase over previous models. High Veto Points again nullifies any effect that Elite Split has on land redistribution. Revolution mostly remains statistically significant. Its estimated effect on land redistribution, however, is dramatically lower in the absence of an elite split. GDP is now positive and statistically significant in Models 5–7.

Models 8 and 9 in Table 8.2 mirror Models 5 and 7 but use a conditional logit specification with data grouped by country. These models therefore analyze the determinants of within-country variation in land redistribution. They consequently drop the roughly one-third of cases pertaining to those countries where the majority of the population works in agriculture but in which there was no variation in land redistribution over time. These are all countries where land redistribution was absent. The main results hold despite this relatively high empirical bar given the data structure. Elite Split again increases in magnitude and is positive and highly statistically significant, whereas its interaction with Veto Points is negative and statistically significant in both models. Revolution is again positive and significant in Model 8. Percent Urban becomes positive and statistically significant in Models 8–9, and Prior Land Redistribution is now negative and statistically significant, indicating that a long history of previous land redistribution within a country places downward pressure on the onset of a new land redistribution program.

I also tested the robustness of the Table 8.2 findings to a host of alternative explanations along the lines of those discussed in Chapter 5. Rival explanations such as ideology, trade openness, foreign aid, geographical endowments, autocratic regime type, declining land prices, and inequality consistently failed as robust predictors of land redistribution. The findings on land redistribution from Latin America therefore travel well beyond that region.

FOUR CASE STUDIES OF LAND REDISTRIBUTION

Land redistribution has occurred the world over during the last century, largely in the context of low institutional constraints and coalitional splits between landed elites and ruling political elites. This section examines four cases of major land redistribution in depth: Egypt, Hungary, Taiwan, and Zimbabwe. In doing so, it seeks to demonstrate how elite splits and low institutional constraints arose and how they were causally linked to land redistribution in each case. The cases of Hungary, Taiwan, and Zimbabwe help illustrate the foreign occupation and ethnic difference paths to elite splits that did not operate in the Latin American cases.

Egypt under the Free Officers

From 1922 until 1952, the Muhammad Ali dynasty ruled Egypt as a kingdom. Despite formally gaining its independence from Great Britain in 1922, Egypt continued to be occupied by British military forces. Yet there was little incentive for land reform during this period. Both King Fuad (1922–1936) and King Farouk (1936–1952) were large landowners. Landed interests also dominated the Parliament (Radwan 1977, 8). The only political party to embrace land reform was the socialist party (Daly and Petry 1998, 323). The Parliament therefore rejected land reform bills in 1945 and 1950 (Warriner 1962, 11–12). This changed dramatically when the Kingdom of Egypt was overthrown in 1952 through a military coup led by the Free Officers Movement. The Free Officers' first decree in office was an ambitious land reform program based on the expropriation of elite land in favor of the peasantry.

Conditions Prior to Land Reform

Warriner (1962) divides the landed elites that were dominant in Egypt in the first half of the twentieth century into two categories. The first was a set of very large and generally absentee landowners who financed their lavish lifestyles by renting out their estates to numerous tenants. The second was a set of landowners who owned 300 or 400 *feddans* (one *feddan* is equal to 0.42 hectares) and either were professional agriculturalists or left management of the farm to an agent.

Many large landholdings were the legacy of nineteenth-century land distribution trends. Throughout the nineteenth century, leaders like Muhammad Ali accumulated massive amounts of land through the *Udha*, *Ib'adiya*, and *Jiflik* systems, which allowed them to grant large plots to their family members and political allies (Baer 1962, 13–17). Under the *Udha* system, high officials, army officers, and others who had become rich during the wars of the nineteenth century were able to pay the tax arrears of indebted villages in exchange for ownership over the villages (Baer 1962, 13). *Udhas* typically ranged from 300 to 800 *feddans* in area (Baer 1962, 13). Although it was abolished by 1868, the *Udha* system "undoubtedly provided a basis for the creation of large estates" (Baer 1962, 15). Under *Ib'adiya*, some uncultivated land was not included in the national cadastre. The land was then granted, free of charge, to high officials and other elites, on the condition that they improve the land and prepare it for cultivation (Baer 1962, 16). The *Ib'adiya* was created through a 1929 decree by Muhammad Ali, and it comprised an estimated 200,000 *feddans* (Baer 1962, 17). The *Jiflik* system mainly benefited the ruler himself, as well as his family. Under the *Jiflik* system, many villages that had been abandoned because of the heavy tax burden – some as large as 20,000 *feddans* – were transferred to the royal family (Baer 1962, 18).

Prior to 1952, the largest plots were managed as plantation estates, with central management, large administrative and technical staffs, and some leasing to tenants (Warriner 1962, 26). The relationship between landowners and the peasantry (*fellahin*) was regularly described as feudal. Radwan (1977, 8) details the circumstances:

The village scene was dominated by the large landlord usually referred to as the Pasha. His manor house, which overshadowed the mud houses of the fellahin, was run by a small army of permanent workers and their families. Invariably, he, as the Umda (or village mayor), was the representative of the State. In short, he represented the political and social power in the village, and he certainly used his power to ensure his master. Tales of social subjection, illegal abuses, repression and human degradation of the fellahin were a pale description of the grim reality of Egyptian rural life.

Land distribution statistics on the eve of the 1952 coup reflect this situation. A total of 72 percent of landholdings were one *feddan* or less, whereas just 0.1 percent of landholdings were larger than 200 hectares and together comprised 19.8 percent of the country's agricultural land (Warriner 1962, 24). In addition to the high level of landholding inequality, there was an extremely high rate of landlessness. In 1950, 1.5 million families representing 60 percent of the rural population neither rented nor owned land, an increase from 37 percent in 1929 (Radwan 1977, 6).

The Free Officers Coup and Land Redistribution

Egypt's King Farouk was overthrown in 1952 through a military coup led by the Free Officers Movement. The Free Officers, founded in the aftermath of Egypt's loss in the Arab-Israeli War of 1948, were a group of junior Egyptian military officers led by Gamal Abdel Nasser. Nasser had commanded an army unit in the 1948 war and lamented the incompetence of Egypt's leaders in organizing the operation. The Free Officers were also vehement opponents of the ongoing British occupation.

Despite the lack of any major episodes of rural protest or unrest, the Free Officers immediately implemented an ambitious land reform program through Law 178, which expropriated landed elites and distributed their land to peasants (Tai 1974, 62). The 1952 land reform decree also regulated tenancy relations. It set land rental ceilings at seven times the basic land tax value for a given plot, mandated a minimum land lease term of three years, and banned arbitrary evictions (Saad 2002). The law initially barred any individual from holding more than 200 *feddans*, although large landowners were allowed to allot 50 *feddans* to each of two children. All land in excess of this maximum would be requisitioned by the government over a period of five years (Warriner 1962, 32). The ceiling dropped from 200 *feddans* to 100 *feddans* in 1961 (Tai 1974, 176–177). Former owners of expropriated land received compensation at the rate of ten times the rental value, itself assessed at seven times the basic land tax (compensation was thus set at seventy times the basic land tax). Because the land tax ranged from £2 to £4 per *feddan*, compensation ranged from £140 to £280, and it could be higher when it also covered improvements and capital assets. In reality, however, rental values in many cases far exceeded seven times the land tax. A purely market-rate level of compensation would therefore have ranged between £400 and £600 per *feddan* (Warriner 1962, 38). Compensation was paid not in cash but rather in state bonds bearing 3 percent interest that were redeemable after thirty years. Nasser cancelled interest payments on these bonds in 1964 and declared that they would not be redeemable (Forte 1978, 275).

Expropriated land was to be distributed to farmers and agricultural laborers in increments of two to five *feddans* per family. The Free Officers saw land distribution to the peasantry as a way to broaden the base of support for the military regime and to ensure stability (Tai 1974). Families that owned more than five *feddans* were not eligible for land. Administratively, great care was taken to ensure that land was given to peasants that had substantial experience cultivating land. Beneficiaries of land redistribution were required to pay back the full purchase price over a period of thirty years, plus 3 percent interest and an additional 15 percent for administrative costs (Warriner 1962, 34). From

1952 to 1964, a total of 840,000 *feddans* of land were redistributed to more than 260,000 farmers under the various land reform laws (Tai 1974, 540).

Peasants who received land as part of the land reform program were required to join cooperatives overseen by the Ministry of Agrarian Reform. The Egyptian land reform thus came to be described as the "supervised cooperative system." Average membership for a cooperative was 300 farmers covering about 1,000 *feddans* of land. Each cooperative ostensibly elected its own manager, although in practice the Cooperative Administration within the Ministry of Agrarian Reform played the largest role in this process (Tai 1974, 249). Cooperatives were responsible for various tasks, including the marketing of joint farming, the acquisition of inputs, rural extension programs, and issuing loans. The success of the cooperatives, in terms of their effect on agricultural productivity, ultimately prompted the government to extend cooperatives to non-reform lands as well (Tai 1974, 250).

The two key factors critical to land reform in most cases in Table 8.1, an elite split and low institutional constraints, aptly characterize rule by the Free Officers following the 1952 coup. The Free Officers were mainly of middle-class origin and had no ties to large landowners (Trimberger 1978). As Tai (1974, 62) writes, "With predominantly middle-class backgrounds, these officers felt no internal restraints in acting against the landed gentry; at the same time they could design a program which sacrificed no interests of their own but was bound to be popular with the masses." Warriner (1962, 13) makes a somewhat stronger claim, arguing that breaking the power of the old oligarchy was one of the key motivations for the Free Officers' land reform. The consequential rise of middle-class officers in the military can be traced back to the 1936 Wafd government decision following the Anglo-Egyptian Treaty to allow sons of non-aristocratic families into the military.

The absence of institutional constraints to the Free Officers' rule facilitated the declaration and execution of the reform. With the small, cohesive group of core military officers being in favor of land reform, it quickly became the law of the land. The Free Officers dissolved the landowner-dominated Parliament and the constitution. The original nine core Free Officers, along with several others, then formed the Revolutionary Command Council (RCC) under Nasser. The RCC outlawed all political parties and dictated major policies, including land reform. The Free Officers created an agency charged with implementing the land reform and staffed it with an adequate number of faithful bureaucrats. Funding was equally unproblematic; they simply reallocated the government budget to support land reform (Tai 1974, 473). Reform therefore proceeded rapidly.

Land Reform Stalled: Land Concentration since Nasser
Since Nasser's death in 1970, many of the steps toward more egalitarian land distribution have been reversed.[13] The 1982 agricultural census pointed to

---

[13] On the broader reversal of radical policies in Egypt since Nasser, see, e.g., Ansari (1986).

growing inequality of land access, increasing rural poverty, land loss by small-holders, and the consolidation of holdings by larger owners (Springborg 1990, 28). These trends generally began in the mid-1970s under Sadat through legal and administrative changes to the Nasser-era land laws. Rents on agricultural land were increased, it became easier to evict tenants, and land ownership ceilings were raised (Springborg 1991, 234). In 1992, the Egyptian Parliament passed a law that reversed the 1952 agrarian relations law. The new law removed rental ceilings and reinstated landlords' eviction rights for the first time in decades. It stripped roughly 1 million registered tenant families of their permanent and heritable land rights (USAID 2010, 1). This reversal on land issues was part of Egypt's broader economic transformation toward a capitalist economy (Hinnebusch 1993).

Notwithstanding subsequent policies that unwound some of the Free Officers' reforms, most scholars view the land reform as a success. Saad (2002, 103), for instance, writes that the reform resulted in "drastic improvements in the lives of millions of rural dwellers." The Gini index of landholding inequality dropped by 0.14 from 0.81 in 1952 to 0.67 in 1964, and by the latter date, 98.8 percent of agricultural holdings were less than five hectares in size (Tai 1974, 310–312). Furthermore, agricultural productivity increased substantially, easily outpacing population growth (Tai 1974, 313–314). The land reform program therefore simultaneously contributed to both equity and efficiency.

Alternative Explanations for Egypt's Land Reform

There are several alternative explanations for the Egyptian land reform. The first, which cuts across all of the cases, is that perhaps the agenda of land reform was the cause of the elite split. This potential endogeneity concern is not strong in the Egyptian case. With King Fuad and King Farouk at the helm in the decades leading up to 1952 and landowning interests dominating Parliament, any land reform agenda was practically nonexistent. Nor might such an agenda have itself radicalized junior military officers. The seeds of an elite split instead rose organically in the military following the 1936 decision to expand the military and the subsequent recruitment from the middle class. What brought this split to the fore was not land reform but rather opposition to ongoing British occupation and a bungled campaign in the 1948 Arab-Israeli War.

Warriner (1962, 13) offers two of the more common alternative explanations. The first is that the Free Officers had an ideologically humanitarian motivation to redistribute wealth in a deeply unequal society. The second is that international pressure for land reform, particularly from the US State Department, led the Free Officers to pursue reform. Neither of these explanations fits well with several key aspects of the land reform. Critically, land was not distributed to the poorest peasants first and foremost. It went instead first to peasants that had substantial experience cultivating land. The largest families were next in line, followed last by the poorer village members and those in outlying areas (Margold 1957, 13). This belies the strictly humanitarian explanation for the reform. Tai (1974, 60) concurs, stating that the Free Officers movement "in the beginning was innocent of either political ideology or doctrinal guidance." At the same time, the United States and other foreign countries were hardly key players in the Free Officers' land reform decisions (Tai 1974, 89). The Free Officers coup clearly sought to eliminate foreign (and especially British) meddling in domestic affairs (Trimberger 1978). Egypt joined the nonaligned movement, accepted Soviet aid over US aid, and nationalized the Suez Canal. All of these actions aroused the ire of the United States. Furthermore, the Egyptian land reform was heavily redistributive, in contrast to prevailing contemporary US advice to foreign governments to compensate private property that was used for the purposes of land reform.

Hungary since World War I

The rural sector in Hungary prior to World War I was one of vast inequities. It was dominated by a small number of elite landowners that commanded "large estates operated in a backward, feudal manner" alongside a large number of landless agrarian laborers and peasants that had extremely small landholdings (Marrese 1983, 332). The Hungarian kings were themselves large landowners and depended on the landed aristocracy for stability and the extraction of rural surplus. They therefore had a vested interest in the status quo distribution of property. Change began immediately after World War I when King Charles IV was pushed aside and the peasantry was mobilized in favor of reform. Hungary passed a land reform law in 1920. But a circumscribed electoral system and the dominance of Admiral Horthy, in alliance with the aristocracy, limited reform. It therefore proceeded at a glacial pace. World War II drastically altered the rural landscape. The absence of large landowners at the end of the war in concert with pressure from the occupying Soviet army resulted in a major land reform decree. The Hungarian Communists, followed by the Independent Smallholders, implemented the reform rigorously with little political or institutional opposition, destroying large- and middle-sized landowners in favor of mobilized peasants.

Conditions Prior to Land Reform

Land distribution in Hungary in the late 1800s and early 1900s was highly unequal, and agriculture depended on a feudal system in which landless peasants worked on large estates owned by aristocrats (Mathijs 1997, 34). A total of 53.6 percent of farms smaller than 2.9 hectares comprised 5.8 percent of all the agricultural land in the country in 1895, whereas the 0.2 percent of largest farms of more than 575 hectares collectively held 32.3 percent of all agricultural land (Berend and Ránki 1974, 33). Roughly 2 million peasants were landless or had landholdings too small for subsistence farming (Stowe 1947, 491). Conditions worsened after the harvesters' strike in 1897. Parliament tightened regulation of agricultural workers' conditions in 1898 and 1907 legislation known as the "slave acts," which criminalized strikes, made labor contracts inviolable, and required the police to return fugitive laborers in breach of contract to their landowners (Janos 1971, 50).

Hungary's First Attempt at Land Redistribution: Interwar Reforms

Political instability in Hungary was severe at the end of World War I. The years 1918 to 1920 witnessed rapid government overturn. In October 1918, Count Mihály Károlyi and his Hungarian National Council seized power in a coup and founded the Hungarian Democratic Republic with support from disaffected army elements and peasant groups. Károlyi declared the expropriation of all estates larger than 284 acres for the purposes of redistribution to peasants (Stowe 1947, 491). Károlyi was rapidly overthrown by the Bolshevik Béla Kun before the reform law could take effect. Kun attracted even greater peasant support. He seized power in March 1919 and then attempted to nationalize the economy and convert the peasantry to communism. Demanding ownership of their own property, peasants quickly withdrew their support from Kun and most supported a counterrevolution that, dovetailing with the Romanian invasion in July 1919, ousted Kun within four months (Stowe 1947, 492).

The Romanian occupiers assisted the counterrevolution and its organization under Admiral Miklós Horthy. When Romanian troops left Hungary in late February 1920, the National Assembly reestablished the Kingdom of Hungary. Under intense pressure from the Hungarian army, as well as from Entente powers that refused to accept the return of King Charles IV, the National Assembly appointed Admiral Horthy as regent on March 1, 1920. The peasant-oriented but bourgeois National Smallholders Party–led government simultaneously took office in March 1920. The government, however, was dissolved on June 4 of that year upon the signing of the Trianon Treaty, which radically shrunk the geographical delimitations of the Hungarian state.

The counterrevolution restored much, but not all, of the old social and political system (Vardy 1983, 22). Horthy, who dominated Hungarian politics during the interwar period, depended a great deal on the support of the aristocracy and thus had little interest in implementing land reform measures (Mathijs 1997, 37). Yet despite being a gradualist and having wide-ranging formal powers, Horthy largely allowed Parliament to function (Vardy 1983, 26). The National Assembly under Prime Minister Pál Teleki passed a mild agrarian reform law in December 1920. Unlike the reforms of the previous few years, Teleki's reform was not quickly overturned. A total of 6 percent of the country's arable land was redistributed under the law until the eve of World War II (Mathijs 1997). But the 1920 land reform was hardly major. Roughly 400,000 landless laborers received an average of one hectare of land each by breaking up several large estates. This was well below what was required for subsistence (Stowe 1947, 492). As Stowe (1947, 492) writes, "[T]he grip of big landowners was scarcely shaken…feudal groups remained well entrenched and politically supreme." The prospects for the 1920 reform were dimmed from the outset when in 1922 the Smallholders Party merged with the conservative nationalist Christian National Unity Party to form the Party of Unity (Vardy 1983, 28), which dominated the first decade of the interwar period. Hungary's large estates therefore survived the interwar period.

Major Land Redistribution in Hungary after World War II

Land reform in Hungary following World War II had a significantly greater redistributive impact than the interwar reforms. The majority of farmers at the time were either landless or owned less than 2.8 hectares of land (Mathijs 1997, 45). The Red Army marched into Hungary in September 1944, and in January 1945 it established a provisional government dominated by the Hungarian Communist Party. The provisional government implemented a March 15, 1945 decree declaring that estates of more than 575 hectares were to be expropriated in their entirety (Mathijs 1997, 45). Smaller estates also faced expropriation, with landowners of noble estates being allowed to retain a maximum of twenty-nine to fifty-eight hectares depending on their location (Gutteridge 1952, 15). The landholding ceiling for peasant estates was somewhat higher at 115 hectares (Varga 2009, 225). Compensation was based on the value of the land that had been reported in cadastral registers fifty to eighty years earlier, and it was only provided if the state had the capacity to pay compensation (Gutteridge 1952, 15). Landowners therefore forfeited their property at rates far below market value.

A total of 64 percent of the land in Hungary was redistributed as a result of Hungary's postwar reform, mostly to former farmhands, agricultural laborers, smallholders, and village tradesmen (Mathijs 1997). Within just a few years of the decree, 95 percent of the rural population owned land, with plot sizes averaging just under three hectares (Mathijs 1997, 46). The former landowning class lost almost all of its economic power (Varga 2009, 224). Mathijs (1997, 46) concludes that the "communists succeeded in overturning the social structure of the countryside."

In contrast to the interwar reform, there was an overwhelming elite split when Hungary's post–World War II land reform was initiated. As Marrese (1983, 332) notes, "[M]any pre-war landowners were absent as the war drew to a close" because of the severe dislocations and damage the war had inflicted in the countryside. The elite split was made complete by the Soviet occupation of Hungary. The Red Army occupation not only severed the connection of landowners to political decision makers; it also enhanced political elites' capacity to act autonomously from landed elites by temporarily gutting institutional constraints. The Hungarian Communist Party, which dominated Hungary's provisional government at the time with support from the Red Army, issued the March 15, 1945 land reform decree. As Varga (2009, 225) matter-of-factly observes, "[D]ue to a transformation of the political institutions, the representatives of the aristocratic and gentry classes were excluded from parliament and the state administration." Clearly neither the Red Army nor the

Hungarian Communists had any ties to landowners. Indeed, the Hungarian Communists were a minority party at the time in the country as a whole.

The Independent Smallholders, Agrarian Workers, and Civic Party swept the newly reinstated elections in November 1945 over the Communists and placed Zoltán Tildy as prime minister. The Independent Smallholders formed in 1930 as an opposition party that had its social base in the peasantry (Palasik 2011, 31). The Independent Smallholders also had a large central faction of middle-class Christians and a disjointed right-wing faction that grew somewhat in 1945 when conservatives saw little other viable political representation (Palasik 2011, 31–32). Nonetheless, they strongly supported land reform because of the role of peasants in the party and in the country more broadly. The official party program on the eve of the 1945 elections stated, "The peasants are the absolute majority of the nation. Thus we must expect that, in a democracy, the peasantry becomes the decisive factor in politics" (Palasik 2011, 34). The Independent Smallholders continued the Communists' land reform while in office and as conflict between them and the Communists deepened. By the time land reform was almost complete in 1949, the Independent Smallholders were absorbed into the People's Independent Front, which was led by the Hungarian Working People's Party.

As mentioned earlier in this section, in addition to a clear elite split there were also few institutional constraints when Hungary's provisional government issued the land reform decree. The occupying Red Army enforced the provisional government's decrees, giving them the broad capacity to set policies in motion. They did not face legislative or judicial barriers. Nor did they rely on the entrenched bureaucracy that had been largely pushed aside by the war. The Independent Smallholders, by contrast, governed during the reconstruction of many state institutions and political bodies, including the National Assembly. Institutional constraints nonetheless remained relatively weak. The 1946 Act I Constitution provided few details about the courts (Palasik 2011, 57), which left them subject to executive influence. And the ongoing Soviet occupation challenged the independence and ability of executives to rule contrary to the Soviets' fundamental interests. The success and early relative autonomy of the Independent Smallholders gave way to communist meddling before long. Moscow aided the Hungarian Communists in pressuring for posts in Tildy's first coalition cabinet (Palasik 2011, 52–54). The 1947 elections were marred by fraud, and the Communists arrested or exiled many prominent Independent Smallholder politicians. Lajos Dinnyés of the Independent Smallholders was prime minister after the 1947 elections, but he was heavily influenced by the Communists. The openly pro-communist Independent Smallholder István Dobi became premier in December 1948 and purged the party of anticommunists. By 1949, the Communists had asserted control over all branches of government.

Land taken from large landowners was turned over mainly to peasants that had been agitating for redistribution. The powerful Hungarian Peasant Alliance had local, organized branches of peasant associations across the country that favored redistribution (Palasik 2011, 31). Furthermore, peasants had started seizing landed estates in substantial numbers in early 1945. These peasants, "sensing the power vacuum caused by the chaos of the time, began an unauthorized distribution of large estates" (Marrese 1983, 332). These were some of the first peasant groups to receive land under the 1945 reform.

Collectivization and Post-Communist Privatization

Hungary's post–World War II agrarian reforms were precursors to land collectivization under communist rule. Collectivization began in force in 1949. Having decimated large estates, the state next turned its gaze to wealthy, independent peasant landowners who were influential in villages and who not infrequently leased portions of their land. Rebranded as "Kulaks" and distinguished from smallholders, these peasant owners were demonized, hounded, and then often imprisoned and expropriated. Three-fourths of all the land owned by Kulaks was taken by the state by 1953 (Varga 2009, 226), after which land seizures and forced sales continued more intermittently. Collectivization was mostly completed by 1962, and collective farming came to replace peasant agriculture (Mathijs 1997, 52). Yet collectivization foundered. Hungary then began to adopt reforms that embraced market capitalism, such as the 1968 New Economic Mechanism and a host of liberalizing reforms in the 1980s. Nonetheless, by 1987, 71.4 percent of agricultural land was still in collective hands (Mathijs 1997, 45).

The collapse of communism led to another wave of major agrarian reforms in the 1990s. Most of these reforms stemmed from privatization and were uniformly dramatically different from earlier land redistribution. The debate centered on redressing the historical injustice stemming from the demands of pre-1945 landowners for land restitution, social equity, and efficiency (Swinnen 1999, 638). Ultimately about one-third of the collective farmland was restituted to former owners, one-third was auctioned for compensation bonds, and another one-third was distributed to the farm workers of the collectives (Swinnen 1999, 639). Restitution was based on 1948 ownership – after the 1945 decree but before collectivization (Swinnen 1999, 643). Hungarians who had lost their land between 1939 and 1948 were partially compensated with option rights or bonds that could be used to buy land or other privatized assets or to establish a life annuity (Swinnen 1999; Varga 2009).

Alternative Explanations for Hungary's Land Reform

There are two main competing explanations for Hungary's major post–World War II land reform. The principal one is the imposition of communism. Mathijs (1997), for instance, argues that the success of post–World War II reforms is largely attributable to the political and technical support of the Soviet Red Army, as well as popular support for communism among Hungary's smallholders. It is certainly true that land redistribution in Hungary could not have been undertaken on such a massive scale if the Red Army had actively opposed it. However, popular support for communism among the peasantry was rather low at the war's close. The Independent Smallholders won 57 percent of the national vote over the Communists' 17 percent in the first relatively fair postwar elections. Furthermore, support for communism was not a necessary condition for reform. Land redistribution proceeded rapidly when the Independent Smallholders held office. This was because the Independent Smallholders, like the Communists, had few ties to large landowners and therefore had similar incentives for reform. It is also noteworthy that peasants had started seizing landed estates in substantial numbers in early 1945, prior to the Communists' land reform decree. Finally, it bears pointing out that interwar land reform occurred in Hungary despite the anticommunist rule of Horthy and the small amount of peasant support for communism. In short, communism in Hungary was imposed on ground that was already fertile for land reform.

A second explanation for Hungary's reform is that simmering discussion of reform catalyzed an elite split to begin with. This is somewhat hard to countenance. Although the threat of land reform during the Károlyi-Kun scuffle in 1919 had served as something of a shot across the bow of landed elites, they emerged unscathed and took great solace from the fact that peasants themselves supported the counterrevolution against the Communist Kun because of their opposition to collectivization (Stowe 1947). The military and large landowners were then largely shielded during the interwar period by their ally Admiral Horthy. The principal origins of the elite split in post–World War II Hungary – Soviet occupation and the temporary displacement of landowners because of the war – were hardly motivated by land reform. Neither was such an outcome foreseen; many landowners were forced to rapidly and haphazardly abandon their estates as the chaos of war intensified. Soviet occupation did initially strengthen the hand of the Independent Smallholders before they were ultimately smothered. But the introduction of land reform by the Soviets did not cause the Independent Smallholders to split from landowners. Their strong social base in the peasantry had oriented them against landed elites and in favor of reform since 1930 (Palasik 2011).

Taiwan under the Kuomintang

Under Japanese rule from 1895 to 1945, an indigenous Taiwanese landowning elite developed alongside numerous large Japanese landholders (Tai 1974, 398). Taiwan during this time was a major exporter of rice, sugar, and other agricultural products to its colonial ruler (Barraclough 1999, 35). When the Chinese Nationalists retreated to Taiwan after their 1949 defeat on the Chinese mainland, the Kuomintang (KMT) swiftly adopted land reform measures in 1949, 1951, and 1953, and it implemented them with sustained political support, effective bureaucratic institutions, and adequate staffing (Tai 1974). Indigenous landed elites were eliminated in favor of smallholders. Land reform helped set the stage for decades of relatively equitable and robust economic growth.

Conditions Prior to Land Reform

Taiwan was a densely populated territory with extreme landholding inequality when the Japanese arrived in 1895. The Japanese constructed an oppressive colonial regime that heavily taxed the local population and blocked Taiwanese participation in policymaking but nonetheless built colonial structures on top of existing, powerful local landed elites (Matsuzaki 2012). Japan's occupation of Taiwan ended in the wake of World War II. Yet just a few years later, the KMT arrived after retreating from the Chinese mainland during the Chinese Civil War. Taiwan was a largely agrarian society when the KMT arrived. The majority of the population – 52.49 percent in 1952 – was engaged in agriculture (Huang 1998, 18).

The Chinese Civil War broke out in the aftermath of World War II as the Japanese were leaving Taiwan. The Chinese Nationalists under Chiang Kai-Shek and the KMT sought to eliminate Communist insurgents in mainland China. Infighting between the KMT party organization and the bureaucracy, military, and Youth Corps weakened the Nationalists. This was compounded by the Nationalists' inability to control their local branches and party members (Myers 2009, 189). The KMT was forced to retreat to Taiwan by 1949 in the face of withering Communist attacks on the mainland. The KMT and other refugees from the mainland would likely have been conquered in Taiwan had it not been for the outbreak of the Korean War on June 25, 1950 (Myers 2009). On June 27, the United States ordered the Seventh Fleet to occupy the Strait of Taiwan and prevent the Communists from attacking the island. Chiang Kai-Shek seized this opportunity to reorganize the KMT and implement several major reforms on the island to stabilize the KMT's rule.

Land Redistribution as the KMT Consolidates

Three main KMT laws formed the basis for Taiwan's land reforms: the 1949 Farm Rent Reduction Act, the 1951 Regulations on Sale of Public Land, and the 1953 Land-to-the-Tiller Act. The Rent Reduction Act mandated that landlords could not charge rent that exceeded 37.5 percent of the land's total annual yield (Tai 1974, 523). The rent program, according to a 1966 UN report, raised tenant incomes by an amount varying between 11 percent and 37 percent, and it was extremely popular among rural households (Tai 1974, 383). The 1951 measure granted public land to agricultural workers at well below market prices. Roughly one-fifth of all the arable land in the country was offered for sale, and more than 150,000 tenant farm families purchased land under this law (Myers 2009, 197).

The 1953 Land-to-the-Tiller Act went even further than the 1949 and 1951 acts. It set a landholding limit on private tenanted land at only three hectares of paddy land (Apthorpe 1979, 522). The state compensated those who lost their land with 70 percent of the compensation in land bonds and 30 percent in shares in four state-run companies that had been seized from the retreating Japanese (Myers 2009, 197). Yet these payments were considerably below market value. Land bonds were distributed in rice bonds and sweet potato bonds, had an annual interest rate of 4 percent, and were paid in equal installments over ten years; rice bonds were paid primarily in rice and sweet potato bonds were paid in cash (Tai 1974, 193). Yet a three-month bank deposit at the time paid 16 percent. Furthermore, the market value of all four state-run companies sank well below the par value of the stocks. Through the land-to-the-tiller program, "by 1954 the Taiwanese government had purchased more than 344,000 acres of land and resold it to 194,823 tenants, with 85 percent of the land consisting of high-grade paddy fields" (Mennen 2009).

The 1951 and 1953 reform laws together resulted in two-thirds of the island's agricultural families owning land, most with less than one hectare (Tai 1974, 476). The combined initial effect of the three programs was thus a steep rise in farm incomes and a significant increase in land ownership. More than 2 million Taiwanese gained property rights and the incomes of farmers almost doubled within a decade of the first reform in 1949 (Myers 2009, 197).

What enabled the KMT to swiftly and effectively implement land reform in Taiwan? The first critical factor was a clean split between ruling political elites (KMT leaders) and the powerful indigenous Taiwanese landowners. There were no significant ethnic, historical, ideological, or political ties between the KMT and the landlords whose land was redistributed. As Taiwanese land expert Shih-Jung Hsu notes, "[T]he key to Taiwan's successful land reform was that the people who implemented the policy had no relation whatsoever with landowners" (Yueh 2009). The KMT therefore had no obligations to indigenous landed elites (Barraclough 1999, 35). The elite split was made even more salient by the fact that indigenous Taiwanese elites posed a potential threat to the KMT if the former were not eliminated. The KMT feared that indigenous Taiwanese elites would try to establish an indigenous-led Taiwanese state separate from China; therefore, acquiring the land of the rich indigenous farming class would aid in neutralizing this threat (Pearse 1980).

The KMT was never infiltrated or captured by indigenous Taiwanese landed elites as it developed on the island and conducted land reform. Although Chiang Kai-Shek was dedicated to reforming the party on its new territory in order to attract members, he did not reach out to landed elites. Chiang Kai-Shek established a Central Reform Committee (CRC) in 1950 and hand-picked each of its sixteen members. The committee members were young and well educated and nine of them had studied abroad. The CRC quickly established reform goals, including eliminating landed elites and broadening their support base to include the peasantry (Myers 2009, 189). By October 1952, the party had increased its membership on the island from 50,000 in 1949 to almost 282,000 (Myers 2009, 193).

The second critical factor that enabled swift land reform implementation was the authoritarian nature of the Nationalist government. The fact that power was centralized in the hands of KMT political elites denied landed elites the opportunity to frustrate the reform process (Tai 1974, 469). As in the Hungarian case, the capacity to implement policy was sweeping. Major decisions were made by Chiang Kai-Shek and his small, hand-picked CRC. Indigenous elites were not the only ones sidelined; other cliques within the KMT that had undermined the cohesiveness of the party were also sidelined into the honorary but powerless Central Advisory Committee (Myers 2009). These steps consolidated party leadership. Chiang and the CRC were assisted by a twenty-five-member advisory group. Together, this new structure took charge of thirteen new agencies, seven of which were directly responsible for carrying out reform duties such as land reform. The political architecture for land reform was therefore unimpeded by independent legislative, judicial, or administrative bodies that could be captured by elites who were opposed to reform.

The actual administrative implementation of land reform in Taiwan was aided by the presence of strong state institutions that had been developed during Japanese colonial rule in Taiwan. These colonial legacies facilitated the KMT in building a large and centralized bureaucracy, an administrative structure that penetrated society via a powerful police organization, and a comprehensive banking and credit system that provided an efficient alternative to informal lending by merchants and landlords (Matsuzaki 2012). The KMT also benefited from early technical and financial support for land reform from the United States, although it was the state's role and not foreign financial assistance that was critical for reform (Barraclough 1999, 35).

The KMT distributed property mainly to peasant groups upon seizing land from indigenous landowners. In doing so, it sought to broaden its support base and reduce the threat of unrest from below (Myers 2009). Many in the KMT leadership attributed its loss on the mainland to its lack of peasant support, and thus the KMT was adamant about not repeating this mistake on the island (Tai 1974, 67–68). Peasant producers were relatively well organized in cooperatives and rural associations when the KMT arrived (Barraclough 1999, 35). Nonetheless, rural associations under Japanese rule tended to be dominated by large landholders who manipulated association activities to serve their own interests. Chiang Kai-Shek's government reorganized the organizations to empower tenants and small farmer-owners (Tai 1974, 398). The most important of these organizations were Farm Tenancy Committees, on which farmer-owners, tenants, and landlords sat. These committees, which were dominated by farmer-owners and tenants, were charged with settling tenancy disputes brought about by the reform laws and were effective "in curbing the landlords' evasive and resistant tactics" (Tai 1974, 401).

The Legacy of Land Reform in an Industrializing Society

As Taiwan modernized in the 1980s and 1990s, agriculture declined as a proportion of the labor force and GDP. Individuals in agricultural households declined significantly from 30.4 percent in 1979 to 16.2 percent in 1994 (Bourguignon, Fournier, and Gurgand 2001, 141). Yet largely because of the continued implementation of land reform, the proportion of owner-cultivators within the total agricultural population increased dramatically: full owner-cultivators increased from 32.7 percent of the farming population in 1946 to 59 percent in 1955, 80 percent in 1974, and 84 percent in 1992 (Huang 1998, 18). The government also put substantial subsidies and incentives in place to make farming more attractive. On top of encouraging cooperative farming and joint-family farms in the 1970s (Tai 1974, 476), it subsequently introduced price support for paddy rice, the 95 scheme, payments for resource retirement and producer retirement, natural disaster relief, and aged farmer allowances (Lin and Chen 2006, 8). In an effort to construct larger farms to boost agricultural output and improve food security, the government initiated its Small Landlord, Large Tenant program in 2009.

Although some scholars have criticized the outcomes of Taiwan's land reform (e.g., Apthorpe 1979), the majority consider it a model for successful reform (Bourguignon et al. 2001; Galor, Moav, and Vollrath 2009; Myers 2009; Tai 1974). Myers (2009, 197), for instance, writes that land reform in Taiwan "brought an important socioeconomic boost to a large segment of the population." Furthermore, it laid the groundwork for rapid and relatively equitable growth (Bourguignon et al. 2001; Galor et al. 2009), in contrast to the elite-biased economy that had been in place prior to land reform.

Alternative Explanations for Taiwan's Land Reform

There are two main alternative explanations for the KMT's land reform. The first is that the KMT had an ideological desire to create a society of smallholder peasants that owned their own property, and the second is that the KMT was seeking to eliminate an internal communist threat (e.g., Wang and Chang 1953). Yet these explanations fail to explain several important KMT choices regarding land reform. The ideological underpinnings for land reform within the KMT stemmed from Sun Yat-sen's "Three Principles of the People," which emphasized peasant land ownership. The First and Second National Congresses of the party incorporated this idea into the party platform. Yet the KMT did not implement these ideas when it ruled on the mainland from 1928 to 1949: "[I]n contrast to its avowed intention [to carry out agrarian reform], the KMT took little action during its mainland rule" (Tai 1974, 85). A related rival explanation that was raised in the other cases in this chapter – that a land reform agenda spurred an elite split and subsequent redistribution – therefore also falls flat in the Taiwan case. The agenda of land reform lacked credibility and in any case was more relevant to mainland China than it was to Taiwan. Land reform was the least of the KMT's concerns as they scrambled across the Strait of Taiwan in 1949 in a last-ditch effort to save themselves. Furthermore, the KMT had not initiated land reform on the mainland despite an evident communist threat (Tai 1974, 85), which undermines the second alternative explanation. Instead, the clear split between the KMT and potentially threatening indigenous Taiwanese elites motivated the newly arrived KMT to pursue reform. Reform also helped Chiang Kai-Shek shore up the KMT's fragmenting internal structure

(Myers 2009). The KMT's efforts at reform were facilitated by a lack of institutional constraints. They then chose to redistribute land to peasants in order to gain popular support. This latter decision dovetailed with the desire to forestall a communist threat on the island.

Zimbabwe after Independence

Land grabbing by the British South Africa Company in 1890 in what is now Zimbabwe marked the beginning of a ninety-year era characterized by "systematic subjugation of the indigenous black population and the dispossession of its land resources" (Gonese et al. 2002, 7). Especially after World War II, hundreds of thousands of blacks were evicted from their land for the benefit of white farmers, who came to dominate the rural landscape (Palmer 1990). Independence in 1980 turned the table on white landowners. Although the negotiated Lancaster House Constitution barred the expropriation of those landowners for ten years and British financing enabled land reform compensation until the late 1990s, the withdrawal of British funding and political challenges to President Mugabe's power resulted in a quick move to redistribute white land. Almost all white farmers were expropriated in favor of indigenous black smallholders and black commercial farmers in the 2000s.

Conditions Prior to Land Reform
The first group of white British miners entered Zimbabwe in the 1880s under Cecil Rhodes. White colonizers passed laws that designated certain lands for whites and other lands for blacks. The most consequential law was the 1930 Land Apportionment Act, which ensured that whites would farm the most fertile land and blacks would be concentrated in areas with low rainfall and low soil quality (Gonese et al. 2002). Congestion exacerbated soil degradation of the so-called "communal land" to which the colonists resettled the natives, making living conditions for blacks worse (Pazvakavambwa and Hungwe 2009). As a result, by 1980 the population density in black areas was three times higher than that in white areas, and 42 percent of the country's agricultural land was owned by 6,000 white commercial farmers (Palmer 1990, 165). The small amount of land owned by blacks tended to be of much lower quality than white land in terms of its productivity and vulnerability to drought (Gonese et al. 2002, 7). White farmers produced 90 percent of the country's marketed food. While peasant farmers had previously cultivated maize and other crops for the home market and white farmers cultivated cash crops for export such as tobacco, international sanctions against the Smith regime after 1965 squeezed export agriculture, turning white farmers back to domestic markets to the detriment of peasants (Palmer 1990, 167).

Independence and the Push for Land Reform
Land redistribution was one of the principal rallying cries during the War of Liberation in the 1960s and 1970s that ravaged the country then known as

Rhodesia (Palmer 1990, 165). It therefore became an important topic during independence negotiations between the black independence leaders, the white Rhodesian regime, and the British government at Lancaster House in 1979. At the insistence of the British government, the independence constitution developed at Lancaster House imposed a ten-year moratorium on the expropriation of white land, resulting in what Gonese et al. (2002, 11) characterized as a decade of "entrenched protection of white farmer interests." The Lancaster House Agreement also preserved 20 seats out of the 100 total in Parliament to be chosen from the "white roll" of voters – those who had been enfranchised under pre-independence rule. Institutional constraints largely explain why land redistribution did not occur in the first decade after Zimbabwe's independence: "[T]he Lancaster House Constitution of 1980, while protecting the rights of the White minority, notably the right to private property, significantly constrained the ability of the Zimbabwean government to undertake substantial land reform" (Alden and Makumbe 2001, 233).

Land reform in Zimbabwe in the 1980s was thus characterized entirely by resettlement efforts that were based on the principle of willing buyer–willing seller. Large landowners interested in selling their land were legally required to offer their land to the government first and only subsequently on the private market if the government declined to purchase their land. The only exception to this approach applied to abandoned or underutilized white-owned farms. But even in those cases, owners would be compensated immediately at full market rates, remittable in foreign currency (Palmer 1990, 166). The British government agreed to match the Zimbabwe government pound-for-pound to carry out these resettlement efforts (Gonese et al. 2002, 11).

Most resettlement carried out in the 1980s occurred before 1983, when the World Bank pressured the Zimbabwean government to cut its budget deficit. The government responded by significantly scaling back funding for resettlement. Overall, by 1989 a total of 52,000 black families had been resettled on 2.8 million hectares of land, 32 percent of the 162,000-family target that had been previously articulated by the post-independence government (Pazvakavambwa and Hungwe 2009, 143). The number of commercial farmers declined from 6,000 in 1980 to 4,300 in October 1989, and by the latter date the commercial farming sector was no longer comprised of exclusively white farmers. The percentage of agricultural land owned by commercial farmers dropped from 42 percent to 29 percent between 1980 and 1989 (Palmer 1990, 170). On top of government-facilitated transfers, roughly 400 farmers sold land in the private sector after the government had issued "no present interest" certificates as part of its right of first refusal. More than 1 million hectares of land were transferred on the private market this way, many to Zimbabwe's ascendant black ruling elite (Palmer 1990, 170).

The Lancaster House Constitution expired in 1990. By that time, former Prime Minister Robert Mugabe had reformed the electoral system and won the presidency, repressing his rivals and forging the party ZANU-PF with majority support from the Shona and other, smaller ethnic and political groups. Mugabe and ZANU-PF quickly approved a 1990 constitutional amendment of Section 16, which lifted the ban on compulsory land acquisition (Coldham 1993, 83). The amendment also did an end run around the courts by constitutionally denying owners the opportunity to challenge land reform proceedings (Alden and Makumbe 2001, 225). The 1992 Land Acquisition Act gave the government a statutory basis for the constitutional amendment, eliminating the principle of willing buyer–willing seller. The law stirred fierce opposition both domestically and internationally (De Villiers 2003; Dube and Midgley 2008). Yet declining rural support for ZANU-PF, economic challenges, and the exclusion of whites from a major role in government spurred the radicalization of land redistribution (De Villiers 2003, 17).

The law was nonetheless a compromise between the demand to redress long-standing landholding inequality and the desire to maintain domestic agricultural production and avoid alienating foreign capital. So although the original draft of the bill did not provide for "fair" compensation for farmers who would lose land under the law, white farmers' toehold in the legislature pushed the government to accept an amendment that instituted fair compensation. De Villiers (2003, 17) writes that "[t]he Act was presented as a compromise between commercial farmers, who preferred the continuation of the Lancaster House arrangement, and government, which favoured wider powers to effect land reform that would include the taking of land without compensation."

Land reform in the 1990s was incremental because of this compromise as well as several other factors. First, land prices increased substantially as a consequence of speculation in the land market, relative political stability, and growing confidence in the black government (Gonese et al. 2002, 12). This increase discouraged land purchases under the Land Acquisition Act, which reached their lowest level between 1998 and 2000. Second, the government feared the economic consequences of a sudden loss of white expertise in commercial agriculture (Palmer 1990, 171), as had occurred in neighboring Mozambique when Frelimo seized power. Finally, the Land Acquisition Act and a series of land occupations were challenged in the courts, which maintained a degree of independence and stalled the process of reform (Alden and Makumbe 2001, 226–228).

Between 1990 and 1997, the government redistributed 800,000 hectares to just short of 20,000 families (Pazvakavambwa and Hungwe 2009, 149). Most of this land went to medium-scale producers and blacks who were better off or more capable in the first place (Pazvakavambwa and Hungwe 2009, 149). Some of it also ended up in the hands of corrupt regime officials (De Villiers 2003, 17).

Land squatting and land invasions picked up in the mid- to late 1990s with the slower pace of land transfers. In contrast to previous waves of land invasions, the government eased off on evictions (De Villiers 2003, 19). At the same time, Mugabe was facing a political challenge to his rule with the creation of the National Constitutional Assembly (NCA) in 1997. The NCA sought a re-founding of Zimbabwe's constitution and the reduction of presidential powers. In the context of this political threat and the stalling of land redistribution, Mugabe announced in October 1997 that the government would expropriate 1,500 large farms (Pazvakavambwa and Hungwe 2009, 149). Mugabe made it clear that there would be no compensation for the land, declaring "[w]e fought for the land and now we are going to take it" (Alden and Makumbe 2001, 229). Shortly after this move, Britain's new Labour government declared that it had no obligation to financially support land redistribution.

"Fast-Track" Land Redistribution

Following a failed constitutional referendum in 2000, the government amended the constitution and the Land Acquisition Act again to speed up land reform. The amendment absolved the government from paying compensation to former owners of expropriated land for anything other than improvements absent British financial support (Gonese et al. 2002, 14). Furthermore, landowners could not appeal expropriations on the basis of unfair compensation of those improvements. The government also directed police not to respond to the complaints of white landowners whose land was invaded. This series of changes was announced as a "fast-track" resettlement program.

The fast-track phase of land reform dramatically increased redistribution. By 2005, roughly 5,200 farms had been redistributed, covering 9 million of the 11.7 million hectares of land in the commercial sector as of 1997. Slightly more than 160,000 smallholders received 7 million hectares of this new land, whereas black indigenous commercial farmers were granted 2 million hectares of land during this period (Pazvakavambwa and Hungwe 2009, 156). Fast-track land reform was further buoyed in 2005 by a constitutional amendment that eliminated any legal remedies for former owners of acquired land (Dube and Midgley 2008, 3). As of 2011, only 300 white-owned commercial farms remained in Zimbabwe.

Consequences and Results of Land Reform

Analysis of the success of Zimbabwe's reform has been mixed. A host of observers note corruption in the distribution of land and the enrichment of regime elements (e.g., De Villiers 2003). The media has frequently linked the program to a loss of agricultural productivity and increased economic hardship in the country (e.g., Freeman 2011). Yet several new, in-depth studies suggest that many farmers have indeed benefited from the land reform and that even if the process was at times brutal and violent, the results in terms of land redistribution and rural black empowerment were nonetheless successful (Hanlon, Manjengwa, and Smart 2013; Marongwe et al. 2010).

All observers agree on one fundamental point: that land reform in Zimbabwe has been massively redistributive. White farmers have been all but eliminated in favor of blacks. This episode took place in the context of a clear split between

Mugabe and his ZANU-PF on the one hand and white landed elite farmers on the other hand. Furthermore, the lack of domestic constraints to Mugabe's rule enabled rapid redistribution when the regime decided to move to fast-track land reform.

Alternative Explanations for Zimbabwe's Land Reform

There are four competing explanations for Zimbabwe's post-independence land reform, and particularly for the most redistributive, fast-track phase. The first is that land reform was contrived to enable black elites to corruptly seize land for personal gain (Davies 2004; Makumbe 1999). The second is that spreading land invasions forced the government to act decisively (Moyo 2007). The third, in common with the other cases in this chapter, is that the land reform agenda caused the elite split and subsequently the reform. The last is that Mugabe deepened land reform to shore up his electoral prospects at a moment of political weakness (Sachikonye 2004).

Although there is certainly evidence of corruption in the land reform in Zimbabwe (De Villiers 2003), it is hard to believe that such a consequential policy was constructed simply for this end given that corruption reigned before the land reform and that ZANU-PF's dominance had already enabled officials to generously line their own pockets. Furthermore, several recent studies indicate a large number of peasant beneficiaries and several important program successes (Hanlon et al. 2013; Marongwe et al. 2010). Second, although land invasions ballooned in the mid-1990s and doubtless impacted who received land, the evidence suggests that this was in part a choice by the Mugabe regime to not enforce evictions and even to encourage them (De Villiers 2003, 19). The government had previously suppressed land invasions and popular pressure successfully in the 1980s. It also continued to diffuse selected land invasions that were particularly inconvenient, such as those in the Svosve Communal Area in 1998 (Alden and Makumbe 2001, 229).

The possibility that the agenda of land reform catalyzed the elite split in Zimbabwe also belies several crucial facts. The roots of an elite split rose as a consequence of the systematic and racially based displacement of indigenous blacks from their land by white settlers during colonization (Gonese et al. 2002). What introduced this split at the national level was not land reform but rather the British retraction from Zimbabwe in 1980. The fact that the elite split after independence did not bring about immediate land redistribution but rather land negotiation and snowballing pressure for deeper reform was the result of a devil's pact with the British via the Lancaster House Agreement, which built in white minority elite protections via institutional constraints as a condition for independence. But the dam burst shortly after the expiration of the Lancaster House Constitution, enabling the elite split to operate.

The last alternative explanation for Zimbabwe's accelerated land redistribution – that it stemmed from a political challenge to Mugabe's rule – is not inconsistent with the theory in this book. Institutional constraints via the Lancaster

House Constitution and then legislative minorities and the courts forestalled wholesale reform into the early 1990s. British funding for land expropriation, holdout courts, international pressure, and the threat of plummeting export earnings if white farmers were expropriated aided in delaying land redistribution amid a clear elite split and severely weakened institutional constraints for several years in the mid-1990s. But the seams came undone in 1997 when Mugabe's support coalition frayed in the face of a serious political challenge from the NCA and the increasingly popular opposition political movement the NCA generated, including the Movement for Democratic Change (Boone 2013). Roughly 50,000 independence war veterans of the militant War Veterans Association, which was part of Mugabe's initial support coalition, agitated for compensation for their previous service (Alden and Makumbe 2001, 229). Mugabe paid them out of the dwindling treasury. Even that was not enough. The independent parliamentarian and founding member of the War Veterans Association, Margaret Dongo, accused regime officials of corrupt land deals and advocated for political change (Alden and Makumbe 2001, 233). Mugabe also began to lose his traditional rural support base after years of unfulfilled promises. In a 2000 referendum, these voters rejected Mugabe's proposed constitution, which would have consolidated executive power and legalized the appropriation of white farmers' land. Threatened with the possibility of further defections within his core coalition, Mugabe moved to expropriate white farmers in order to satisfy his key supporters.

CONCLUSION

This chapter puts the book's theory and scope to the test by examining redistributive land reform outside of Latin America. As former landed elites and the rural poor well know, redistributive land reform is prevalent throughout the world. There have been fifty-four episodes of land redistribution since 1900 outside of Latin America spanning every region of the world and affecting hundreds of millions of rural inhabitants. Together with Latin America, more than one-third of all countries have undertaken land redistribution since 1900, and many more have implemented programs of large-scale land negotiation and land colonization.

The conditions most conducive to redistributive land reform outside of Latin America are the same as those within Latin America: elite splits and low institutional constraints to rule. A split between ruling political elites and landed elites provides the former with a coalitional incentive to attack the latter. Low institutional constraints enable ruling political elites to carry out expropriation and redistribution. In addition to coding these two key variables across the world since 1900, I also examine in depth four cases of major land redistribution: Egypt under the Free Officers, Hungary in the wake of World War I and World War II, Taiwan under the KMT, and Zimbabwe since independence. These four congruent cases demonstrate that variation in elite splits and institutional constraints to power provide the best explanation for land reform policies over time.

This chapter also offers additional insight into the origins of elite splits through foreign occupation and ethnic difference, paths that are discussed in Chapter 2 but were not trodden in the Latin American cases. Occupying armies and the negotiated agreements they leave behind them can eclipse or undergird the political power of landed elites. In cases such as Hungary and Poland, war temporarily dislocated landed elites and provided an opportunity for domestic parties to expropriate them. The Soviet occupation forces ensured that major reform was a done deal. In Taiwan, a foreign force (the KMT) occupied the island and quickly set to expropriating indigenous landed elites who posed a potential threat to them and with whom they shared no affinity. In Zimbabwe, foreign influence served to temporarily protect landed elites despite an elite split that was rooted in long-standing ethnically based grievances. The British government negotiated temporary protection for white landowners and then subsidized their compensation as part of a land reform program until Mugabe moved to rapidly confiscate their property after the Lancaster House Agreement expired. In several North African cases, such as Algeria, Morocco, and Tunisia, independence empowered indigenous political elites and left foreign landowners without direct access to political power, creating circumstances conducive to land redistribution. Elite splits arising from international war and independence, although not uncommon, are at the heart of only a minority of cases of redistributive land reform. The balance of cases arises from domestically generated elite splits.

Finally, this chapter introduces a new set of cases that help delineate the outer limits of this book's theory. In many countries in sub-Saharan Africa, although not all, the overwhelming majority of land is held in customary rather than private tenure structures. The more fluid and diverse nature of property rights under authority-based control is difficult to account for within the land reform typology developed here. Whether the expanding push toward privatization spurred by the World Bank and the international community – a point taken up in Chapter 9 – eventually tips the balance in favor of private over customary ownership is a question that remains to be answered.

9

Conclusion

Despite rapid rates of urbanization and development, just less than half of the world's population still lives in the rural sector. Most of these individuals dedicate themselves to agriculture. Those that already own land work feverishly to retain and exploit it. Yet many of them wake up every day dreaming to own a plot of land that they can farm to feed their family, to insure themselves against capital or employment losses, and to have the freedom to allocate their labor as they wish.

This book seeks to explain why governments sometimes choose to allocate land to these rural laborers and at other times guard the privileges of large landowners. In doing so, it marshals a century of evidence spanning from broad cross-country trends to micro-level details about the machinations of elites.

I draw several important conclusions. First, the most redistributive type of land reform is implemented when there is a coalitional split between ruling political elites and landed elites alongside low institutional constraints. Land redistribution of this variety makes waves. With sufficient scope, it has the power to decimate landed elites and create a new class of smallholding peasants. These reforms can be eroded or transformed by subsequent governments in ways that hang peasants out to dry, but they can never be entirely rolled back. The autocratic or majoritarian democratic governments that implement them are thus critical players in a country's long-term political and economic development. Popular rural pressure can ratchet up the scope of land redistribution but only when the political conditions are ripe for redistribution in the first place.

Given the overwhelming strength of this finding, it is surprising that landowners seemingly so often feared democratic transitions, as Barrington Moore, Alexander Gerschenkron, and others have long noted. Large landowners in countries that democratized in the late twentieth century, such as Brazil, Colombia, El Salvador, the Philippines, and South Africa, have not only avoided being soaked by the masses; they have thrived. Perhaps landowners in these countries were not as sanguine as they should have been about their capacity to act as cogs in the wheel of land reform efforts under democracy. Fearing radical, popular democracy, they may have overlooked the fact that holding veto power over major reform in a Madisonian-style democracy is often better armor than an alliance with a pliable or sympathetic political elite under autocracy. One change of mind by an autocratic political elite can spell more harm to landed elites than a string of antagonistic democratic governments.

In any case, large landowners are now good democrats – at least outwardly – in most of the world's democracies. When Hugo Chávez picked up the phone daily in Venezuela in front of a sea of television cameras to threaten the rich and powerful, elites clamored for a more independent judiciary and fair elections that could win them greater political representation in the National Assembly. Brazil's landowners have mostly abandoned the paramilitary tendencies of the Rural Democratic Union and now rely on what is perhaps the most successful sectoral congressional block in the country – the *bancada ruralista* – to do their bidding. In South Africa, white landowners who inherited their privileges from the apartheid era fear nothing more than an unchecked African National Congress (ANC) and therefore were the first to organize to protect the judiciary and to decry the ANC's increasing consolidation of power. Where large landowners are not good democrats in today's autocracies, it is mostly because they have nearly insoluble links with ruling political elites or prefer to keep their heads down. Egypt, Myanmar, and Saudi Arabia are illustrative examples.

A second key conclusion is that the less redistributive types of land reform – land negotiation and land colonization – operate under logics distinct from land redistribution. Although a coalitional split between ruling political elites and landed elites together with low institutional constraints are conducive to land negotiation, their effects are much more muted than on land redistribution. This is because landed elites face little material loss from land negotiation by receiving market-value compensation for their property. Large landowners targeted for land negotiation are not destroyed but rather displaced. Only if landed elites are deeply enmeshed in valuable social and political networks, as indeed they sometimes are, will they vehemently resist land negotiation. But in cases such as Venezuela from the 1960s until the 1990s, when landed elites were offered practically scandalous levels of compensation for their property, they may be happy to rinse their hands of the business and go earn a living and influence politics and policy in the big city.

In contrast to land redistribution, foreign aid contributes to the likelihood and scope of land negotiation. In Latin America, US aid through the Alliance for Progress went toward financing land reform programs, studying reform possibilities, and providing grants for inputs and infrastructure. This aided land reform efforts while freeing resources in order to compensate landowners. Today, much of the foreign aid for land reform comes from the World Bank.

This aid supports land negotiation programs in countries such as Namibia, the Philippines, and South Africa.

Land colonization is distinct from both land redistribution and land negotiation. Unlike these other types of land reform, coalitional elite splits and institutional constraints have little impact on land colonization. In fact, landed elites at times champion land colonization as a way to relieve pressure from the landless on the property of large landowners. Rather than risk losing their own property to land invasions, landed elites much prefer a "Go West, young man" policy that rids them of superfluous rural laborers. In the United States, the West was sparsely populated Native American land; in Brazil, it is the Amazon; in Argentina, it was the Pampas; and in much of sub-Saharan Africa, it is low-quality arid land or forests. The most robust determinant of land colonization is therefore latent popular pressure from the rural sector. Wealth is also linked to greater land colonization. Countries that have the resources to resettle rural dwellers are more likely to do so.

Taken together, land redistribution, land negotiation, and land colonization policies have ordered and reordered the countryside in much of the world in the past century. Every country in Latin America adopted at least one of these programs. A total of 14 percent of all of the land in the entire region – 271 million hectares – transferred hands between 1930 and 2008 as a result of these three types of land reform. Because most of this land was concentrated in productive agricultural zones, more than half of all cultivable land transferred hands through land reform.

Yet land reform is hardly limited to Latin America. Roughly one-third of all countries in the world implemented a land redistribution program in the last century. Many more executed land negotiation and land colonization policies. These policies set the stage for modernization in many countries. They also serve as a backdrop to the massive private land titling efforts that have been sweeping the developing world since the 1980s.

The conditions that paved the way for large-scale land redistribution in the past century are unlikely to repeat themselves on the same scale in the current one. This is more due to the spread of democracy than it is to a decline in elite splits. The third and fourth waves of democracy have brought unprecedented advances in political freedom. But institutional constraints are usually part of the democratic deal. And institutional constraints in most of the world's new democracies have given elites more than just a foothold in government to slow or water down land redistribution; they have given them a platform on which to strangle it.

But land reform is hardly finished. Half of the world still lives in the rural sector, and the urban demand for food is steadily increasing. Land inequality and landlessness remains high in South and Southeast Asia, parts of the Middle East and Latin America, and much of sub-Saharan Africa. As Boone (2013) notes, levels of ruralness in sub-Saharan Africa are comparable to Western Europe around 1850 and Latin America in 1900. The demand for land reform therefore continues unabated in much of the world. Where autocracy is still deeply entrenched, land redistribution may emerge, as Zimbabwe exemplifies. But in democracies and countries that depend critically on foreign aid, it is now the World Bank and foreign donors that must fight land inequality, and they must do so with cash rather than with a military. Their tools may not be as effective or quick-handed as those in a determined autocratic regime, but they are tools nonetheless.

REDISTRIBUTION BEYOND LAND REFORM

Though the theory and empirical analyses in this book focus on land reform, just how deep this critique of the dominant view on the link between regime type and redistribution runs stands to question. Is there something unique about land redistribution that sets it apart from other forms of redistribution and makes it a major and consequential exception to both social conflict theory and power resources theory? Or do other forms of redistribution also occur under elite splits amid low institutional constraints? While the answers to these questions can only be definitively uncovered with further research, a brief survey of several other major forms of redistribution suggests that the insights developed here have broad implications well beyond land reform.

Recall several important features of land redistribution: it is institutionally exacting, requiring consent and coordination between the executive, legislature, bureaucracy, and even the judiciary and military; it tends to target a narrow and powerful social class rather than society more broadly; it often requires individual rather than group enforcement; and it is difficult to reverse. Other major redistributive programs that exhibit several of these key features may therefore occur under conditions similar to those that guide land reform. Furthermore, one could certainly make the case that large-scale, relatively irreversible reforms that are targeted squarely at elites are the most consequential types of redistribution. They affect more lives in a more profound way over the long term than, for instance, minor tweaks to fiscal redistribution that come from fiddling with marginal tax rates or the progressivity of spending.[1]

The large-scale expropriation and distribution of resource rents and financial assets, for instance, often occurs under autocracy when there are splits between incumbent elites and preexisting economic elites (e.g., Albertus 2015a; Albertus and Menaldo 2012a). To name just a few Latin American examples, these conditions set the stage for the expropriation and nationalization of banks in Brazil under Getúlio Vargas, Cuba under Fidel Castro, El Salvador under José Napoleón Duarte, Mexico under José López Portillo, and Nicaragua under Daniel Ortega. Similar conditions paved the way for the nationalization of mining and oil interests under several autocratic regimes in Bolivia, under several

---

[1] Major shifts in fiscal redistribution, of course, can have a much broader impact and be difficult to entirely peel back.

military rulers in Ecuador, and again under Castro in Cuba and the PRI in Mexico. In many of these cases, resource rents were used to finance more generous social programs, and banking terms became more favorable for a broader swath of the population.

As indicated in Chapter 6, the Peruvian military regime under General Velasco did not just redistribute land; it also forged a statist economic policy as it split from powerful industrial elites. The military expropriated foreign mining companies (e.g., the Cerro de Pasco copper company and the Marcona iron mine) and privately owned Peruvian companies including banks (e.g., Banco Popular), utilities, fishing enterprises, and all five major presses. Furthermore, it created manufacturing laws that specified worker participation in profit distributions, worker shareholding, and company management in all industries.

Legal changes that extend human rights (e.g., the abolition of forced servitude) and yield economic and social redistribution over the long term are also in many cases – although certainly not all – implemented under conditions similar to land redistribution. Land tenure reforms that abolished semi-feudalistic tenure and labor arrangements in countries such as Bolivia, Ecuador, Peru, Chile, and Mexico destroyed some of the most exploitative labor conditions in the Americas and enabled peasants to increase their political and social independence vis-à-vis landlords. All of these reforms occurred when leaders' political coalitions were split from landowners and when these leaders faced low institutional constraints to rule. Exploitative land tenure relations were upended under similar conditions in Egypt, Russia, Taiwan, and elsewhere. Chapter 8, for instance, details how new authoritarian regimes that came to power without the aid of landowners rewrote tenure relations in Egypt and Taiwan by undercutting debt peonage and severing the paternalistic landowner-peasant relations that were at the heart of social subjugation.

Another form of redistribution that is at least partially consistent with the theory here is the centralization and expansion of access to education, which in many cases preceded the establishment of social insurance systems and laid the groundwork for subsequent increases in the quality of and funding for education. When analyzing the origins of the centralization of primary education from 1870 to 1939, for instance, Ansell and Lindvall (2013) find that the centralization of education by the state has typically occurred under either dictatorship or democratic liberalism/social democracy. Some of these dictatorships clearly exhibit elite splits, as was the case with Japan during the Meiji Restoration (Trimberger 1978). Although the authors' predictions are split fairly equally between democracy and dictatorship, the small set of countries in their analysis dramatically oversamples democracies during the era.[2] The centralization of education may actually have been more common under dictatorship if it occurred at an even more frequent rate in the excluded dictatorships.

---

[2] Their intent, however, was to focus on countries that had been examined in early studies of the welfare state.

A preliminary study of primary education in postcolonial Asia, for instance, suggests that almost all of the countries in that region that centralized education or maintained centralized systems (e.g., China, Malaysia, Myanmar, the Philippines, Taiwan, and Vietnam) were dictatorships at the time (Tan 2014). Many of these regimes were forged under elite splits.[3] The KMT, for instance, centralized control of education under the state after it invaded Taiwan and forcibly displaced indigenous Taiwanese elites with mainlanders. The KMT monopolized teacher training and funding via a teachers' college system, curricula and degrees were controlled by the state, and access to education was expanded dramatically in an effort to reshape and control society (Albertus, Fenner, and Slater 2015). By contrast, the two most stable and long-lived democracies in the region – India and Japan – have had decentralized systems since independence. Many other countries in the region decentralized after they became, at least temporarily, democracies (e.g., Indonesia, Nepal, South Korea, Taiwan, and Thailand).

Interestingly, and putting yet another chink in the armor of median voter models of redistribution, the earliest welfare state initiatives also occurred under autocratic rulers. Germany's Otto von Bismarck and Austria's Eduard von Taaffe pioneered modern social insurance through workers' pension benefits and income protection, building off the programs spearheaded by France's Napoleon III (Esping-Andersen 1990). Their model was one of "monarchical socialism," an absolutist model of paternal obligation for the welfare of the state's subjects. Aristocratic rulers such as Benjamin Disraeli in Britain and Jacob Bronnum Estrup in Denmark also initiated relief for the poor. Throughout Western and Northern Europe, conservative authoritarian and aristocratic rulers were some of the first to underpin social rights and to attack the commodification of labor that divorced social welfare from labor arrangements. At the same time, they were more likely than their democratic counterparts to introduce consumption and income taxes (e.g., Mares and Queralt 2014).[4] These rulers often engaged in reform policies with narrow political coalitions that supported the aggrandizement of the state over nascent and still-weak industrial elites. When Bismarck introduced Germany's first social insurance scheme, he did battle against both liberals and conservatives, instead choosing to "chain workers directly to the paternal authority of the monarchy" (Esping-Andersen 1990). This drive for state autonomy is one of the deeper origins of elite splits

---

[3] Another well-known example from Ansell and Lindvall's period of study is 1920s Turkey, where Mustafa Kemal Atatürk abolished separate religious schools and colleges and replaced them with secular schools unified under the state (Trimberger 1978). His support coalition was clearly split from the religious and imperial bureaucratic elite within the Ottoman Empire.

[4] This is also true in Latin America. In Mexico, for instance, it was the autocratic leader Plutarco Elías Calles who first adopted progressive taxation on individual income and corporate profits under the Tax Law of 1924 (Albertus and Menaldo 2012a). Barely one year after income taxation was introduced, 5 percent of Mexico's total government revenue was in the form of income taxation, whereas the level of income taxation had reached 1 percent of GDP.

discussed in Chapter 2, and it squares well with many cases of land redistribution.

Even the more contemporary foundations of the modern welfare state in much of Europe were built in times when institutional constraints were low and leaders were split from major economic interests. This occurred most often during the course of and in the aftermath of major wars and during extraordinary economic crises. Alesina and Glaeser (2004), for instance, argue that the welfare state and the institutions that underpin it in continental Western Europe came about in the wake of World War I and World War II. These wars decimated the strength of the secular right and also brought substantial political instability when armed and disgruntled veterans returned from war unhappy with the status quo. Relatively unconstrained political leaders at the time reformed institutions and rewrote social contracts to empower labor and the left more generally.

Take the case of Germany. At the end of World War I in 1918, Germany lost control of its own military and the Kaiser abdicated. The Spartacist uprising in Berlin provided the opportunity for a shrewd and popular socialist leader, Friedrich Ebert, to strike a deal with the military. In exchange for becoming the president, Ebert allied with the military and the right-wing paramilitary Freikorps to suppress the uprising. Ebert also agreed to keep Paul von Hindenburg as the head of the army (he later followed Ebert as president). In 1919, Ebert then ushered in the Weimar Constitution, which featured proportional representation, few constitutional checks, and key redistributive measures, such as the right for labor to collectively bargain and the eight-hour workday. Hitler continued redistribution. The National Socialists, facing few constitutional constraints, built massive public works programs, pushed for profit sharing in large industries, increased pensions, and threatened land redistribution (Alesina and Glaeser 2004, 116). Further redistributive measures were enshrined in the wake of World War II. Just prior to the end of the Allied occupation, Germany's first postwar chancellor, Konrad Adenauer, promulgated a co-determination law that gave labor unions seats on company supervisory and managerial boards.

In contrast to the types of redistribution detailed above, on which there are surprisingly few broad and explicitly comparative studies, there is a well-developed literature that examines the variation in fiscal redistribution since the 1970s. Annual changes in fiscal redistribution via taxation and social spending are perhaps the types of redistribution that are least similar to land reform: changes in fiscal redistribution are less dependent on institutional agreement, are broad-based, and are reversible, and important elements of enforcement can be aggregated up to a smaller number of actors (e.g., employer income withholding for tax purposes). It is therefore unsurprising that a host of studies find that fiscal redistribution is guided by a much different political logic than land reform (see, e.g., Avelino, Brown, and Hunter 2005; Huber, Mustillo, and Stephens 2008; Timmons 2005). Nonetheless, several recent contributions to this literature can be viewed through the lens of the theory presented in this book. First, as noted in recent work such as Albertus and Menaldo (2014) and Inman and Rubenfeld (2005), not all democracies are equally effective at implementing fiscal redistribution through social spending and progressive taxation. Those democracies that inherit autocratic legacies that are intended to hamstring the median voter actually redistribute less than autocracies on average. These legacies may come in the form of higher constraints on policymaking. Second, Slater, Smith, and Nair (2014) demonstrate that autonomous militaries in the postcolonial world that topple democracy while acting independently of wealthy economic elites tend to uphold – and in some cases expand – the fiscal redistribution policies they inherit upon seizing office. Even fiscal redistribution, therefore, does not operate according to a simple median voter or power resources logic, and it may in some cases become more progressive under the conditions laid out here.[5]

NORMATIVE IMPLICATIONS

Even setting aside the patterns that guide the other types of redistribution discussed in the previous section, the main findings in this book raise a host of thorny normative concerns. If autocratic regimes implement more redistributive land reform in developing states where access to land is critical to rural well-being, then is dictatorship such a bad thing? To take it one step further, should policymakers who are serious about rural poverty promote (or at least turn a blind eye to) dictatorship – or foreign occupation for that matter – as an institutional line of attack rather than democracy? There is certainly evidence that citizens at times look back on dictatorship with nostalgia and at their current democracy with ambivalence (Diamond and Plattner 2008; Inglehart 2003). This is even more likely the case with rural dwellers that benefited from autocratic land redistribution programs.

Unfortunately, dictatorships do not only redistribute land. In cases where economic and political elites are fused, they implement hardly any redistribution at all. At the same time, they squelch freedom of speech, deny citizens fair representation and voice in government by rigging or eliminating competitive and open elections, and in many cases violate human rights and even violently repress their own populations through politically motivated imprisonment, isolation, and murder. It could thus hardly be considered sage advice to foist a Rafael Trujillo or a Bashar al-Assad on any society.

Even when dictatorships do redistribute land, they sometimes introduce market distortions that hobble the independence of peasant beneficiaries. Although

---

[5] The same is true for the provision of public goods. Although it is also very dissimilar in structure to land reform and it is not always redistributive in nature, there are at least some cases in which public goods such as sanitation, rural infrastructure, and education spending are provided at higher rates by authoritarian regimes in which there is an ethnically based elite split (Albertus, Fenner, and Slater 2015).

doing so is not necessarily unique to dictatorship, these regimes typically use land reform as an entrée into cultivating political dependencies to prop up regime support by withholding formal land titles, creating artificial scarcities of credits and inputs, isolating beneficiaries from markets, and failing to invest in human capital that enables social mobility (e.g., Albertus 2013; Albertus et al. 2014; de Janvry, Gonzalez-Navarro, and Sadoulet 2013). Land reform beneficiaries then find themselves bumping up against a politically generated ceiling just as they are establishing themselves.

Yet dictatorship comes in many stripes. Autocrats *can and sometimes do* implement progressive policies. This is not only true when it comes to direct redistribution. Htun (2003), for instance, demonstrates that military regimes in Latin America were often very effective at implementing liberalizing reforms on gender and family issues that extended a wider repertoire of rights to women. In East Asia, the developmental states of South Korea, Hong Kong, Singapore, and Taiwan have generated spectacular economic growth rooted mainly in the broad-based expansion of education and manufacturing (Haggard 1990; Woo-Cumings 1999), which was largely implemented under authoritarian rule. The former Soviet Union and many other communist regimes elevated workers' rights and access to housing, health care, and education (Laclau 1977). Atatürk in Turkey and the Meiji Restoration in Japan led to major reforms from above, including the elimination of powerful bureaucratic ruling elites, judicial reform, and the expansion and secularization of education (Trimberger 1978).

Are rural populations in developing states destined to be stuck between the Scylla of an autocratic regime that may benefit them materially while turning a deaf ear to their broader concerns and the Charybdis of a democratic regime that grants citizens voice but little else? Or does the analysis teach us something about policymaking under autocracy that can inform our understanding of democratic policymaking in a way that could improve it? Similarly, what does the analysis tell us about the potential for land reform in the guise of land negotiation or land colonization?

MAKING LAND NEGOTIATION AND LAND COLONIZATION WORK

For those living in one of the increasing number of democracies in the world, land redistribution is more or less off the table. But as Venezuela's Punto Fijo era of democracy, which was detailed in Chapter 7, demonstrates, democracy does not spell the death of land reform more broadly. Land negotiation and land colonization can operate actively under democracy. And if they are done correctly, these policies can benefit rural dwellers while preventing landed elites from crying foul.

Take the case of Brazil. During the 1988–2008 period, Brazil's National Institute of Colonization and Agrarian Reform transferred nearly 70 million hectares of land, an area equivalent to the size of Texas, to 750,000 families (INCRA 2011). This was hardly a seamless process. Change of this scale required nearly 8,000 land invasions in rural areas – staged by several million individuals – due to the demand-driven nature of Brazil's ongoing land reform. The state responds to land invasions and rural land pressure with expropriation at market value and redistribution rather than leading the process by targeting unproductive land and building a land bank for qualified petitioners. This legal framework protects large landowners from broad, state-initiated land redistribution, and although it creates incentives for rural conflict and land invasions, most observers consider Brazil's large-scale land negotiation in response to popular and partisan pressure leveraged by the Landless Workers' Movement largely a success. Landowners have embraced democracy and many rural families have gained access to land.

South Africa's land reform since its 1994 democratic transition is consistent with the Brazil example. At the end of apartheid, 86 percent of all farmland in the country (82 million hectares) was held by 60,000 white farmers (Lahiff 2009, 170). The 13 million blacks on the remaining poor-quality land, many of whose forebears had been dispossessed through racially discriminatory colonial and post-independence practices such as the 1913 Native Land Act, clamored for the restitution of their land rights. The South African government promised to redistribute 25 million hectares of agricultural land by 1999 to redress historical racially based land dispossession. It then instituted a market-based willing seller–willing buyer reform in line with the World Bank's recommendations. Through this land negotiation program, now known as the Land Redistribution for Agricultural Development (LRAD) program, the South African government purchases voluntarily offered private farmland at market value rates up front in cash and then provides grants to farmers that enable them to purchase land. LRAD and other programs peacefully guided the transfer of 4.2 million hectares of land to black farmers from 1994 to 2007.

Land negotiation and land colonization can even function successfully in the wake of widespread civil conflict rooted in land issues. In Guatemala, a brutal civil war sparked by the unequal distribution of land simmered for thirty years before the Guatemalan National Revolutionary Unity, an umbrella organization that represented the four strongest guerrilla groups, entered into negotiations with the government. The two sides finally reached a deal in 1996 after a decade of UN-brokered negotiations. The peace accords stipulated that land should serve a social function. To that end, the parties created a land agency, FONTIERRAS, that would both ensure that the rural poor got access to land and grant official land titles to rural landholders. Guatemala's Land Access Program provides credits and cheap loans to peasants to use to buy land. The program also provides subsidies to rural communities to help them capitalize their farms. Between 1998, when the program started, and 2010, a total of 94,251 hectares of land had been transferred to peasants. And when land conflicts have arisen, the Secretariat for Agrarian Affairs has mediated disputes and even purchased land for displaced peasant communities. Although FONTIERRAS gets less funding than it needs and thus has only marginally improved land inequality, it has helped alleviate pressing land disputes that could be tinder for wider conflict.

Land reform played a similar role in El Salvador's civil war, which raged for twelve years before a negotiated settlement ended the fighting in 1992. As part of the deal, ex-combatants from both sides as well as civilian supporters of the country's main guerrilla group received land. The land transfer program was also a state-market hybrid: private owners and cooperatives that had space for more members voluntarily sold off plots. El Salvador's national Land Bank served as a broker. Ten percent of the country's agricultural land was transferred through the program to applicants during the first six years after the peace accords. There were more than 36,000 beneficiaries by 2000. The program was far from perfect: many of those who resisted demobilization or received insufficient agricultural credits and training joined gangs and organized crime outfits. Yet land conflict in the countryside has largely subsided.

These experiences show that market-based reforms are a viable option for gaining consensus among negotiating parties and getting land to the tiller. Although such reforms do not guarantee decreases in rural inequality, they ameliorate some of the most destabilizing land conflicts and a broader turn to organized rural violence.

Land negotiation and land colonization programs extend far beyond Brazil, El Salvador, Guatemala, and South Africa. These policies are also being implemented on a substantial scale in Malawi, Namibia, the Philippines, Venezuela, and a host of other countries. Furthermore, countries such as Kenya are actively rewriting laws that impact land allocation and define what constitutes property rights over land.

Land Negotiation and Land Colonization Shortcomings and the Path Forward

From the perspective of keeping the peace and curtailing broader rural unrest, the land negotiation and land colonization projects discussed in the previous section have been largely successful. They have also improved the lives of millions of rural beneficiaries that have received land. Yet they are uniformly too small in scale. And they are much less redistributive than land redistribution. The Gini coefficient for landholding inequality in Brazil in 2006, for instance, was an incredible 0.857, which is exactly the same figure as it was in 1985. In South Africa, a host of analysts have long decried the fact that it will take a lifetime or more for land negotiation at this pace to deliver 30 percent of agricultural land to blacks as was promised in 1994 (see, e.g., Thwala 2006, 68). It is therefore not surprising that President Jacob Zuma announced in 2013 that the willing seller–willing buyer principle would be dropped in favor of a "just and equitable" redistribution principle that enables the expropriation of private land, encapsulated in the Expropriation Bill. The deadline for land restitution claims, which previously had to be submitted by the end of 1998, was extended to 2018 by Parliament in February 2014. Broad new legislation guiding land reform looks set to pass in 2015.

How can land negotiation and land colonization programs be modified to make them more effective and more popular? The first and most obvious answer is better funding from the top down. If high institutional constraints effectively grant landed elites veto power over reform and foreclose reform by imposition, then the proponents of reform can only move forward if landed elites are a willing partner. Compensation must substitute for force in acquiring private property, and creativity in making state land available is paramount. Although South Africa's LRAD has been slowed by an inefficient bureaucracy and incomplete land registries, for instance, there is little question that much more land could be transferred with greater access to funding. When governments themselves lack the funding, the World Bank or foreign donors could step in, perhaps by matching government investments in land purchases or colonization schemes.

Colombia is one interesting case of how such a solution may come to fruition. Landed elite resistance, along with an agonizing and drawn-out conflict with the Revolutionary Armed Forces of Colombia (FARC), stymied substantial agrarian reform for fifty years. Yet a 2013 preliminary agreement on agrarian reform that is part of the peace negotiations with the FARC would distribute some 3 million hectares of land to small landowners and landless farmers through a series of regional "land funds." These funds would distribute lands that have been illegally or improperly attained and consequently seized by the state as well as underutilized private lands in some cases. This builds on top of the Victims Law that President Juan Manuel Santos signed in 2011, which offers reparations in the form of land to victims of civil conflict. Some 350,000 families are eligible to reclaim roughly 2 million hectares of land through the law. The price tag is hefty – somewhere around $20 billion for the Victims Law alone. The United Nations has promised to help Colombia implement the Victims Law, and a host of actors such as Brazil, the United States, Spain, the Organization of American States, the European Union, and the United Nations have spoken out in favor of the peace negotiations. These parties should help fund the Colombian government's investments in land purchases and loans if they want to push reform forward.

A second possible solution for improving the efficacy and scope of land negotiation and land colonization programs is to create a parallel reform track that operates from the bottom up. It is not hard to imagine an NGO – or even a World Bank program – that deploys mobile units to areas of particularly high rural pressure or rural poverty. These areas could be identified with the help of widely available mapping technology paired with data on land invasions, droughts, agricultural product prices, or crime. They could also be identified through social media or mobile platforms given the increasing penetration of cell phones in rural areas. Mobile units could then work with existing land reform agencies to identify target properties and match peasant demands with private or public properties that could be purchased through a World Bank fund or through a crowd-sourcing method along the lines of Heifer International. This would have the added benefit that the host country land reform agency could claim partial credit for the land transfer. In cases where a land reform agency is either absent or unwilling to participate, mobile units could use local information to identify available properties in the land market and then match peasants to these properties once funds were raised. The most obvious downside of such a program is that it is unlikely to approach the scale of an effective government program of land negotiation or land colonization. Yet it has the advantage that it does not require large-scale collective action or necessarily even state participation in order to institute change.

A final solution for making land negotiation programs in particular more effective – especially where there is a paucity of unoccupied and potentially productive land for colonization – is to push the boundaries of negotiation into what actually constitutes "land redistribution light": in other words, to loosen the compensation standards for land negotiation. This would only work if international organizations such as the World Bank sign on and aid in generating standards for – or signaling approval of – "fair" expropriation that is short of market-value compensation yet does not cause capital to flee in unison. Although this sounds naïvely optimistic on its face, it has in fact received substantial discussion. The prominent World Bank consultant and former World Bank senior advisor to Africa Hans Binswanger-Mkhize writes in the recent volume, *Agricultural Land Redistribution: Toward Greater Consensus* (Binswanger-Mkhize, Bourguignon, and van den Brink 2009, 27),

[T]he fear of adverse economic repercussions associated with the use of the expropriation instrument should not be a deterrent to its use, provided the state is using due process and is willing to pay amounts ultimately judged reasonable by the broader class of owners and the general public, if not by individual owners.

South Africa seems poised to move toward this type of land redistribution light after years of land negotiation and land colonization. The Expropriation Bill that would enable a shift to "just and equitable" redistribution from the current willing seller–willing buyer is anticipated to be brought to Parliament shortly. This, of course, occurs as the ANC continues to tighten its grip on power amid widespread allegations of corruption and cronyism. Some observers are therefore fearful that South Africa may mimic its northern neighbor Zimbabwe and focus more on the "equitable" over the "just" in future land redistribution and restitution. Nonetheless, the enticement of access to capital may lead governments such as that in South Africa to calculate that a slow program of land redistribution light is better than a Mugabe-style fast-track land confiscation program.

SOWING THE LAND AND HARVESTING THE FUTURE

Given the rural demand for land, the fact that agricultural productivity can be enhanced by putting more land into the hands of those who would farm it regularly, and the obvious short-term benefits of rural poverty reduction, investing in land reform seems like an uncontroversial proposition. But land reform can also risk stoking a backlash by large landowners or generating distributional conflict. Furthermore, development trends come and go, which can leave popular programs and their beneficiaries in the lurch once a strategy has changed. So even though the World Bank is turning its focus back to land reform after several decades of disfavor toward it, should countries and foreign donors do the same?

Aside from the substantial number of countries where the rural status quo cries out for land reform regardless of other considerations, the answer to this question depends in part on the long-term consequences of land reform. Yet the research on long-term effects is still in its nascent stages, in part because researchers have not previously compiled systematic land reform data.

There are several facts that are fairly well established. First, land redistribution can spur sustained economic growth by creating greater equality in the distribution of land and more efficient exploitation (Alesina and Rodrik 1994; Lipton 2009). This is perhaps best demonstrated by Japan, South Korea, and Taiwan, where massive land redistribution paved the way for modernization and spectacular subsequent economic growth. Yet land redistribution does not always generate such virtuous outcomes. In Mexico, for instance, land redistribution generated short-term economic growth that then turned negative in the long run as economic distortions and political dependencies associated with the reform derailed progress (Albertus et al. 2014). This was likely a result of the perverse incentives created in the *ejido* structure that deterred investment and also insufficient state provision of credits, inputs such as seeds and fertilizer, and infrastructure. This bolsters the case for pursuing "integral" land reform. There is little evidence on the long-term economic consequences of land negotiation and land colonization.

Land reform also clearly impacts rural stability and conflict, although not always in positive ways. The demand-driven structure of reform in Brazil essentially requires land invasions in order to yield reform, a process that creates incentives for rural conflict and land threats (Albertus, Brambor, and Ceneviva 2015). In Russia following the emancipation of serfs in 1861, land-based rural rebellion actually increased as landlords hijacked the reform implementation process to win favorable land allotments (Finkel, Gehlbach and Olsen 2012). And in Colombia, land titling in conflictive rural areas led to spillover effects in which nearby communities recognized the need to support rebel groups in order to garner the attention of Colombia's land reform agency (Albertus and Kaplan 2013). The key to tamping down conflict in selected areas in Colombia was sustained, large-scale reform coupled with inputs, credits, services, and the development of local infrastructure.

There is less research on the long-term impacts of land reform on education and on income inequality. Yet research on land inequality suggests that differences in the distribution of land ownership contributed to the "great divergence" in income per capita around the world between 1800 and today. Galor, Moav, and Vollrath (2009) argue in favor of this hypothesis and provide consistent empirical evidence to explain public spending on education across US states. They also attribute major education reforms in Japan, Russia, South Korea, and Taiwan to the role that land redistribution played in destroying many landed elites that blocked access to education and changing the calculus of others. Further research is required to determine how generalizable these examples are and how dependent they are on land redistribution over land negotiation or land colonization.

Finally, land reform – or the possibility of land reform – may also have political consequences in the long run. A dictator or a series of dictators who implement large-scale land redistribution can condition the future likelihood of democratic transition and consolidation. This could operate through several channels. Land redistribution may abolish traditional land tenure relations, destroying rural patron-client relations that landlords can use to dominate electoral competition by influencing rural votes. The elimination of landholding elites can also reduce the capture of local officials and activists that can be used to manipulate election outcomes. Lastly, a redistributive dictator can make powerful elites more wary of autocratic rule and therefore more likely to support democracy, particularly if they can disproportionately influence policy.

The potential for a nondemocratic leader to favor a support coalition that is distinct from landed elites can deter those elites from mounting a coup if they imperfectly control a dictator's behavior or potential countercoups and dictator cycling. It can also lead landed elites to support a more predictable, mildly redistributive democracy rather than the prospect of irregular leader replacement and possible reformist autocratic rule. As Schmitter (2010) notes of Latin America, democratization in many states followed after elites that had formerly supported autocratic rule started to realize that democracy would better safeguard their interests moving forward. This line of argument is consistent with the fact that democratization is often initiated by elites from a position of relative strength (Slater and Wong 2013). Democratic transition in unequal countries where elites are powerful, such as Colombia and Venezuela in 1958 and Brazil in 1985, are less surprising under this account than most of the current literature anticipates. Indeed, this may help explain the lack of a general relationship between inequality and democratization (e.g., Houle 2009).

Governments have a number of arrows in the quiver when it comes to development policy. Given its subsequent effects, the discussion here suggests that land reform is one of the first arrows that should be drawn. But it must be drawn carefully. Land reform must come in tandem with supportive policies such as land titling, the provision of credits and inputs, the development of rural infrastructure, and access to basic schooling. It may otherwise land wide of the mark.

References

Aberbach, Joel, Robert Putnam, and Bert Rockman. 1981. *Bureaucrats and Politicians in Western Democracies*. Cambridge, MA: Harvard University Press.

Acemoglu, Daron, and James Robinson. 2001. "A Theory of Political Transitions." *American Economic Review* 91: 938–963.

———. 2006. *Economic Origins of Dictatorship and Democracy*. Cambridge: Cambridge University Press.

———. 2008. "Persistence of Power, Elites, and Institutions." *American Economic Review* 98: 267–293.

Acemoglu, Daron, James Robinson, and Thierry Verdier. 2004. "Kleptocracy and Divide-and-Rule." *Journal of the European Economic Association Papers and Proceedings* 2: 162–192.

Alamgir, Muhiuddin Khan, ed. 1981. *Land Reform in Bangladesh*. Dacca: Centre for Social Studies, Dacca University.

Albertus, Michael. 2013. "Vote Buying with Multiple Distributive Goods." *Comparative Political Studies* 46(9): 1082–1111.

———. 2015a. "Explaining Patterns of Redistribution under Autocracy: The Case of Peru's Revolution from Above." *Latin American Research Review* 50(2): 107–134.

———. 2015b. "The Role of Subnational Politicians in Distributive Politics: Political Bias in Venezuela's Land Reform under Chávez." Forthcoming, *Comparative Political Studies*.

Albertus, Michael, Thomas Brambor, and Ricardo Ceneviva. 2015. "Land Reform and Land Invasions in Brazil." Working paper.

Albertus, Michael, Alberto Diaz-Cayeros, Beatriz Magaloni, and Barry Weingast. 2014. "Authoritarian Survival and Poverty Traps: Land Reform in Mexico." Working paper.

Albertus, Michael, Sofia Fenner, and Dan Slater. 2015. "Coercive Distribution: Authoritarian Public Goods in Ethnically Divided Societies." Working paper, University of Chicago.

Albertus, Michael, and Oliver Kaplan. 2013. "Land Reform as a Counterinsurgency Policy: Evidence from Colombia." *Journal of Conflict Resolution* 57(2): 198–231.

Albertus, Michael, and Victor Menaldo. 2012a. "If You're against Them You're with Us: The Effect of Expropriation on Autocratic Survival." *Comparative Political Studies* 45(8): 973–1003.

———. 2012b. "Dictators as Founding Fathers? The Role of Constitutions under Autocracy." *Economics & Politics* 24(3): 279–306.

———. 2014. "Gaming Democracy: Elite Dominance during Transition and the Prospects for Redistribution." *British Journal of Political Science* 44(3): 575–603.

Alden, Patricia, and John Makumbe. 2001. "The Zimbabwe Constitution: Race, Land Reform and Social Justice." In Grant Hermans Cornwell and Eve Walsh Stoddard, eds., *Global Multiculturalism*, 215–237. Lanham: Rowman& Littlefield.

Alesina, Alberto, and Edward Glaeser. 2004. *Fighting Poverty in the US and Europe: A World of Difference*. Oxford: Oxford University Press.

Alesina, Alberto, and Dani Rodrik. 1994. "Distributive Politics and Economic Growth." *Quarterly Journal of Economics* 109: 465–490.

Alexander, Gerard. 2002. *The Sources of Democratic Consolidation*. Ithaca, NY: Cornell University Press.

Alexander, Robert Jackson. 1973. *Latin American Political Parties*. Vol. 2. New York: Praeger.

Alexander, Robert Jackson. 1982. *Rómulo Betancourt and the Transformation of Venezuela*. New Brunswick: Transaction Publishers.

Almeida, Paul. 2008. *Waves of Protest: Popular Struggle in El Salvador, 1925–2005*. Minneapolis: University of Minnesota Press.

Alston, Lee, Gary Libecap, and Bernardo Mueller. 2000. "Land Reform Policies, the Sources of Violent Conflict, and Implications for Deforestation in the Brazilian Amazon." *Journal of Environmental Economics and Management* 39(2): 162–188.

Amemiya, Takeshi. 1973. "Regression Analysis when the Dependent Variable is Truncated Normal." *Econometrica* 41(6): 997–1016.

Ames, Barry. 1976. "Rhetoric and Reality in a Militarized Regime: Brazil since 1964." In Abraham Lowenthal, ed., *Armies and Politics in Latin America*, 261–290. New York: Holmes & Meier Publishers.

Amstutz, J. Bruce. 1986. *Afghanistan: The First Five Years of Soviet Occupation*. Washington, DC: National Defense University.

Anderson, Charles. 1967. *Politics and Economic Change in Latin America: The Governing of Restless Nations*. Princeton: Van Nostrand.

Andreyeva, Natalya. 2008. "The Baltic German Nobility and Russia's Policies in the Early 20th Century." *Social Sciences* 39(3): 43–52.

Angrist, Joshua, and Jörn-Steffen Pischke. 2008. *Mostly Harmless Econometrics: An Empiricist's Companion*. Princeton: Princeton University Press.

Ansari, Hamied. 1986. *Egypt: The Stalled Society*. New York: SUNY Press.

Ansell, Ben, and Johannes Lindvall. 2013. "The Political Origins of Primary Education Systems: Ideology, Institutions, and Interdenominational Conflict in an Era of Nation-Building." *American Political Science Review* 107(3): 505–522.

Ansell, Ben, and David Samuels. 2010. "Inequality and Democratization." *Comparative Political Studies* 43: 1543–1574.

———. 2014. *Inequality and Democracy: An Elite-Competition Approach*. New York: Cambridge University Press.

Anzia, Sarah. 2011. "Election Timing and the Electoral Influence of Interest Groups." *Journal of Politics* 73(2): 412–427.

Apthorpe, Raymond. 1979. "The Burden of Land Reform in Taiwan: An Asian Model Land Reform." *World Development* 7: 519–530.

Aristotle. 1992. *The Politics*. Translated by T. A. Sinclair. Edited by Trevor Saunders. London: Penguin Books.

Ashford, Douglas. 1969. "The Politics of Rural Mobilisation in North Africa." *Journal of Modern African Studies* 7(2): 187–202.

Assunção, Juliano. 2006. "Land Reform and Landholdings in Brazil." UNU-WIDER Research Paper 2006/137.

Atkinson, Dorothy. 1983. *The End of the Russian Land Commune: 1905–1930*. Stanford, CA: Stanford University Press.

Augelli, John. 1963. "La colonización agrícola en la República Dominicana." *Revista Geográfica* 58: 181–197.

Avelino, George, David Brown, and Wendy Hunter. 2005. "The Effects of Capital Mobility, Trade Openness, and Democracy on Social Spending in Latin America, 1980–1999." *American Journal of Political Science* 49: 625–641.

Aylwin, José. 2005. "Implementacion de legislación y jurisprudencia nacional relativa a los derechos de los pueblos indígenas: La experiencia de Chile." Unpublished ms.

Babones, Salvatore, and Maria Jose Alvarez-Rivadulla. 2007. "Standardized Income Inequality Data for Use in Cross-National Research." *Sociological Inquiry* 77(1): 3–22.

Baer, Gabriel. 1962. *A History of Landownership in Modern Egypt, 1800–1950*. Oxford: Oxford University Press.

Baland, Jean Marie, and James Robinson. 2008. "Land and Power: Theory and Evidence from Chile." *American Economic Review* 98(5): 1737–1765.

Ballantyne, Brian, Michael Bristow, Buster Davison, Sean Harrington, and Khaleel Khan. 2000. "How Can Land Tenure and Cadastral Reform Succeed? An Inter-Regional Comparison of Rural Reforms." *Canadian Journal of Development Studies* 21(3): 693–723.

Balli, Hatice Ozer, and Bent E. Sorensen. 2013. "Interaction Effects in Econometrics." *Empirical Economics* 45(1): 583–603.

Bardhan, Pranab, and Dilip Mookherjee. 2010. "Determinants of Redistributive Politics: An Empirical Analysis of Land Reforms in West Bengal, India." *American Economic Review* 100(4): 1572–1600.

Barraclough, Solon, ed. 1973. *Agrarian Structure in Latin America*. Lexington, MA: D. C. Heath.

————. 1999. *Land Reform in Developing Countries: The Role of the State and Other Actors*. Vol. 101. Geneva: United Nations Research Institute for Social Development.

Bates, Robert. 1981. *Markets and States in Tropical Africa: The Political Basis of Agricultural Policies*. Berkeley: University of California Press.

Bawden, Charles. 1968. *The Modern History of Mongolia*. London: Weidenfeld& Nicolson.

Beck, Nathaniel, Jonathan Katz, and Richard Tucker. 1998. "Taking Time Seriously: Time-Series-Cross-Section Analysis with a Binary Dependent Variable." *American Journal of Political Science* 42(4): 1260–1288.

Béjar, Héctor. 1969. *Peru 1965: Notes on a Guerrilla Experience*. New York: Monthly Review Press.

Berend, Iván, and György Ránki. 1974. *Economic Development in East-Central Europe in the 19th and 20th Centuries*. New York: Columbia University Press.

Bermeo, Nancy. 2010. "Interests, Inequality, and Illusion in the Choice for Fair Elections." *Comparative Political Studies* 43(8/9): 1119–1147.

Berry, Albert, and William Cline. 1979. *Agrarian Structure and Productivity in Developing Countries.* Baltimore: Johns Hopkins University Press.

Bertram, Geoffrey. 1991. "Peru, 1930–60." In Leslie Bethell, ed., *The Cambridge History of Latin America*, vol. 8, 385–450. Cambridge: Cambridge University Press.

Besley, Timothy, and Robin Burgess. 2000. "Land Reform, Poverty Reduction, and Growth: Evidence from India." *Quarterly Journal of Economics* 115(2): 389–430.

Bienen, Henry. 1985. "Populist Military Regimes in West Africa." *Armed Forces & Society* 11: 357–377.

Bill, James. 1969. "The Military and Modernization in the Middle East." *Comparative Politics* 2(1): 41–62.

Binswanger, Hans, Klaus Deininger, and Gershon Feder. 1995. "Power, Distortions, Revolt and Reform in Agricultural Land Relations." In Jere Behrman and T. N. Srinivasan, eds., *The Handbook of Developmental Economics*, vol. III, 2659–2772. Amsterdam: North-Holland.

Binswanger-Mkhize, Hans, Camille Bourguignon, and Rogier van den Brink, eds. 2009. *Agricultural Land Redistribution: Toward Greater Consensus.* Washington, DC: The World Bank.

Bird, Richard, and Enid Slack, eds. 2004. *International Handbook of Land and Property Taxation.* Cheltenham: Edward Elgar.

Boix, Carles. 1998. *Political Parties, Growth and Equality: Conservative and Social Democratic Economic Strategies in the World Economy.* Cambridge: Cambridge University Press.

Boix, Carles. 2003. *Democracy and Redistribution.* Cambridge: Cambridge University Press.

Boix, Carles. 2010. "Electoral markets, party strategies, and proportional representation." *American Political Science Review* 104(2): 404–413.

Boone, Catherine. 2009. "Electoral Populism Where Property Rights Are Weak: Land Politics in Contemporary Sub-Saharan Africa." *Comparative Politics* 41(2): 183–201.

———. 2013. *Property and Political Order: Land Rights and the Structure of Politics in Africa.* New York: Cambridge University Press.

Borras, Saturnino, Jr. 2007. *Pro-Poor Land Reform: A Critique.* Ottawa: University of Ottawa Press.

Bourguignon, François, Martin Fournier, and Marc Gurgand. 2001. "Fast Development with a Stable Income Distribution: Taiwan, 1979–94." *Review of Income and Wealth* 47(2): 139–163.

Bradley, David, Evelyne Huber, Stephanie Moller, François Nielsen, and John Stephens. 2003. "Distribution and Redistribution in Postindustrial Democracies." *World Politics* 55(2): 193–228.

Brenan, Gerald. 1990. *The Spanish Labyrinth: An Account of the Social and Political Background of the Spanish Civil War.* Cambridge: Cambridge University Press.

Brenner, Robert. 1976. "Agrarian Class Structure and Economic Development in Pre-Industrial Europe." *Past and Present* 70(February): 30–75.

Bueno de Mesquita, Bruce, Alastair Smith, Randolph M. Siverson, and James D. Morrow. 2003. *The Logic of Political Survival.* Boston: MIT Press.

Caballero, José María, and Elena Alvarez. 1980. *Aspectos cuantitativos de la reforma agraria, 1969–1979*. Vol. 12. Lima: Institutode EstudiosPeruanos.

Calvo, Ernest, and Maria Murillo. 2004. "Who Delivers? Partisan Clients in the Argentine Electoral Market." *American Journal of Political Science* 48: 742–757.

Canache, Damarys. 2004. "Urban Poor and Political Order." In Jennifer McCoy and David Myers, eds., *The Unraveling of Representative Democracy in Venezuela*, 33–49. Baltimore: Johns Hopkins University Press.

Cannadine, David. 1999. *The Rise and Fall of Class in Britain*. New York: Columbia University Press.

Canovan, Margaret. 1981. *Populism*. New York: Harcourt Brace Jovanovich.

Cant, Anna. 2012. "'Land for Those Who Work It': A Visual Analysis of Agrarian Reform Posters in Velasco's Peru." *Journal of Latin American Studies* 44(1): 1–37.

Carey, John. 1996. *Term Limits and Legislative Representation*. Cambridge: Cambridge University Press.

Carter, David, and Curtis Signorino. 2010. "Back to the Future: Modeling Time Dependence in Binary Data." *Political Analysis* 18(3): 271–292.

Carter, Michael, and Elena Alvarez. 1989. "Changing Paths: The Decollectivization of Agrarian Reform Agriculture in Coastal Peru." In William Thiesenhusen, ed., *Searching for Agrarian Reform in Latin America*, 156–187. Boston: Unwin Hyman.

Carter, Michael, and Luis Galeano. 1995. *Campesinos, tierra y mercado*. Asunción: Centro Paraguayo de Estudios Sociológicos.

Cheibub, Jose, Jennifer Gandhi, and James Vreeland. 2010. "Democracy and Dictatorship Revisited." *Public Choice* 143: 67–101.

Chen, Yan, and Sherry Xin Li. 2009. "Group Identity and Social Preferences." *American Economic Review* 99(1): 431–457.

Cleaves, Peter, and Martin Scurrah. 1980. *Agriculture, Bureaucracy, and Military Government in Peru*. Ithaca, NY: Cornell University Press.

COCOCH. 2008. "Reforma agraria, agricultura, y medio rural en Honduras." Unpublished manuscript. Tegucigalpa: Consejo Coordinador de Organizaciones Campesinas de Honduras.

COFOPRI. 2008. "Saneamiento físico legal de la propiedad informal y titulación." Lima, Peru: COFOPRI.

Coldham, Simon. 1993. "The Land Acquisition Act, 1992 of Zimbabwe." *Journal of African Law* 37(1): 82–88.

Collier, Ruth Berins. 1999. *Paths toward Democracy: The Working Class and Elites in Western Europe and South America*. Cambridge: Cambridge University Press.

Conaghan, Catherine, and James Malloy. 1994. *Unsettling Statecraft*. Pittsburgh: University of Pittsburgh Press.

Condarco Morales, Ramiro. 1965. *Zárate, El Temible Willka*. La Paz: Editorial, Imprenta y Librería Renovación.

Coppedge, Michael. 1994. *Strong Parties and Lame Ducks: Presidential Partyarchy and Factionalism in Venezuela*. Stanford, CA: Stanford University Press.

———. 1997. "A Classification of Latin American Political Parties." Kellogg Institute Working Paper 244, University of Notre Dame.

———. 2000. "Venezuelan Parties and the Representation of Elite Interests." In Kevin Middlebrook, ed., *Conservative Parties, the Right, and Democracy in Latin America*, 110–136. Baltimore: Johns Hopkins University Press.

Corden, Warner Max. 1984. "Booming Sector and Dutch Disease Economics: Survey and Consolidation." *Oxford Economic Papers* 36(3): 359–380.

Corrales, Javier, and Michael Penfold. 2007. "Venezuela: Crowding Out the Opposition." *Journal of Democracy* 18(2): 99–113.

Cotler, Julio. 1970. "Political Crisis and Military Populism in Peru." *Studies in Comparative International Development* 6: 95–113.

Cox, Gary. 1997. *Making Votes Count: Strategic Coordination in the World's Electoral Systems.* New York: Cambridge University Press.

——. 2009. "Swing Voters, Core Voters and Distributive Politics." In Ian Shapiro, ed., *Political Representation*, 342–357. Cambridge: Cambridge University Press.

Cox, Gary, and Mathew McCubbins. 1986. "Electoral Politics as a Redistributive Game." *Journal of Politics* 48: 370–389.

Crabtree, John. 2002. "The Impact of Neo-Liberal Economics on Peruvian Peasant Agriculture in the 1990s." *The Journal of Peasant Studies* 29(3–4): 131–161.

Crespo Valdivia, Fernando. 1991. *An Analysis Of Land Distribution And Concentration In Bolivia.* No. 11003. Michigan State University, Department of Agricultural, Food, and Resource Economics.

Crisp, Brian. 2000. *Democratic Institutional Design: The Powers and Incentives of Venezuelan Politicians and Interest Groups.* Stanford, CA: Stanford University Press.

Crisp, Brian, Daniel Levine, and José Molina. 2003. "The Rise and Decline of COPEI in Venezuela." In Scott Mainwaring and Timothy Scully, eds., *Christian Democracy in Latin America: Electoral Competition and Regime Conflicts*, 275–300. Stanford, CA: Stanford University Press.

D'Aragona, G. Gaetani. 1954. "A Critical Evaluation of Land Reform in Italy." *Land Economics* 30(1): 12–20.

Dacy, Douglas. 1986. *Foreign Aid, War, and Economic Development: South Vietnam, 1955–1975.* New York: Cambridge University Press.

Dahl, Robert. 1971. *Polyarchy: Participation and Opposition.* New Haven: Yale University Press.

Dahlberg, Matz, and Eva Johansson. 2002. "On the Vote-Purchasing Behavior of Incumbent Governments." *American Political Science Review* 96: 27–40.

Daly, Martin W., and Carl Petry. 1998. *The Cambridge History of Egypt, Volume 2: Modern Egypt, from 1517 to the End of the Twentieth Century.* M. W. Daly, ed. Cambridge: Cambridge University Press.

Davies, Rob. 2004. "Memories of Underdevelopment: A Personal Interpretation of Zimbabwe's Economic Decline." In Brian Raftopoulous and Tyrone Savage, eds., *Zimbabwe: Injustice and Political Reconciliation*, 19–42. Cape Town: Institute for Justice and Reconciliation.

de Janvry, Alain. 1981. *The Agrarian Question and Reformism in Latin America.* Baltimore: Johns Hopkins University Press.

de Janvry, Alain, Marco Gonzalez-Navarro, and Elisabeth Sadoulet. "Are Land Reforms Granting Complete Property Rights Politically Risky? Electoral Outcomes of Mexico's Certification Program." *Journal of Development Economics* 110 (2014): 216–225.

de Janvry, Alain, and Elisabeth Sadoulet. 2011. "The Three Puzzles of Land Reform." Unpublished manuscript.

De Soto, Hernando. 2003. *The Mystery of Capital: Why Capitalism Triumphs in the West and Fails Everywhere Else.* New York: Basic Books.

De Villiers, Bertus. 2003. *Land Reform: Issues and Challenges: A Comparative Overview of Experiences in Zimbabwe, Namibia, South Africa and Australia.* Johannesburg: Konrad Adenauer Foundation.

Deininger, Klaus. 1999. "Making Negotiated Land Reform Work: Initial Experience from Colombia, Brazil, and South Africa." Mimeo.

———. 2003. "Land Policies for Growth and Poverty Reduction." Washington, DC: World Bank.

Deininger, Klaus, and Lynn Squire. 1996. "A New Data Set Measuring Income Inequality." *World Bank Economic Review* 10: 565–591.

Delahaye, Olivier. 2001. *Políticas de tierras de Venezuela en el Siglo XX.* Caracas: Fondo Editorial Tropykos.

Delahaye, Olivier. 2006. "Tenencia de la tierra y desarrollo rural sostenible: Algunos puntos para la reflexión en el caso venezolano." *Agroalimentaria* 23: 11–20.

Derham, Michael. 2010. *Politics in Venezuela: Explaining Hugo Chávez.* New York: Peter Lang.

Diamond, Larry, and Marc Plattner, eds. 2008. *How People View Democracy.* Baltimore: Johns Hopkins University Press.

Dixit, Avinash, and John Londregan. 1996. "The Determinants of the Success of Special Interests in Redistributive Politics." *Journal of Politics* 58: 1132–1155.

Dorner, Peter. 1992. *Latin American Land Reforms.* Madison: University of Wisconsin Press.

Dovring, Folke. 1970. *Land Reform in Yugoslavia.* Washington, DC: Agency for International Development.

Dube, Memory, and Rob Midgley. 2008. "Land Reform in Zimbabwe: Context, Process, Legal and Constitutional Issues and Implications for the SADC Region." In Anton Bösl, Willie Breytenbach, Trudi Hartzenberg, Colin McCarthy, and Klaus Schade, eds., *Monitoring Regional Integration in Southern Africa Yearbook, vol. 8,* 303–341. Stellenbosch: Trade Law Centre for Southern Africa.

Duff, Ernest A. 1968. *Agrarian Reform in Colombia.* New York: Praeger.

Dugas, John. 2000. "The Conservative Party and the Crisis of Political Legitimacy in Colombia." In Kevin Middlebrook, ed., *Conservative Parties, the Right, and Democracy in Latin America,* 80–109. Baltimore: Johns Hopkins University Press.

Duque Corredor, Román. 2009. *Procesos sobre la propiedad y la posesión.* Caracas: Academia de Ciencias Políticas y Sociales.

Easterly, William. 2007. "Inequality Does Cause Underdevelopment." *Journal of Development Economics* 84: 755–776.

Eastwood, David, and H. J. Pollard. 1985. "The Development of Colonization in Lowland Bolivia." *Boletín de Estudios Latinoamericanos y del Caribe* 38: 61–82.

Eckstein, Susan. 1986. "The Impact of the Cuban Revolution: A Comparative Perspective." *Comparative Studies in Society and History* 28(3): 502–534.

Einaudi, Luigi R. 1973. "Revolution from Within? Military Rule in Peru since 1968." *Studies in Comparative International Development* 8(1): 71–87.

El-Ghonemy, Mohamad Riad. 2002. *Political Economy of Rural Poverty: The Case for Land Reform.* New York: Routledge.

Ellis, Frank. 1992. *Agricultural Policies in Developing Countries*. New York: Cambridge University Press.

Engerman, Stanley, and Kenneth Sokoloff. 2002. "Factor Endowments, Inequality, and Paths of Development among New World Economies." National Bureau of Economic Research Working Paper 9259.

Esping-Andersen, Gosta. 1990. *The Three Worlds of Welfare Capitalism*. Princeton: Princeton University Press.

FAO (Food and Agriculture Organization of the United Nations). 1981. *1970 World Census of Agriculture: Analysis and International Comparison of the Results*. Rome: Food and Agriculture Organization.

———. 2000. *Irrigation in Latin American and the Caribbean in Figures*. Rome: Food and Agriculture Organization.

Figueroa, Valentín, and Marcelo Leiras. 2014. "Tierra, clubes y poder: la influencia política de los terratenientes en las repúblicas oligárquicas." Working paper.

Finkel, Evgeny, Scott Gehlbach, and Tricia Olsen. Forthcoming. "Does Reform Prevent Rebellion? Evidence from Russia's Emancipation of the Serfs." *Comparative Political Science*.

Forte, David. 1978. "Egyptian Land Law: An Evaluation." *The American Journal of Comparative Law* 26(2): 273–278.

Frankema, Ewout. 2010. "The Colonial Roots of Land Inequality: Geography, Factor Endowments, or Institutions?" *Economic History Review* 63(2): 418–451.

Franzese, Robert. 2002. *Macroeconomic Policies of Developed Democracies*. New York: Cambridge University Press.

Fredericks, L., and R. Wells. 1978. "Some Aspects of Tenancy Reform Measures in Southeast Asia." *Asian Survey* 18(6): 644–658.

Freeman, Colin. 2011. "The End of an Era for Zimbabwe's Last White Farmers?" *The Telegraph*. June 26, 2011.

Freeman, John, and Dennis Quinn. 2012. "The Economic Origins of Democracy Reconsidered." *American Political Science Review* 106: 58–80.

Gagnon, Valere. 1995. "Ethnic Nationalism and International Conflict: The Case of Serbia." *International Security* 19(3): 130–166.

Galiani, Sebastian, and Ernesto Schargrodsky. 2010. "Property Rights for the Poor: Effects of Land Titling." *Journal of Public Economics* 94: 700–729.

Gallup, John Luke, Jeffrey Sachs, and Andrew Mellinger. 1999. "Geography and Economic Development." *International Regional Science Review* 22(2): 179–232.

Galor, Oded, Omer Moav, and Dietrich Vollrath. 2009. "Inequality in Landownership, the Emergence of Human-Capital Promoting Institutions, and the Great Divergence." *Review of Economic Studies* 76(1): 143–179.

Gandhi, Jennifer. *Political Institutions under Dictatorship*. Cambridge: Cambridge University Press, 2008.

Gandhi, Jennifer, and Adam Przeworski. 2006. "Cooperation, Cooptation and Rebellion under Dictatorship." *Economics and Politics* 18(1): 1–26.

Garrido, José, ed. 1988. *Historia de la reforma agraria en Chile*. Santiago: Editorial Universitaria.

Geddes, Barbara. 2003. *Paradigms and Sand Castles*. Ann Arbor: University of Michigan Press.

Gellner, Ernest. 1983. *Nations and Nationalism*. Ithaca, NY: Cornell University Press.

Germani, Gino, and Kalman Silvert. 1961. "Politics, Social Structure and Military Intervention in Latin America." *Archives Européennes de Sociologie* 2(1): 62–81.

Gerschenkron, Alexander. 1946. *Bread and Democracy in Germany*. Ithaca, NY: Cornell University Press.

Gibson, Edward. 1997. "The Populist Road to Market Reform." *World Politics* 49: 339–370.

Gilbert, Dennis. 1977. "The Oligarchy and the Old Regime in Peru." PhD diss., Cornell University.

Gill, Anthony. 1998. *Rendering unto Caesar: The Catholic Church and the State in Latin America*. Chicago: University of Chicago Press.

Gill, Anthony, and Arang Keshavarzian. 1999. "State Building and Religious Resources: An Institutional Theory of Church-State Relations in Iran and Mexico." *Politics and Society* 27: 431–465.

Ginsborg, Paul. 1990. *A History of Contemporary Italy: Society and Politics, 1943–1988*. New York: Penguin Books.

Gleditsch, Kristian, and Michael Ward. 2006. "Diffusion and the International Context of Democratization." *International Organization* 60: 911–933.

Goemans, H. E., Kristian Skrede Gleditsch, and Giacomo Chiozza. 2009. "Introducing Archigos: A Dataset of Political Leaders." *Journal of Peace Research* 46: 269–283.

Gold, Martin. 1977. *Law and Social Change: A Study of Land Reform in Sri Lanka*. Nellen: Bibliotheksverbund Bayern.

Gonese, Francis, Nelson Marongwe, Charles Mukora, and Bill Kinse. 2002. "Land Reform and Resettlement Implementation in Zimbabwe: An Overview of the Programme against Selected International Experiences." Mimeo.

Gorman, Stephen. 1997. "Antipolitics in Peru." In Brian Loveman and Thomas Davies, eds., *The Politics of Antipolitics*, 300–326. Wilmington: Scholarly Resources.

Granovsky-Larsen, Simon. 2010. "*Fincas recuperadas*: Land Access in Post-War Guatemala." Unpublished ms.

Griffin, Keith. 1975. "Income Inequality and Land Redistribution in Morocco." *The Bangladesh Development Studies* 3(3): 319–348.

Griffin, Keith, Azizur Rahman Khan, and Amy Ickowitz. 2002. "Poverty and the Distribution of Land." *Journal of Agrarian Change* 2(3): 279–330.

Gutteridge, Joyce. 1952. "Expropriation and Nationalisation in Hungary, Bulgaria and Roumania." *The International and Comparative Law Quarterly* 1(1): 14–28.

Haber, Stephen. 2006. "Authoritarian Government." In Barry Weingast and Donald Wittman, eds., *The Oxford Handbook of Political Economy*, 693–707. Oxford: Oxford University Press.

Haber, Stephen, and Victor Menaldo. 2011. "Do Natural Resources Fuel Authoritarianism? A Reappraisal of the Resource Curse." *American Political Science Review* 105(1): 1–26.

Haber, Stephen, Armando Razo, and Noel Mauerer. 2003. *The Politics of Property Rights*. New York: Cambridge University Press.

Habyarimana, James, Macartan Humphreys, Daniel Posner, and Jeremy Weinstein. 2007. "Why Does Ethnic Diversity Undermine Public Goods Provision?" *American Political Science Review* 101(4): 709–725.

Haddadin, Munther. 2009. "A Jordanian Socio-Legal Perspective on Water Management in the Jordan River-Dead Sea Basin." In Clive Lipchin, Deborah Sandler, and

Emily Cushman, eds., *The Jordan River and Dead Sea Basin: Cooperation Amid Conflict*, 41–60. Dordrecht: Springer.

Haggard, Stephan. 1990. *Pathways from the Periphery: The Politics of Growth in the Newly Industrializing Countries*. Ithaca, NY: Cornell University Press.

Haggard, Stephan, and Robert Kaufman. 1995. *The Political Economy of Democratic Transitions*. Princeton: Princeton University Press.

———. 2008. *Development, Democracy, and Welfare States: Latin America, East Asia, and Eastern Europe*. Princeton, NJ: Princeton University Press.

———. 2012. "Inequality and Regime Change: Democratic Transitions and the Stability of Democratic Rule." *American Political Science Review* 106: 495–516.

Handelman, Howard. 1975. *Struggle in the Andes*. Austin: University of Texas Press.

Handlin, Samuel. 2013. "Survey Research and Social Class in Venezuela: Evaluating Alternative Measures and Their Impact on Assessments of Class Voting." *Latin American Politics and Society* 55(1): 141–167.

Haney, Emil, and Wava Haney. 1987. "Transformation of the Agrarian Structure in Ecuador with Specific Reference to the Province of Chimborazo." Land Tenure Center Research Paper 86.

Hanlon, Joseph, Jeanette Marie Manjengwa, and Teresa Smart. 2013. *Zimbabwe Takes Back Its Land*. Sterling, VA: Kumarian Press.

Hazleton, Jared. 1979. "Land Reform in Jordan: The East Ghor Canal Project." *Middle Eastern Studies* 15(2): 258–269.

Hellman, Joel S., Geraint Jones, and Daniel Kaufmann. 2003. "Seize the State, Seize the Day: State Capture and Influence in Transition Economies." *Journal of Comparative Economics* 31(4): 751–773.

Helmke, Gretchen, and Julio Ríos-Figueroa, eds. 2011. *Courts in Latin America*. Cambridge: Cambridge University Press.

Hendrix, Steven. 1996. "Tensions in Cuban Property Law." *Hastings International & Comparative Law Review* 20(1): 1–101.

Henisz, Witold. 2000. "The Institutional Environment for Economic Growth." *Economics and Politics* 12: 1–31.

———. 2002. "The Institutional Environment for Infrastructure Investment." *Industrial and Corporate Change* 11(2): 355–389.

Herman, Donald. 1986. "Agriculture." In John Martz and David Myers, eds., *Venezuela: The Democratic Experience*, 329–363. New York: Praeger.

Herring, Ronald. 1983. *Land to the Tiller: The Political Economy of Agrarian Reform in South Asia*. New Haven: Yale University Press.

Hetherington, Kregg. 2009. "Privatizing the Private in Rural Paraguay: Precarious Lots and the Materiality of Rights." *American Ethnologist* 36(2): 224–241.

Hinnebusch, Robert. 1993. "The Politics of Economic Reform in Egypt." *Third World Quarterly* 14(1): 159–171.

Hirschman, Albert. 1963. *Journeys toward Progress: Studies of Economic Policy-Making in Latin America*. New York: W. W. Norton.

———. 1968. "The Political Economy of Import-Substituting Industrialization in Latin America." *Quarterly Journal of Economics* 82(1): 1–32.

Hooker, Juliet. 2005. "Indigenous Inclusion/Black Exclusion: Race, Ethnicity and Multicultural Citizenship in Latin America." *Journal of Latin American Studies* 37(2): 285–310.

Horiuchi, Yusaka. 2004. "Malapportionment and Income Inequality." *British Journal of Political Science* 34: 179–183.

Horowitz, Donald. 1985. *Ethnic Groups in Conflict*. Berkeley: University of California Press.

Houle, Christian. 2009. "Inequality and Democracy." *World Politics* 61: 589–622.

Howe, Keith. 1998. "Politics, Equity, and Efficiency: Objectives and Outcomes in Bulgarian Land Reform." In Stephen, Wegren, ed., *Land Reform in the Former Soviet Union and Eastern Europe*, 208–223. New York: Routledge.

Hsieh, Chang-Tai, Edward Miguel, Daniel Ortega, and Francisco Rodríguez. 2011. "The Price of Political Opposition: Evidence from Venezuela's *Maisanta*." *American Economic Journal: Applied Economics* 3(2): 196–214.

Htun, Mala. 2003. *Sex and the State: Abortion, Divorce, and the Family under Latin American Dictatorships and Democracies*. New York: Cambridge University Press.

Huang, Chun-Chieh. 1998. "Historical Reflections on the Postwar Taiwan Experience from an Agrarian Perspective." *Postwar Taiwan in Historical Perspective* 1: 17–35.

Huber, Evelyne, Thomas Mustillo, and John Stephens. 2008. "Politics and Social Spending in Latin America." *Journal of Politics* 70: 420–436.

Huber, Evelyne, and John Stephens. 2012. *Democracy and the Left: Social Policy and Inequality in Latin America*. Chicago: University of Chicago Press.

Huber, Evelyne, John Stephens, Thomas Mustillo, and Jennifer Pribble. 2012. Latin America and the Caribbean Political Dataset, 1945–2008. University of North Carolina.

Hunefeldt, Christine. 1997. "Enterprises, Agrarian Producers, and Peasant Communities, 1969–1994." In Maxwell Cameron and Philip Mauceri, eds., *The Peruvian Labyrinth: Polity, Society, Economy*, 107–133. University Park: Pennsylvania State University Press.

Huntington, Samuel. 1968. *Political Order in Changing Societies*. New Haven: Yale University Press.

IBRD (International Bank for Reconstruction and Development). 1961. *The Economic Development of Venezuela*. Baltimore: Johns Hopkins University Press.

Ikenberry, John, and Charles Kupchan. 1990. "Socialization and Hegemonic Power." *International Organization* 44(3): 283–315.

INA (Instituto Nacional Agraria). 1965. *Memoria 1965*. Tegucigalpa: Instituto Nacional Agraria.

INCRA (Instituto Nacional de Colonização e Reforma Agrária). 2011. INCRA Database on Land Reforms in Brazil.

INEGI (Instituto Nacional de Estadística, Geografía e Informática). 1985. *Estadísticas históricas de México*. Mexico City: Instituto Nacional de Estadística, Geografía e Informática.

Inglehart, Ronald. 2003. "How Solid is Mass Support for Democracy – and How Can We Measure It?" *Political Science and Politics* 36(1): 51–57.

Inman, Robert, and Daniel Rubenfeld. 2005. "Federalism and the Democratic Transition: Lessons from South Africa." *American Economic Review* 95(2): 39–43.

INRA (Instituto Nacional de Reforma Agraria). 2007. *Plan estratégico nacional de distribución de tierras y asentamientos humanos (PENDTAH)*. La Paz: INRA, Viceministerio de Tierras.

———. 2011. *Informe de gestión 2010: Logros y resultados*. La Paz: INRA.

Iversen, Torben, and David Soskice. 2006. "Electoral Systems and the Politics of Coalitions." *American Political Science Review* 100(2): 165–181.

————. 2009. "Distribution and Redistribution: The Shadow of the Nineteenth Century." *World Politics* 61(3): 438–486.

Janos, Andrew. 1971. "The Decline of Oligarchy: Bureaucratic and Mass Politics in an Age of Dualism (1867–1918)." In Andrew Janos and William Slottman, eds., *Revolution in Perspective: Essays on the Hungarian Soviet Republic of 1919*, 1–60. Berkeley: University of California Press.

Janowitz, Morris. 1977. *Military Institutions and Coercion in the Developing Nations.* Chicago: University of Chicago Press.

Jones, Benjamin F., and Benjamin A. Olken. 2005. "Do Leaders Matter? National Leadership and Growth Since World War II." *The Quarterly Journal of Economics* 120(3): 835–864.

Jörgensen, Hans. 2006. "The Inter-War Land Reforms in Estonia, Finland and Bulgaria: A Comparative Study." *Scandinavian Economic History Review* 54(1): 64–97.

Kain, Roger, and Elizabeth Baigent. 1992. *The Cadastral Map in the Service of the State.* Chicago: University of Chicago Press.

Karl, Terry Lynn. 1987. "Petroleum and Political Pacts: The Transition to Democracy in Venezuela." *Latin American Research Review* 22(1): 63–94.

————. 1990. "Dilemmas of Democratization in Latin America." *Comparative Politics* 23: 1–21.

Kaufman, Robert, and Alex Segura-Ubiergo. 2001. "Globalization, Domestic Politics, and Social Spending in Latin America." *World Politics* 53: 553–587.

Kawagoe, Toshihiko. 1993. "Deregulation and Protectionism in Japanese Agriculture." In Juro Teranishi and Yutaka Kosai, eds., *The Japanese Experience of Economic Reforms*, 366–391. London: MacMillan Press.

Kawagoe, Toshihiko. 1999. *Agricultural Land Reform In Postwar Japan: Experiences and Issues.* Washington, DC: World Bank.

Kay, Cristóbal. 1998. "Latin America's Agrarian Reform: Lights and Shadows." *Land Reform* 2: 8–31.

Keefer, Philip. 2004. "What Does Political Economy Tell Us about Economic Development – and Vice Versa?" *Annual Review of Political Science* 7: 247–272.

————. 2007. "Clientelism, Credibility, and the Policy Choices of Young Democracies." *American Journal of Political Science* 51(4): 804–821.

Khader, Bichara. 1975. "Propriété agricole et réforme agraire en Syrie." *Civilisations* 25(1–2): 62–83.

King, Russell. 1973. *Land Reform: The Italian Experience.* London: Butterworth.

Klein, Herbert. 1992. *Bolivia: The Evolution of a Multi-Ethnic Society.* 2nd ed. Oxford: Oxford University Press.

Kleinpenning, J.M.G. 1984. "Rural Development Policy in Paraguay Since 1960." *Journal of Economic and Social Geography* 75(3): 164–176.

Kohli, Atul. 1987. *The State and Poverty in India: The Politics of Reform.* New York: Cambridge University Press.

Kontogiorgi, Elisabeth. 2006. *Population Exchange in Greek Macedonia: The Rural Settlement of Refugees 1922–1930.* Oxford: Oxford University Press.

Korpi, Walter. 1983. *The Democratic Class Struggle.* London: Routledge and Kegan Paul.

Koťátko, Jiří. [1948]. *Land Reform in Czechoslovakia.* Translated by B. Rohan and Fr. Stein. Prague, Orbis.

Kruijt, Dirk. 1994. *Revolution by Decree: Peru 1968–1975.* Amsterdam: The la Publishers.

Kung, James Kai-Sing, Xiaogang Wu, and Yuxiao Wu. 2012. "Inequality of Land Tenure and Revolutionary Outcome: An Economic Analysis of China's Land Reform of 1946–1952." *Explorations in Economic History* 49: 482–497.

Kerkvliet, Benedict. 1979. "Land Reform: Emancipation or Counterinsurgency?" In D. A. Rosenberg, ed., *Marcos and Martial Law in the Philippines*, 113–144. Berkeley: University of California Press.

Kurtz, Marcus. 2004. "The Dilemmas of Democracy in the Open Economy." *World Politics* 56: 262–302.

Kuznets, Simon. 1955. "Economic Growth and Income Inequality." *American Economic Review* 45(1): 1–28.

Laakso, Markku, and Rein Taagepera. 1979. "The 'Effective' Number of Parties: A Measure with Application to West Europe." *Comparative Political Studies* 12(1): 3–27.

Laclau, Ernesto. 1977. *Politics and Ideology in Marxist Theory*. London: NLB.

Lahiff, Edward. 2009. "Land Redistribution in South Africa." In Hans Binswanger-Mkhize, Camille Bourguignon, and Rogerius van den Brink, eds., *Agricultural Land Redistribution: Toward Greater Consensus*, 169–200. Washington, DC: World Bank Publications.

Lapp, Nancy. 2004. *Landing Votes: Representation and Land Reform in Latin America*. New York: Palgrave Macmillan.

Lastarria-Cornhiel, Susana. 1989. "Agrarian Reforms of the 1960s and 1970s in Peru." In William Thiesenhusen, ed., *Searching for Agrarian Reform in Latin America*, 156–187. Boston: Unwin Hyman.

Lee, Chong-Sik. 1963. "Land Reform, Collectivisation and the Peasants in North Korea." *China Quarterly* 14 (April–June): 65–81.

LeGrand, Catherine. 1986. *Frontier Expansion and Peasant Protest in Colombia, 1850–1936*. Albuquerque: University of New Mexico Press.

Levi, Margaret. 1989. *Of Rule and Revenue*. Berkeley: University of California Press.

Levine, Robert. 1998. *Father of the Poor? Vargas and His Era*. Cambridge: Cambridge University Press.

Levinson, Jerome, and Juan de Onís. 1970. *The Alliance That Lost Its Way: A Critical Report on the Alliance for Progress*. Chicago: Quadrangle Books.

Levitsky, Steven, and Lucan Way. 2010. *Competitive Authoritarianism: Hybrid Regimes after the Cold War*. New York: Cambridge University Press.

Lewis, Paul. 1980. *Paraguay under Stroessner*. Chapel Hill: University of North Carolina Press.

Lewis, Paul. 1991. "Paraguay since 1930." In Bethell, ed., *The Cambridge History of Latin America* Vol. VIII, 234–256. Cambridge: Cambridge University Press.

Lewis, Paul. 2006. *Authoritarian Regimes in Latin America*. Oxford: Rowman & Littlefield.

Lin, Kuo-Chin, and Yu-Hui Chen. 2006. "The Future Challenges of Agricultural Policy Reform in Taiwan." Unpublished ms.

Lindbeck, A., and J. Weibull. 1987. "Balanced Budget Redistribution and the Outcome of Political Competition." *Public Choice* 52: 273–297.

Lipset, Seymour Martin. 1959. "Some social requisites of democracy: Economic development and political legitimacy." *American Political Science Review* 53(1): 69–105.

Lipset, Seymour M., and Stein Rokkan. 1967. *Party Systems and Voter Alignments: Cross-National Perspectives*. New York: The Free Press.

Lipton, Michael. 2009. *Land Reform in Developing Countries: Property Rights and Property Wrongs*. New York: Routledge.

Lizzeri, Alessandro, and Nicola Persico. 2004. "Why Did the Elites Extend the Suffrage?" *Quarterly Journal of Economics* 119: 707–765.

Llavador, Humberto, and Robert Oxoby. 2005. "Partisan Competition, Growth, and the Franchise." *Quarterly Journal of Economics* 120(3): 1155–1189.

Lowenthal, Abraham F. 1974. "Armies and Politics in Latin America." *World Politics* 27(1): 107–130.

Lupu, Noam. 2010. "Who Votes for Chavismo? Class Voting in Hugo Chávez's Venezuela." *Latin American Research Review* 45(1): 7–32.

Lynch, Edward. 1993. *Latin America's Christian Democratic Parties: A Political Economy*. Westport, CT: Praeger.

Mabogunje, Akin. 1992. "Perspective on Urban Land and Urban Management Policies in Sub-Saharan Africa." World Bank Technical Paper 196.

MAC, IAN, and IICA. 1995. *Evaluación de la reforma agraria*. Caracas: MAC.

Machado, Absalón. 1998. *La cuestión agrarian en Colombia a fines del milenio*. Bogotá: El Áncora Editores.

Madison, James, Alexander Hamilton, and John Jay (Publius). [1788] 1998. *The Federalist Papers*. New York: Mentor.

Magaloni, Beatriz. 2006. *Voting for Autocracy: Hegemonic Party Survival and Its Demise in Mexico*. New York: Cambridge University Press.

———. 2008. "Credible Power-Sharing and the Longevity of Authoritarian Rule." *Comparative Political Studies* 41(4–5): 715–741.

Mahoney, James. 2003. "Knowledge Accumulation in Comparative Historical Research: The Case of Democracy and Authoritarianism." In James Mahoney and Dietrich Rueschemeyer, eds., *Comparative Historical Analysis in the Social Sciences*, 131–176. Cambridge: Cambridge University Press.

Mainwaring, Scott. 1999. *Rethinking Party Systems in the Third Wave*. Stanford, CA: Stanford University Press.

Mainwaring, Scott, and Aníbal Pérez-Liñán. 2014. *Democracies and Dictatorships in Latin America: Emergence, Survival, and Fall*. Cambridge: Cambridge University Press.

Mainwaring, Scott, Daniel Brinks, and Aníbal Pérez-Liñán. 2001. "Classifying Political Regimes in Latin." *Studies in Comparative International Development* 36(1): 37–65.

Majd, Mohammad, and Vahid Nowshirvani. 1993. "Land Reform in Iran Revisited: New Evidence on the Results of Land Reform in Nine Provinces." *The Journal of Peasant Studies* 20(3): 442–458.

Makumbe, John. 1999. "The Political Dimension of the Land Reform Process in Zimbabwe." Unpublished ms. University of Zimbabwe.

Malefakis, Edward. 1970. *Agrarian Reform and Peasant Revolution in Spain*. New Haven, CT: Yale University Press.

Malloy, James. 1974. "Authoritarianism, Corporatism and Mobilization in Peru." In Frederick Pike and Thomas Stritch, eds., *The New Corporatism*, 36–54. South Bend, IN: University of Notre Dame Press.

Mamdani, Mahmood. 1996. *Citizen and Subject: Contemporary Africa and the Legacy of Late Colonialism*. Princeton: Princeton University Press.

Margold, Stella. 1957. "Agrarian Land Reform in Egypt." *American Journal of Economics and Sociology* 17(1): 9–19.

Maríñez, Pablo. 1993. *Agroindustria, estado y clases sociales en la era de Trujillo (1935–1960)*. Santo Domingo: Fundación Cultural Dominicana.

Marongwe, Nelson, Blasio Mavedzenge, Jacob Mahenehene, Felix Murimbarimba, and Chrispen Sukume. 2010. *Zimbabwe's Land Reform: Myths & Realities*. Oxford: James Currey.

Marrese, Michael. 1983. "Agricultural Policy and Performance in Hungary." *Journal of Comparative Economics* 7: 329–345.

Martz, John, and David Myers, eds. 1986. *Venezuela: The Democratic Experience*. New York: Praeger.

Marx, Karl. [1848] 1998. *The Communist Manifesto*. New York: Signet Classic.

———. [1852] 1963. *The Eighteenth Brumaire of Louis Bonaparte*. New York: International Publishers.

Mason, T. David. 1998. "'Take Two Acres and Call Me in the Morning': Is Land Reform a Prescription for Peasant Unrest?" *Journal of Politics* 60(1): 199–230.

Masterson, Daniel. 1991. *Militarism and Politics in Latin America*. New York: Greenwood Press.

Mathijs, Erik. 1997. "An Historical Overview of Central and Eastern European Land Reform." In Johan Swinnen, ed., *Political Economy of Agrarian Reform in Central and Eastern Europe*, 33–55. Aldershot: Ashgate Publishing.

Matsuzaki, Reo. 2011. "Institutions by Imposition: Colonial Lessons for Contemporary State-Building." PhD diss., MIT.

———. 2012. "Do Effective Colonial Institutions Make Successful Postcolonial States? Taiwan, the Philippines, and Their Contrasting Colonial Legacies." Unpublished ms.

Mayer, Enrique. 2009. *Ugly Stories from the Peruvian Agrarian Reform*. Durham: Duke University Press.

McBride, George McCutchen. 1936. *Chile: Land and Society*. New York: American Geographical Society.

McClintock, Cynthia. 1981. *Peasant Cooperatives and Political Change in Peru*. Princeton: Princeton University Press.

———. 1983. "Velasco, Officers, and Citizens: The Politics of Stealth." In Cynthia McClintock and Abraham Lowenthal, eds., *The Peruvian Experiment Reconsidered*, 275–308. Princeton: Princeton University Press.

———. 1999. "Peru: Precarious Regimes, Authoritarian and Democratic." In Larry Diamond, Juan Linz, and Seymour Martin Lipset, eds., *Democracy in Developing Countries*, 308–366. Boulder: Lynne Rienner.

McCormick, John. 2011. *Machiavellian Democracy*. New York: Cambridge University Press.

McElhinny, Vincent. 2006. "Inequality and Empowerment: The Political Foundations of Post-War Decentralization and Development in El Salvador, 1992–2000." PhD diss., University of Pittsburgh.

McPherson, James. 1964. *The Struggle for Equality*. Princeton: Princeton University Press.

Mejía, José Manuel, and José Matos Mar. 1980. *La reforma agraria en al Perú*. Lima: Instituto de Estudios Peruanos.

Melmed-Sanjak, Jolyne, Peter Bloch, and Robert Hanson. 1998. *Project for the Analysis of Land Tenure and Agricultural Productivity in the Republic of Macedonia*. Madison: Land Tenure Center, University of Wisconsin-Madison.

Meltzer, Allan, and Scott Richard. 1981. "A Rational Theory of the Size of Government." *Journal of Political Economy* 89: 914–927.

Mennen, Tiernan. 2009. "Land Reform Revisited: Can Latin America Get It Right and Should It Even Try?" *International Affairs Review* 28(1). http://www.iar-gwu.org/node/62.

Ministerio de Agricultura. 1991. "Estadísticas de la agricultura." Lima: Ministerio de Agricultura, Dirección General de Agricultura.

Ministerio de Asuntos Campesinos y Agropecuarios. 1951. *I censo agropecuario de 1950*. La Paz: Ministerio de Asuntos Campesinos y Agropecuarios.

Ministerio de Guerra. 1966. *Las guerrillas en el Perú y su represión*. Lima: Ministerio de Guerra.

Moïse, Edwin. 1983. *Land Reform in China and North Vietnam: Consolidating the Revolution at the Village Level*. Chapel Hill: University of North Carolina Press.

Molina, José. 2004. "The Unraveling of Venezuela's Party System: From Party Rule to Personalistic Politics and Deinstitutionalization." In Jennifer McCoy and David Myers, eds., *The Unraveling of Representative Democracy in Venezuela*, 152–180. Baltimore: Johns Hopkins University Press.

Montgomery, John. 1957. *Forced to Be Free: The Artificial Revolution in Germany and Japan*. Chicago: University of Chicago Press.

———, ed. 1984. *International Dimensions of Land Reform*. Boulder: Westview Press.

Moore, Barrington, Jr. 1966. *Social Origins of Dictatorship and Democracy: Lord and Peasant in the Making of the Modern World*. Boston: Beacon Press.

Morrison, Kevin. 2009. "Oil, Nontax Revenue, and the Redistributional Foundations of Regime Stability." *International Organization* 63: 107–138.

Moustafa, Tamir. 2007. *The Struggle for Constitutional Power*. Cambridge: Cambridge University Press.

Moyo, Sam. 2007. "Land Policy, Poverty Reduction and Public Action in Zimbabwe." In Haroon Akram-Lodhi, Saturnino Borras Jr., and Cristóbal Kay, eds., *Land, Poverty and Livelihoods in an Era of Globalization: Perspectives from Developing and Transition Countries*, 344–382. New York: Routledge.

Mulligan, Casey, Ricard Gil, and Xavier Sala-i-Martin. 2004. "Do Democracies Have Different Public Policies than Nondemocracies?" *Journal of Economic Perspectives* 18(1): 51–74.

Muñoz, Jorge, and Isabel Lavadenz. 1997. "Reforming the Agrarian Reform in Bolivia." Harvard Institute for International Development Discussion Paper 589.

Muratorio, Blanca. 1966. "Changing Bases of Social Stratification in a Bolivian Community." Paper presented at the American Anthropological Association, Pittsburgh, PA.

Myers, David. 1986. "The Venezuelan Party System: Regime Maintenance under Stress." In John Martz and David Myers, eds., *Venezuela: The Democratic Experience*, 109–147. New York: Praeger.

———. 2004. "The Normalization of Punto Fijo Democracy." In Jennifer McCoy and David Myers, eds., *The Unraveling of Representative Democracy in Venezuela*, 11–32. Baltimore: Johns Hopkins University Press.

Myers, David, and Robert O'Connor. 1983. "The Undecided Respondent in Mandatory Voting Settings." *Political Research Quarterly* 36: 420–433.

Myers, Ramon. 2009. "Towards an Enlightened Authoritarian Polity: The Kuomintang Central Reform Committee on Taiwan, 1950–1952." *Journal of Contemporary China* 18(59): 185–199.

Naimak, Norman. 1995. *The Russians in Germany: A History of the Soviet Zone of Occupation, 1945–1949*. Cambridge, MA: Harvard University Press.

Negretto, Gabriel. 2006. "Choosing How to Choose Presidents." *Journal of Politics* 68(2): 421–433.

Neuhouser, Kevin. 1992. "Democratic Stability in Venezuela: Elite Consensus or Class Compromise?" *American Sociological Review* 57(1): 117–135.

———. 1996. "Limits on Authoritarian Implementation of Policy." *Comparative Political Studies* 29(6): 635–659.

Nordlinger, Eric. 1970. "Soldiers in Mufti: The Impact of Military Rule upon Economic and Social Change in the Non-Western States." *American Political Science Review* 64(4): 1131–1148.

———. 1977. *Soldiers in Politics*. Englewood Cliffs, NJ: Prentice Hall.

North, Douglass. 1990. *Institutions, Institutional Change and Economic Performance*. New York: Cambridge University Press.

North, Douglass, and Barry Weingast. 1989. "Constitutions and Commitment." *Journal of Economic History* 49: 803–832.

Nun, José. 1976. "The Middle-Class Military Coup Revisited." In Abraham Lowenthal, ed., *Armies and Politics in Latin America*, 49–86. New York: Holmes & Meier Publishers.

O'Donnell, Guillermo, and Philippe Schmitter. 1986. *Transitions from Authoritarian Rule*. Baltimore: Johns Hopkins University Press.

OECD. 2000. *Review of Agricultural Policies: Romania 2000*. Paris: OECD.

Olson, Mancur. 1993. "Dictatorship, Democracy, and Development." *American Political Science Review* 87: 567–576.

Ondetti, Gabriel. 2008. *Land, Protest, and Politics: The Landless Movement and the Struggle for Agrarian Reform in Brazil*. University Park: Pennsylvania State University Press.

Otero, Gerardo. 1989. "Agrarian Reform in Mexico: Capitalism and the State." In William Thiesenhusen, ed., *Searching for Agrarian Reform in Latin America*, 276–304. Boston: Unwin Hyman.

Paige, Jeffery. 1975. *Agrarian Revolution*. New York: The Free Press.

Palasik, Mária. 2011. *Chess Game for Democracy: Hungary between East and West, 1944–1947*. Montreal: McGill-Queen's University Press.

Palmer, David Scott. 1973. "'Revolution from Above': Military Government and Popular Participation in Peru, 1968–1972." PhD diss., Cornell University.

Palmer, Robin. 1990. "Land Reform in Zimbabwe, 1980–1990." *African Affairs* 89: 163–181.

Parry, Geraint. 2005. *Political Elites*. Colchester: ECPR Press.

Payne, Leigh. 1992. "Brazilian Business and the Democratic Transition: New Attitudes and Influence." Working Paper 179, University of Notre Dame, Kellogg Institute.

Pazvakavambwa, Simon, and Vincent Hungwe. 2009. "Land Redistribution in Zimbabwe." In Hans Binswanger-Mkhize, Camille Bourguignon, and Rogerius Johannes Eugenius van den Brink, eds., *Agricultural Land Redistribution: Towards Greater Consensus on the "How,"* 137–168. Washington, DC: World Bank Publications.

Pearse, Andrew. 1972. "Peasants and Revolution: The Case of Bolivia." *Economy and Society* 1(3): 255–280.

Pearse, Andrew. 1980. *Seeds of Plenty, Seeds of Want: Social and Economic Implications of the Green Revolution*. Oxford: Oxford University Press.

Pease García, Henry. 1977. *El ocaso del poder oligárquico*. Lima: DESCO.

Perotti, Roberto. 1996. "Growth, Income Distribution, and Democracy: What the Data Say." *Journal of Economic Growth* 1(2): 149–187.

Petras, James. 1969. *Politics and Social Forces in Chilean Development*. Berkeley: University of California Press.

Philip, George. 1978. *The Rise and Fall of the Peruvian Military Radicals, 1968–1976*. London: Athlone Press.

———. 2013. "Nationalism and the Rise of Peru's General Velasco." *Bulletin of Latin American Research* 32(3): 279–293.

Piketty, Thomas. 2014. "Capital in the Twenty-First Century." Cambridge, MA: Harvard University Press.

Pires de Almeida, Maria Antónia. 2007. "Memory and Trauma of the Portuguese Agrarian Reform: A Case Study." *Portuguese Journal of Social Science* 6(2): 63–76.

Powell, John. 1964. "A Brief Political History of Agrarian Reform in Venezuela." Unpublished ms.

———. 1971. *Political Mobilization of the Venezuelan Peasant*. Cambridge, MA: Harvard University Press.

Powelson, John H., and Richard Stock. 1990. *The Peasant Betrayed: Agriculture and Land Reform in the Third World*. Washington, DC: Cato Institute.

Prado, Manuel. 1962. "Mensaje que debía presentar el Presidente Constitucional del Perú, Doctor Manuel Prado y Ugarteche, al Congreso Nacional, el 28 de julio de 1962." Lima: Congreso Nacional.

Pronin, Dimitri. 1949. "Land Reform in Poland: 1920–1945." *Land Economics* 25: 133–145.

Prosterman, Roy, Mary Temple, and Timothy Hanstad. 1990. *Agrarian Reform and Grassroots Development: Ten Case Studies*. Amsterdam: Lynne Rienner.

Przeworski, Adam. 2009. "Conquered or Granted? A History of Suffrage Extensions." *British Journal of Political Science* 39(2): 291–321.

Przeworski, Adam, Michael Alvarez, José Antonio Cheibub, and Fernando Limongi. 2000. *Democracy and Development: Political Institutions and Well-Being in the World, 1950–1990*. New York: Cambridge University Press.

Przeworski, Adam, and Michael Wallerstein. 1988. "Structural Dependence of the State on Capital." *American Political Science Review* 82(1): 11–29.

Quevedo, Rafael Isidro. 2007. *Temas agrarios*. Caracas: Editorial Serwaca C. A.

Radwan, Samir. 1977. *Agrarian Reform and Rural Poverty, Egypt, 1952–1975*. Geneva: International Labour Office.

Rajan, Raghuram. 2009. "Rent Preservation and the Persistence of Underdevelopment." *American Economic Journal: Macroeconomics* 1: 178–218.

Rajan, Raghuram, and Rodney Ramcharan. 2011. "Land and Credit: A Study of the Political Economy of Banking in the United States in the Early 20th Century." *Journal of Finance* 66(6): 1895–1931.

Ramsay, James. 1982. "The Limits of Land Reform in Thailand." *The Journal of Developing Areas* 16(2): 173–196.

Rashid, Shaikh Muhammad. 1985. "Land Reforms in Pakistan." *Social Scientist* 13(9): 44–52.

Roberts, Kenneth. 2003. "Social Correlates of Party System Demise and Populist Resurgence in Venezuela." *Latin American Politics and Society* 45(3): 35–57.

———. 2007. "Latin America's Populist Revival." *SAIS Review of International Affairs* 27(1): 3–15.

Rodríguez, Francisco. 2004. "Inequality, Redistribution, and Rent-Seeking." *Economics and Politics* 16(3): 287–320.

Rodríguez Weber, Javier. 2009. "Los tiempos de la desigualdad: La distribución del ingreso en Chile." Master's thesis, Programa de Historia económica y social, Universidad de la República, Montevideo.

Roemer, Michael. 1983. *Dutch Disease in Developing Countries: Swallowing Bitter Medicine.* Cambridge, MA: Harvard Institute for International Development, Harvard University.

Ropp, Steve. 1992. "Explaining the Long-Term Maintenance of a Military Regime: Panama before the US Invasion." *World Politics* 44(2): 210–234.

Ross, Michael. 2006. "Is Democracy Good for the Poor?" *American Journal of Political Science* 50: 860–874.

Rosset, Peter, Raj Patel, and Michael Courville, eds. 2006. *Promised Land: Competing Visions of Agrarian Reform.* New York: Institute for Food and Development Policy.

Rowles, James. 1985. *Law and Agrarian Reform in Costa Rica.* Boulder: Westview Press.

Roy, Denny. 2003. *Taiwan: A Political History.* Ithaca, NY: Cornell University Press.

Rudra, Nita. 2002. "Globalization and the Decline of the Welfare State in Less-Developed Countries." *International Organization* 56(2): 411–445.

Rueschemeyer, Dietrich, Evelyn Stephens, and John Stephens. 1992. *Capitalist Development and Democracy.* Chicago: University of Chicago Press.

Russett, Bruce. 1964. "Inequality and Instability: The Relation of Land Tenure to Politics." *World Politics* 16(3): 442–454.

Saad, Reem. 2002. "Egyptian Politics and the Tenancy Law." In Ray Bush, ed., *Counter-Revolution in Egypt's Countryside: Land and Farmers in the Era of Economic Reform,* 103–125. London: Zed Books.

Sabates-Wheeler, Rachel, and Myrtha Waite. 2003. "Albania Country Brief: Property Rights and Land Markets." Mimeo, University of Wisconsin, Madison.

Sachikonye, Lloyd. 2004. "The Promised Land: From Expropriation to Reconciliation and Jambanja." In Brian Raftopoulous and Tyrone Savage, eds., *Zimbabwe: Injustice and Political Reconciliation,* 1–18. Cape Town: Institute for Justice and Reconciliation.

Samaraweera, Vijaya. 1982. "Land Reform in Sri Lanka." *Third World Legal Studies* 1(7): 104–122.

Sanderson, Susan Walsh. 1984. *Land Reform in Mexico: 1910–1980.* Orlando: Academic Press.

Saulniers, Alfred. 1988. *Public Enterprises in Peru: Public Sector Growth and Reform.* Boulder: Westview Press.

Schady, Norbert. 2000. "The Political Economy of Expenditures by the Peruvian Social Fund (FONCODES), 1991–95." *American Political Science Review* 94: 289–304.

Scheve, Kenneth, and David Stasavage. 2011. "Democracy, War, and Wealth: Evidence from Two Centuries of Inheritance Taxation." *American Political Science Review* 106: 81–102.

Schmitt, Carl. 1923. *The Crisis of Parliamentary Democracy*. Berlin: Duncker & Humblot.

Schmitter, Philippe. 2010. "Twenty Five Years, Fifteen Findings." *Journal of Democracy* 21: 18–28.

Scott, James. 1985. *Weapons of the Weak*. New Haven: Yale University Press.

Seligmann, Linda. 1995. *Between Reform and Revolution: Political Struggle in the Peruvian Andes, 1969–1991*. Stanford, CA: Stanford University Press.

Seligson, Mitchell. 1980. *Peasants of Costa Rica and the Development of Agrarian Capitalism*. Madison: University of Wisconsin Press.

———. 1984. "Implementing Land Reform: The Case of Costa Rica." *Managing International Development* 1(2): 29–46.

Shleifer, Andrei, and Robert Vishny. 1998. *The Grabbing Hand: Government Pathologies and Their Cures*. Cambridge, MA: Harvard University Press.

Simmons, John. 1970. "Agricultural Cooperatives and Tunisian Development." *Middle East Journal* 24(4): 455–465.

Skocpol, Theda. 1979. *States and Social Revolutions: A Comparative Analysis of France, Russia and China*. New York: Cambridge University Press.

———. 1985. "Bringing the State Back In: Strategies of Analysis in Current Research." In Peter Evans, Dietrich Rueschemeyer, and Theda Skocpol, eds., *Bringing the State Back In*, 3–37. Cambridge: Cambridge University Press.

Slater, Dan. 2010. *Ordering Power: Contentious Politics and Authoritarian Leviathans in Southeast Asia*. New York: Cambridge University Press.

———. 2013. "Democratic Careening." *World Politics* 65(4): 729–763.

Slater, Dan, Benjamin Smith, and Gautam Nair. 2014. "Economic Origins of Democratic Breakdown? The Redistributive Model and the Postcolonial State." *Perspectives of Politics* 12(2): 353–374.

Slater, Dan, and Joseph Wong. 2013. "The Strength to Concede: Ruling Parties and Democratization in Developmental Asia." *Perspectives on Politics* 11(3): 717–733.

Smith, Adam. [1776] 1863. *An Inquiry into the Nature and Causes of the Wealth of Nations*. Edinburgh: Adam & Charles Black.

Smith, Benjamin. 2005. "The Origins of Regime Breakdown and Persistence under Single-Party Rule." *World Politics* 57: 421–451.

Smith, Tony. 1975. "The Political and Economic Ambitions of Algerian Land Reform, 1962–1974." *Middle East Journal* 29: 259–278.

Snyder, Richard, and David Samuels. 2004. "Legislative Malapportionment in Latin America." In Edward Gibson, ed., *Federalism and Democracy in Latin America*, 131–172. Baltimore: Johns Hopkins University Press.

Sokoloff, Kenneth, and Eric Zolt. 2007. "Inequality and the Evolution of Institutions of Taxation: Evidence from the Economic History of the Americas." In Sebastian Edwards, Gerardo Esquivel, and Graciela Márquez, eds., *The Decline of Latin American Economies: Growth, Institutions, and Crises*, 83–136. Chicago: University of Chicago Press.

Soto, Oscar David. 2006. *La cuestión agraria en Venezuela*. Mérida: Universidad de Los Andes.

Springborg, Robert. 1990. "Rolling Back Egypt's Agrarian Reform." *Middle East Report* 166: 28–38.

———. 1991. "State-Society Relations in Egypt: The Debate over Owner-Tenant Relations." *Middle East Journal* 45(2): 232–249.

SRA (Secretaría de la Reforma Agraria). 2010. "FANAR: Fondo de apoyo para núcleos agrarios sin regularizar." Unpublished ms.

Staiger, Douglas, and James Stock. 1997. "Instrumental Variables Regression with Weak Instruments." *Econometrica* 65: 557–586.

Stanfield, J. David. 1989. "Agrarian Reform in the Dominican Republic." In William Thiesenhusen, ed., *Searching for Agrarian Reform in Latin America*, 305–337. Boston: Unwin Hyman.

Stearman, Allyn MacLean. 1984. "Colonization in Santa Cruz, Bolivia: A Comparative Study of the Yapacaní and San Julián Projects." In Marianne Schmink and Charles Wood, eds., *Frontier Expansion in Amazonia*, 231–260. Gainesville: University of Florida Press.

Stepan, Alfred. 1971. *The Military in Politics*. Princeton: Princeton University Press.

———. 1978. *The State and Society: Peru in Comparative Perspective*. Princeton: Princeton University Press.

———. 1988. *Rethinking Military Politics*. Princeton: Princeton University Press.

Stephens, John. 1979. *The Transition from Capitalism to Socialism*. London: Macmillan.

Stokes, Susan. 2005. "Perverse Accountability: A Formal Model of Machine Politics with Evidence from Argentina." *American Political Science Review* 99: 315–325.

Stowe, Leland. 1947. "Hungary's Agrarian Revolution." *Foreign Affairs* 25(3): 490–502.

Stringer, Randy. 1989. "Honduras: Toward Conflict and Agrarian Reform." In William Thiesenhusen, ed., *Searching for Agrarian Reform in Latin America*, 358–383. Boston: Unwin Hyman.

Suehiro, Akira. 1981. "Land Reform in Thailand: The Concept and Background of the Agricultural Land Reform Act of 1975." *The Developing Economies* 19(4), 314–347.

Svolik, Milan. 2009. "Power Sharing and Leadership Dynamics in Authoritarian Regimes." *American Journal of Political Science* 53: 477–494.

———. 2012. *The Politics of Authoritarian Rule*. Cambridge: Cambridge University Press.

Swinnen, Johan. 1999. "The Political Economy of Land Reform Choices in Central and Eastern Europe." *Economics of Transition* 7(3): 637–664.

———. 2002. "Political Reforms, Rural Crises, and Land Tenure in Western Europe." *Food Policy* 27: 371–394.

Tai, Hung-Chao. 1974. *Land Reform and Politics*. Berkeley: University of California Press.

Tan, Hanqiang. 2014. "The Confluence of History, Politics and Circumstance that Shaped the Beginnings of Primary Education Systems in Asia." Master's thesis, University of Chicago.

Tannenbaum, Frank. 1962. *Ten Keys to Latin America*. New York: Knopf.

Teichman, Judith. 2002. "Private Sector Power and Market Reform." *Third World Quarterly* 23: 491–512.

Themnér, Lotta, and Peter Wallensteen. 2013. "Armed Conflict, 1946–2012." *Journal of Peace Research* 50(4): 509–521.

Thies, Cameron. 2005. "War, Rivalry, and State Building in Latin America." *American Journal of Political Science* 49(3): 451–465.

Thiesenhusen, William, ed. 1989. *Searching for Agrarian Reform in Latin America.* Boston: Unwin Hyman.

———. 1995. *Broken Promises: Agrarian Reform and the Latin American* Campesino. Boulder: Westview Press.

Thomas, Hugh. 1971. *Cuba: The Pursuit of Freedom.* New York: Harper & Row.

Thome, Joseph. 1970. *Expropriation and Title Distribution under the Bolivian Agrarian Reform: 1953–1967.* Madison: Land Tenure Center, University of Wisconsin.

———. 1989. "Law, Conflict, and Change: Frei's Law and Allende's Agrarian Reform." In William Thiesenhusen, ed., *Searching for Agrarian Reform in Latin America*, 188–215. Boston: Unwin Hyman.

Thwala, Wellington Didibhuku. 2006. "Land and Agrarian Reform in South Africa." In Peter Rosset, Raj Patel, and Michael Courville, eds., *Promised Land: Competing Visions of Agrarian Reform*, 57–72. New York: Institute for Food and Development Policy.

Timmons, Jeffrey. 2005. "The Fiscal Contract: States, Taxes, and Public Services." *World Politics* 57(4): 530–567.

Tjondronegoro, Sediono. 1972. *Land Reform or Land Settlement: Shifts in Indonesia's Land Policy.* Land Tenure Center 81. Madison: Land Tenure Center, University of Wisconsin, Madison.

Trimberger, Ellen. 1978. *Revolution from Above: Military Bureaucrats and Development in Japan, Turkey, Egypt and Peru.* New Brunswick: Transaction Books.

Trinkunas, Harold. 2004. "The Military: From Marginalization to Center Stage." In Jennifer McCoy and David Myers, eds., *The Unraveling of Representative Democracy in Venezuela*, 50–70. Baltimore: Johns Hopkins University Press.

Tsebelis, George. 2002. *Veto Players.* Princeton: Princeton University Press.

Tuma, Elias. 1965. *Twenty-Six Centuries of Agrarian Reform: A Comparative Analysis.* Berkeley: University of California Press.

Turits, Richard Lee. 2003. *Foundations of Despotism: Peasants, the Trujillo Regime, and Modernity in Dominican History.* Stanford, CA: Stanford University Press.

Turovsky, Paul. 1980. "Bolivian Haciendas: Before and after the Revolution." PhD diss., University of California, Los Angeles.

Urioste, Miguel. 1987. *Segunda reforma agraria: Campesinos, tierra y educación popular.* La Paz: CEDLA.

USAID. 2010. "Property Rights and Resource Governance Country Profile: Egypt." Washington, DC: USAID.

Vandewalle, Dirk. 1998. *Libya since Independence: Oil and State-Building.* Ithaca, NY: Cornell University Press.

Vanhanen, Tatu. 2009. Index of Power Resources (IPR) 2007. FSD2420, version 1.0. Tampere: Finnish Social Science Data Archive.

Vardy, Steven. 1983. "The Impact of Trianon upon Hungary and the Hungarian Mind: The Nature of Interwar Hungarian Irredentism." *Hungarian Studies Review* 10(1): 21–42.

Varga, Zsuzsanna. 2009. "The Agrarian Elite in Hungary before and after the Political Transition." In Friederike Sattler and Christoph Boyer, eds., *European Economic Elites: Between a New Spirit of Capitalism and the Erosion of State Socialism*, 223–250. Berlin: Duncker & Humblot.

Vaskela, Gediminas. 1996. *The Land Reform of 1919–1940: Lithuania and the Countries of East and Central Europe*. Vilnius: Arlila.

Velasco Alvarado, Juan. 1997. "Speech by Juan Velasco Alvarado, 1969." In Brian Loveman and Thomas Davies, eds., *The Politics of Antipolitics*. 188–194. Wilmington: Scholarly Resources.

Verdery, Katherine. 1991. *National Ideology under Socialism: Identity and Cultural Politics in Ceausescu's Romania*. Berkeley: University of California Press.

Vollrath, Dietrich, and Lennart Erickson. 2007. "Land Distribution and Financial System Development." IMF Working Paper WP/07/83.

Walinsky, Louis. 1962. *Economic Development in Burma, 1951–1960*. Hartford: Twentieth Century Fund.

———, ed. 1977. *Agrarian Reform as Unfinished Business: The Selected Papers of Wolf Ladejinsky*. Oxford: Oxford University Press.

Wang, Ch'ang-hsi, and Wei-kuang Chang. 1953. *Land Reform in Taiwan*. 3rd ed. Taipei: HsinTung Li Ch'u Pan Shê.

Warriner, Doreen. 1962. *Land Reform and Development in the Middle East: A Study of Egypt, Syria, and Iraq*. London: Greenwood Press.

Wegren, Stephen K., ed. 2003. *Land Reform in the Former Soviet Union and Eastern Europe*. London: Routledge.

Weitz, Richard. 1986. "Insurgency and Counterinsurgency in Latin America, 1960–1980." *Political Science Quarterly* 101(3): 397–413.

Weyland, Kurt. 1996. *Democracy without Equity*. Pittsburgh: University of Pittsburgh Press.

———. 2003. "Economic Voting Reconsidered: Crisis and Charisma in the Election of Hugo Chávez." *Comparative Political Studies* 36(7): 822–848.

———. 2009. "The Rise of Latin America's Two Lefts: Insights from Rentier State Theory." *Comparative Politics* 41(2): 145–164.

Wilpert, Gregory. 2006. "Land for People Not for Profit in Venezuela." In Peter Rosset, Raj Patel, and Michael Courville, eds., *Promised Land: Competing Visions of Agrarian Reform*, 249–264. Oakland, CA: Food First Books.

Winters, Jeffrey. 2011. *Oligarchy*. New York: Cambridge University Press.

Wittman, Hannah, and Laura Saldivar-Tanaka. 2006. "The Agrarian Question in Guatemala." In Peter Rosset, Raj Patel, and Michael Courville, eds., *Promised Land: Competing Visions of Agrarian Reform*, 23–39. New York: Institute for Food and Development Policy.

Woo-Cumings, Meredith, ed. 1999. *The Developmental State*. Ithaca, NY: Cornell University Press.

Wood, Elisabeth. 2000. *Forging Democracy from Below*. New York: Cambridge University Press.

Wooldridge, J. M. 2002. *Econometric Analysis of Panel Data*. Cambridge, MA: The MIT Press.

World Bank. 1975. "Land Reform: Sector Policy Paper." Washington, DC: World Bank.

Wright, Joseph. 2008. "Do Authoritarian Institutions Constrain? How Legislatures Affect Growth and Investment." *American Journal of Political Science* 52(2): 322–343.

———. 2009. "How Foreign Aid Can Foster Democratization in Authoritarian Regimes." *American Journal of Political Science* 53(3): 552–571.

Wright, Thomas. 2001. *Latin America in the Era of the Cuban Revolution.* 3rd ed. Westport: Greenwood Publishing Group.

Wurfel, David. 1983. "The Development of Post-War Philippine Land Reform: Political and Sociological Explanations." In A. Ledesma, P. Makil, and V. Miralao, eds., *Second View from the Paddy*, 1–14. Quezon City: Institute of Philippine Culture, Ateneo de Manila University.

Wurfel, David. 1989. "Land Reform: Contexts, Accomplishments and Prospects under Marcos and Aquino." *Pilipinas* 12 (3).

Yashar, Deborah. 1999. "Democracy, Indigenous Movements, and the Postliberal Challenge in Latin America." *World Politics* 52(1): 76–104.

Yoo, Dongwoo, and Richard Steckel. 2012. "Property Rights and Financial Development: The Legacy of Japanese Colonial Institutions." National Bureau of Economic Research Working Paper 16551.

Young, John. 1997. *Peasant Revolution in Ethiopia: The Tigray People's Liberation Front, 1975–1991.* New York: Cambridge University Press.

Yueh, Jean. 2009. "Sharing Successful Land Reform with the Rest of the World." *Taiwan Today.* September 11, 2009.

Zamosc, Léon. 1986. *The Agrarian Question and the Peasant Movement in Colombia.* Cambridge: Cambridge University Press.

Ziblatt, Daniel. 2006. "How Did Europe Democratize?" *World Politics* 58: 311–338.

_____. 2008. "Does Landholding Inequality Block Democratization?" *World Politics* 60: 610–641.

_____. 2009. "Shaping Democratic Practice and the Causes of Electoral Fraud: The Case of Nineteenth-Century Germany." *American Political Science Review* 103(1): 1–21.

_____. 2013. *Conservative Political Parties and the Birth of Modern Democracy in Europe, 1848–1950.* Ms.

Zúquete, José Pedro. 2008. "The Missionary Politics of Hugo Chávez." *Latin American Politics and Society* 50(1): 91–121.

Index

Lily Lee Tsai, *Accountability without Democracy: How Solidary Groups Provide Public Goods in Rural China*

Joshua Tucker, *Regional Economic Voting: Russia, Poland, Hungary, Slovakia and the Czech Republic, 1990–1999*

Ashutosh Varshney, *Democracy, Development, and the Countryside*

Jeremy M. Weinstein, *Inside Rebellion: The Politics of Insurgent Violence*

Stephen I. Wilkinson, *Votes and Violence: Electoral Competition and Ethnic Riots in India*

Jason Wittenberg, *Crucibles of Political Loyalty: Church Institutions and Electoral Continuity in Hungary*

Elisabeth J. Wood, *Forging Democracy from Below: Insurgent Transitions in South Africa and El Salvador*

Elisabeth J. Wood, *Insurgent Collective Action and Civil War in El Salvador*